The Spirit Speaks Today

But—Is the Christian Church Listening Today?

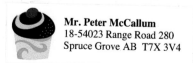

MY READERS,

Before you start to read, consider the following: my book explains my theme, my burden, and my purpose in writing to warn Christian churches that Christ is Coming Soon to claim what He desires, namely a "Holy, Radiant, Sinless, and Blameless church as Bride." He will give such a church rewards for faithfulness, and give them a happy, eternal future with Him in Heaven.

My urgent desire for my brothers in Christ is based upon our Lord's Will and Purpose for His "Body" as stated in His Great Commission (Matt. 28) as well as on His urgent words in Rev. 2 and 3. In a Divine Revelation to the Apostle John, He warns Seven named churches before the deaths of the Apostles to "hear what the Spirit says to His churches"—then and down the centuries to today. To those who remain obedient to all He asks (us, too!) He Promises rewards and Himself as the future Bridegroom. To those who "have lost their First Love, who tolerate false teachers, who are spiritually dead, dying, lukewarm or disobedient, etc." He Promises His wrath and "removal of their 'lampstands' (church) from His Presence" when He Comes.

These and other Scriptural statements led me, under the Spirit's urging, to write this book of warning, using Christ's Words and His Divine example of warning named, actual, disobedient churches and their members (and the Apostle Paul's inspired writings to churches at Corinth and Rome).

I write this message so that there will be no misunderstanding of my motives, opinions, and of His message conveyed in my own words to you. In certain chapters of my book, especially, when I deal with Christ's Orders to His church: "Go, and make disciples... baptize them (and add them to the church)... and teach them to obey all that I have commanded you," I have named some denominations or church groups. I specifically did so, not to condemn or judge them (that is Christ's prerogative alone) but to show them and all who read my book, that they and unknown thousands of churches or groups have, by their publicly observed actions or practices in connection to our Lord's teachings and commands, and knowingly or not have been disobedient to Him and to His inspired Word to His church. They must be warned, in the same way our Lord named early churches who disobeyed Him in many diverse ways.

I, as author, take full responsibility for my words in this book, for my Scriptural interpretations and my expressed opinions—although my opinions and words are always written in consultation with the Spirit of Truth, given to me and to you to lead us to His Truth. I also state that my Publisher, *Essence Publishing*, is not to be held responsible or liable in any way for my opinions, my quotes, or my interpretation of specific churches' doctrinal statements or practices discussed here by me. They are made by me alone. Every Christian church, in the past, today, and until our Lord Comes, must decide whether "their church" pleases Christ, their Divine Head, or not. If not, they must "hear what the Spirit says to the churches" and make their own decisions for their eternal future. This is not a "How-To book" but a warning from Christ's inspired, inerrant Word of Truth.

Bob Williamson.

The Spirit Speaks Today

*"He who has an ear to hear, let him hear
what the Spirit says to the churches"*

—Christ, in a loving Command to all His church
(Rev. Chapters 2 and 3)

But—Is the Christian Church Listening Today?

*A book of scriptural warnings for
"those who have an ear to hear,"
echoing our Lord's warnings to
His church 2,000 years ago.*

W.R.WILLIAMSON, TH.D

The Spirit Speaks Today

Copyright © 2001, W.R. Williamson

Except where otherwise indicated, all Scripture quotations in this book are taken from the *NIV Study Bible*, (New International Version) copyright 1985 by the Zondervan Corporation. The Holy Bible, New International Version copyright 1973, 1978, 1984 by the International Bible Society. Used by permission.

ISBN: 1-55306-274-4

**For more information or
to order additional copies, please contact:**

W.R. Williamson
#63–13320 124 St.
Edmonton, AB T5L 5B7

Guardian Books is an imprint of *Essence Publishing*.
For more information, contact:
44 Moira Street West, Belleville, Ontario, Canada K8P 1S3.
Phone: 1-800-238-6376. Fax: (613) 962-3055.
E-mail: info@essencegroup.com
Internet: www.essencegroup.com

Printed in Canada
by

Guardian
B O O K S

Table of Contents

"He who has an ear to hear, let him hear
what the Spirit says to the churches"
—Revelation 2,3

But—Is the Christian Church Listening Today?

*"He who testifies to these things says
'Yes, I am coming soon.'
Amen. Come Lord Jesus."*
Rev. 22:20.

Acknowledgements

First, I want to give thanks to God, the Father; God, the Son; and God, the Holy Spirit, Who Omnisciently know how their Holy Presence in my "born-again" life has drawn me to God, allowed me to become His adopted human "Son" through belief in the Risen Son; added me to the Son's "Body, His church on earth"; and Who continually and spiritually nourished and encouraged me (by the *Spirit of Truth*) to become a spiritually-mature believer, teacher, servant and witness in His Christian church, and in the world.

I would like to acknowledge the love, patience and forbearance exhibited by my wife, Vi, during the months of research, writing, editing, re-editing, re-writing, and, finally the printing of this humble book intended to warn the disobedient Christian church today, on behalf of Jesus Christ. It was only her love, sympathy, and support that sustained me through this creative task and burden from the Lord. Book #5 was tough to write! Thanks for sticking by me through it all!

I also want to thank many godly Christian writers, most of whom I do not know personally, but only through their Christian writings. They are unaware of their influence on would-be Christian writers, such as myself, whose writing is encouraged and sustained by these men's Christian books, with their knowledge, discernment, and Spirit-led love to others in their roles as teachers, Pastors, and members of Christ's Body clearly in evidence. There are too many to thank personally, but I thank them here for their mutual love and concern for God's Truth and His Son's often-failing church.

I thank my Saviour and Lord, too, for showing me His Truth, Love, Mercy and Favour throughout my life of service to Him in His church and in the world, and for giving me a great thirst for His Word and His Truth, and especially for His "Body," the church. I thank Him for the gift of God's Spirit, Who gave me this burden and purpose to write about His church today, often found *wrinkled, not radiant; stained with sin, not pure and holy; failing not blameless; forsaking their first love; spiritually asleep, not spiritually repentant and awake* (Rev. 2,3; Eph. 5:27). I pray that the Lord will take this book of spiritual warning to the Christian church, and place it before failing and failed Christian churches; will take its scriptural Words from Him and His inspired servants of New Testament times, and show them that this book is about (and from) God, His Spirit, and the Divine Head of the Christian church—not alone from a frail, weak (but joyfully Christian) writer.

I acknowledge, too, the present work of the Holy *Spirit of Truth* in my life, and in the lives of every believer in every Christian church in the past and today. I pray that He will allow the publication and distribution of this book as Christ's loving warning to failing or failed Christians in the many disobedient churches of today's End Times. Finally, I pray that my book's urgings (echoing those of our Lord's) will cause Christ's failing people and churches to seek the Spirit's aid—and that He will Counsel, Guide, Teach, Remind, Convict, and Strengthen His necessary and urgent Revival and Reform process. And return all today's failing members, leaders, and churches to full obedience, before Christ comes to earth to claim His holy, *radiant* Bride.

Behold, I am coming soon, JESUS says (Rev. 22:7). Join with the Apostle John and all faithful Christians, in replying in love, gratefulness and obedience, welcoming our Saviour and Lord—and in saying: *Amen, come Lord Jesus* (Rev. 22:20). Pray for His coming—but also pray that failing and presently disobedient Christian churches will *hear what the Spirit says to the churches,* repent, and return to *do the things* they *did before* in faithful obedience to Him (see Rev. 2,3) before it is too late.

Preface

Let me explain why this book of warning to disobedient Christian churches today is so **important** and **necessary now**, and **today**. The "Contents" page preceding this preface lets every reader know, in a brief summary, why and how this book came to be written, and of course, what Christian readers can expect to find within the six main *parts*, and 15 included *chapters*. There is even a final chapter, called *"Conclusion—Choose Your Future,"* that some may read first—for some Christians like to see the ending before the beginning! From Contents to Conclusion, readers will receive a heavy (even staggering) "dose" of scriptural information—all explaining the book's title and subtitle: *"The Spirit Speaks Today, But Are Christians in His Church Listening?"* Then why have a preface you may ask?

The answer to the last question is found in the writer's mind, as well as in the reader's minds—the latter being, I hope, mostly church leaders; then secondly, church members; and finally (a small proportion, I believe), a few church and seminary or Bible school theologians and teachers.

You see, this writer, a Christian for nearly four decades, has been intimately involved in the Christian church in the Western world, as a Bible student, a church teacher, and a church Deacon for all this time—and he loves the church of Jesus Christ, for it has been a second family to him. Latterly, too, this writer has authored several Christian books, all presently unpublished.

In preparing for, and actually writing these books (all on the general subject of the church of Jesus Christ, Who is the Divine Head of His "Body" on earth—the One Who is God Incarnate), I have read and studied not only the Christian Bible, particularly the New Testament for His Church, but have studied Christian church history, from the death of the Apostles, down through the centuries to today.

I, the writer of this humble book, as an advocate for our Saviour and Lord, have also, in my own way as God has led me in these few decades, been a small part of several Christian churches, and been part of Christian church history—which has affected me deeply. Part One gives some details of this writer's particular "pilgrimage" in this sinful world, as well as revealing, to all my readers and those who know me personally, how much I love my Saviour, Lord, and church Head.

Why have a preface, if my book is so organized into parts and chapters, and a conclusion? I said, a few paragraphs back, that the answer is not completely in this rather large book, with dozens of experiences, examples, and scores of scriptural verses. But it has to be explained by my mind revealing to you what prompted me to write this book on this particular, hidden, forgotten, and almost ignored subject of God's Spirit speaking today to churches—who probably aren't the least bit concerned! Readers' minds are involved, too, as I wrote this book, for what can explain how so many churches today are disobedient to Jesus Christ, the Head, other than their members' mind-sets, lack of interest in religious matters, and ignorance of what is happening, what will happen, what could happen, depending upon their personal and corporate (church) decisions at an early date?

I'm getting mysterious again, I hear readers say! Why don't you sit back and let me explain, in this preface, the *key elements found in this book's* wonderful/terrible, hidden/exposed, forgotten/remembered, obeyed and disobeyed Words of Jesus Christ to all His church Bodies *today.*

*The key elements readers must understand (and obey) when the Spirit Speaks to all Christian churches today—small or large, groups or "Empires," faithful or unfaithful to the Divine Head, **Jesus Christ**.*

1. The first element of understanding this book, with its contents revealing Christ's Will and purpose for His Body, the church, and how it applies to the reader, is ***understanding, reading and believing the inspired, inerrant, and infallible Holy Word of God, the Bible—especially the New Testament, for Christians making up Christ's church on earth.***

Unless the readers (members and leaders, and Spirit-Gifted church teachers), understand, accept and believe that the Bible is what it says it is—God's revealed Word to mankind (first to the Jews, then to the Christians; Old and New Testaments)—***and read, teach and obey it faithfully***, then not only is this book of warning from Christ useless in trying to communicate His Word to failing churches today. Without this key element in church life, worship, and service accepted, believed and acted upon in every church, the church today—divided, divisive, spiritually *asleep*, and immature—cannot resist *false teachers*, and will fail the Head.

The Bible is discussed in Chapter 2 of this book, as the only and final source for what the Spirit, Christ, and God say they require of Christians in Christ's church on earth. The elements that follow are taken, not from this writer's words or beliefs, but directly from the Bible, as they relate to the individual parts of this book.

2. The second "element of understanding this book" lies ***in the scriptural subject of obedience to Christ, the Head.*** Chapter 3 asks: ***What does Christ require of all Christians?*** And answers it, from Scripture, so that even if it has not been taught or studied or preached in disobedient churches today, this book's readers will be awakened to what the Lord asks of them. And they will know, by self-examination and comparison, just how well—or how badly—they have served Him in His church.

3. The third element further explores *the **scriptural subject of obedience to the head, by the church,*** as Chapter 4 reveals how the church through history has often failed the Lord. This chapter contains many historical instances of disobedience, from the New Testament church down the centuries until today.

4. The fourth element, covered in Part 3, over three chapters (5,6, and 7) returns from history of the church to our Lord's "Great Commission for His Church," in Matthew 28. The Composite three commands express the Will and purpose for the then-unformed Christian church, to *Go, and make disciples of all nations...baptize them...and teach them to obey all that I have commanded you* (His first apostles and disciples before His death, burial, Resurrection, and ascension). Readers will not only have scriptural explanations of this important set of duties from the Head to His then-future church, from Pentecost until today, but will understand the importance of obedience, then, now, and in the future, when the Head comes to claim His Perfect Bride—His church.

5. The fifth element, covered in Part 4 (Chapters 8 and 9) reveals a little-known, little-taught, critical portion of Scripture for the Church of all ages (not just for a few churches of long-ago historical failings). *Chapter 8 discusses what this writer calls "Christ's first 'Audit and Review' of His church"* (Rev. 2,3). The first element in this list must be considered as we read our Lord's two chapters, early in His Revelation to the Apostle John. If the Christian church of all ages to today does not accept the Holy Bible as *God's inspired, inerrant and infallible Word of Truth to men and His church,* they will fail Christ by not accepting *all of it* (including Rev. 2 and 3)—*intended not only for the Seven churches described, but for ALL and EVERY CHURCH down the centuries, including today (our churches).*

The chapters quoted and explained in this book are applicable to every church that does (or does not) do the things that Christ asks His church of all centuries to be, and do, for Him. Because this writer believes in "the faith once delivered to the saints" (and contained in, especially, the New Testament for the church), he has utilized Revelation 2 and 3 (and the introduction in Chapter 1 of Revelation) as a key element to remind failing churches of all they must do and be for Him before He comes again.

Chapter 9 of Part 4 of this book, like chapter 4, again applies the disobedience revealed to us in Revelation 2 and 3, to disobedience of later churches—and again down to today's evidence of church failures.

6. The sixth element of understanding important for churches today to know is that of *scriptural and eternal Consequences of failure, and how members and leaders of failing or failed Christian churches must act to avoid Christ's wrath and terrible consequences.* Chapter 10 of Part 5 discusses these consequences, from Scripture. Not all churches, from the New Testament era down past the death of the Apostles, through the so-called "Protestant Reformation," down to today have been or are disobedient and unfaithful, and the Divine Head of His church speaks about rewards for them. As well, He speaks of rewards for obedience and faithfulness to all His Commands in Revelation 2 and 3 (for all churches, including today), and I have discussed these in Chapter 10.

7. The seventh, connected to 6, is explained in Chapter 11, as it is allied to *consequences of disobedience and failure. It is discussed and scripturally explained, from our Lord's Words to all churches in Revelation 2 and 3, as "action words."* Here, I write to readers, quoting our mutual Lord, and begin to speak what the Lord says about *how failing or failed churches (members and leaders) can do His Will, by overcoming sin, repenting, reviving, and reforming their disobedient ways, and returning to all He has asked them to be and do for Him in His Words found in Scripture alone.*

In Part 5, Chapter 12, this writer sums up the "Consequence" portion of this book by writing a chapter entitled "Listening to what The Spirit (not men) *says to the churches*"—the title of this book.

What the Spirit says comes from the seven individual statements made by the Lord to the Seven Churches of Asia, in Revelation 2 and 3. His full quote is *He who has an ear, let him hear what the Spirit says to the churches.* Chapter 12 (as in earlier and later chapters) reminds churches, and their often "unlistening" members, that what the Spirit says to each church member and leaders is, in God's own Truth, exactly what the Living and Risen Lord has said in His Word— and still applies to every church down through history, including today. Many *false teachers*, encouraged by Satan, have entered the churches. They have neither listened to the Spirit, nor obeyed what He reminds us the Lord has told us to be and do for Him, obediently and faithfully—or face His wrath and consequences.

8. The eighth and final element of understanding for all Christian churches today, as represented by readers of this book of warning for failing or failed churches: to repent and reform themselves to meet Him, when He returns soon to claim His *radiant*, holy, Sinless and Blameless Bride. If they do not repent and reform themselves, with the Spirit's Leading them to God's Truth, they will remain what the inspired Paul said will be Wrinkled, stained with sin, unholy, and disobedient churches, not fit or worthy to be His Bride when He comes. Their "candlestick" (representing each church down through the centuries until He comes—see Rev. 2,3 again) will be "removed from their place in His Presence," and they will not be part of the Spiritual marriage with the Lamb, as described in Scripture.

Chapter 13 talks about a scriptural Reform Process, that this writer suggests (based upon Christ's Words) will lead disobedient churches out of their errant ways, into the radiant light of His Presence. Chapter 14 gives readers from small churches a "Scenario," or practical example, of how the Reform Process, based upon Christ's Words of instructions to all his churches, can result in *Scriptural action, with prayer and the Guiding of the Spirit—please Christ—and ensure His Love and Favour when He Comes to Rapture us to Heaven as Faithful churches, according to His Word.*

Finally, chapter 15 speaks of applying a different reform process to very large groups of disobedient churches. These have unscriptural church hierarchies of leadership, which have proved to resist all attempts to urge them to reform their many disobedient actions, doctrines, and Scripture-opposing church life and work. Martin Luther tried, about 5 centuries ago, to "nudge" a very large, autocratic, authoritarian, and errant church towards reform, but could not withstand the power of disobedient, Satan-influenced men. Luther, however—contrary to this writer's "plan of scriptural reform"—seemingly did not take advantage of the Holy Spirit's purpose and role to lead him and his church to Spiritual truth and obedience to the Lord. This scripturally-based book, however, in recommending prayer, and the convicting power of the *Spirit of Truth*, in an effort to warn disobedient churches (of any size or degree of failing the Lord), speaks not from men's wisdom or lack of it. This writer only urges that failing churches **must** be made aware that our mutual Lord has said He is coming Soon. If such churches do not *wake up…repent…and do the things they did at first* (in full obedience to Christ and His Holy Word), they will face a terrible earthly—yet spiritual and eternal—future, together with Satan, and all who have rejected our Lord and His Holy Word.

Finally, the last part of this book (*Conclusion—Choose Your Future*) speaks of exactly these choices that must be made by every failing or failed Christian church, if they desire to please Christ, and go with Him to Heaven, as God's plans for Israel, for Christians, and for a lost world without the True God.

This book, as I review it before attempting to have it published and distributed to as many failing churches as I, with the Spirit can arrange, has been a difficult book to write. For Satan still roams the world, seeking who he can destroy. No-one—and Christian churches and leaders are no exception—likes to be criticized, even if it is Christ's own words that offend and condemn them. But, with prayer, the Holy Spirit, and God's inspired, infallible Word, I know that His Grace, Mercy and Truth will lead disobedient ones back to their *first love,* **Jesus Christ**. For our Lord said, *You will remain in my love if you obey my commands.*

Choose now, and choose aright with the Spirit's help—the One who is in every True believer. Return back to the Bible, God's inspired, inerrant and infallible Word, and repent and reform your undiscovered disobedience, so that you might join with faithful brothers and sisters in Christ, and please the Bridegroom who will, at a time no man knows, only God.

Read on, pray and ask the *Spirit of Truth* to convict you of your urgent need as part of His Body.

Chapter 1

A Burden and a Purpose From the Lord

For Christians, *a burden* may be one of several things. It may be a physical burden that is taken up voluntarily or given to them through circumstances such as an illness that restricts them from being able to live as freely as they choose or desire. It may be merely a possession or item used in their work, or conditions of their home lives weighing them down. However, these burdens are usually accepted as a necessary condition of life. To a Christian who is maturing (*...growing up in all things into Him Who is the Head, that is Christ* [Eph. 4:15]), it can mean something not physical, but involving the heart, mind, body and soul—usually spiritual in nature. This kind of spiritual burden may be recognized as from the Lord, and the burden may be uniquely for one Christian or a number of them organized for a Scriptural purpose.

A Burden From the Lord for This Writer

My spiritual burden—spiritual, yet involving every sense and my entire heart, mind and being—was given personally to me at this time of my spiritual life, maturity and my service for my Lord. The inspired Paul was guided by the Holy Spirit to write the quoted verse, in Ephesians 4:15, for every Christian's guidance in their spiritual journey to maturity through this life on earth. Through the same Spirit, I recognize that "growing up" (spiritually and in every other way—wisdom, knowledge, etc.) applies to me personally in reference also to the spiritual burden I must assume, uniquely at this time, in and for the service of our mutual Lord. Uniquely for me; but others have had similar burdens over the years. I have discovered, through my experiences in life—as well as those of other Christians I meet in life, or encounter through their writings about their Christian faith and their experiences—that a Christian must learn to recognize a spiritual burden from the Lord when he or she encounters the supernatural and material signs surrounding it. If not, a wonderful, though perhaps difficult, experience given them by the Spirit will be missed.

Let me explain what my burden is; how I received it; how I recognized it, accepted it, and have now acted upon it to carry out the purpose of the Lord in giving it to me. I am now able, with the Spirit's guidance, to explain it to other Christians and Christian churches who may become involved or touched by my burden's purpose from the Lord.

As a Christian, I have observed the Christian church in the world for several decades, through personal contact, membership, worship, visitation, and through member and church literature, radio and television programs. I have compared the church's observed or recorded faith, worship, service, life, and obedience, with Jesus Christ's requirements from Scripture. Through these personal observations, I believe that I know part of what the diverse, divided, and often-disobedient Christian church is and does today, in faithful response or otherwise, to Christ, the Divine Head of His Body that He willed to build so long ago for His Service.

I have studied the New Testament church; the church in history after the deaths of the Apostles, and I have read some "modern" Christian church history. Recorded church history has allowed me to observe the "public face" of the church of past centuries; after the impact of schisms and non-Christian sects of the early centuries; after the "Reformation," called Protestant; of the church passing through the convulsions of Puritanism, Modernism, neo-Orthodoxy, New Age, and other "-isms," down to today's innumerable divisions, cults, and sects. I have observed the "orthodox church's" battles with the church of "the social gospel;" "the church of 'man alone'"; "the church of the Bible alone"; the church of the Bible and "church traditions"; and the church of "an errant and inapplicable Bible" (they say!). I have observed, and participated in and with a few churches very close to the faithful church of the New Testament. Churches who claim to be "people of the Book" (the inspired, inerrant written Word of God)—many of whom live up to their claim. There are few of the latter—and regrettably, many of them today are turning away from the Bible also. Many churches, I find, have given up doing what they did at first for Christ (i.e. being faithful and obedient in all things [Rev. 2,3]). They are compromising, perverting and disobeying Christ's Words and Commands, by listening to false teachers and to Satan.

I am neither a Bible historian, nor a Christian theologian, nor a philosopher. I am a repentant sinner, saved by God's Grace—a believer in the Risen Christ, added by New Testament faith and baptism to Christ's Body on earth: the church. A Christian disciple of Christ, I am a *fellow citizen of God's people, and member of God's Household* (Eph. 2:19). I don't claim to "know it all," with respect to the Christian churches I speak about, pray about, and now write about in this book; this is outweighed, however, by the fact that I love my Lord and His church—and my brethren in Christ. Now, I want to warn them, using Christ's own words of Scriptural warning! I love, respect and follow the inspired, inerrant and infallible Word of God to mankind, and especially to His **adopted** sons and daughters—Christian believers. I certainly feel I have a more than average love for Christ's Body, the church on earth, for I am very concerned about the Church's future, as I know Christ is concerned. All of these things, I believe, have led to my being given Christ's burden by His Spirit, to accept it, and describe it to you.

My burden from the Lord, simply stated, is **to alert and warn all disobedient Christian churches in this world** that Jesus Christ has spoken Divine Words of warning to them. In His written Word, He has told each disobedient member and local leader of every such church to obey His commands, to reject *false teachers* and false gods, and to carry out faithfully all that He asks of them, until He returns to earth. He has told every Christian member of His *Body on earth* (Eph. 5:30) to repent of the sins that have resulted in His Body often to *forsake* Him, their *first love;* while being *lukewarm* or *asleep* (Rev. 2,3).

Yes, He has given some of His early church commendations to those who have overcome evil and persecution in their midst, and have been faithful. He has promised them rewards and encouraged them (and us now) to continue in faithfulness. But, my burden is to urgently warn those churches *today* who are failing Him (or have already failed Him Who is the Head)—for the consequences of continued failure, without full repentance and reform, are terrible to consider.

In view of *the observed, almost universal nature and condition of the whole Christian Body of Christ*, the Lord compels me to write a universal warning to all the failing Christian churches in the world today. But who will listen to one frail voice in this world, out of many thousands of voices, speaking, preaching, writing, communicating on television and radio, on daily newspapers' "religious pages"—especially if I, and others, only express our personal views or opinions? *False teachers*, in and out of the church, do this every day—attracting millions to their ideas that may be sincere, but are often sincerely wrong, according to God's inspired Word to man.

The Spirit of God and His inspired Word tells me that I must be only a "message-carrier" of what the Divine One, Who uttered the original Words of Truth I quote here, would have me say from the inspired, inerrant, infallible written Word of God alone. My warning must not only be conveyed from my human concerns—it must bear always the imprint of the Divine Truth, the actual inspired Words of Scripture. Anything less will surely fail, as other human ideas have failed. My universal warning message from God in this book consists only of inspired and inerrant Scripture (primarily the New Testament for the church) quoting the Words of Truth Jesus Christ has spoken in Scripture nearly 2,000 years ago, telling Christians of all ages what disobedient churches (members and leaders) must do to please Him or suffer His stated consequences. What I say must have its source in Scripture, given to the church by godly men *moved to write* by the Spirit, in every believer.

The Divine church Head, Jesus Christ, gave His "Body" of all ages His written Words of warnings, consequences, discipline, and rejection of those who do not—or will not—act to repent and obey

Him in all things before He comes again. Inspired New Testament scriptural writers, on behalf of Christ, have spoken of disobedient, unfaithful churches as *wrinkled–not radiant churches* (Eph. 5:27), so that their readers—past, present and future—might, with the Spirit's aid and guidance, repent and return to full obedience before Christ's second coming (Rev. 22:7) to claim **His Bride, the Church**.

My burden of warning, given me from the Lord, written with no human hate or spiritual bias, but with the love and requested help of the Spirit available to all true Christians, is to simply point out from Scripture what Jesus Christ requires of His church—or suffer His wrath for failure. I warn the failing churches of today not to heed or practise what *false teachers* have required and still say in sinful church bodies. The Apostle Peter warned us that *there will be false teachers among you* (2 Pet. 2:1). As well, Christ condemns, in Rev. 2 and 3, those Christians in past churches who have listened to such teachers and acted observably in disobedience to Him.

How My Burden Was Given to Me

I did not receive my burden from the Lord in a spectacular flash of light, or a vision such as we read of in the Bible. Instead, like most of the spiritual burdens of Christian men and women that I have met, read about, heard about, or watched recounting burdens in this "TV age," I received my burden quietly over a period of years.

My burden came to me over some 20 years, later in life, while I was studying God's inspired, inerrant Word—in a way, and at a time, that I felt led to do. When I first became a Christian believer, although I had a great thirst for God's Word, I was forced to set aside academic Bible studies because of pressures of my work, family, and other circumstances of life. I attended church Bible classes, but felt I could not go further then. A time eventually came (the Lord knew all about it!) when I could retire from my secular career. I was a church Bible teacher, a "Sunday School Superintendent," a Deacon, and a Board Chairman for a number of years. Yes, I was "busy" for Him, but a time came when I had less pressures of life, of family and secular business. The Lord spoke to my spirit, and said "you wanted time to study my Word—now you have time!" (Retirement time!)

So, while not neglecting my home, my wife, or the church in which I became involved in my retirement, I found I could now study God's Word (by correspondence) to a greater depth. Completion of my studies (and even application of many parts of my several years of studies to teaching Bible studies in home groups and in the local church) was unknowingly, but slowly, forming my "special burden" for the Lord within my heart, mind and soul.

I don't mean to imply that only intense Bible studies entirely formed my burden, or my purpose to speak out for the Lord to the *wrinkled* Christian church I observed in the world. The Lord was also using my church experiences in our new location to make my studies real, and my burden more urgent. In my case and my specific burden's formation, then, I found that the Lord was not only urging me to study His Word—He seemed to be placing me in various church situations where my Bible knowledge and increased learning allowed me to see more clearly His Word in action, or inaction, in several local bodies of Christ throughout my retirement area.

The Lord led my wife and I to join, leave, and rejoin several churches over the course of a decade of retirement life, in a different part of the country from our "baptismal church." In our early baptismal church, we were taught to obey all that Christ commanded us, learned to grow spiritually mature, and serve Him and strengthen the "Body of Christ." I firmly believe that the Lord, by arranging for me after secular retirement to study His Word more intensively, also used our retirement move to prepare me for His burden. His preparation included adding us, by "church letter and testimony," to a new, smaller community church.

Prior to my retirement and move to the new location, our "new church" had lost their Pastor when he resigned and moved to another location. The church was in the process of "calling a new Pastor" to become their local leader. When I retired, we built and moved into our retirement home, and joined the little church in the new community—looking forward to contributing to the Lord's work wherever we could help God's people. I was invited to join the Deacon's church board, teach Bible (adults) and Sunday school (children's) classes, and worship with the small congregation who seemed to genuinely love the Lord. My wife also offered her *gifts of the Spirit,* and served the Christians there, too. We assisted with Christian camp work nearby, helping to lead youth to Christ therein.

All went well in the new little church, but not for long! Satan was and is still active, *roaming the world, seeking those he would destroy* (1 Pet. 5:8). The new Pastor was, sadly, found to be under Satan's control. He betrayed his marriage vows and was found guilty of immorality with a female church member, as well as betraying his Lord. He resigned, but left behind a legacy of church division, false teaching, and loss of trust and leadership confidence within the Body of Christ there. The "divisions" caused by Satan emerged when some untaught members supported the unrepentant and immoral Pastor, against Scripture and the advice of godly members and Deacons.

We were unhappy, not only with the immoral Pastor, but unsettled with the unspiritual divisions he left behind in the small church. We could not worship with unspiritual, unrepentant members who could neither see, nor scripturally justify, their spiritual divisions in the congregation. "Outside" reconciliation did not help the matter. We found another church in a town a few miles away from our home, and worshipped there for a few months.

Unhappily, this new church was also found to be in an unspiritual condition. For the last year, they had been looking for ways in which to "dispose of" (that is, discharge) their Pastor, rather than seeking God's scriptural pattern of understanding, forgiveness, reconciliation, and a united way of witnessing, preaching, and teaching Christ in the community. We only joined this church near the end of this "Pastor discharge event."

It appeared to my wife and I that God was using these two churches to show us that all was not well with the church of Jesus Christ! While I do not say the two diverse church situations were produced by God to teach us what was happening, I do believe Christ used these two churches, under personal and corporate attack by Satan, to point out something almost unbelievable. He showed me that the Christian church, and its members and leaders were not, in truth, all spiritually alive and well. Instead, many were under attack by Satan, and close to failing the Lord in their human disobedient acts, words and deeds. Nor were they *one*, as Christ said, *as I and the Father are One* (John 17:21) *so that the world may believe that You sent Me.* Their internal divisions, too, resembled those encountered and described by the Apostle Paul in 1 Corinthians 1 and 11!

The second church, unfortunately, did "drive out" their Pastor unilaterally. An unspiritual attitude of unforgiveness, denial of recon- ciliation, and lack of reform where needed caused other unfortunate events as well. The Devil was still at work in the church. The congre- gation split into two groups. One group (among them my wife and I as members) felt they (we) could no longer continue associating with the other group's decidedly unforgiving Christian attitudes and unrepentant actions, and we left. The others decided to seek a Pastor who would go along with their un-biblical ideas of a Christian church and its governance. The second group remained in the church build- ing and location, but the first group was "dispossessed." Calmer members of both groups tried to hold the "Body of Christ" together, using scriptural principles and outside counsel, but didn't succeed.

With "hindsight" (and my later in-depth Bible studies under the Spirit's guidance), I feel today that Satan was perhaps aided, in both church examples given, by a failure of both Pastors to preach and teach God's Word fully. The majority of the members could have become more spiritually and scripturally mature and knowledge- able, and prepared to overcome Satan's work of defeat in the churches. The inspired Paul, in Ephesians 4, gives the church God's good reason for Christian Education (by preaching and teaching)— spiritually training mature members to avoid church divisions, and combat Satan's work.

We, and the other longer-term members of the second church, with much trepidation and prayer, felt in our hearts that some Christ- like action was required. Since we could not return to worship with the original Body members who disagreed so strongly with us and God's scriptural principles, God led us to arrange a place of worship, in a building that another church denomination did not use on Sunday. We began planning a permanent place of worship, with prayer. We sought the guidance of God and His Spirit, so that we could serve Him and the unsaved of the same community with His aid, and with no conflict between His purpose for the church we had left and the church we proposed to build for His Son.

We felt God's leading again, when we were able to buy a lot and build a church building—on the other side of town, yet readily accessible to lost sinners, for His purposes of *making disciples, baptizing them, and teaching them to obey all that His Son commanded* (Matt. 28:18–20). Again, within a space of just a few years, my wife and I (and others) felt that the events precipitated by Satan within several church congregations a few miles from each other not only could be seen as a warning to those who were spiritually "awake" enough to see it as such, but were working out for our and their edification—and His gospel purpose. From a spiritual standpoint, and in obedience to Christ's Commission to His church, the events—although sad and often unChristian in many respects—were leading each part of the divided church (including the newly-founded church) to witness and serve the Lord, with some impetus from Him towards revival, reform and spiritual growth.

I began by relating to you these unhappy church situations, in an effort to show how I personally was able, slowly, to understand and accept a "burden from the Lord" which prompted writing this book. I want my readers to note that, at the time, my burden was forming in my spirit and mind. While my wife and I were undergoing this spiritual "trauma," of discovering that many Christian churches around us in our time were changing and failing Christ, we did not look ahead to using our broken church lives as the precipitating events for a warning book to the churches! On the contrary, even though I was studying the Bible in correspondence Seminary instruction, and serving Christ within these same churches as a Deacon and a Bible teacher, I did not see clearly what God was saying to me, particularly, through these unfortunate events. Whether I saw it clearly or not, God was at work in my life for His purpose for me! Not all burdens from the Lord are disclosed immediately—His time is not our time, and His ways not like our ways, for He is altogether Holy!

Later, I saw that He and His Spirit wanted, specifically, to have me, when He considered me prepared, warn all Christian churches today against sin and disobedience. He was using these sad events in my church life, together with what He had said in His inspired Word about past and present church sin, about His Son's warnings and their unheeded consequences, to convince me of His Will and His need of me.

My burden from the Lord continued to be formed in my heart, mind, and spirit. The time came, after some 12 years of secular retirement, when my wife and I decided to return to Edmonton, Alberta. We wanted to enjoy more often, as we aged, the love and company of our families and our grandchildren. Quite naturally, we looked for a "good" Christian church, reasonably close to our two daughters and their families. My formal theological education was completed by now. I felt in my heart no call to serve as a Christian church Elder or Pastor. Instead, I felt that my Bible studies had equipped me to better aid the Pastor and the church Body in serving as Bible teacher, and Deacon-administrator (two obvious Spirit gifts)—releasing the Pastor for his work of preaching, teaching and leading the flock of Christ under the Divine Head, Christ.

We found a Christian church near our new home, and joined the little Body, even though they, too, were in the process of changing Pastors (sound familiar? I, too, was beginning to learn how the Lord was speaking to me more urgently now). This time, the denominational "headquarters" (although the church was self-governing in most things) had called this church's Pastor to serve in another area-wide post. So, the church began looking for a Pastor to serve as leader, according to New Testament principles. An "Interim Pastor" served for almost a year before a "long-term" Pastor was called, and came to serve the small church. God was still working observably for good in the congregation, although Satan's persuasions to error were still evident in the actions of some members of this church, also. This small, relatively young church— through circumstances existing at the time of the "old Pastor's" leaving and the "Interim Pastor's" temporary service—showed some also to be "unspiritual and scripturally untaught" in many ways. After my wife and I joined, I was offered by the church and the Board members, and had accepted, a term as Deacon. I had also been chosen by the church Board of Deacons to serve them, and the new church, as Chairman of the Board of Deacons. Until the Interim Pastor (or new Pastor) was selected and approved by the church, the church's policy was that the Deacon's Board would lead the church in accord with the Church Constitution, which contained good scriptural principles for governance in a New Testament church. The Interim Pastor would preach, teach, and guide the church as temporary overseer, with the help of the Deacons.

The Interim Pastor proved to be a sound preacher and teacher, well-founded in the Bible and in the Christian faith. But within a few months, something showed Satan at work in the hearts of some members and some Deacons. Satan used their unspirituality, and lack of adequate Bible learning, their weak faith, and worldly leanings, to challenge the church-work of both the Interim Pastor and myself, as Chairman of the Deacons.

This church was unusual in being composed of a **minority** of scriptural, Christian members, and a **majority** of "non-members" or "adherents." The latter majority had been Christian members of a wide variety of denominational churches across the country and across the world. Some were not baptized; some were previously members of churches not generally acceptable to the "denomination," or to the group forming the membership of this church. Despite New Testament statements about selecting Elders and Deacons, and *testing the latter before appointing them to the New Testament positions as church leaders* (*paraphrased, author*—see 1 Tim. 3), this church (with Satan whispering to some in the background) had quite obviously appointed untested, often untrained and unspiritual men as Deacons, before my being selected by the church and Board to be both Deacon and Board Chairman.

The small church, probably because it had such a small number of committed Christian church members, and a majority of uncommitted attendees (non-members), allowed non-members to teach Bible classes, to influence others, and to speak up (but not vote) at church business meetings.

Lacking sufficient members and funds to keep up the church's weak finances, the spiritually weak Deacon-Treasurer resigned (at the time of the Interim Pastor's arrival, and with the support of some other Deacons), and suggested worldly, rather than New Testament, methods of financing the failing church. While the Interim Pastor carried out his Scriptural preaching, teaching, and leadership duties, it was left up to myself as Chairman, with the Pastor's agreement and support, to encourage the Deacons and through them, weak and uncertain church members. My wife and I were new to the church; the Board, except for myself, was not well guided by the previous long-term Pastor. The latter utilized a controlling, untrained, and hence, unspiritual Board of Deacons, rather than a spiritual, Bible-trained "Board," for all church business except Pastoral preaching, teaching and Oversight. This weakness resulted in a poorly chosen, untrained number of weak Deacons. The church was divided, with baptized church members only a minority among the congregation. The new Interim Pastor, in just a few months, found that the majority of untested Deacons of this small church were attempting to apply, not scriptural principles, but secular, worldly, management knowledge, to control the Interim Pastor and the church—simply because he was temporary (not "called," but selected primarily by their "Headquarters organization").

Christian principles and New Testament church governance writings and principles were almost abandoned. The Interim Pastor and the Chairman (myself) came under vitriolic attack by biblically untaught and unspiritual church members, along with a number of weak Deacons. Both the Pastor and myself pleaded with these individuals, in the privacy of the Board meetings, not to wrongly disturb the church now, but to actively support the Interim Pastor in this precarious time while a permanent Pastor was being actively sought. To visitors, the Lord's work in the church appeared to continue, but Satan's work of hardening divisive hearts, and attempting to defeat Christ's witness through this small church, was well under way in the hearts of several Deacons and some members.

The unruly Deacons, under Satan's evil persuasions, tried to bring the Interim Pastor and myself before the church Headquarter officers, for a "church trial" that would wrongly attack our Christian actions and characters. The Interim Pastor felt (as did I) that, if the church officers or even individual church members had something against us, New Testament principles required that they made their charges within the church Body before taking it to a Headquarters group for discipline that was, itself, unscriptural in relation to this local church matter. We both refused to face even an informal, external "Board of Enquiry"—for that would negate what our Lord asked members of His Body to do, to keep problems and discipline within the Body and its leadership. If found guilty, and no repentance is offered by guilty ones, then Scripture supports only excommunication. This weakened little Body of Christ (weak because they were unspiritual, and wrongly considered an "Interim Pastor" as not being their current true leader under Christ) acted without Christian love, in trying to lead their church in secular and worldly, not scriptural ways.

The upshot? God gave this church a more permanent Pastor, shortly after the aborted inquiry by church outsiders was refused by the Interim Pastor and the Chairman of the Board of Deacons (myself). The Interim Pastor, deeply hurt, refused when asked by some to informally remain as Pastor. He left without being reconciled to the congregation of Christ he had been asked to serve for a short time (and had served well). My wife and I also considered it wiser to remove ourselves from this congregation, for the hostility and unforgiveness of these few Deacons (and some church members) remained. It has not been tempered in mercy or in Christian love since.

I hold no grudge against my brothers and sisters in Christ for these acts, or those of any other church for their often un-Christlike ways, words or actions. I only sought then, and seek still, to follow Christ and His Word for His Body, its doctrines, its faith, and its practices. But, like others before me, and others even in the early church, I have found it is not wise to remain in close association with those who are found to be "not of Christ" through unforgiving words and actions that oppose Christ's love. Martin Luther and his supporters, in their failed "Protestant Reformation" of the Roman Catholic church in the 16th century, also found it was better to leave—even to be excommunicated wrongly—than to remain and deny their Lord's scriptural teachings and principles. Satan-led opposition, leading to church "splits" or "separations" is often not lasting, when a Pastor can intervene and effect reconciliation by Godly and Scriptural counsel. But where full repentance, reform, and reconciliation are denied, Christ has shown us in His Word that it is better to depart and not live among spiritually misled Christians, who are unwilling to obey Christ and His Word for His Body, the church.

Outright sin, as described in Revelation 2 and 3 in Christ's Body—such as accepting and tolerating *false teachers*, or outright heresy and false gods—must be erased by immediate repentance, reforms, and the dismissal of those who will not return to their *first love*. But I have found that a Pastor-less church can best be handled by simply leaving the Body, and trusting that God will send a wise Pastor who will discern the hidden, unaddressed problems of his new flock, and try to reconcile all members with those who have left.

The subject matter of this chapter demonstrates how God can lead a Christian to observe, and suffer as a result, a lack of spirituality, faith and obedience in His church Body in these final days before Christ comes again, as He has promised in His Word (Rev. 22 and elsewhere). I have mentioned my sad experiences with these few churches also to reinforce my good experiences—and, at the same time, describe how God can give a Christian such as myself an ever-growing burden and concern for some unspiritual acts and spiritual failings in Christ's church. My experiences (very similar to those of many people, as you will find by asking Christians why they do not now attend church regularly) have not only shown me Satan-inspired church failure and disobedience in a general way. They have affirmed, in my mind and spirit, my specific burden from Christ about His church, and have led me to a specific purpose and specific purposeful action for our mutual Saviour.

The Purpose of This Writer, From and For the Lord.

I will leave my own church experiences and problems now, and go directly to discuss what the Head of the church (Jesus Christ) asks, demands, and orders individuals and His corporate church to do for Him, and to be for Him, in this world. My purpose from the

Lord has become firmed up from my concern for, and personal experience of, church sin and disobedience, as well as observations of many other churches of our Lord today. My book, arising from my burden, is only like a sign post. It points to Christ's Way and Will and Purpose; reminds the churches to *hear what the Spirit says to the churches* (Rev. 2,3)—and tells them of His consequences for failing Him and not reforming sin.

You see—and I pray that you do, as you read His Word, with the guidance of the Holy Spirit—for then, you will see (especially in John 14 and 16), that the important thing about my burden, and my purpose in writing this book, is not *my* words, *my* experiences, or *my* church and academic knowledge. But it is what our Lord has asked us in His Word to be and do for Him—for Him alone, *as new creations* (2 Cor. 5:17), added to His church.

As I continue in this book, referring the Christian reader, whether church member or leader, to inspired inerrant Scripture—sacred writings from God, His Son and inspired by His Spirit—I will also suggest an obvious and vital set of scriptural actions for all failing Christian churches to embark upon. These "sets of actions" (later I call them a "church reform process") are not part of a "How-To" book for Christians, but a serious approach to please the Lord by reforming disobedient acts that He abhors. The Lord wants us to *return to do the things we did at first* (Rev.2:5), which means: return to do what the early New Testament church did in obedience to Christ. **Obey all His teachings and Commands** in all areas of scriptural faith, doctrine and practice—**and not obey the false teachings and disobedient commands of men,** in His Inspired, Inerrant Word.

I pray that this book will be examined and read without presuppositions or personal bias—and found to be what I say it is, and what a Christian, guided by the Spirit, will find from Scripture it really is—God's inspired, inerrant Truth. It is a book that simply asks all Christian churches to examine themselves and their work, service, witness and actions for Christ—and to **compare honestly what they are doing,** and **publicly saying** as a Body of Christ, **with what Christ has asked them to be and do for Him**.

The authority of the Lord to ask full obedience of Christians is Supreme, since He, alone, is Head of the church—not unscriptural human "heads." Disobedience to Him and His inspired Word of Truth brings loss, of rewards and His presence, to those who deliberately fail Him. Only when they search, using His Words and holy standards found in His written Word, for hidden (or overt) sin in their church life—and please Him, with repentance and reform—only then will they revert from being a sin-stained and "wrinkled" church, and be holy and *radiant* when He comes to claim Her as His Bride.

I neither say now, nor anywhere in this book, that **all** churches or **all** Christians are disobedient to Christ and His Word. Some churches, some members, and some leaders, I know from history and Scripture, began as we all do—as "Born-Again spiritual *infants*." They determined, with Spirit-gifted church teachers and the written Word of God, to mature spiritually by the Word, to serve the Lord faithfully as He desires. They have done so—and will have His rewards. Many Christians and churches are, and will be, rightfully commended, and praised and rewarded by Christ for faithful obedience over the years until He comes again.

Finally, I write, not judgmentally, but only echoing Christ's Words of command, of commendation, even of His wrath against those who fail Him. I urge today's churches and members to re-examine their life (and church) in Christ for disobedience to His Word. If sin is found, the Spirit will reveal it, convict all who seek His counsel, and guide them to repent of their error and sin. With the help of the *Spirit of Truth* in each believer, He will revive, reform and return them to be and do what He requires—so that He will find them a *Radiant not Stained or Wrinkled church* (Eph. 5:27) when He comes again.

Reader, is it your purpose to faithfully follow Christ's purpose for His church, as it is brought to your memory through the Scripture I will quote in the following chapters? The *"Spirit of Truth,"* the Divine Head of His church on earth, says *I am coming soon* (Rev. 22:20). Will His church and His people be ready? I pray for this, and pray also that doubters and waverers will ask the Spirit to guide them to the Truth of His Word.

Chapter 2

"Sanctify Them by the Truth... Thy Word is Truth"

With this chapter, I discuss a fundamental Divine statement of Jesus Christ, about God's Word being Truth (John 17:17). As the Head of His then-future church—that men were to call "Christian" in the earliest years of the formation of His Body He Willed to build (Matt. 16:18)—He was concerned, even before His rejection as the Messiah by the Jews, about being obedient to His Heavenly Father. God's Plan, which only Jesus Christ knew then, was to allow His Only begotten Son to be unjustly betrayed, condemned, and brought to die on Calvary's Cross. This was necessary, as Scripture tells us, in order that He might bear the sins of the world in His death, and justify the whole sinful, Gentile world before a Holy God. God now determined to extend His loving grace and mercy to all nations—not alone to His Chosen People, the almost continually disobedient Jews. Jesus, when He taught and prayed and spoke to His disciples before His death, prepared them (and us) to accept and obey His Will to build a unique Body of believers for Him very soon.

During this teaching, praying and learning period, before the Lord was to leave His then-disciples for a period in Heaven with His Heavenly Father, the inspired Apostle John (see John 14–17) conveys Christ's wonderful message about the fact that God's Word is Divine Truth revealed to man. We also learn more truths from His inspired written Word. That He wanted His present and all future disciples to be **Truly One**—as He was and is One in all things with the Heavenly Father (John 17:11,21). At this time, too, the Lord spoke another Divine Truth when He told us in His then-future church that *if we love Him, we will obey His Commands* (John 15:10). These are but a few of His important Words, from the One Who is *the Way, the Truth, and the Life* (John 14:6) to we present disciples also. These basic truths form a critical part of this book's background, and will be brought forward and re-examined in later chapters.

This is *a book of love*—Christ's love—but *also a book of warning* to those in His church, in the past and today, who have forgotten His Divine commands and teachings to His church, or have deliberately disobeyed Him and His inspired Word. Some readers, at this point, may begin to defend their disobedience to the Lord by saying, "but my church never taught me these things you write about." I will have more to say about this defense and church teaching problem in Chapter 7 of this book.

God, in the fullness of His Time, gave Christ, His Only begotten Son, to the world—but particularly and first to His Chosen People, the Jews, as the prophesied Messiah of the Old Testament. Jesus, called **the Christ** or **Saviour**, first went to the Jewish people, and acknowledged His mission from God by stating His purpose clearly: *For the Son of Man came to seek and to save what was lost* (Luke 19:10). He was the Prophesied, the Messiah, the Incarnate form of the *Son of Man*. The *lost* were His own people, the Jews, as He said in Scripture after choosing 12 disciples for God's saving purpose for Israel. These Words of Christ are found in the Gospel of Matthew: *Do not go among the Gentiles or enter any town of the Samaritans. Go rather to the lost sheep of Israel* (Matt. 10:5,6) with His message to them about the salvation He offered on God's behalf following this passage. He confirmed it later in **His first mission to the Jews only**, in Matthew 15:24, although He responded to faith in Him by a Canaanite (outside the Jewish race), who pleaded for healing for her ill daughter. The Lord made an exception, in His first mission to the lost of Israel, and healed her daughter.

I quote these things from the Word of God to make a important point, often lost upon the Christian church formed after many highly-placed Jews rejected Jesus, the Christ. The Saviour-Messiah was sent first to offer salvation to the Jews only, upon their repentance and return to God, and a demonstration of their obedience to Him by their repenting and doing works of righteousness.

My point (God's point!) is simply this: only when the Jews largely rejected the prophesied Messiah (and many disobedient Jews continue to do so to this day), God softened His wrath to the Jews who rejected Him, and offered His great gift of salvation through His Son to the Gentile races of the world, then and now. ("Gentile" is the Biblical composite name of all races other than the Jewish "Chosen Nation" described in the Old Testament history of God dealing with one particular group of people, out of all men in His Created world.) Most Christians are Gentile believers.

Spirit-inspired, John, the beloved of Jesus among His 12 chosen Apostles, describes Jesus' new purpose and new mission among men after His rejection as the Messiah by certain Jews. I quote here: *For God so loved the world, that He gave His One and Only Son* (only-begotten Son) *that whoever believes in Him shall not perish but have eternal life* (John 3:16). His **new mission,** which I call His second mission, followed Christ's First Mission to the Jews only and became another unique mission for God, "Headed" by His Son on earth.

This time, the Resurrected Christ asked His disciples (with the Holy Spirit's help) to go beyond the **lost Jews alone,** and offer the Heavenly Father's Mercy, Love, and Grace to the Gentiles (all other races). It was all made possible by God's plan to extend His saving Grace and salvation by allowing His Only Son to be betrayed by the Jews and go to Calvary's Cross. And there He would die, in expiation of the sins of the entire world to a Holy God, redeeming all mankind (if they repented and believed by faith alone in the Risen Christ). God's plan was to resurrect Christ to Heaven, to sit at the Right Hand of this Holy, Merciful, and Just Creator-God. The Trinity remains One in all things; His Word tells us Christ will return soon to claim His *radiant* church, at a time only the Father knows.

Our Lord explained to His faithful disciples—excluding Judas, who was tempted by Satan to betray him to the highly-placed Jews of Jerusalem before His Death, Burial and Resurrection—that it was

His Will to build a then-future "church or assembly" called "Chris-tian" (those belonging to Christ's Body on earth). The "First Baptist church" of Jerusalem, formed on that long-ago Pentecost day, obe-diently began to carry out His earlier-given "Great Commission to His church" (Matt. 28:18–220). His Commission Commands are found in Part 3 of this book.

Using the inspired, inerrant Word of God, I must point out to my readers a few basic truths about God's plan, and **Christ's two missions for God**—the first to **the lost of Israel alone** (which ended in apparent failure, but was really just a "postponement" of God's promises to Israel)—and the second, salvation mission, to **all (Gen-tile) nations**, that began with Christ's Atonement for the sins of the whole world. Thanks be to God, the story didn't end in a martyr's death, but continued with His Son's (our Lord's) Resurrection after His death and burial; and with a Divine Statement of Christ that **He Willed to build His church of believers,** whose souls and glorified bodies would be resurrected to Eternal Life after bodily death. Thus, through reading Christ's Words, and the inspired Word of God written by the Spirit's moving in the hearts of holy men of old, we later members of the present church called Christian (all of us, whatever we name the local churches)—we all can know the full nature and extent of our Lord's Will, Purpose and Plan. His plan involves each member of His church serving Him, obeying Him, and pleasing Him, until He returns to claim each *radiant* church, composed of faithful, obedient disciples.

I point these things out in my book because my personal experi-ences in the church of Jesus Christ, my studies of New Testament Scripture, and my scriptural observation of His church after the death of the Apostles, down to today's Christian churches, has led me to dis-cover that very many past churches **did not teach all their members** to *obey all that I have commanded you* (Christ, in Matt. 28:20). Many churches today appear disobedient to His "Great Commission." I must quote portions of Christ's teachings, His authority, His commands, and His desires. Those members and leaders, reminded of them, will be touched by the Spirit of God, and want to do something for Him: dis-cover disobedience, repent, and reform their churches to please Him.

The Divine Standard of Truth—
God's Inspired, Inerrant and Infallible Written Word.

I must go further with my burden and purpose, which I declare is God's and His Son's purpose and Will in building His church, by defining how it must function; by declaring His Will and purpose to have His "Body" do as He commands, requires, and expects of us as Head, in the church and in the world. I quoted a portion of God's Truth in John 3:16 (read also verse 17) that describes a fundamental reason for the church's existence. It is vitally important for the church to carry out all Christ commanded in His Great Commission, and the first (the "Make disciples") purpose must be carried out before the last two commands of Christ, in Matthew 28.

The gospel message, the "Good News of Salvation from God" to all lost and sinful people (Jew or Gentile) requires the church, as Christ's Body on earth, to first *make disciples,* so that the following commands will accomplish all that He requires of the new as well as the old, or earlier .disciples. His church, Jesus commands, is to be composed of changed sinners—who, when they hear the gospel, are convicted by the Spirit, and repent and believe by faith alone in the Risen Lord. Then only can the church obey His following command, to baptize the believers—thus, adding them to His Body, the church on earth. The church must then take these baptized, repentant Christian believers, **teaching them** to obey all Christ requires, to mature them, strengthen the Body, reject *false teachers*, and serve Him.

All the things I have spoken of previously, as well as those I propose to discuss from God's inspired, inerrant Word, must be entirely based—not on men's words—but on the **Divine Standard of Truth: the Bible.** An important part of my burden and purpose from the Lord is to join together my referencing the inspired Word of Truth, concerning Christ's church, with my purpose to urge all Christian churches today to join with all other failing local churches in repentance, reform, and obedience—with the aid of the Spirit of God.

But what is truth, some might ask? Pontius Pilate asked this question after his encounter with Jesus Christ, with the hostile Jews asking Pilate to judge Him guilty by Roman, not Jewish, law. Jesus had said (see John 18:37), *I came into the world to testify to the Truth. Every one on the side of Truth listens to me.* He was speaking of Who He Was; but Pilate, blind to spiritual truth, asked *What is truth?* Jesus earlier had declared Himself *the Truth, the Way and the Life* in talking to His disciples (see John 14:6). Jesus also declared an important truth for all lost persons as well as for the church, when He added: *No man comes to the Father except through me,* in the same verse. The Divine Truth in the Divinely inspired, inerrant, written Word of God is, for Christians and His church, something that alone must guide them—not only to their own salvation, and later sanctification (being made Holy, or set apart for God's service)—but in the church's life, growth, training of members, and essential service and worship to the Lord. It is a vital church necessity to know **where to find truth**, and how to use **and follow it alone** in the church, and in the world. *God's Word is Truth,* Christ claims in John 17:17. If our Lord Himself is Truth, and **the only way to God;** and if the church must mature new Christians (spiritual *infants* Ephesians 4:14), and "grow" all Christians into *the faith and knowledge of the Son of God,* and recognize false teaching that destroys these purposes (Eph. 4:16)—then it is obviously important to discover, learn, and teach all church members (and leaders!) to know where to find God's Truth. And it is important to teach His Divine Truth to all members, as He orders us to do in His Great Commission for His church.

Now, I refer to Spiritual truth—distinct from worldly knowledge and secular wisdom; the truth that God speaks, His Son represents and teaches, and to which the Holy Spirit guides us. The church must teach God's Truth in contrast to men's false teachings about spiritual subjects, with Satan's ever-present lies clouding Divine Truth.

Many kinds and conditions of learning and teaching are evidenced publicly by many "diverse kinds" of so-called "Christian churches." Some of these churches show to the world, by their words and actions, that their sins are very similar to some of the disobediences found in the Seven Churches of Revelation 2 and 3 that I will write about in more detail later. These Seven early churches were, to varying degrees, under temptation and severe persecution during those ancient times. Some had failed, or were failing their

Lord. Just as many nominally Christian churches in the past have failed, or are failing God in our day, Satan, with the help of *false teachers* in many of these churches, is causing Christians to fail Christ.

Christ says, about new believers—*Teach them.* And He says *God's Word is Truth—making believers sanctified* (John 17:17, paraphrased by author). I say in this book, do what Scripture tells us: obey our Lord and God's Word. Teach all church members to obey all that the Lord asks. But I see, in my own church experience and in church history, that **many churches do not teach members fully, as Christ asks and commands**. Therefore, I feel a burden to remind the disobedient churches to do as the Lord asks: *teach all disciples in My church* (Matt. 28:20, paraphrased by author). This reminder of Christ's Words to Pastors and teachers of today's churches must necessarily consist primarily of Scripture. I can only apologize if I seem to be talking down to teachers in Christian churches, who may "know" Scripture better than I do—I am not! I pray that the Spirit of God will act upon their hearts, and they will hear me out as I warn them, on Christ's behalf, to *hear* (and obey) *what the Spirit says to the churches* (Rev. 2,3).

The title of this book is taken from Christ's universal request, in Revelation 2 and 3, to all His churches of every age. Readers will note my paraphased form of this verse on the title page and other pages of this book as a reminder to all readers! The Spirit of God speaks only the things the Divine Head of His Church, Jesus Christ, says (John 16:13–15). Hear the Spirit speaking through the Word of God!

I write these things about truth, and Eternal Life, and the Way (of life) of our Lord, and quote Scripture—not to imply I am more mature or knowledgeable about Scripture than my readers, but to emphasize the possibility that some of you who read this book are failing Christ right now—and don't know His Truth. If so, you need to know (or recall, or learn again from the Spirit and the Word) that you may be presently far from having Christ's approval for you and your church. In truth, your church may be failing Him now.

Back to my chapter heading, concerning **The Divine Standard of Truth**—I use, and recommend to all my readers, God's Truth as the only truth that all members and leaders in the church must teach, learn, know and obey, if we are to *remain in His love* (John 15:9,10).

It is part of this book—but far more important, it is part of the Christian church's required knowledge that will allow all members and leaders to faithfully carry out all of Christ's commands. Only by knowing the inspired Word of God, **and** teaching it to every new Christian added to the church, will every church be strengthened by having all its members become spiritually mature, and able to discern and reject false teaching (Eph. 4:14). The Apostle Peter said, in the Divine Word of Truth (2 Pet. 2:1ff), there were also false prophets among you, (in Peter's time and prior to it) just as there will be false teachers among you (the church, in the future, and in our time). The Spirit leads each believer to vital Truths of God's Word, concerning our churches in the past and today, and by this means, reveals there are false teachers among us today. If we don't know what is truth, or where to find it (in Christ, and in God's Word), Peter is inspired to tell us of a continuing problem, so that we can recognize and cast false teachers out before they harm the spiritual life of new (or old!) Christians. Or before the church does and says things sinfully contrary to the True Head—disobeying and failing Him.

I say, too, on the authority of God's Word, and on the authority of the Holy Spirit, that the *Divine Counselor,* the *Teacher of Truth* sent to us when we believed in the Name of Jesus—the One Who is *the Spirit of Truth* is also the One Who will teach us all things about our Lord and *guide us to all Truth* (John 14,16). And He will teach failing **church teachers** to return to teach all members what Christ requires in His Great Commission for the church (Matt. 28:18–20). If the church is faithful to do these things, in accordance with God's Truth, for Christ Who is the church's Head (Eph. 5:23), we will have repentant, revived and reformed churches, returned to their *first love,* and restored as *Radiant churches, unstained by sin.* Then the church will, at last, become *the Bride of Christ, Obedient, Radiant and unstained by sin* (Eph. 5:27) when He comes again and soon (Rev. 22:7).

The Early Christian Church and Their Divine Standard of Truth.

If an unbiased Christian approaches the Divine history of Christ's Body on earth, in the inspired Gospel books, the Book of Acts, and the record of Paul's and others' inspired Letters—all in the New Testament for the Christian church—clear evidence of Christ's Will, purpose and commands to build His church emerges. But these records, in the written form in which the later church (and today's churches) has them, were not, of course, available to the early church in the same way we today have received the Divine Standard of Truth. The life and purpose of Jesus Christ, His two consecutive missions on earth received from His Heavenly Father—the Divine Standard of Truth about about His Will to *build His church*, and His instructions as to achieving this purpose—was available to the very early church only through verbal Apostolic instruction (most Apostles received the truth directly from the Lord over some 3 1/2 years). Some inspired teachings became available in handwritten, manuscript letter form (2 Pet. 1:21) much later on, as seen by us in the "New Testament Canon" or "inspired collection" of this portion of the Bible.

What the first—and earliest—of the Christian churches had of God's Truth was received from their Master-Teacher, the Lord Himself, through the Apostles, who were with Jesus on His first mission to *lost Israel.* Later disciples (the Apostle Paul, among others) received further instructions by the Spirit's moving them (2 Pet. 1:21) to record what He wished passed on to the church of His second mission. And, as Christ's "Commission to the church" tells us (Matt. 28:18–20—the *teach them* part), the Apostles and inspired disciples passed the truths on to the first church members, and to the later missionary churches, by teaching visits. All of these truths were given orally to the Jerusalem and later bodies of Christ. Christ told His disciples then, and us now (He **commissioned** us all), to *teach them*—the new disciples, who had repented and believed in the Risen Christ, and who had been baptized and added to the "Body of Christ"—to: *obey all* (everything) *that I* (Christ) *have commanded you.*

Unbiased obedient Christian churches today must recognize—as they study, learn, and teach the Divine Standard of Truth to all new members—that the "*all* (or everything)" in the third part of His Commission referred to above, includes **all** of Christ's teachings, imparted to the Apostles and disciples over three-and-a-half years, as well as those things that the Holy Spirit *moved* (inspired) other disciples to

43

write down, as Divinely-inspired instructions, to other disciples in the widespread new bodies of Christ. Not only were all the "original teachings of Christ" taught; the Spirit moved some Apostles to "clarify—but without change" some of His teachings. Some examples are Paul's inspired teachings to the Corinthian church (and others), concerning abuse and false teachings about Christian baptism, the Lord's Supper, church organization and practices, qualifications and gender of church leaders (Elders), teachers, and Deacons under Christ, the Head—and, of course, many other inspired, substantive doctrines of Christianity. Paul wrote them to disobedient churches, upon the Spirit's urging, to correct disobedience, false teachings, interpretations and false practices even then creeping into the early church.

My point here is that the first church of Christ at Jerusalem, and missionary churches formed in obedience to Christ's commands to *Go, and make disciples of all nations...baptize them...* (Matt. 28:18,19), also obeyed **His third command** (V. 20, *teach them*), and faithfully did so throughout the New Testament record—with few exceptions. The teaching in the Jerusalem church was done primarily by the Apostles—while in the spreading church outside Jerusalem, the teaching was carried out by those Christians who had been instructed by the Apostles, and later forced into the adjoining provinces by Jewish persecution. Later, others like Paul, who had met the Lord after His return to His Throne in Heaven (in visions, or in Spirit-given instructions to be passed on to Christians in other nations), carried out Christ's command to teach the new disciples, as the Church spread out to a lost world through the Spirit's urging.

The word-of-mouth form of teaching Christ's Words, as the Church grew and spread abroad, became supplemented by other means of passing on and teaching these inspired Divine Truths. These provided clarification and amplification of what His church Body must be and do in all things for Him. This is apparent as we read the New Testament books, with the *Spirit of Truth*—available from copies of original hand-written letters, on parchment—forming a "Canon," or church-approved list, of Sacred writings. They include many copies, in letter form, written to special churches ("special" to the inspired writer—but soon dear and special to all Christians who read the inspired New Testament record). These scriptural letters were passed around by Christians travelling on their business of trade, etc., to the Christian leaders and to the brethren in the new missionary churches. All these truths (Holy writings) then and now are valuable—even vital—to the Christian reader of all ages, simply because they were and are seen and believed to be Divine in their origin, as God's Word to the church. God inspired these writings of holy men, and preserved them for His church.

All Scripture...is God-breathed (Spirit-inspired) *and is useful for teaching, rebuking, correcting and training in righteousness, so that the man of God may be thoroughly equipped for every good work* (2 Tim. 3:16,17—Paul's inspired word of instruction to his protegé and Pastor in church work, and to all Christians!). Scripture, then, God's Holy writings (first orally transmitted by Christ's personally chosen disciples) was first handwritten, then printed, and today is available for teaching new disciples, in hundreds of languages or dialects represented in His Body. And, by Christ's Commission Command, they **must be taught** to all believers.

Under the conviction and urging of the Spirit within each believer, Christ's church grew in numbers—and more importantly, spiritually. The value of these inspired manuscripts, that began to circulate among the churches, grew as they became known and accepted as Holy Scripture—literally, God's written Word to special groups of men and women. God then led the early Christian churches to gather, assemble and make available the Scriptures, called the New Testament books, in a permanent form. (The Old Testament portion of the Bible, being more ancient, was placed into a "Canon" of God's *Law and Prophets*, including Moses' early five books on the *Beginnings* of God's Creation of His Heavens, Earth, and mankind.)

This is just a brief explanation of our Bible's formation. Interested readers should consult the many excellent, scholarly Christian books for details about how God inspired, preserved, and arranged for His Chosen Nation (the Jews), and His Son's Church, to have His Holy Word in inerrant (and infallible) written form, as His Standard of Truth for all in His Church and in His Chosen Nation.

We Christian believers in Christ's church Body are fortunate today to have the Words of Christ, instituting and instructing His church as to what to do to build His church, and how to organize for His purpose of *making disciples...baptizing them...and teaching them to obey all that I have commanded you.* We have His Word in an inspired, inerrant form that contains His Truth, the Whole Truth, and nothing but the Truth! We must not forget His Love and Grace in providing the Holy Spirit in every new believer, to guide us and lead us to the truth, contained in His inspired Bible.

With many other Christians, I believe in the ***Bible as God's inspired, inerrant, (and infallible) Written Word.*** I believe that the God Who created the world and all that is in it, Who cannot lie, for He is Holy—that this Merciful, Just, Holy and True God is also Omnipresent, Omniscient, Omnipotent, and loves His whole creation, including mankind. I believe He Has spoken to us clearly through His Only Begotten Son, and through His written Word. I believe that Satan, the Devil (that fallen angel, who influenced our first ancestors to disobey God), still roams the world, seeking to destroy God's plans and people, and especially, God's Son's plans for extending God's gift of salvation to the whole lost, Gentile world through His church.

This Devil we call Satan, according to God's Word, remains active in tempting Christ's Body (all Christians, members and leaders) to reject and disobey the One True Creator-God and His written Word. I believe that Satan has placed *false teachers*, in the church and in the world, to cause Christians to question God, Christ, and the inspired, inerrant Word of God.

What is truth? It is God's inspired Word for all mankind—especially for His Body, the church on earth. Readers who truly believe that the Christian Bible, especially the New Testament for the Christian church, is completely inspired of God, and is inerrant and infallible in **all** that it says for **all** Christians (all Christ's Body on earth), must rely upon it **alone** as our guide. I pray many will recognize, with the aid and guidance of the *Spirit of Truth*, that the Bible is completely True—and is, in fact, the only Divine Standard of God's Truth that sanctifies all believers (in all stages of spiritual maturity) in the Church (John 17:17). Satan's *false teachers*, in and out of the church, are causing many churches to give up *their first love* (Christ)—causing *lukewarmness* and *spiritual deadness*. All of these things and more will inevitably cause alienation from the Head of the church. If these sins are not repented of, and reform and revival instituted, they will cause Christ *to spit them,* the failing or failed churches, *out of His mouth... remove their candlestick from His presence* (italics above—Christ's own Words in Rev. 2,3). Failings and failures in many churches are seen and known to the world today, and also reveal an absence of "Oneness," or "church Unity" that the Lord desires (John 17:21).

The Word of God, written, is completely of and from God. It is the only Standard of Truth that we Christians in the Body of Christ have, and against which we can measure the false teachings, the "additions," the "perversions," the Satan-inspired "modern" opinions and false teachings of men. Christ and the Bible both declare God's Word is Truth, and that men's words that oppose or pervert the Holy Scriptures are wrong. *False teachers*, in or out of the church, or in false organizations, cults or sects or failing denominations, can only be seen by comparing their false words with the Spirit's Guidance to God's written Word. This is what I advocate and urge upon the many failing Christian churches.

Always in my spirit, soul, mind and heart, I am urged on in my burden and my purpose from Christ: to prepare this humble book containing God's Standard of Truth and warning for His Son's church quickly, for I know—as any Bible student and Christian who reads the Word can see for themselves—that our Lord, the Head of the church says *I am coming soon* (Rev. 22:7,20).

Some Words About the Divine Standard of God's Word, and the Form in Which We Have It.

With the development of the printing press, the availability of God's Written Word, the Bible, to all Christians in the world became feasible and relatively economical. But, as church history shows, this did not mean that all Christians in all churches either were taught, or read, God's Word. Nor did it change some churches' habitual patterns of **not** teaching all Christians to *obey all that I* (Christ) *have commanded you* from the newly available printed Word of God.

47

Instances are recorded of Christians not even being allowed to possess and read the Holy Scriptures for themselves.

Part of the past and present disobedience of many churches is demonstrated through some churches' "traditional" practice of perverting Scripture by teaching new disciples only a brief extract from God's Word, in the form of a brief "catechism" (or incomplete "creed"), and **not teaching** ...*all that I* (Christ) *have commanded you.* Despite Paul's inspired words in 2 Timothy 3:16, Christians in some churches fail to realize that the church's required duty, given by the Head, Jesus Christ, to the leaders and gifted teachers, is to observe, preach and teach all of Scripture—not a part of it only.

Incomplete teaching is disobedience to Christ's commands, and will be mentioned later in this book as I analyze past and present patterns of established church disobedience to Christ that merit His anger and warrant His punishment. Recall that Christ said to all disciples: *If you love me, you will obey my commands and will remain in my love* (John 14:15; 15:10).

Many churches are faithful in having Bible classes for all ages of believers, not merely "Sunday School" for children. But again, the full teaching of all of God's Word to equip each believing member for service and *every good work* is often neglected. Some disobedient churches today also teach adult Christians God's Word only on a *voluntary* basis, rather than exhorting from the pulpit that *everyone* who is a Christian needs to be equipped for His service (2 Tim. 3:16,17). All must be taught, as the inspired writer of Ephesians 4 states, to strengthen the whole Body; to bring each new Spiritual infant-Christian to full maturity, and all His bodies, the church, into the Unity that Christ prayed for in John 17:20,21. Within the last few centuries, extensive printing and publishing has allowed the Church to provide Bibles for all its members in many languages. But this does not always mean the Christian church faithfully applies God's Word to Christ's stated purposes for all Christians in the local churches. Satan has led some to deliberately misuse and disuse the Bible. Furthermore, many sects calling themselves Christian have perverted the Sacred Word with additions to, or mistranslation of, the Holy Bible—to justify *false,* Scripture-opposed teachings. But I write here to Christians only.

Some Christian churches and seminaries have produced or allowed, with Satan's help, *false teachers and theologians* (as Peter prophesied!)—with the end result that reading some Bible versions may lead men to eternal destruction if they trust what false Bible versions and *false teachers* say. If that isn't enough, some well-organized groups of disobedient Christians, seminaries, and Pastors have opposed the inerrant written Word of God—the Bible—by telling gullible Christians that, while the Bible is true in matters of salvation, in matters of history and science, the Bible contains many errors. Others say the Bible was written by unschooled men in a completely different and patriarchal society—and so, they state, "we cannot always trust the Bible when it comes to Christian and church life, faith, form, or some practices, and so these errors must be discarded in our advanced technological society." These things are wrong, for God had holy men write down His Revelation for **all** ages, and His Word is mandatory for all Christians to follow until He comes again to claim a Holy, Radiant, Sinless, and Fully obedient church.

These *false teachers* and their deceitful schemes, prompted by Satan to destroy Christ's church and those believers who compose it, and who are trying to serve Him obediently in all things, must be opposed by those who know God's inspired Word is Truth. And the *false teachers* must be ejected from Christ's Church, unless they give up their false ways. These *false teachers* often do not recognize their errors as such, and do not accept God's Truth, because their *minds are darkened* (Rom. 1) in their rejection of God. Nor do they tell us how they alone, and not their followers, can discern truth from error. Believers, well-taught by the church, along with Spirit-gifted leaders and members, can and will know the truth, if they subject the claimed "new truth" (actually error) to the guiding Divine Spirit of God, Who can and will teach us Divine Truth. See John 14,16 on the Spirit's role. Only the Holy Spirit within each believer—only the *Holy Spirit of Truth*—can lead us to the Divine Truth, while rejecting everything of man not in accord with the only Word of Truth that man can trust: the inspired, inerrant Bible as we have it today.

A word of caution concerning the many available Bible versions, as produced by a great variety of Christian teachers, theologians, historians, and translators, and printed and made available to the great variety of Christian churches, and denominations. I do not include the "mistranslated Bibles" or "additions" to the Bible produced by false Christian cults. My caution concerns the fact that some Christian Bible versions have been produced using "recent" ancient documents (that is, closer to today's times, as compared to closer to the events written about) instead of the more accurate materials from closer in time to New Testament events. These Bible versions are not as faithful as they might be, because of poor material, or faulty and careless translations from older languages to ours. Some older Bible versions also contain mistranslations, besides less accurate source material, and often particularly obsolete and archaic words and expressions that hinder the reader (removed in time from the translator's time, society and culture) from fully understanding what God is truthfully saying to men of all ages. Copyist's errors too, unless carefully removed, may cause some little-taught churches and their members, to conclude the Bible is "full of errors"—and, therefore, is not to be trusted.

Elsewhere in this book, I speak about some Christian denominations who recommend that their members teach the Bible as either "myth" or "truth." If our God is the Only True God, whose *Word of Truth sanctifies Christian believers* (as Christ said in John 17:17), then of course we know that this Almighty, Omniscient, Omnipotent, and Holy God would not allow "untruths" to creep into His Word! He has preserved His Word of Truth over the centuries, so that we believers in His church (and Righteous Jews, in their religion) might have His Truth to help us all become Holy, as He is Holy. I spoke of copyist errors, deliberate cultist errors, and a few mistranslations from Hebrew or Greek, to English of today, and of the past; none of these errors, Christian and Jewish researchers tell us, **seriously** affect the Word of God today. So, for all Christian churches, it is important to trust the new versions of the Bible—for most contain God's Holy Word, relatively untouched by evil, Satan-inspired men over time. Most importantly, with the Gift of the Holy Spirit of God within each believer, the Word of God can be understood and obeyed as never before, for the *Spirit of Truth* (John 14,16) will remind us of Christ's Words, teach us to obey them, and guide us to the truth.

Too, I do not suggest that paraphrased Bible versions do not have the merit of leading young or unmotivated Christians to read the Bible and find salvation. I only suggest they be used with caution, and not be used by Church teachers in obedience to Christ's Great Commission (*teach them*), for they often are not fully accurate interpretations of important teachings and doctrines. The only spiritual corrective I know for "Bible version problems" is the asked-for Counsel, Aid and Guidance of the Holy Spirit, given to each Christian for these and other purposes of Christ.

After all these cautions, I will say that there are, today, many excellent translations and Bible versions available for Christians and the teaching ministries, in churches, Bible schools and seminaries. Some versions are more accurate than earlier versions (Christian scholars tell us), simply because more very early Greek and Hebrew documents are available today to translators than were available in past centuries. And many of these accurate versions, we are also told by Bible scholars, are now entirely free of early editing and translating errors, cultural language errors, and errors of personal or editorial bias. Therefore we can be and are assured that, in all important respects, we Christians today have God's Word, accurate and very close to the original documents. But we still must teach God's inspired Word with the Spirit to all church members—not kept the personal property of Priest or Pastor alone!

Why the Christian Church Today Needs to Return to the Bible Standard of God's Truth.

After my experience of Christian churches, my Bible training, reading Christian church history, and my reliance upon the *Spirit of Truth* (even though I have been a Christian for only some 37 years), I believe that I know the source of much of Christian church disobedience and sin. It is that, primarily, many church members, leaders, and theologians do not fully trust or rely on God's inspired, inerrant, and infallible written Word that the Spirit has given us in Bible form—especially the New Testament portion He has given for personal and corporate church guidance. While Satan is, doubtless, the prime instigator, the source of error, sin ,and disobedience lies in the initial and Original Sin of man: of listening to and obeying men and Satan, rather than listening to and obeying God's Word (first in oral teaching, then in written Words).

I would like to close this chapter on God's written Word of Truth, that sanctifies men who follow and obey it (Christ, in John 17:17), by speaking of the absolute trustworthiness and reliability of the Bible today to guide each Christian member and leader, and lead each Christian church, to this Truth of God. And to act upon His inspired Word in full obedience before the Lord returns.

I mention elsewhere in this book, but will do so here in this chapter, that I personally prefer to read, study, and use the New International Study Bible, because I believe it is based upon the most reliable, "early" documents now available to Bible scholars, historians and translators. And it uses the most reliable and earliest Hebrew and Greek material available. It also eliminates other, earlier, Bible versions' use of material and translations that contain archaic words, editor and copyist's errors, and translations made for societies and languages much different from ours today.

I can also recommend to readers two recent books: *The Making of the NIV* and *The Accuracy of the NIV* (plus another I do not have, *The Balance of the NIV*) all by Kenneth L. Barker, published by Baker Books and copyright 1991 by the International Bible Society. Both describe how the Society, with approximately 125 Christian historians and translators, put together a Bible over 11 years, ending in 1978, that is as accurate and readable as Christian men, under the guidance of the Holy Spirit, can make it. They have this, without the originals, but with very many ancient Hebrew and Greek documents, some just a few decades from the New Testament events.

I believe that we have in our hands, today, a Bible version very close to the *God-breathed* Revelation to man, described in 2 Timothy 3:16 and elsewhere. I believe that God and His Spirit guided modern historians and translators to discover His Word of Truth from the old God-preserved documents, and to faithfully put it into many languages and dialects for the multitudinous societies of mankind. I thank God for their faithful, Spirit-led work.

Because I believe and trust my God and His Spirit, I do not believe the claims of *false teachers* and theologians who try to tell their followers that the Bible as we have it—as God inspired holy men of old to write His Truth and Revelations down for all ages (2 Tim. 3:16,17)—is errant in part or whole. They say, wrongly, it is written by sinful men in differing societies and situations; and, in short, that we cannot trust God alone as Divine Author of His Word of Truth. I believe the Creator-God, Who created men for His pleasure and worship—the Omnipotent, Omniscient, Just, Holy and Loving God and Saviour—could not, would not, **and did not** allow His Revelation to man to be perverted, distorted, added to or subtracted from, so as to lead either Jews or Christians astray spiritually. **God would not and did not lead men astray** in His inspired, infallible Word. Nor did He allow errors affecting Christian believers to lead His church astray—in truth, He gave us His Holy Spirit, Who ensures that we can discern and reject error—even if *false teachers*, cults, or anyone rejects God's Word or changes it, by misinterpretation, mistranslation, deliberate *false teachings*, or by Satan's work.

We Christians today have the inspired, inerrant Truth of God; and we have the gift of the Holy *Spirit of Truth* to guide us to all truth; we have full scriptural knowledge of what Christ, our Divine Church Head, teaches, asks, expects and demands of His Body on earth— and we know that He is coming soon, **expecting to find a** *holy, radiant, sinless and obedient* **church Body, all united,** all one, just as He and His Heavenly Father are One in all things. His Word is Truth, indeed—but His church must fail unless each one reads, teaches, preaches and practises it in obedience!

Chapter 3

What Does Jesus Christ Require of All Christians?

Before we answer this chapter's urgent question, let me recapitulate some of the familiar, but perhaps forgotten "history" of the events leading to the Will and purpose of our Lord to build His church.

Preceded on His First Mission by John the Baptist, the prophesied forerunner of the long-awaited Messiah sent by God, Jesus would bring salvation to the Jews. As recounted in the gospels, Jesus gathered twelve Apostles, who He prepared and taught to accompany Him on His mission to preach to His people only and offer God's Mercy and Reconciliation to those Jews who would, under the Law, repent and return in full obedience to their God.

Near the end of the Gospel of John, we read that Jesus made a momentous statement to His assembled Apostles and disciples, about His future and their new mission to the Gentiles of *"all nations"* on this earth . It was a very troubling time for Jesus, the Christ (the "Anointed One," or "Messiah" of God). It was near the end of His First Mission for God *to seek and save the lost of Isreal* (Matthew 15:24), and hate, opposition, rejection, extreme jealousy, and hostility by some religious Heads and teachers was clearly seen. These things revealed to the disciples' Lord that His time on earth with them was coming to a close, in accordance with God's Plan of salvation for the whole lost world—not only for the Jews. Our Lord, too, was becoming aware of the suffering He must endure on earth, before He could rejoin His Heavenly Father (John 14:2).

Beginning in John, chapter 12, and continuing to the end of chapter 17, we find the whole intense narrative of Jewish hostility, Christ's betrayal by Judas, the Lord's sudden change of teachings, and His preparation of the Apostles (and present and future disciples) for what must happen—to Him, and to them (and to us in the distant future). There are, indeed, many books for Christians about these few scriptural chapters that have been noted—but the best cannot reveal these events and teachings to we latter-day disciples as well as can the inspired Word, itself. Nor can these Sacred passages give us the True teachings of our Lord for His Body on earth, when read in isolation as history alone, without the guidance of the Holy Spirit living in each True Christian.

In this large portion of Holy Scripture, in the Gospel of John, I want to extract a few verses, in Jesus' own Words, to illustrate this Part 2 heading: "Disobedience to the Divine Church Head." As this book proceeds, readers will see that the verses used in these chapters are not taken out of context at all—for the few are all set in the overall body of teachings of Christ as He finished His first mission for His Heavenly Father, and saw ever more clearly that He would have to leave the world temporarily. He knew His Apostles, along with His present and future disciples, had to carry out His new mission until His return, and knew they needed His help during his absence. The present disciples could not be left alone to carry out the new mission (for they did not fully understand how they could do it, with their Lord leaving this world). The Promised Gift of God, a Spiritual Counselor (John 14:16), however, was soon to be given to them, and each new future believer. But then they needed to understand what was happening to Him, as God's time-table for these barely-understandable events moved on ever more quickly—toward Calvary's cross.

After His overheard prayer, in John 17, the Apostles would understand more. And certainly, when the Holy Spirit came upon them in Jerusalem, after the Lord's death, burial and resurrection, these things became clear to His waiting and grieving followers.

What does Christ require of all Christians?

In these chapters of the Gospel of John, we are told of the temporary closing off of Christ's first mission to the Jews (temporary, for
God is Faithful and Just and will keep His Promises to the Jews). The
text enters into a new phase of communications between the Lord
and His faithful few disciples and Apostles—dealing with Christ's
new mission to the Gentiles, and a sad postponement of the first
mission of Jesus (for God) to the Jews. I use the word "**postponement**" although it is not stated, as such, in the Scriptures. But the
events leading up to Chapters 12–17, and concluding with Chapter 18 to the close of John's Gospel, cannot but show us that the
Lord's first mission—*to seek and save the lost of Israel*—will shortly be
postponed until the Messiah's later and predicted return to earth. It
will be deferred until long after His coming betrayal, rejection by
Jewish leaders, and His death on Calvary's cross.

A Spirit-guided Christian, looking at Scripture, cannot fail to
come to any other conclusion. It is seen as "God's postponement"
of the first mission, and the start of an entirely new mission, to **offer
God's Mercy and salvation to the Gentiles**. When we take up John's
inspired writings in Chapter 18, we see the events God foresaw and
allowed to proceed: Christ's death and burial after His Atoning
death on the cross, His glorious Resurrection, and His meeting with
His disciples before being taken up into Heaven.

These chapters contain our Lord's Words describing, to them
and all future disciples, what they must undergo for Him in building
His Church (Matthew 16), and why obedience to Him—in the world
and in the church—is vitally important for Christian believers to
understand. Reading them with the Holy Spirit as our guide is urged,
so that all readers might understand why His early disciples were
confused and at a loss to understand or accept what was happening
to them and their Lord—and what He requires of them and us today.

Chapter 12 of John's Gospel reveals to Jesus' Apostles and disciples something of Christ's news of His coming "Glorification"
(12:23); that He will be *lifted up from the earth* (12:32) after the
coming days at Calvary and, later, in His Ascension. He said these

things as John was inspired to write—*to show the kind of death He was going to die* (12:33). But recall that John wrote these things much later, after the establishment of the Christian church. The Jewish leaders, other Christ-seekers, and the Apostles who heard these revelations, did not really understand Jesus' Words, and could not put them into a clear pattern until Calvary's tragedy took place. And, in the case of the soon-to-be-formed Christian church, the Apostles could not believe what He told them until the coming *Spirit of Truth* (John 14:17) brought all these things back to their still-grieving memories. But we have them in Holy Writing now, and we have the Spirit in each Christian believer to teach us the Divine Truth, Divine meaning, and God's plan behind these events and Words, and show us the way to obediently serve our Risen Lord.

John **Chapter 13** tells us of many last events and last words— among them being Christ's Words about His coming betrayal (John 13:21). Subsequent verses in this chapter tell us how Satan entered into Judas, one of the original twelve Apostles, and how Judas formed his intent to betray Jesus falsely to the Jews in high places in Israel. These hostile Jews remained unbelieving that Jesus was the true Messiah Who had come to save His People, Israel. We also find Christ predicting Peter's denial of Him, by disowning His Lord, in the terrible events to follow his betrayal (John 13:38).

Many wonderful teachings of Christ for His present and future disciples in His future church are revealed in **Chapter 14** by the inspired Apostle Paul, and they are explained to us as Divine Truth by the Holy Spirit. The promised gift of the Holy Spirit came upon the believers waiting in the Upper Room in Jerusalem, just prior to the establishment of Christ's first church. This great spiritual event, Willed by the Lord, was preceded by the Spirit coming upon the waiting Apostles and disciples, causing them to speak in many different languages, in order to draw visiting Jews from other countries to hear Peter's first gospel message of salvation (see Acts 2, with the Spirit leading you!)

The early verses of John's Gospel, in Chapter 14, contain much comfort and information to all Christ's disciples, then and now. Christ speaks to us today as He did to the early disciples of His

future church by revealing His imminent death and departure—
but He speaks also of His soon-to-be-fulfilled plans of asking His
Father to send them (and us) *a Counselor, to be with you forever* as
the Spirit of Truth (John 14:16ff). Note this passage carefully, for
He tells them and us that *the world neither sees or knows Him* (the
Spirit) *but you know Him, for He lives with you and will be in you*
(14:17). Because He lives within true believers, we are able to *live
in accordance with the Spirit, and have our minds set on what the
Spirit desires* (Rom. 8:6). Also, *if anyone does not have the Spirit of
Christ* (within him) *he does not belong to Christ* (8:9). This explains
why, in the church Christ Willed to build (after His Resurrection),
the inspired, Spirit-occupied-and-led Apostles and missionaries
were obediently devoted to the Lord, and faithfully carried out
(with the Spirit's conviction of sinners), all the "steps" I write about
in Part 3. That is, following His commands concerning **the making
of disciples...the baptizing of them following repentance and belief...and
the careful teaching of the new baptized believers to obey all Christ had
commanded them** (Matt. 28, paraphrased by the author).

John 14:17, confirmed by Romans 8:6,9 is, in my opinion, one
of the least-publicized or even least-known Divine teachings given
to the Body of Christ in the world. I say this because personal and
public awareness of the lack of obedience by many Christian
churches leads me, and other concerned Christians, to the knowledge that the average Christian today is simply not taught that
each believer has the Spirit of God in them (*He lives with you, and
will be in you...*John 14:17), and that the Spirit's role and purpose
is as described in John 14 and 16, among other places in God's
inspired Word. Yet, it is seen to be the key to being obedient to
Him. And it is the key to discovering disobedience, repentance,
and reform, as I point out later. This book's title (in Christ's own
Words to each New Testament church example in Revelation 2 and
3, and in all ages) says **The Spirit Speaks Today**. We in His church
must listen to what He says, and act in obedience to *Christ who
loved the Church, and gave Himself up for Her* (Eph. 5:25).

After describing His Father's gift of the Spirit, Jesus continues
His words of teaching and comfort to His present and future disci-

ples in His new Body to be formed later. In John **Chapter 15**, He speaks to them (and us today!) of the analogy of "the Vine and the Branches," in which the Head of the future church, Jesus Christ, is the "true Vine," we Christians are "branches in Him," and God is the "Gardener." The fruit of good works in Christian lives will only be produced plentifully, as God requires, if He prunes (disciplines) us, and we thus remain in Christ (being faithful to the One Who died for the sins of the world, and Who asks all Christians in His Body, the church, to obey Him). In this parable, Jesus tells us: *As the Father has loved me, so have I loved you. Now remain in my love* (i.e. don't disobey or fail me). *IF YOU OBEY MY COMMANDS, YOU WILL REMAIN IN MY LOVE.* Our Lord adds: *just as I have obeyed my Father's commands and remain in His love* (John 15:9). **What does Jesus Christ require of all Christians in His church? First, love Him—then obedience will follow naturally! But the converse is true: we will not remain in His love if we are disobedient and fail Hi m, our Lord!**

Some church examples of the Apostle John's later years, as recorded in Revelation 2 and 3 when Christ came to him in a vision (Rev. 1), contain some of these same injunctions, and warnings Christ gave to His Apostles even before the first church was formed, according to His Will after His Resurrection. Then, the subject was general obedience, in a clear response to love. In Revelation 2 and 3, the subject of obedience or loss of His Love becomes very urgent and specific for all churches. They will be discussed in more detail later for the benefit of some Christian churches who are often disobedient, according to the public evidence of their sin.

This is not a detailed analysis of Christ's Words to His disciples as He tells them of what must happen soon in connection with His imminent death. This is, rather, an introduction to more detailed and specific Words of Truth directed to His yet-to-be-formed churches (to us today!), addressing their individual and personal relationship to Him and their status and standing with their Lord in this world, through the coming gift of God—the Holy Spirit in each believer (see Acts 2:38, His coming to the first Christian church).

Pressing on, we reach the close of John, Chapter 15—in which our Lord makes reference to His leaving them bodily, but not leaving them alone spiritually to face a hostile, unbelieving world. In John 15:26,27, Jesus tells the shocked disciples that *When the Counselor comes, whom I will send to you from the Father—the Spirit of Truth, who goes out from the Father—He will testify about Me. And you also must testify* (about me) *for you have been with me from the beginning.* With these few words, Jesus sets the stage, preparing them for God's plan for Himself and for them. As well, He gives them advance confirmation of His Words to them about His Commission to the future church (Matt. 28). They will receive and must follow the *Counselor,* the Holy *Spirit of Truth,* and they must add their testimony about Christ to that of the Spirit's, in dealing with the sinful Jew or Gentile.

In **Chapter 16** of John's Gospel, Jesus first warns His faithful few of coming persecution, and expulsion from the Jewish synagogues, which have been a large part of their Jewish life and religion. The hostile, radical Jews, He said, might even kill you, supposing they are doing a service for God. This reveals the great misunderstanding of the leaders and many of His people, concerning the Truth that Jesus was the long-promised (prophesied) Messiah sent by God to seek and save the *lost of Israel* (Luke 19:10; Matt. 15:24). It was not only their misunderstanding, but a complete rejection of the Holy "Anointed One" of God—for, in Jesus' Words: *they have not known the Father or Me* (John 16:3). These things He said to His disciples and Apostles for the first time because while He was with them, on His first mission, He protected them. Now, He would leave them, and warns them of trouble, though they will soon have the Spirit with them when He left this world.

From John 14:16,17; John 14:26ff, and then from John 15:26, we read about the coming of the *Spirit of Truth*, the gift of God to every repentant, convicted believer, *born again* by the same Spirit. We learn, in these great passages of Scripture for the Christian church, much more of what the Spirit will do for those who receive Him, after repentance and belief in their new, *born-again* lives, and seek His guiding Counsel and Teachings of Truth. This passage, as well as the portion in John 14, is one of the most vital portions of Divine Truth that the church should teach to every new believer, every spiritual *infant* (Eph. 4), baptized and added to the church after being *born again* by faith alone. But, regrettably, many churches in the past and today, have not and do not obey Christ's command in Matthew 28:18–20, to *teach them to obey all that I have commanded you...* That is: teach them to grow and become spiritually mature (and knowledgeable) members of the Body, *all united in the faith and ...in the knowledge of the Son of God...and in all things growing up into him who is the Head, that is Christ* (Eph. 4:13–15).

This "lack of teaching" kind of disobedience weakens the church and their members' service for Christ. It exposes weak Christians and the church itself to *every* (false) *wind of teaching, and... the cunning and craftiness of men in their deceitful scheming* (more Ephesians 4!), and is a particular form of Satan-induced rebellion and disobedience against God and His Son. Peter, Paul, John and others note, and warn us against, the presence of *false teachers within the church* (see, for ex: 2 Pet. 2:1). This disobedience extends to Christ's Revelation to the Apostle John in chapters 2 and 3. So, *false* church *teachers* are covered in this book in greater detail than in these introductory statements and early words of Christ.

After speaking to his disciples in more detail about the coming of the Holy Spirit soon to every believer in Him, in Chapter 16 of John's Gospel, Jesus speaks again of His (obedient) necessity to leave them. But now, He speaks of their grief that will soon turn to joy, even while the unbelieving world (and many disobedient Jews) rejoices in His coming death. Read the latter portion of Ch. 16, with the teaching of the Holy Spirit, and rejoice with the early disciples, who—unlike us later saints—did not then know the outcome of their Lord's leaving them. They had to, and did, trust Him that they would not be left alone, but would have His Holy Spirit to dispel their grief and guide them to His Truth.

We, however, have the inspired, inerrant Scripture, and know that God's plan to extend His salvation to the Gentiles (while setting aside temporarily His promise of a coming King to Israel) required a Sinless One to take on the sins of the whole world—to make propitiation to God for the sins of all humanity, and allow His Mercy to be extended to the lost world. We Christians remember our Lord, and His death, burial, and Resurrection, in the **enactment of the "Lord's Supper"** or "Memorial Service" that He gave His disciples (us too!) and asked us to do as an act of Remembrance of Him (see Matt. 26:17–29; Mark 14:12–25; Luke 22:17–22; 1 Cor. 11:23–30).

The Corinthian passage, later given by the Lord to Paul, was made necessary because the church Christ Willed to build sometimes made a mockery of Christ's Intent to give His disciples a True recognition and Blessing, concerning what the Lord had undergone for them and for all future believers. Because it was blasphemed by the sinful actions of some in the Corinthian church, Paul was undoubtedly inspired to write these words to the later church and to us today. He cautioned them, and all future Christian readers, about the importance of being faithful to their Risen Lord—to remember the truth, behind the symbolism expressed in the Lord's Supper, about His great act of propitiation and redemption at Calvary, and His great love for the world.

I must, and will, say more later in this book, about the Corinthian church's disobedience and sin in connection with the Lord's Supper, along with how the later Christian churches also blasphemed the Lord, showing contempt and disrespect for God, His Son, and His Spirit in their often disobedient ways of conduction the Lord's Supper. Their disobedience—opposing Scripture—still occurs to this day in many churches, in their not faithfully following the clear scriptural instructions of the Lord (and Paul's inspired corrective to their errant actions).

What does Christ require of all Christians, the title of this chapter asks? **Nothing less than full, faithful, and loving obedience to Him in all that He Commands us to do, and be, for Him** in His Words of Truth in Holy Scripture.

I continue on now with these vital few chapters in John's Gospel, dealing with Christ's revelations to His Apostles concerning the end of His First Mission (because of hostile Jewish rejection of Him as the Prophesied Messiah) and their need to know about His soon leaving them physically. He would soon be asking them to carry out a new Mission for Him in His church that He had earlier told them *He Willed to Build* (Matt. 16:18).

In the course of these few chapters, but especially in John 14 and 16, Jesus tells the Apostles (and us!) that while He must return to the Father, He will not leave them, or us alone, but will provide the Holy Spirit of God to all His disciples. He describes the Spirit's work in them as a: *Counselor, Teacher, Spirit of Truth,* and other titles, describing His purpose to guide the future "body of disciples" to witness to Him and serve Him in the world, until His return. I propose to thoroughly describe the importance of seeking the Spirit's aid in areas of Christian need as above, including convicting the world of *sin, judgment and righteousness* (John 16:8).

Chapter 17 of the Gospel of John is a favourite portion of God's Word to me and to many born-again believers in the Christian church. "Favourite," because seldom are we as privy to our Lord's thoughts and concerns and love for us all, as in this overheard passage of prayer given to us through the inspiration of the Apostle John. Usually, we read in Scripture that *Jesus went apart from His disciples to pray to His Heavenly Father;* here, we read that one moment He was teaching, consoling, and talking to them as friends—and the next, He (obviously) prayed audibly a beautiful prayer to God, concerning all His disciples, present, and future.

Reading this prayer for His Church, I am always uplifted spiritually from earth to Heaven as I read again, and realize in my heart, mind and spirit, that my Lord died for me. That He loves me, and is concerned for my (and your) peace of mind and heart and spirit; my well-being and protection; and is overseeing my human frailties and concerns. I always thank God for this special prayer of our Lord to His and my Heavenly Father—and I hope my readers do, also!

I urge all readers to **study John 17**, with the guidance of the Holy Spirit in us. He will explain it all fully as we study. He, if we seek His aid, will be our Counselor, *Spirit of Truth*, guide to all truth, Reminder of all Christ said to us, and Teacher of all things. These truths from our Lord, found only in the Christian Bible, can only be known, and obeyed, with the Holy Spirit's Help. The Christian church must return, often and always, to God's written Word, His inspired, inerrant, and infallible Truth, and, with the Spirit's counsel, determine whether they are fully faithful to the Living **Word**—the Divine Head of His church on earth.

Yes, the *Spirit Speaks Today* (Rev. 2,3) —but are the churches listening? I pray so, for the time of our Lord's return is near, and the Spirit wants to speak to us of our personal and church disobedience to the Head of His Body on earth.

In His prayer, in John 17, the Lord says many important things about His relationship to His Heavenly Father-God and His own relationship to us, and about His requests to His Father concerning our life for Him in this world. It is perhaps strange to new believers (but the Spirit will explain it if asked) when they discover, in this prayer, that the Lord does not ask His Father to remove us from this hateful, evil and sinful world! Instead, He asks God to protect us from the Evil one (Satan), while leaving us here to serve Him in His church for our human lifetime! I will have some things also to say about this portion of Scripture later, as I discuss how some Christian organizations handle, act upon, reject or pervert these Divine facts among other portions of God's Truth.

Turning From Church History to Present Church Life; An Introduction to Required Church Unity.

Now, I want to direct all Christians to a special portion of the Lord's urgent appeal in prayer to God—in which He speaks about future Christian disciples, not only those Apostles and disciples who were with Him on His first mission. In John 17:20ff, Christ says *My prayer is not for them alone. I pray also for those who will believe in me through their* (the early disciples') *message*—then see Acts 2 and Peter's first gospel sermon. Read with me, now, His special prayer for his later disciples: *I pray also for those who will believe in me through their message. I pray that all of them may be one, Father, just as you are in me, and I am in you* (John 17:20,21).

This very prayer portion about Christ's prayer for "oneness of the church Body"—for **complete unity of all Christians**—is a vital part of Christ's Will and purpose. He prays that it may be an undivided church—with **no divisions within each local church**—but also a **total unified church Body** of perhaps millions of local churches (described as *His*

Body, the church on earth (see Rom. 12:4,5 and elsewhere in Scripture). Jesus said, and inspired John to write down for us, the significance of obedience and "Body unity" of the entire Christian church for future disciples, gathered as Christians in the Body of Christ on earth. They are to be His True witnesses to a lost, sinful, world.

Note that our Lord, the Head of His total church Body on earth (Eph. 5:23), clearly **defines the church unity He is speaking about in John 17**. There is no lack of clarity or truth in His Words, and there should be no mistakes made by *false teachers* under Satan's ever-present persuasions. Christ's definition of Christian (church) unity is, unlike man's: *One...just as you are in me, Father and I am in you...* (I pray) *that they may be One as We are One* (John 17:21,22).

To understand this special form of Oneness, Christians must know, and be taught, about the special relationship between the "Three Divine Persons in One"—between God the Father, God the Son, and God the Holy Spirit, summed up in the all-encompassing phrase, "The Trinity of God." The relationship is not called "Trinity" in the Word, but is best described this way, as God in Three Person, Holy Trinity.

New Christians are required by Christ, in His Great Commission to the Church (Matt. 28:18-20), to be taught by Spirit-gifted Pastors and teachers (Eph. 4). Therein, the inspired Paul is "moved" (led and inspired to write God's Truth, by the Spirit of God) to clearly state that new (and old, if untaught) Christians are, at first, **spiritual infants**—who must mature spiritually, if they are to be of use to the Head in the church and in the world. Without full teaching, the church will not be strong and built up in the faith, and the church will not recognize *false teaching*. Also, the desire of Christ in Ephesians 4:12,13—*that the Body of Christ may be built up until we all reach unity in the faith and in the knowledge of the Son of God*—will not be realized until we become truly "One" in all things spiritual, as He and the Father are One in all things.

Christ's definition of unity, in John 17—concerning His Oneness with the Heavenly Father—is echoed later for the new church when Paul talks to Timothy, a young protegé and Pastor, of the same unity in practical terms (Eph. 4) for the Christian church: i.e., **unity** *in the faith once entrusted to the saints* (Jude 3), and in the knowledge of the Son of God.

How does Christ's plea to His Father for church Oneness become a very practical church unity after Christ's death, burial and resurrection, and the Lord's Will to build His church becomes obediently reflected in the inspired Paul's statements about unity in the "Body of Christ" a few decades later? The answer lies in the full implications of **Divine Unity**, the Oneness shown in Scripture as being required in the future churches, just as *God is in Christ, and Christ is in God,* as Jesus stated in His prayer in Gethsemane (John. 17:20ff). The promised gift of God (the Holy Spirit), promised to all disciples in John 14 and 16, as well as in the Book of Acts (Ch. 1), was first given to each new believer first at Pentecost in Jerusalem (Acts 2), and from there, given down through the centuries.

The Holy Spirit, the Third Person of the Trinity, is not a "force," nor an inferior agent of God (as some cults say). He is God's Spirit, sent by the Father-God, at the request of the Son then on earth. And He, the *Spirit of Truth*, has the same Divine Oneness with God and His Son that Jesus described in His Prayer of John 17.

It is the full, Divine Oneness of the Trinity as to God's Will, purpose, Love and Grace for man that commands His Son's believing disciples to be formed into a unified church—a Body of Christ in the world, intended to carry out His Will and purposes for all mankind. Note here that when Scripture speaks of "a church" or "a Body" (singular), it speaks for convenience and understanding to describe one part only of a unified whole. The "whole"—all the local, individual, churches of Christ, gathered by the Spirit into a world-wide Body of Christ—is singular. He had one human Body, incarnate on earth; He has only "one, composite"—but not entirely unified— "Body on earth." His church, composed of many local churches = His "Body" on earth. Sound difficult? Ask the Spirit (if you are a Christian believer) to explain the references to Christ's church found in the New Testament, and He will teach you the truth, together with True Spirit-Gifted Pastors and member-teachers.

The earthly Unity and Oneness of all Christian believers, assembled into the Christian Church on earth, is Divinely Willed, prayed for, and expected of His church until He comes. But, in the past, and today, church unity is not evident to the world; to many Christians, or to Christ. This church unity is required in the Word of God (Eph. 4 and elsewhere) to be taught, practised, and shown to the world, as a Christian goal of *"unity in the faith, and in the knowledge of the Son of God."* Such ideal human-practiced and human-observed unity, however, is often lacking, sadly, and this displeases the Divine Head, while incurring His future Wrath, if present disunity is not reformed before He returns.

When the church teaches believers, with the aid of the Spirit, obedience to Christ's commands, the strengthening of the Body by maturing the individual believers in the Christian church is achieved. Because of unity and the full teaching of new believers by the church, *false teachers* will be recognized and removed from the church when their teaching is seen to be *false*, compared with God's Truth. More on disunited churches later!

As I try to summarize a little-recognized doctrine of the Christian church **(Christ-required Church unity)**, I can say, **by examining the** Lord's Prayer in John 17:20,21, and **comparing it** with the inspired words of Paul the great missionary, church founder and teacher of the early church in Ephesians 4 and elsewhere, that **one great, single, supernatural truth knits both Divinely-inspired statements together.** God's definition of "unity," and men's wrongful approaches to, and application of, "church unity" can only converge in the Body of Christ in the world, when men yield to the Spirit's teaching of God's Truth and give up Scripture-opposing false doctrines. **Churches today must strive to obey Him and eliminate the differences between what Christ teaches, and what men propose and oppose Scripture.** Only through accepting the Divine work of the Spirit (described in Jesus' words in John 14,16) can church members and leaders (believers all) recognize what True unity and Christ-desired oneness really is—and, through church teaching with the *Spirit of Truth*, actually achieve it, in **all** the church bodies of Christ in the world.

I repeat, on the Authority of God's Word: full unity can only be accomplished when each and every Christian local church (or unscriptural groups, denominations, or "empires of churches") asks the Holy Spirit to reveal to them their disobedience—individual and collective—and act to repent and reform their sins to please Him.

In John 17:21, the Lord closes His brief prayer for Christian unity, with an incredible statement as to what will result, if His prayed-for unity of all His disciples would be realized and achieved by His future church (us!). He says, in John 17:21b: *May they also be in Us* (in the Trinity of God; Father, Son and Spirit, three Persons in One Person, called "God"); In us, in Divine Will and purpose, for this reason: ***So that the world may believe that you have sent me.*** I emphasize His final words, since they seem to be forgotten by, or hidden from, many churches' understanding—although they are fundamental to Christ's Will and purpose, to *build my church* and *…that it may be One.* If the sinful, lost world does not believe that God sent His Only begotten Son into the world, of what purpose is the church in the world? John 3:16 tells us that *God so loved the world, that He gave His only son that whosoever believes in Him shall not perish, but have eternal life.* The Spirit of God—as I read Jesus' prayer of unity, and John's inspired word of truth concerning God's proffered salvation to the Jews, first, and then to the Gentiles—tells me that Christ's prayer and great desire for the unity of all Christians, assembled in thousands of Christian churches in the past and today, has been rejected and disobeyed in large measure.

How can I say this? Because men have applied their own definition and purpose of unity to "their churches," down through the years to today. They have divided sinners and seekers, divided Christians, and destroyed their witness to Christ, by showing the world the utter chaos of divided, divisive and ineffective, supposedly Christian, churches. Churches of today are divided because they reject Christ as the scriptural (Eph. 5:23), Divine Head of His whole "Body on earth"—and insist (wrongly) that they, sinful men saved by God's Grace alone—have Divine authority to "rule" their "own" particular group of Christian believers. Many churches, in the past and today, show the world that they are separated, under leaders whose authority and doctrines come from *false teachers* in the church, who in turn often oppose Scripture, and refuse any call to unite with others, except under their false headship!

This chapter asks: What does Christ require of all Christians? Christ requires obedience first of all from Christians. Obedience that is based on His Love for us, and our love for Him. I repeat what our Lord said to us, and all His disciples, in John 15: 9,10: *...now remain in my love. If you obey my commands, you will remain in my love.* This powerful statement is rarely preached or taught in divided churches today, for its converse condemns unhearing, divided, and disobedient churches with the loss of our Saviour's Love. In Part 4, I will examine our Lord's wrath against some early Christian churches who were not only disobedient, but spiritually *asleep,* or *dead.* **Remaining in His Love,** or **losing His Love** will be explained in more detail, and applied to churches then, in later centuries, **and today.**

Chapter 4

What Forms of Disobedience are Observed in Past and Present Church History?

This is not the kind of "How-To Book," available in today's modern bookstores, with social subjects taught in "modern churches," to please the nominal, untaught Christian congregation. I simply point out, in my book, that our Lord tells us, in the Scriptures I speak about, that errant Churches must *hear what the Spirit says to the churches* (Rev. 2,3) and obey Him. Or, suffer His wrath and terrible consequences!

My burden and resultant purpose for Christ, however, is to warn and urge disobedient churches to examine their words, actions, and every aspect of church life, against the Inspired, Inerrant Word of God, as a Divine Standard for Christ's Body. It is only partially carried out when I simply quote some old, familiar Bible passages. I must also take into account (as I realize from the Holy Spirit's work in my life, as well as in the lives of other mature believers) whether past and present churches of Christ have obediently followed Christ's commands and teachings, or have continued to follow past and present "*false teachers*" in the church. I ask my readers to consider my purpose—which is really Christ's purpose, to *build my church...and obey me.* Whether disobedient Christian churches, in the past and today, have refused to preach or teach God's Word, and have *forsaken their first love* (Rev. 2:4) over the years may be academically interesting—but their fate, if they do not repent and return to faithfully serve Him, will be tragic if they do not relate their current life to past unfaithful churches.

The only way I can activate my Spirit-led purpose to do what the Spirit leads me to do for failing or failed churches, on behalf of Christ, is to stimulate their scriptural recall process. All humans seem to be forgetful, and Christians are no exception. Christ said, to an ancient Christian church at Sardis (see Rev. 3:3): *Remember, therefore, what you have received and heard; obey it and repent.* I will speak in detail of this church, and the six other, largely disobedient, churches Christ "reviewed" in Revelation 2 and 3, in part 4 of this book; but for now, it illustrates what I write in this chapter about my efforts to warn disobedient churches today.

Have their members and leaders forgotten our Lord? Or have they not been taught what they need to know from God's Word, about obedience, failure and consequences? If disobedient churches today, as in the past, selectively discard God's infallible inspired Written Words to them, and substitute the *false teacher's* words that oppose them, Christian church members and leaders will fail their Divine Head, and suffer a terrible fate when He returns to this earth soon to claim His Holy, Radiant, sinless and blameless Bride.

At this point in this humble book, quoting only scriptural Words as a Divine standard against which all Christian responses, actions, and deeds for the True Head of His Body must be determined by Him, **it is time to shock the untaught, forgetful, Christians in spiritually sleeping churches, or the deliberate sinners against Christ, with some "real-life" examples of sin against Jesus Christ**. It is time to give you some **actual examples** of Christian disobedience to what Christ has asked His Church to be and do for Him *as born-again disciples in His church body* through nearly 2,000 years to today.

Where the New Testament Words of Christ demand a **"united Body of Christ"** —see John17:11,21 (although troubled at times by *false teachers)*, how does the Lord react when past and present church history reveals a **divided Body of Christ**? What does He require of today's unscriptural, un-Christian, "denominations" of churches, divided "main-line" churches, or large groups of churches, divided under unscriptural leaders—**all** divided from other Christians in their beliefs, words, and actions, with many false doctrines increasingly opposing the inspired, inerrant written Word of God? As you will read here, the

Apostle Peter's *"false teacher"* prophecy (2 Pet. 2:1) came true in his past, in his day, and today. Many Christian church members are divided and untaught. Thus, spiritually untaught (or forgetful) Christians are subject to *every wind of teaching,* and *to the cunning and craftiness of men in their deceitful scheming* (Eph. 4:14). If untaught by their church, such Christians in divided and disobedient churches do not strengthen, but only weaken, the local Body. If untaught, they cannot be united with scriptural teaching churches, and so, are divided. The lost world, observing today's and past churches, perceives that God really didn't **send His Son into the world, and loves the lost** (See John 17:23 on unity)—for even pagans know that Christian churches are often unspiritual, disobedient, as well as separated by *false teachers.*

These things said, let me list only a few of the church errors that are observed in the New Testament inspired record, in the ancient past, and in today's church history record. This list is multiplied many times over as today's churches displease the Lord and ignore His Commands and Teachings.

An Introduction to the Shameful, Disobedient Acts of Christian Church Members, In the Past and Today.

Almost 2,000 years of church history, beginning with the First church of Jerusalem, have passed. The church slowly but obediently spread abroad *to all nations* (Matt. 28:19), with the result that there have been, and are, hundreds of thousands of Christian "bodies of Christ" formed. Sympathetic readers can imagine the near-impossible task I have undertaken, to choose and review even a few church errors in one brief chapter of one small book! I am tempted to compare it with the task of the Apostle John, who, at the close of His Gospel book in John 21:25 spoke about...*Jesus doing many other things as well!*

Since I cannot begin to quote all the errors of even one errant division of the Body of Christ over the years, I must—with the guidance of the Spirit—only select a few typical examples of just a few churches of Christ in the past and present centuries. Examples that will illustrate just why Christ said to His early errant churches in Revelation 2, and 3: *Nevertheless, I have a few things against you*—and went on to give some examples of "typical churches" disobeying Him in one small region of the world. New Testament-type church sins continue to this day, regrettably—but Christ knows of them all, and *will repay them,* as He said, *according to their deeds.* Revelation 2,3 details some of our Lord's views of failing churches.

In all my seemingly human-engineered recommendations, warnings, and advice you will read throughout this book, please believe me when I say they are not my, or my professor's, or any one human's advice to the churches. Faithful readers, without preconceived or traditional church biases, will soon discern—with the *Spirit of Truth* within them—that these are **Christ's recommendations, warnings, advice and commands alone.** This book is not enjoyable to write—nor, probably, a pleasure to read, for those who may know in their hearts, minds, and spirits that "their" church is disobedient to the Lord.

My book is written as Christ's warning. It quotes Jesus, the Head of His church on earth; urges readers to listen to the *Spirit of Truth* (not to *false teachers,* or sinful, disobedient men); and urges the church to *wake up; to repent; to return to Him; to change* (reform) *their ways* and to conform to the Divine, inspired, inerrant Word of God. That said, let us examine a very small part of what is public knowledge, and, sadly, what is known and seen of the sinful presence of church disobedience.

Forms of disobedience seen in the past and present churches are many and varied—but they all have the same underlying pattern, of human rejection of God's Word, and following *false teachers.* From the first disobedience of our ancestors in the Garden of Eden (Gen. 3) to the present day, we Christians (with Jews, the first Chosen People of God, and all sinful, lost *Gentiles*) carry the mark of that Original Sin in our lives. We, like our ancestors, all have the choice of accepting or rejecting God; of obeying Him or not as racial Jews; as Christians, repenting and believing by Grace and Faith alone in Jesus Christ; or as all God-rejecting lost sinners, lost unless they hear and respond in faith alone to the call of a Merciful Creator-God. We in the Christian church have the Divinely commanded task of carrying out His Great Commission (see Part 3 of this book): to seek and save all the lost souls till He comes again.

This book, however, is about the Christian church alone, and I must now ask readers to examine your status as Christian believers, and the status of the local church of Christ to which the Spirit of God has led you. Whether members or leaders, I urge you to read this book, to especially read the New Testament for the church, and urge you to ask the Holy Spirit to be your guide to what Christ requires of you in His Body on earth. But don't stop with hearing or reading alone—ask the *Spirit of Truth* to **show you** where Christ's "Body" has gone astray from the truth. If sin, error or disobedience is found—follow Christ's urging in Revelation 2 and 3, and His call for you and your church's obedience in many other Scriptures. Repent of your sins, and return in full obedience to *do the things you did at first* (Rev.2:5) for Him Who is our Saviour, Lord, and Head of His church Body on earth.

Disobedience in past Church history— a few examples for your consideration.

"Church history" needs to be defined here. We have the inspired New Testament canon in our Bible, so the first church in Jerusalem and the spreading "missionary" church record therein can be accurately seen as ancient (past) church history—but relevant to all later churches as well.

As the church of Christ continued to grow (see Acts), it expanded to *all nations* (Matt. 28:19) as Christ commanded—at least to the small, known nations surrounding the Mediterranean (largely Roman-governed areas of the then-known world). First, ancient manuscripts, and then the inspired canon of the Bible, that God has preserved for us over the centuries, was closed. Divinely-recorded New Testament history was followed by human-recorded church history, until today. I will provide some examples of disobedience to Christ for some churches in this period also (spanning many centuries)—calling these centuries "early church history." Finally, I will select some examples from today's church history which covers the 20th century to A.D. 2000. They, too, will be only representative, since the purpose of this book is to warn Christ's church today—not to slander, denigrate, or otherwise incite hatred against those who, if they are true *born-again* believers, are truly my, and your "brothers and sisters in Christ."

In these necessarily few cases, I will cite ancient disobedience and errors (some continuing down the centuries until today) observed in church history, and show the actual scriptural Standard of Obedience required by our Saviour and Lord, Head of His Body. I will also show why *false teachers*, disobedient men in and out of the church, have, with Satan's assistance, committed or tolerated grievous errors. The things I discuss here, then, from church history past or present, are *the things that* **Christ** *holds against* **the Christian church of any age** (Rev. 2:4, paraphrased by this writer).

Some Ancient Christian church errors:

1. The first church's sin and disobedience

One of the first church sins (against God and the Spirit) was committed in the first church of Jerusalem, as described in Acts 5. It is the case of Ananias and Sapphira. I urge you to read verses 1 to 11, with the guidance of the Spirit of God, to discover its meaning—not alone for the Jerusalem church, but for all churches, past and present, even "our (really His) church."

Briefly, God sent the Promised Spirit to the Apostles and disciples gathered in Jerusalem, as the Lord asked (see Acts 1). The Spirit came, as described in Acts 2, and the disciples heard *a sound like the blowing of a violent wind from Heaven* and saw what seemed *like tongues of fire* resting on each believer's head. The Spirit entered their bodies, *tongues of fire rested on them,* and *they began to speak in other tongues* or languages. Crowds of Jews, come from many countries for the Feast of Pentecost, heard the sound of *a violent wind* as well as the *praising of God* in their diverse languages coming from the disciples, who were urged by the Spirit to go into the streets.

It was there that Peter, hearing the crowd's confusion as to the sound of *Spirit filled disciples speaking their* (the crowd's) *own languages,* was led by the Spirit to preach the first gospel sermon (Good News from God about Christ). Many of the crowd were convicted of sin by the Spirit hovering in their midst. They asked: *"Brothers, what shall we do?"* (that is, "to be saved"—for Peter had preached of their sin, and their need to return, with repentance and life reform, to their

God). Peter told the convicted ones of the process of salvation (of repentance, and belief in the Risen Christ, as later Scripture confirms). He told them to be baptized, and added to the new church, or Body of Christ (as we know from Scripture, and the Apostles knew from the teachings of Christ and later inspired writings by Paul and others).

Many Jews, and a few Gentiles were added, in those early days, to the church (described in Acts 2:41,47), as Peter and the other Apostles gave the message of salvation to the people on the streets of Jerusalem. Over 3,000 were baptized after repenting, *believing the Gospel message by faith, and receiving Christ and the Gift of the Holy Spirit.* Saved by their belief, they were then added by baptism to the Body of new Christians forming the First Christian church in Jerusalem. The church, under the obedient teaching of the Apostles (all of Christ's teachings they had received from Him), was an active fellowship, as described in Acts 2:42ff. With this brief summary, we now go to Acts 5, when the church had been in fellowship and under the Apostles' teaching and preaching for some weeks or months—and discover the "first sin and disobedience" among the congregation of the saved, and its deadly consequences, applicable equally today.

This first recorded disobedience to the Lord is described as *lying to the Holy Spirit* (Acts 5:3). Early church members Ananias and his wife Sapphira were prompted by Satan *filling their hearts.* They deceived their church leaders and members, concerning the sale of a material piece of property. With lies, Ananias and Sapphira withheld part of the sum of money received from donation to the poor of the church. It was not so much their greed, but their withholding of the money from His needy "Body" that troubled the Apostle Peter. It was the fact, too, that they had lied to the Holy Spirit, and to Peter (as well as to the other members of the Body) that was sinful. The Holy Spirit revealed to Peter what Ananias and Sapphira had done, with Satan's leading, in their greedy and sinful act. The consequences were that, because the church members had not only *lied to men but to God* (5:4), both Ananias and his wife, confronted by the enormity of their sin against God and the Spirit, fell down and died, separately.

Acts 5:11 (the closing record of this incident) states that, as a consequence of the sudden deaths of two church members, *great fear seized the whole church and all who heard about these events.*

It is noteworthy that Luke, who wrote the history of the New Testament church under the "moving of the Spirit," and God, Who preserved this record for the later church, wanted us to know that disobedience within the church, and sin against the Spirit (as well as lies to God and men) are not to be tolerated as Christian conduct in the Body of Christ. Then and today, lying to the Holy Spirit is *still* not tolerated by the Divine Head of the church. We Christians are *new Creations* in Christ, by virtue of His salvation grace Offer, and its receipt by us in faith alone. Old sins and worldly practises must pass away and the teachings of Christ must grow us spiritually, so that we all become *mature in the faith and in the knowledge of Christ* (Eph. 4). Sins in and against the Body of Christ, the inspired Paul tells us (1 Cor. 11:29,30)—while not always leading to the awful consequences that happened to the two sinners in Acts 5—often lead to death, and worse. Teaching of Christ and obedience is vital in the Body of Christ.

2. Other sins in the early church

The inspired Paul writes of the problems of sin and disobedience of the Christian church at Corinth in 1 Corinthians 11. Commencing with verse 17, he speaks briefly of the sin of *divisions among you.* Additionally, from the following verses, it is clear that these early Christians, taught by Paul after their formation, continued to deny Christ's plea that *they,* (his future disciples in Jerusalem, Corinth, Antioch, Ephesus; and in His later churches, then and now) *may be one, just as you are in me, and I in you...I in them, and you in me* (John 17:21-23). Some also denied the inspired teachings of Paul and other more mature Christians, and abused the Lord's supper and "Christian etiquette," by pushing aside weaker persons in their haste to eat.

They denied the true meaning of Christian teachings, and the Lord's Will and purpose in establishing the *Lord's Supper.* Paul repeats the actual ritual and Words of Christ, in asking *all* His disciples to do these things, *in Remembrance of Me.* The Spirit-led Paul, in chapter 11, uses this opportunity to amplify the importance of not only carrying out this Sacred Remembrance of the Lord's Body and blood, and His Sacrifice on Calvary's cross exactly as He asked, but also to think about what they (all disciples) are doing as they partake of His Remembrance Symbolic Supper. They must do so with self-examination, and in a worthy manner.

The statement, *anyone who eats and drinks* (the elements of the Lord's Supper) *without recognizing the Body of the Lord* is seen, with the guidance of the *Spirit of Truth*, to refer particularly to considering other church members participating with them. This we see, when we read 1 Corinthians 11:29,30. Those who don't consider the other church members—who, together with each participating member, constitute the local *Body of Christ*—have forgotten Paul's teachings from the Lord. In verses 29 and 30, Paul is led by the Spirit to speak to the Corinthian Christians (as well as all later Christians yet to be "added" to the church) of the *judgment* that he or she brings on themselves by acting disobediently. He speaks of Christ's judgment causing *many among you to be weak and sick,...and some to fall asleep* (die). Verse 32 speaks of this kind of disobedience and judgment by the Lord, as *being discipline, so that we will not be condemned with the world* (of lost sinners).

3. Yet another disobedient sin in the early church

Not recognizing the truth that our Lord *Willed to build* His church, and made all members equal in spiritual worth in His eyes—or not appreciating that all believers are part of His Body—resulted in unworthy members being judged by the Lord and disciplined by illness, even bodily death. This "other sin," allied to the major sin noted in 2 above, has to do with the actual practice of carrying out the Lord's Will and purpose, in giving **all** His present and future disciples the privilege and duty to remember Him and what He did on the Cross for all mankind, including His church—by the obedient practice of *eating and drinking the Lord's* (symbolic)*Supper*. The Apostles were instructed by the Lord concerning the *Lord's Supper* after first celebrating (as good Jews) the Passover meal, described in Matthew 26:17-30 and some other Gospel books. In establishing His symbolic "Memorial Supper," the Lord was thinking about the necessity of His leaving them soon, as well as about forming His church on a new basis apart from the religion of the Jews.

The Apostles, after Christ's Resurrection, taught and instituted *His* Christian "Memorial Supper"—in Jerusalem, as well as in all the Lord's new churches, spread *to all nations* in obedience to Him—after the martyrdom of Stephen in Acts 7, and the scattering of the disciples, under the Holy Spirit, in Acts 8. Later, with the conversion of Paul (then Saul) to Christ on the Damascus Road, the church spread rapidly and obediently, and was established under the missionary teachings of Christian believers—such as Paul, Barnabas, and many others who had been with Jesus personally or in the Spirit. Paul received teachings and instructions from the Lord, and was inspired by the Spirit to not only establish new churches, but *teach them, and correct them* with Divine Truth when they were found to have disobeyed Christ and His commands as taught by their human leaders. The church at Jerusalem, we see in Acts 2ff, thrived and grew in numbers and in spirituality—new members *devoted themselves to the Apostles' teachings* (Acts 2:42), as the latter received them personally from Christ Himself. Worship, fellowship, prayer and other Christian elements of the True Oneness they experienced in the Body of Christ were necessary and present, to please the Divine Head.

But Paul heard of abuse, disobedience, and sin going on in the Corinth Christian church. He wrote to them, telling them again of the Lord's Memorial Supper requirements; of their disobedience to their Lord in practicing it wrongly; and of the Divine consequences if not repented of, within the Lord's congregation at Corinth. I want to speak briefly here, too, of how later churches abused the Lord's Supper after the New Testament canon was closed, the church spread abroad, and after the death of the Apostles. *Later abuses occurred,* not in the manner of the Corinthians, by listening to *false teachers* among them (prompted by Satan)—but by *accepting the teaching of men* who wrongly decided that "their churches" must be headed by Supreme Heads (called sometimes "Popes" or "Patriarchs"): despite the fact that the inspired, inerrant, written Word of God speaks only of Elders (or Overseers or Bishops—all synonymous) and deacons, as the only Scriptural leaders for Christian churches under Christ, the Divine Head.

Inspired, inerrant Scripture does not speak of "theologians" advising "Supreme church Leaders" of their interpretations of God's

Word, nor of these leaders forming large groups of churches under their authority. The written Word tells us (and them) that these "Supreme Leaders" are illegitimate, wrongly chosen by *false teachers* who deliberately misinterpreted Matthew 16:18—*the rock upon which Christ planned to build His church*—while neglecting other inspired Scripture, such as 1 Timothy 3, which specifically and inerrantly defines human leadership of the church under Christ, the Head. More on this subject later in this book; now, back to the later church's "Lord's Supper abuses" derived from men, not Scripture!

After the deaths of the Apostles, the early church taught members based upon knowledge of Christ's verbal teachings, as some of His inspired Words were available to the growing church in written manuscript form in the Gospel books, Acts, and the letters of some Apostles.

But, under Satan, some churches began to heed *false teachers* (errant members or leaders infiltrating the Body) who entered the church as Peter predicted (2 Pet. 2:1), and led church leaders and others astray. These perverted "heads" continued to state that whatever new doctrine their leader issued from the (false) "throne of Peter" was as inspired and authoritative as if from Christ Himself. Over the centuries, however, many of these authoritative—often false—commands from these Supreme Leaders to their groups of churches were seen to oppose Scripture as the Truth of God.

The abuse of the Lord's Supper by some early churches, under falsely-placed "Supreme Leaders," involves the publicly known, wrongly practiced, and perverted "Lord's Supper" (or "Mass," as they have wrongly chosen to name the Christ-given "Memorial Remembrance Ceremony" or "Lord's Supper"—1 Cor. 11:20), as practised by the Roman Catholic church in the past centuries and today. Instead of faithfully following the inspired, inerrant Scriptures (including Paul's inspired writing on the subject and the Lord's statements to us in Matthew 26:17ff), the "Roman Catholic" church, under an early Pope, denied the Christ-ordered *Bread* **and** *Wine representing Christ's Body and blood* to the members of "their church" and gave members only the *Bread,* Christ's symbolic Body. They **wrongly reserved the Wine** for the wrongly-named "Priest" only, and

wrongly withheld it from the members. Scripture reveals—and the teacher of Truth, the Holy Spirit, confirms—that the Lord, in His inspired Scriptures and teachings, clearly gave his Disciples **both** His symbolic Body and His symbolic Blood (represented by ordinary bread and wine). The Lord told believing disciples to eat and drink as they "remembered Him and His death" in this Sacred way (as Paul was inspired by the Spirit to remind the disobedient Corinthians, in New Testament times, in 1 Cor. 11).

This continuing Roman Catholic church abuse of the Lord's Supper must rank as equal, if not worse, than the sin of those ancient worshippers at Corinth, who completely and deliberately misunderstood what Paul, Christ's "Apostle out of time" as some called him, had taught Christ's disciples and passed on to the churches about this very necessary symbolic Remembrance act for all Christians to faithfully observe. Why did the disobedient Corinthians, then, and why do the Roman Catholics and others, today, still deny Scriptural Truth and choose to pervert the very Words, Will and Commands of Christ? The basic answer is *that all men have sinned and fall short of the Glory of God* (Rom. 3:23). An additional scriptural answer, with the Spirit's guidance, tells me and other believers that these distortions and perversions of Scripture can be laid at Satan's door, as his *false teachers* convince false church leaders to do these things at Satan's urging.

The Spirit of God has many things to tell us, in Christ's church; among them is His task of *convicting the world of sin and righteousness, ...judgment in regard to sin* (John 16:8,9). **By my quoting the Inspired Words of Christ, not writing from my opinion, or those of the disobedient church leaders of the past, and today—as the Spirit guides me—I fervently pray that all church teachers and leaders will see a similar necessity to return to our Lord's Words. And cast out all man-made rules, doctrines, commands, and teachings that oppose Scripture, and displease Christ, the True Church Head.** I pray, with other True Christian leaders and members, that the Words of Christ, concerning His sending His Spirit to live in all Christian believers, and His many tasks for the obedient church, will be reread and re-learned; and sins repented of, when their interpretations and actions are found false. They must be reformed and correctly applied with scriptural truth to all things done for Christ in His Body on earth.

4. Some further examples of the sins and disobedient acts of the early church *(often carried over as false "traditions" of men in today's churches).*

Christian Baptism. Another basic perversion of Scripture by the early church, often found in many errant Christian churches today, is sin and abuse related to Christian (Scriptural) believer's baptism. This is described in Acts, and in the Spirit-inspired words of the Apostle Paul in Romans 6:3ff.

Readers may recall, by reading the New Testament Gospels, or by recalling what the Church was required to teach *all new believers:* that through immersion water baptism, and in the name of the Father, Son and Holy Spirit, new believers were *added to* the Christian church as Scripture teaches.

John the Baptist, the forerunner of the prophesied Messiah to the Jewish People, baptized his Jewish disciples in a form of water baptism that "symbolically *washed* away their sins," that they acknowledged had kept them apart from their Holy God. Their sins were to be repented of publicly. When they did so, John baptized them by immersion in any nearby river or lake. This was not Christian baptism, however. It was John the Baptist's way of assuring the Jews of God's approval of their repentance, and confirming their return to a former, Righteous relationship with their God.

Christians who love, read and are taught the inspired Word of God, written, will know from the New Testament inspired Gospel writings, that the incarnate Jesus, in the fullness of God's time, came to the knowledge that *He was the Christ,* the prophesied Messiah of His often-disobedient people of Israel. He went out from His human home and, realizing that He was sent by His Heavenly Father to *save the lost* (of Israel), (Luke 19:10), entered into what I call (from scriptural evidence) His "first mission" to the Jews alone. Matthew 3:13ff describes Jesus going from Galilee to the Jordan to be baptized by John. Many, including John then, and some now, are mystified by Jesus' request to (seemingly) "be baptized," i.e., have his sins washed away as a sign of repen-

83

tance, in the waters of John's baptism. Matthew tells us that, despite John the Baptist's knowing that Jesus was the *Lamb of God* and the prophesied Messiah, and his statement that he, John, needed to be baptized by this sinless Divine person, Jesus insisted John baptize *Him*. But Jesus insisted that John baptize Him *only to fulfill all Righteousness* (3:15). No scriptural mention is made of "washing Him for removal of sin" by either Jesus or John—because we know Jesus was uniquely **without sin** as the Incarnate "Great I Am."

Scripture records an amazing confirmation that Jesus was the Messiah, come at last to *seek and save* the disobedient and *lost ones* of Israel. After His baptism, in the waters of the Jordan river, Heaven was opened (Matt. 3:16,17); the Spirit of God descended upon Him, and the voice of God from Heaven announced: THIS IS MY SON, WHOM *I* LOVE; WITH *HIM I* AM WELL PLEASED. For Christ, it was necessary that He be publicly baptized in water; but not as John's followers, sinful men, were baptized after repentance—for Christ was both sinless and Divine. It was also necessary for God to publicly fit His Son for His work on earth; to "accredit Him," and confirm Who and What His Son was and must do and endure for God's salvation purpose—first for the Jews' salvation, later for the Gentiles'.

Many Christians have misunderstood the passage about Jesus' baptism by John. Many have wrongly inferred from the passage (obviously without the Spirit's guidance), that Jesus was simply a man, as John's followers were. Many churches wrongly say (and some say today) that "we must follow Jesus in baptism." But as we will see from Scripture, no man can imitate Jesus' baptism. We believers instead follow a baptism that Christ asked His church to give to all sinful but now repentant believers. Our baptism represents unique Christian and church significance, as Scripture tells us.

The inspired Apostle Paul, in Romans 6, wrote to tell Christians of all ages what Christ wants us to know and follow about Christian baptism, and our "addition" to His church, through baptism *after conscious repentance and belief.* It is highly significant, as the Spirit reveals in the phrase Paul uses in Romans 6:3: *Or don't you know...?* to his readers at Rome and all later Christians elsewhere. As we discussed earlier, in regard to Paul's corrective words (inspired of God) to the Corinthian church about their abuse of the Lord's Supper, other churches have displayed ignorance of what Christ wanted them to know and obey. So, Paul wrote to reinforce his and other's teachings from Christ, for Romans 6:3ff is Spirit-inspired knowledge for Christians. The New Testament church should have known about true baptism of Christian believers (since they had received Christ's teachings from Paul and others)—but they gave evidence of false church teachers leading them astray, as Satan led Adam and Eve astray after their creation by God.

Paul was inspired to write in Chapter 6 of his letter to the church at Rome, the infallible truth of Christian baptism. ***The Divine Truth?:*** Christian baptism is no less than a vital symbolic act required to be practised by the church (see Matt. 28:18-20, Christ's Commission to the church). As the church *made disciples* by preaching or telling the gospel message of salvation, aided by the Spirit's conviction of the sinner and the sinner's belief, repentance of sins, and profession of the new believer's faith in the risen Lord—the church must baptize the "born again" person in this special way of immersion in water. This special Christian mode differentiates the True Way of baptism from the false way and false understanding that came into the later New Testament church (obviously into the church at Rome also, from Paul's expression—*Or don't you know?*)

In the few short, inspired verses following Romans 6:3, *false teachers* and untaught Christians of that day (and all others down to today!) should understand the symbolism expressed by immersing the newly convicted and knowing believer in water: burying (immersing) him or her in this "watery grave;" then raising the believer up out of the depths of the "grave," is the Christ-required way of expressing the believer's new, full identification with their Saviour, and now with his (or her) new Lord.

Only this act of Christian baptism, and only this *specific* Scriptural method of baptism, can fully express the inspired truth about this symbolic act that also adds the new, *born again* and now Scripturally *baptized* believer to the *Body of Christ*, His church on earth, of which He is the sole Head. Only immersion baptism conforms fully to God's Word of Truth, Christ's Commands. Christian churches following some other form of baptism cannot give the one baptized, or the congregation, or observers, the True significance that Christ desired each *born again, baptized* believer to understand as he or she identifies with the death, burial and resurrection of the Lord.

5. Another major act of disobedience to Christ:

Leaders (Overseers, Bishops, Elders, Pastors—and Deacons, only) *were to govern the church under the Divine Head, Christ.* I mentioned 1 Timothy 3, earlier, as Scripture reveals Christ's inspired teachings about local leaders in the church (under the Divine Head)—and I have talked about "Supreme leaders" (my words) wrongly placed over the church, some, but not all, after the death of the Apostles. But now I bring it up in relation to sins committed by "human authorities in the church" not under Christ's authority as Head, in the past and today.

I draw attention to Christ's Words to His Apostles concerning His future church, made to His first-mission disciples (and Apostles) in Matthew 16:17–19 before He fully revealed to them that He must die and leave them. Within these few verses, Christ *apparently* connects the man, Peter, with Christ's plans apparent plans to have Peter assume *some form* of supreme leadership when the church is formed. I say "apparently," for Scripture (and His Spirit) tells us in Christ's words that the designation of Peter (and so-called successors) by some later portions of Christ's Body on earth is not at all what Christ meant. The Roman Catholic church, at an early stage following the death of the Apostles (and continuing today), was not guided by the Holy Spirit in this instance. Instead they allowed disobedient "church teachers" to recommend that "successors" to the Apostle Peter be (wrongly) appointed in an entirely new and unscriptural way. The result has been division of His Body, for when we disobey Christ and His inspired Word, we grieve Him and His Spirit.

Scripture tells us that the Roman Catholic church (and others who choose unscriptural leaders as human "Heads of His church") are wrong and scripturally disobedient in appointing a "Supreme Leader," a "Pope," or "Holy Father," etc., as "Head" of "their" Christian church, to act (unscripturally) as the "Vicar," or so-called "Supreme

Representative" of Christ on earth. Conveniently-forgotten verses (Matt. 16:13–16) precede the often-quoted following verses which some churches view as Christ's authorization to choose Peter and his "successors" as "Supreme church leaders." They wrongly chose a few somewhat unclear verses, rather than following the inspired writings of Paul, in 1 Timothy 3 and elsewhere, which give the only True authority for male human leaders in Christ's church—as "Overseers" and "Deacons" only.

Verses 13 to 16 in Matthew 16, in Christ's own Words, tells the Roman Catholics, Greek "Orthodox," and all other religious groups calling themselves "the true Christian church" (as well as other "named" churches down through the centuries) that the Lord did **not** want a human "Supreme Leader," "Pope," or a "Patriarch" or a "Vicar of Christ" to rule over His church, in His place—then or now. These verses tell we Christians, who ask the Spirit to guide us, the true meaning of all that He and other inspired Scripture writers say to us, for He is the *Spirit of Truth* (John 14). In Matthew 16:13–16, Christ was deliberately probing His disciples' (and Apostles') minds, so that His God-planned transition from *seeking the lost of Israel* (on His first mission to the Jews only) to extending God's Grace, Mercy and salvation to the "Gentiles" (His second mission "through His church" to *all nations*)—and His coming death on the Cross—would clearly teach new Truths for His followers, who would also serve Him in the future church *He Willed to build*. The probing Words of Christ, in verses 13–16, should now be read again by all Christians, with the *Spirit of Truth*—while dismissing from our minds what past church "traditions" have taught, often wrongly.

Jesus (Matt. 16:13) first asked His small group of disciples: *Who do people say the Son of Man is?* (that is, "Who do they, the *lost of Israel* we met on My first mission as the prophesied Messiah, say I, Jesus, am?"). The disciples relayed the wide range of human responses by the Jews—all wrong! Then the Messiah, the Christ sent by God to earth, to be born of a virgin—the Holy One, Incarnate in human flesh—asked all His disciples another question, the answer to which He already knew (Omnisciently) would come—*But what about you? Who do you say that I am?*

The impulsive fisherman, Peter—the one who continually blurted out his quick, often-ignorant responses, and the one who would not many days later deny his Lord—said the wisest, truest truth he or any of us can say about our Lord: *You are the Christ, the Son of the Living God.* Then, in more vital words, almost forgotten today, Jesus said: *Blessed are you, Simon, son of Jonah, for this was not revealed to you by man* (as were the earlier responses to His first question) *but by my Father in Heaven* (16:17). Now follows the ***apparent, but errant*** assignment of ***"Supreme authority to Peter,"*** which it is not—except by the declarations of *false teachers* who distort Scripture. In 16:18, after telling Simon that he is Blessed by God revealing to him the truth of Who He Is (the Prophesied Messiah, the Christ, Who is God's Son), the Lord says: *And I tell you that you are Peter.* Bible scholars who understand the Aramaic language of Jesus—as well as the Greek into which the Aramaic of the original documents which we have as the "Gospels" were translated—tell us that the word Jesus used, translated in our Bibles as *"Peter" is the Greek word "Petros."* So Christ, speaking of Simon first as the descendant of Jonah, then as his given name "Peter," or "Petros" in the Greek, is about to make a "play on words" in making His next crucial statement. In the latter part of verse 18, Christ says ...*and on this 'rock'* **(Petra) I will build my church.** In this latter statement, the Greek for ***"rock"*** used here **is *"petra."*** Christian Bible language scholars tell us that verse 18, in the first part of which Christ uses the Greek ***"Petros"*** for **Peter**, while in the last part He uses ***"petra,"*** the ***Greek word for rock***, is crucial in our understanding of the Truth. There are two seemingly possible choices to be made by readers, and one crucial determination to be made—for Christ is stating that *I will build my* (future) *church upon something I call a 'rock'–'petra.'*

The two "choices" are these:

1. The church that Christ will build, will seemingly ***either be constructed upon a foundational "rock" of a weak human being, Peter (Greek-'Petros'),*** an impulsive, often failing, human disciple of Christ (and his "successors" some say), ***or:***

2. The church that Christ will build ***will be constructed upon a foundation "rock" of Peter's faith statement (not on a human, fallible***

man)–the faith in God's Son that is first described in the revelation of God to the Apostle Peter, an inspired but weak human disciple—as a *foundational faith in Christ* that must later (and now) be accepted and professed by each and every *born again* human disciple *made, baptized, and taught* by the past, present and future church, as Christ commanded.

The first "choice" (not really a choice, if inerrant, infallible Scripture is always to be interpreted by the *Spirit of Truth* sent by God to every True Christian believer) is quite clear—but, as chosen and interpreted by *false teachers*, is indefensible and in error. We readers must recognize that later portions of inspired, infallible Scripture interpret the earlier passages, and must never oppose the Word of God to man.

The Spirit tells us, in later Scriptures describing the church of Christ yet to be built after His death, burial and resurrection, *that Christ ALONE is Head of His church* (Eph. 5:23). The Lord does require human disciples (and inspired Scripture states the clear truth) *to guide and oversee each church, under Christ's teachings and Headship, with the Spirit's interpretations of Scripture to them.* But never would He, nor does He, state or allow human men, impulsive, sinful, failing often, and subject to *false teachers* and Satan's persuasion, to be the Christian church's Head on earth (a "Pope," or anyone else who denies Christ's full Divine Headship, and assumes unscriptural human Headship over Christ's Body). Men fail God, from Adam to ourselves.

1 Timothy 3, given later in time than was the Matthew 16 passage to the church *confirms* that every local Body must only have men as "local leaders," and only have two church offices of local church leadership—*Overseers and Deacons.* Their qualifications, responsibilities, and duties, under Christ the Divine Head, are outlined in Scripture and must be followed. Nowhere in Scripture, in the inspired New Testament for the church, does the Spirit or the Word lead men to covet or create "Headship" positions over local churches, or groups, or over unscriptural "denominations" or "universal or 'catholic'" organized groupings of churches.

The second, so-called "choice,"—which also is not really a choice at all—*is really the only true, definitive scriptural answer to the question: What is the "foundation" rock upon which Christ stated the Christian church is to built? Faith in Christ by all believers, or faith in a human, unscriptural "Head"?* I repeat that when *all* of Scripture on this subject of Headship of the church is read, and not just one phrase from one verse (here in Matthew 16), there is really only one true interpretation for the (foundation) rock upon which Christ Willed to build His church. And that is: *He will not build it on a sinful man as Head, even an Apostle* (or "successors," who are also human and fail often). But *He will build it on a foundation 'rock' (petra), on a scriptural faith statement that is Divinely prompted by the Spirit—universal, eternal, and, in the New Testament church, faithfully followed, as 1 Timothy 3 requires.*

The Roman Catholic and other errant churches, by their faulty choice of leaders adopted through *false teachers'* unscriptural recommendations, and by their "traditions" of past errant actions, are clearly seen in history as disobedient to God's Word, and to Christ's Will and written purpose for His Body. Many such churches, by allowing frail, often sinful men to act as "Supreme Heads of Christ's church," have taken this unscriptural action to extremes—confirmed by their other sinful words, doctrines, and deeds that often oppose Scripture. Many "Supreme Leaders," called "Popes," "Patriarchs," etc. have produced false Edicts and Statements that their members are called upon to obey, which are often Scripture-opposing, and Satan-pleasing. They speak of being "a Vicar of Christ" on earth in the Lord's absence—but this, too, is denied by the clear teaching of Scripture, which never mentions a human "vicar, but only 'Overseers,' (or 'Elders,' "Bishops' or modern 'Pastors'), together with their assistants: Deacons.

Their obvious disobedience to Christ and His Word have resulted in centuries-old church divisions, and worse—which opposes the prayer of Christ that all His disciples (in His Body on earth) be one in all things, as *He and the Father are One* (John 17:21,22). Even after the so-called Protestant Reformation—involving those who protested what the Roman Catholic church had wrongly said and become—many Protestant Christians today follow in the errant footsteps of the Roman church group from which they separated. Many accept doctrines that still oppose Scripture. Many Protestants also split and divide, instead of becoming one, as Christ desires. All is a result of continuing disobedience caused by Satan and *false teachers* in the church. All oppose Christ, God, the Holy Spirit and inspired, inerrant Scriptures, and many sin by denying the Word of God's inspiration. Second Timothy 3:16,17, and many other passages of Scripture support what I have said above—as does the Spirit.

But, if Christ alone is the Head of His Church (Eph. 5:23) why would some churches, on the basis of other Scripture (Matt. 16:17–19) reverse this Truth, and declare fallible men (Peter and his successors) as Head (Pope or Patriach) to be the Head? The answer lies in an early misinterpretation by Satan-led false teachings—namely that "the rock" upon which His, then future, church is to be built is a man, Peter. As I quote further Scripture, Spirit-led readers will see that Christ alone is the *"foundation of His church"* (1 Cor. 3:11). From this, it follows, with the Spirit's guidance, that the "rock" (Matt. 16:18) cannot mean a fallible human (Peter), but must refer to the "rock" of faith expressed by every believer, added by faith alone, to the future church Christ Willed to build. Finally, all these Scriptural arguments are settled as we read 1 Timothy 3 and discover that church leaders on earth are overseers, Pastors, or Elders—all under Christ—the True and only Head of His body, the church on earth.

Disobedience to Christ and His Word in Today's Churches.

Disobedient churches often use the term "traditions" to defend their Scripture-opposing doctrines and actions. They ask their untaught members to accept something as God's Truth because it has been done (disobediently) for centuries, without attracting God's Wrath.

Without self-examination under the *Spirit of Truth*'s guidance, without repentance where sin is found, and without spiritual Revival and true Reform to all that Christ requires (as revealed in Scripture), the church today that disobeys their Lord in any respect is in great danger of **losing His Love** (Rev. 2,3). His True teachings and His commands have asked us not only *to remain in His love by obeying Him* (John 15:9,10) but also to *wake up...do the things you did at first...to come back to Him, their first love...and repent, and obey Him in all things* (Paraphrased, author—see Rev. 2,3). Christ, the Divine Head, says He is coming back to earth soon, and this writer and all obedient Christians say *Amen. Come Lord Jesus* (Rev. 22:20). But Scripture and many discerning Christians, now and in past centuries, have warned their brothers and sisters—in their own and other Christian churches—to repent, and return in full obedience to their True Head before He comes again. Our avowed Lord says also (Eph. 5:27), in His inspired, inerrant Word, that when He comes, He intends to present to Himself His church, as Bride to Him, the Divine Head and Bridegroom. He wants, He says in this verse, to have a *Radiant church, without stain or wrinkle or any other blemish, but holy and blameless* (writer—of sin or disobedience). Which kind of church will He find? And what will we do then, when the True Head of His church finds not a *Radiant, sinless, obedient church,* but divided, divisive church bodies *stained, wrinkled, and blemished* by sin and disobedience to Him?

This last question troubles me, and I am sure every true Christian. It is my burden from the Lord, and the reason I write this book about the Christian church today—to urge repentance.

We know, from Scripture and the *Spirit of Truth*'s teachings, that Satan still roams the world seeking to destroy God's people, Christians, and their assemblies called churches. We can put this truth together with our knowledge of the disobedience to Christ of the ancient, New Testament church (Rev. 2,3), and the 2 Pet.1 and Ephesians 4 inspired statements, that Satan is working through *the cunning and deceitful scheming of men (false,* Satan-inspired *teachers* in the church). Observing the New Testament record of the church, as well as early, late, and present church history records (and often our personal church experiences!), disobedience as a fact of much church life today is seen as ever-present, even increasing. But knowing the sad truth of omnipresent disobedience (from the Bible, church history, and experience) is one thing—recognizing disobedience in "our" Christian church, or even understanding the awful consequences of it, and repenting and reforming the sinning Christian Body, is quite another! Fortunately (for eternal Christian optimists, such as myself, who love the Lord and His church, and others who have written books on this same subject), we know that with recognition of sin, prayer, repentance, revival, and reform (and the Leading of the *Spirit of Truth*) sinners can (even as in the past) repent, revive, and reform the church to please the Lord, and return His church to be the *radiant* Bride He requires when He, the Divine Bridegroom, the Head of the church, comes again.

In this section on disobediences in today's churches, I want to include here a noticeable recent pattern of disobedience among Baptist churches in the city, provinces, and country in which I live. Baptist "denominations"—like other groups often formed by well-meaning, sincere, but often sincerely wrong Christians—are a fairly recent group of Christians, when compared, say, to Roman Catholics and others. Baptists owe their name, according to historical writings, to other groups of churches, who found that the "Baptist baptism" is the true, scriptural **Christian baptism**—not **"infant baptisms"** or other's **"sprinklings"** or **"pouring** or affusion" attributed to some early "Baptists," or their own unscriptural, but traditional teachings. These churches, who called themselves Christian, but often were not scripturally so in many ways, observed the Baptists' scriptural practices in connection with unknowing believers and infant baptism, and gave them what they thought was an insulting name among the world's Christians. But later Baptists generally accepted the name willingly, for it emphasized at least one significant part of their Scriptural beliefs—even if it gave them a false sense of pride! Baptists re-read Romans 6, and confirmed that they were biblically correct in immersing only knowing believers—not sprinkling adults or unknowing children.

Latecomer Baptists also became known (with a few other church bodies in the world) as "People of the Book" (the Christian Bible), and were known, internally, and externally to the world, as "those peculiar Christians who stick to the 'literal' truth of the inspired Word of God, especially the New Testament Word for the church." Not only in Believers', (not infant), Christian baptism, but with regard to every Word found in the Bible that Christ asks or commands His disciples to obey. When I say "literal," I can assure readers from other churches that Baptists (at least conservative Baptists) do **not** believe that all of the Bible must be read literally, but they (and I) understand that many scriptural Words, of Christ or other inspired men of old, are written in parabolic, symbolic, or metaphoric forms. These need to be treated, not literally, but by seeking the truth hidden in the non-literal words. Seeking truth from Scripture means seeking the Guidance of the *Teacher of Truth,* the Holy Spirit within each Christian believer, whose roles include this kind of guidance as listed in John 14 ,16 and in other places in Scripture.

Back to some Baptist disobediences now. I said above that conservative, Bible-believing Baptists—those who believed the Bible was fully inspired of God and *useful for training in righteousness,* etc. (2 Tim. 3:16), who believed that it was fully of God, inerrant and infallible in **all** that it speaks about (not only in salvation matters, as *false teachers* say)—accepted it as all Divine Truth. But attacks from early 19th-century "modernists" along with the later rise of some German theologians and philosophers, with their "God is dead; the Bible is errant in part" teachings, and other defiances of God and His written Word, affected the Baptist church. *False teachers* not only entered the church, but even some Baptist seminaries. Even the "People of the Book" (as some called the Baptists), and their inviolable doctrines of the faith *once for all entrusted to the saints* (Jude 3) were affected adversely as their new, young, seminary-trained Pastors came onto the scene, and began to serve in Baptist churches throughout the land. Some Baptist churches began to accept these *false teachings,* and gave up, in part, some of the truth of the Word—for a partly errant Bible, and false teachings of their own.

One "Baptist example" of disobedience, that has become noticeable to me, occurred when relocations of myself and family became necessary, due to conditions of employment in my secular career. This caused us to seek out new local churches in new locations in new cities, and other Canadian provinces. My spiritual insights, academic training, and spiritual brushes with *"false teachers"* or different and divided groups of Baptists within the overall Baptist "denominations" alarmed and disturbed me with what I saw and heard within several churches.

Some years ago, I had become spiritually mature and gained more knowledge concerning my burden for disobedient churches. I began my search for a Christian church Body to unite with, by attending worship services in a certain Baptist church in a Western Canadian city. After attending a few Sundays, I requested a meeting with the Pastor. At this meeting, I told the Pastor that my wife and I were seeking a "good church home" for us to attend, and that we were looking for a *"New Testament church"* (meaning a church believing and obeying Christ in all scriptural, Christian matters of faith and practice). I told him I was looking for a church that had adopted *the faith once delivered to the saints by the Apostles* (Jude 3, *paraphrased by author*)—one that *faithfully practiced and preached all those things Christ asked His new Body to do.* I sought (I told him) a church completely faithful to their *first love.* One that had the *Spirit of Truth* in and among them, to alert and warn them of *false teachers*, so that the church might be mature and fully obedient to all that Christ required of them, as the Apostles taught, and as the New Testament Word we have teaches us. Was this an unreasonable search, on my part, to find a New Testament, Bible-believing, Worshipping, preaching, teaching and obedient church, one in which the Bible is taught to all members, and the Spirit reveals His Truth to guide the church? Many of the Baptist Pastors to whom I put the question or requirement didn't think so! This pastor and most others say something like: "stop your search, for I can say, humbly, **we** are, in deed and in truth, a true New Testament church here!"

Unfortunately, the Baptist Pastor's statements (of which the above is but a representative sample) proved—on examination against the New Testament, and the physical evidence seen and heard in the local Body—not to be the whole truth. Some of these churches preached the Old Testament 95 percent of the time, while the New Testament teachings and Words of Christ for His Body were sadly lacking in their pulpit sermons. The congregation was small, not growing, and remained largely Scripturally untaught. They were not able to mature spiritually, nor to grow or strengthen the Body, nor to discern *false teaching*, nor even know what Christ asked of His Body (and their church), because of this lack of New Testament preaching and teaching.

In some other churches—surprisingly to myself, who had been a part of several "Baptist" bodies of Christ, and who had taught Bible

classes, and had worshipped and served the Lord therein as Deacon—
I found that the younger Pastors, who had attended seminaries of
other denominations (because Baptist seminaries were not close at
hand in much of Canada) had absorbed much *false teaching* and false
traditions, and were "passing it on" to their congregations. When my
wife and I asked the young Pastors if this or that local church was a
"New Testament" church, again I was assured that this was so in their
case. But when I asked (for example) if they appointed female Deacons (or in a few cases, female Pastors), the response was yes. Scripture leaves no doubt that these offices were, in New Testament teachings, to be filled **only by males.** This was scripturally required, for the
inspired reason given by the Apostle Paul, in 1 Timothy 2:12–14, prior
to his stating the qualifications (including gender) for the two church
offices of Overseer or Pastor, and Deacon, in 1 Tim. 3.

Bible students (and well-taught new Christians) should recall
that, *moved by the Spirit* in 1 Timothy 2:12–14, the inspired Paul stated, *I do not permit a woman to teach or have authority over a man; she
must be silent* (verse 12). The reason for this, he gives in verses 13 and
14—*For Adam was formed first* (by God), *then Eve. And Adam was
not the one deceived* (first) *it was the woman who was deceived* (first)
and became a sinner (Interpolations are this writer's, to make it easier
for the new Bible student to fully understand these verses; but they
do not alter the inspired doctrine as written).

Those Christian churches (Baptist or others) who today approve
and appoint women Pastors, Elders, Deacons or as teachers of male
Christians are opposing Scripture' teachings, and likely will continue on, if no-one complains, to another disobedient act...then
another—until they reach the point where the Bible is discarded,
and *false teachers* govern the church. They will become a non-Christian sect if they do not *listen to what the Spirit says to the churches,*
as Christ asks them to do in Revelation 2,3 where He reveals His displeasure with such church failings and sin. They must be warned by
godly men, who will recall to their memory the dangers of committing such acts; that Christ *holds these sins against them.*

In discussing these particular acts that outwardly Christian
churches perpetrate in opposition to Christ's inspired Words to His

church and stubbornly continue, even if someone points out that it is scripturally in error, I have found many Pastors—although aware of what they have done—try to justify their false and weak leadership by admitting that they are pressured by so-called "liberated women" who attend the local church. These women say they want complete Scriptural "equality" in all areas of church government and service. The Pastor, disliking friction and divisions within the church, accepts their unscriptural reasoning. He advises the church that he will support the appointment of women as Deacons and even Pastors, even when his acceptance directly contradicts Holy Scripture—see 1 Timothy 2 and 3.

These women's reasoning often goes like this: "If the Word of God says in Galatians 3:28 that *there is neither Jew nor Greek, slave nor free, male nor female, for you are all one in Christ Jesus*—then male and female are completely equal in God's eyes, and Paul's advice (inspired or not, they say) about *women not teaching or having authority over men in the church* or not being appointed as Elder or Deacon, is completely unfair and opposed to Galatians 3:28."

By this false argument, they push aside specific inspired instructions of Christ for His church, and say the Galatians verse overrules Paul, since it talks about "unity in Christ transcending race, freedom and gender." But this is incorrect reasoning, made without the Spirit's counsel, and neglecting applicable Bible hermeneutics or rules of interpretation. When applied correctly, with the Spirit, a Pastor or church member must take both verses into account, and assess whether they are both given in the same context, or are completely out of the context one with the other.

The second argument against clear scriptural doctrines (one that often succeeds where the first does not), is made on a sociological basis. Some women who desire equality with males in the two church offices mentioned in the Bible say that "the New Testament was written in a society dominated by males, with women in complete subjection to males, even in regard to the church leadership positions. We feel that the Bible is also written by males, (Error! God is the author—inspired men the writers) and thus only represents the view of men in **their secular** society." This 'male-domination view,' they say, was transferred from society to the Christian church when the first church was formed by male Apostles. (Wrong! Christ built His church, the Apostles and the Spirit formed it!) The Bible, some (*false*) teachers tell us, is full of errors, and this picture of male dominance in the church is an error that needs to be opposed today, in our modern society, where women are now finally reaching full equality in the family, in the workplace, and soon (they hope!) in the Christian church.

This argument succeeds better than the first, it seems today, for it appeals to the modern, liberal Pastor and his liberal flock. Often the Pastor has been taught, in his liberal seminary by liberal professors, that these things about New Testament society and ours are true today, and as a result, the modern church must take into account that the Bible is neither inspired, nor inerrant in all it says.

These errant views opposing the One, True Creator—God has, by His Holy Spirit, moved holy men of old to write down for the guidance of Christians in His Son's church are the direct result of what God's Word warns us about. Namely: that Christian born-again believers in Christ's Body, the church on earth today, have been, will be, and are, infiltrated by "*false teachers*" whose Scripture-opposing teachings demonstrate that they are not believers in the God of the Bible, but in "a god—a false god" called Satan, whose only purpose is to destroy Christ's work and God's purpose and plan for His creation.

Christ's resurrection in the power of His Heavenly Father, after His expiatory death on the cross, has overcome death and Satan for those who are His and overcome Satan by His (Christ's) Resurrection. Our Lord's Revelation to John, in the final book of the Bible, tells us of the certain judgment to follow His return to earth, the tribulation, the millennium of peace on earth, Armageddon, His Judgment, and the casting into Hell of Satan, His Fallen angels— and all those whose names are not written in the Lamb's Book of Life (i.e. both unbelievers, and unrepentant disobedient, sin-stained churches, members, and leaders).

Because of God's plans, and His Son's obedience in all things to His Heavenly Father, and because God has saved sinful men by His

Mercy and Grace (granted when His Son offered Himself to pay the sin penalty for the whole world to a Holy God)—because of these things and more—we Christians, *if we remain faithful, true and obedient to Him and His Word*—for *Scripture cannot be broken* (John 10:35)—we will remain in His Love always. If the Christian church and its scripturally-appointed male shepherd-leaders or Pastors, under Christ the Head of the church for which He gave Himself up, teach *all* new (and old) repentant believers to obey all that He has commanded us (in His Word!), *all* the Body of Christ will be able to overcome their sin. Not only that, but the church, with spiritually-educated and mature disciples making up "Christ's Body," will be built up—will become spiritually discerning people. Then only will the church resist *false teachers*, cast them out, and grow into a Holy church. Then, and then only, will the church cast off all sin and disobedience, every stain and blemish of sin. All churches, transformed by the Spirit's Teachings and Leading, will become what our Saviour and True Lord want us to be—truly One in the faith and the knowledge of the Son of God.

My illustrations from actual Baptist church experiences, with congregations led often by weak, failing, and wrongly-taught Pastors, is not meant to shame them by their inclusion within these pages. To the contrary, these and other examples only point to the serious erosion of many formerly faithful churches by *false teachers* and the need for Christian churches to act to discover their sin, repent, and reform their errors against God's inspired Word before our Lord comes to claim a Holy church.

Understand that it is the Lord's Will that the Christian church *wake up...for I have not found your deeds complete in the sight of my God* (Christ's Words in Rev. 3:2). The Revelation messages to some early, often disobedient churches in the remote Roman Province of Asia—found in the New Testament written Word of God—are not just for those small, struggling, missionary churches in an ancient, ignorant society of the past. Nor was the Word given in hopes *these churches only would hear and obey, and only they would suffer terrible consequences*. If God's Word in Revelation 2 and 3 were *only* for the Seven Churches then, Satan and his *"false teachers"* in disobedien† churches would win their rebellion against the Son of God, and present-day churches will continue to fail to hear and respond to Christ's Will for His Body on earth. They would continue to **spiritually sleep in sin**—continue to **reject what the Spirit says to the churches**, and allow Satan to thwart Christ's Will.

False teachers and misguided members and leaders of many churches today continue to refuse to do the Lord's Will for His Body on earth.

Truly obedient Christians must not give up, but pray that God's Holy Word and His Son's Divine teachings will continue to be the Divine Rule and Holy Standard for individual Christian churches. New believers, baptized, and "added" to His Christian church, His "Body of Christ on earth," must all be taught and so mature, that they may strengthen the Body to be One in His Will and purpose, and overcome the world by obeying our Lord in all things till He comes again.

Christ's warnings are my burden for all my brothers and sisters in Christ, for all the church of Christ in the past and today. Those who have forgotten; who have fallen "*asleep;*" who have not listened to what the Spirit (and the Word) says to His churches; have been warned; their sins keep errant church bodies from becoming sin-*Overcomers* and from *being all one, as I* (Christ) *and the Father are One*. These examples are placed here only to echo Christ's warning, to disobedient churches of today, to: *wake up… repent and do the things you did before* (Revelation 2, and 3 in Christ's own Words of Truth).

I know the **Spirit speaks today** to our mutual Lord's churches—but I am concerned that the churches are not listening. The Lord says, in the final page of the final, Sacred book in the Bible: *Behold, I am coming soon* (Rev. 22: 7,20). But do lukewarm, failing, spiritually sleeping and outright disobedient and sinful churches understand what the Spirit and the Word tells all Christians to hear? If we are found by Christ to be unrepentant, disunited, unloving, and unprepared to meet Him, perhaps tomorrow! Our fate will be dreadful! Read on—and obey Him, our Saviour and Lord!

Chapter 5

Command #1: "Go...Make Disciples of All Nations" —Matthew 28:18

The Spirit has led me to communicate, to *disobedient and to faithful churches* alike, what Christ requires each Christian and each of His local churches comprising His "Body on earth" to be and do for the Love of Him Who first loved us. For whom He died; and Who seeks our love and obedience. Reading this book of warning, other concerned and obedient Christians—perhaps with the same burden and purpose given them in the same way by the same Spirit in each of us—will know something of what I feel as I write. And they will know with certainty, from the written Inspired and Inerrant Word of God, the Holy Spirit and Christ's teachings and pleadings in His Name, that a written book such as this (and others written by godly men in the past) will serve their and His purposes to warn a sleeping church far better than all the sermons from luke-warm, sleeping, and disobedient Pastors in similar churches around the world.

Without certain basic spiritual and scriptural truths, no Christian book will succeed, in Christ's eyes. These truths are to be found, not in the human author's beliefs or teachings (although they may have much academic knowledge, and church "experience") but always, and *only*, in the inspired, inerrant and infallible written Word of God and His Son, as mediated to all who read them by the *Spirit of Truth* within each believer.

I purpose to tell God's Truth from His Word—His Truth, the Whole Truth, and nothing but the Truth—so, help me, God! I will relate some of my experiences; some of other Christians' experiences; and some open, flagrant, and sinful actions of past and present churches, who deny or pervert His Word of Truth. Every experience and action I write about will be related to the inspired, infallible Standard of Truth, the Christian Bible, with the Spirit of Truth's Guidance. As you read on, ask this same Spirit to guide you personally to the Truth about you and your church's present obedience and unity (or lack of it!).

If, upon prayerful self-examination, and with the Spirit's guidance, the scales do not fall from the eyes of those failing to obey the Head of the church, Jesus Christ—if they do not wake up spiritually, and conform to all that He commands—they will suffer awful scriptural consequences.

This said, now allow me to speak out boldly for your Lord and mine, as I purposely proceed to remind the Christian church of one of our Lord's most eternally important plans for His church that He has given us who are saved to serve Him. I must remind we members and leaders of Christ's Body on earth to fully obey and perform His tasks, as revealed in His *"Great Commission for His church,"* because they are an important key to our pleasing Him, now and when He comes again. It is our choice to obey our Lord, or reject Him by spiritually and practically perverting His commands, as many churches have done in the past, and still do today. Please consult the *Spirit of Truth*, as Christ urges all Christians to do, while I briefly explain what many may never have heard, or if heard, forgotten.

The "Great Commission of Christ for His Church" —Matthew 28:18-20.

The First Command: "Go...to all nations."

The phrase **Great Commission**, above, is of course a man-made descriptive "tag" describing briefly the three important commands from our Lord to His disciples after He had risen from the dead, but before His ascension to His Heavenly Father. The angel of the Lord greeted the women who came to Jesus' empty tomb, after His death and burial there, and told them (Matt. 28:6,7) that *He is not here, He is risen.* The angel added, *Go quickly and tell His disciples...He is going ahead of you into Galilee. There you will see Him.*

The inspired Gospel of Matthew, from 28:16 to the end of the chapter, tells of how the risen Jesus met the 11 disciples on a certain mountain in Galilee, and told them what He wanted them to do for Him. Before His Transfiguration, He spoke to them of the church He Willed to build—now He had conquered death, would return to His Father in Heaven. Before He ascended, however, He "Commissioned" them with three vital tasks, concerning His church soon to be formed in Jerusalem, with the aid of the promised Holy Spirit. I will discuss the Commission itself in this and the two following chapters, but will first ask you to read Matthew 28, Verses 18 and 20b—as always, with the Spirit's teaching.

Christ's Authority to Give Commands to His Church of All Ages.

In verse 18 of Matthew 28, the Risen Jesus states that all Divine **authority** has been given Him by His Heavenly Father—for the Apostles' benefit and encouragement as well as for all future Christians—to command them to obey Him in the building of His church. This Christ, this Messiah of the Jews, Who was raised a carpenter's son, Who lived among them for just a few years, Who recruited them for His mission *to seek and save the lost of Israel*; the One *who spoke as no man had before Him*, the One Peter called *the Christ, the Son of the Living God*; the One Who showed His people many miracles, the One Who was betrayed by one of their own number, the One Who died on a Roman Cross, was buried, yet rose from the dead, and appears now before their amazed (and even doubting eyes)—He now tells them that **all authority is given Him in Heaven and on earth.**

With these three commands, He exercises His Divine authority, telling them what they (and we, His present disciples) must do for Him, as His Body on earth. He then speaks of a subject they had almost forgotten, in their agony of apparently losing Him forever to the grave. Matthew does not report the Lord's Words as commands to the future church, but only to His present disciples (the few that the Lord recruited on His first mission to the Jews). But later, the Apostles would understand His Words were for the near and distant future, and for all groups of believers called Christian, until He returns to claim His *radiant* Bride.

The church the Lord Willed to build was not to be built before the Holy Spirit came upon the disciples after Jesus' Ascension to His Heavenly Father. But in His Great Commission, now given to them in Galilee, He is established and recognized as their Omnipotent Head, with authority from His Heavenly Father that no "man" has ever been given—only the "Son of Man—God, Incarnate in Jesus Christ."

Christ's Encouragement to His Church

I would like readers to go directly from His "Authority statement" to the latter part of Verse 20 of Matthew 28, and focus now on Christ's closing Words, where He says something extraordinarily important to all His church Body—namely: *And surely I am with you always, to the very end of the age* (Until He comes again to claim His Holy, Radiant and sinless Bride, the Church.) What a wonderful way to close off His Three Commands to His disciples, then, and to us much later in history—and what a wonderful, comforting, and assuring Divine Statement He makes! The disciples then, prior to the church being established with the coming of the Holy Spirit on the disciples, would not fully recognize the nature or importance of the Lord's closing statement. But we, distant heirs of the early church of Christ, can recognize and realize the importance of these closing Words of the Lord.

He, the Divine Head of the future church, promised that He would be with every true Christian in every obedient church formed under His authoritative commands—**Always**. Not just once in a while, not just when we please Him, but always, through His Spirit Promised and given to each believer—and to the very end of the church age! Without this promise and authority of the Holy One Who gives it to each believer, in every Body of Christ, the seal of the Spirit could not empower us to obey what He commanded. With these opening and closing Divine Words of Truth in our hearts and minds, we should and must obey His Words without hesitation. His Spirit in us still speaks to us, His Body, individually and corporately today—if we will listen to His counsel, and not to sinful men.

Command #1—*"Go and make disciples of all nations."*

Because of the importance of the Three Commands of Christ to his future church—to the church established according to His Will in Jerusalem, to the growing church in Judea, Samaria, and beyond into the ancient world of the Apostles' day, and down through the centuries until today—I want to emphasize, for Christ, each individual Command, while restating His authority and presence.

First, while we Christians today have the New Testament canon of holy, inspired manuscripts in many languages available to us, recall that the early church of Matthew's day, while having received His fellowship and commands day by day in verbal teachings, were confused with what was now being said to them. The Lord spoke of **His Will to build His church** on the occasion of God's Revelation to "Peter the rock," as his nickname was (Matt. 16), but with no details given. Now, after His Resurrection, the Lord appears to the Apostles and gives them seemingly confusing commands. We have the Canonized Gospels, inspired to clarify and give Christians, now, what was difficult truth for the Apostles and disciples then. The Truth that Jesus told them in person, concerning their part in building an "institution" for Him, would first require them to actually *Go, and make disciples of all nations.* The Apostles heard Him, but did not fully understand His new message, especially the phrase *"Go, to all nations."* Leave Israel and their Jewish people? What was He **saying**?

The Apostles accepted His commands to travel with their Lord in His Jewish Nation—their people, too—and had accepted His commands **not** to go to either the Samaritans or to the Gentiles (Matt. 10:5,6). Recall that Christ's first mission from and for God was among **only** His own People, and their Lord was being obedient in all things to His Heavenly Father. He sent His willing disciples out before Him to prepare His way, with His authority to cast out evil spirits, and heal the people. They obeyed Him, their Teacher, just as He obeyed His Father's Will as Christ, the Messiah.

But things had changed for their Lord, and for them, as His obedient disciples. The Sanhedrin and individual Jews became increasingly hostile to Jesus—even sought to kill him, the true Messiah. Only

He knew that He would go soon to Calvary, and be the sacrificial *Lamb of God* (John 1:29) for the sins of His People, and for the whole lost world, not just the *lost of Israel.* The Lord told His disciples that not only must He leave them, but He expected them to *build* (His) *church.*

The Apostles were confused, and it seems, as we read Scripture (the inspired Gospels), they could not humanly accept these prophesied changes—particularly the true significance of His first Commission Command, to *Go and make disciples of all nations.* All nations? "The Gentile nations that you told us to avoid, together with the Samaritans, not long ago?" (an unscriptural and hypothetical statement, by this author, of what the Apostles must have been thinking during their Lord's Commissioning them to *build His church*).

The confusion remained with the Apostles and disciples, as Luke describes in Acts' early chapters. He relates how the promised Spirit came upon all Christ's servants, together with the sound of a mighty wind. This sound attracted expatriate Jews from many lands, now in the streets of Jerusalem to attend the Feast of Pentecost. The confusion as to exactly how the Lord wanted them to build His church, along with a strange new process of going to make disciples of **all nations**, remained—but the Holy Spirit in each disciple and Apostle enabled them to overcome their fears. The Spirit used the audible sounds of His coming on the disciples to attract a crowd of Jews in the street. The crowd were amazed to hear the disciples of Christ coming to them, and speaking in many foreign languages—in their own languages of the lands outside Israel in which they now lived and worked.

What a strange way for the church of Jesus Christ to be formed! This "church" would become a "Body," or assembly, that would contain "a new people," a spiritually-changed people who would receive by faith the Spirit of God within them after being spiritually "born-again," and who would be added by baptism to His new Body that He Willed to build just a few days or weeks ago! How strange that the first new believing members, of this First church of Christ in Jerusalem, would be mostly God-fearing Jews like themselves, attracted to hear the first gospel message about the crucified, dead, and Resurrected Christ, God's Son, and about God's proffered Grace, salvation to men of all nations, as preached by the Apostle Peter! It was doubly strange to the Apostles, for they had been told earlier by the Risen, but not yet Ascended, Lord that it was their first duty to *Go...to all nations...to make disciples*—and here in Jerusalem, it was their people from many nations who had been brought **to them** by the Spirit!

Nevertheless, the leaders of the first church of Jerusalem followed Christ's Commands (all three of them, noted in Matthew 28:18–20). They honoured His Divine authority, and obediently *made disciples* in the way described in Acts 2 and elsewhere. The absent Lord honoured them with His Spirit (His Presence within them), to the extent that we read (Acts 2:41): *Those who accepted his* (Peter's) (Gospel) *message* (and repented and believed in the Resurrected Jesus Christ) *were baptized, and about three thousand were added to their number* (the new Body of Christ, His church) *that day.*

As readers know from Scripture, *making disciples* was but the vital first part. The Apostles *made* (produced, with the Spirit) new early disciples that Pentecost day through the convicting Work of the Holy Spirit. Several thousand Jews—from other lands, as well as some, probably, from Jerusalem and vicinity—and a few Gentiles, who perhaps lived and worked in Jerusalem, were *born-again* (John 3:3) through their faith alone. And were *baptized into the church,* and there taught to *obey all that Jesus had commanded them,* by the Apostles and gifted teachers. Acts 2:47; 4:4, and other passages, tell us the first church grew rapidly—but we also note that persecution by the Jews in high places also increased. Acts 6:1 tells us that some Gentiles ("Grecian Jews" who had converted to the Jewish religion, and had now "re-converted," by accepting the Christ preached by the Apostles in Jerusalem) initiated a new need for the growing church there.

Acts 6:1ff describes the church need caused by Jewish Christians discriminating against Grecian Jews' widows (all believing members of the Christian church in Jerusalem), and the solution found. The Apostles appointed seven **male Christian members** in the church to take on the responsibility of ensuring equal treatment of all members of the Body of Christ. These "Seven" men (church helpers) were to be men *full of the Spirit and wisdom*—they would release the Apostles from these tasks, and allow them (the Apostles) to *give* (their) *attention to prayer and the ministry of the Word.*

The seven men chosen, significantly, all had Greek names, and were chosen to ease the potentially divisive widow discrimination situation in the new church. Although not named "Deacons," as such, many believe that these seven men, their spiritual qualifications, their duties, and their nomination by the church to relieve the church leaders (the Apostles) of the time for important (and commanded) pastoral duties in the church, echoes Paul's later Spirit-led writings in his church letters (NB: especially 1 Tim. 3).

This Timothy letter and passage (1 Tim. 3) is the inspired scriptural authority (and command), then and now, for each local church to appoint Deacons and Elders (or Overseers, or Pastors) within the church, with shared duties in some areas, and some special spiritual qualifications for the **male** incumbents of these two scriptural church offices, under Christ as Head of His Body, the church.

With the church well established in Jerusalem, and the Body, under Christ the Head, well-led by the original "Eleven Apostles" (and a new "Twelfth Apostle" chosen by the disciples before Pentecost) as described in Acts 1, the new Christian church seemed to settle down to their "Commanded work." Although well-liked by the people, the Apostles began to be persecuted by hostile Jewish leaders (the *Sanhedrin*, or governing members). The Holy Spirit, however, although apparently content with the obedient actions of the new church in Jerusalem, seemed—as we read later on in Acts—to be committed to making the newly-formed church ever more aware of what the Lord had asked them to do in His Great Commission—particularly the first important part involving *Go... to all nations.*

Many churches of the recent past and today, and those scholars who have produced various translations and versions of the Bible over the years, have referred to the New Testament book of "Acts" (actually, an inspired letter from one Christian to another, telling many details concerning the Spirit's establishing the church that Christ Willed before His death to build) as "The Acts of the Apostles." I understand that this is an editorial addition not included in the text of the early documents, but I personally prefer to think that, if a title for the letter Luke wrote to his friend (and probable Christian brother) Theophilus must be included in the Bible, it should be: "The Acts of the Holy Spirit." My preferred title acknowledges what is apparent, as we read this portion of Scripture (with the Spirit)—namely, that it is the Holy Spirit inspiring and guiding them, not the Apostles themselves.

After my previous paragraphs, today's New Testament readers can return to the events surrounding the contented, growing, but slightly persecuted early church in Jerusalem described in Acts 6. The Holy Spirit "used" the growing persecution of the church to focus the Apostles' thoughts on the Lord's earlier command to "Go," rather than "stay" in Jerusalem. The Lord wanted them to go to all nations (Gentiles). But the church, led by the Apostles, seemed still unsure and confused by a seeming contradiction to His "first mission" commands to **not go to the Gentiles**.

Acts 6 and 7 describe how Stephen, one of the seven helpers chosen to look after the 'widow's assistance' program in the Jerusalem church—being *Full of the Spirit and wisdom* (Acts 6:5), and also *full of God's grace and power* (6:8ff)—began to speak out for His Risen Lord among the people of Jerusalem. His *great wonders and miraculous signs* (given by the Spirit) pleased those who were open to God's Grace, but also offended certain Jews in a certain synagogue of the City of David.

These Jews, offended, stirred up false charges of blasphemy against him, and caused the Sanhedrin governors to examine him. The High Priest asked Stephen if the (false) charges brought against him were true. The Spirit led Stephen to give an impassioned speech about the history of God's dealings with the often stubborn and disobedient Jews (Acts 7). He ended with an accusation that they, the unbelieving Jews, had betrayed Jesus, and had the Romans murder the *Righteous One* (God's Son, Jesus Christ, the Messiah). Then Stephen accused the Sanhedrin in turn of disobeying God and His Law.

The speech, although God's Truth, infuriated the Sanhedrin so much that *they gnashed their teeth at him.* But Stephen (soon to be the new Church's first martyr, full of the Holy Spirit) stood there, and looked up into Heaven. He saw the Glory of God and Jesus standing at God's right hand, and described what he saw to the ruling party of Jews.

Still more infuriated, they would hear no more from this man. They dragged him outside and began to stone Stephen, for the false charge of blasphemy against God. As His Lord said and did on the Cross of Calvary, this new Christian, full of faith and wisdom, and of the Spirit, in dying asked the Lord to receive his spirit...and asked Him to not hold this sin against them. Acts 8:1 says: *And Saul* (Paul, now no longer persecutor, but the converted believer and great church founder) it is said, *was there at the martyr's death of Stephen, giving approval to his death.*

A "New Exodus": The Spirit Acts to Remind the Church to "Go..."—Not "Stay."

Acts 8 continues, saying that *a great persecution broke out at that time against the church at Jerusalem, and all except the Apostles were scattered throughout Judea and Samaria.* The Apostles, shepherds (Elders) and teachers under Christ, the Head, remained to teach a now "underground church"—one attacked by Saul. Saul *dragged off men and women* (Christians) *and put them in prison,* at the urging of the Sanhedrin. A great tragedy for the church? Yes, but much good resulted from Stephen's death, because of the scattering of the church (except for the Apostles, and those who went into hiding against the evil work of Saul) to the adjoining provinces of Judea and Samaria.

The "good" was the result of the scattering of many Christians out of Jerusalem. For, as they fled in this time of great trouble, they, with the urging of the Spirit, began to speak to others about the gospel of Christ, and God's great gift of salvation—which, if accepted, would make them *new creations* and grant them *everlasting life*—in this world and the next. Christ's plan to have them "Go to all the nations" had finally been activated. The Church was on the move.

We discover, after the great increase in the persecution of the church of Jerusalem, that *all except the Apostles* had been driven into adjoining provinces. In Acts 8:4ff, we read: *Those who had been scattered, preached the word wherever they went.* They were seemingly led to obedience by the death of Stephen, by increased Jerusalem persecutions, but basically by the Spirit, Who urged them in Christ's Name, to carry out His Command: *Go to all nations and make disciples* for Me!

The church under the Apostles in Jerusalem, meanwhile—although successful in church numbers, baptisms and teaching, as Christ's Commission had asked—had seemingly forgotten (or ignored, as we humans today often do with God's Word, when the Word tells us to do something that appears difficult, or painful!) that Christ had first Commanded them to *Go, and make disciples of all nations.* Their Lord told them (and us) we must obey. **GO,** not stay at home!

A Hard Lesson For the Early Church and the Apostles: The Samaritan Jews are Part of Christ's Plan.

Acts 8:5 reads: *Philip* (with other scattered Christians from the Jerusalem church) *went down to a city of Samaria and proclaimed the Christ.* Philip was also one of the Jerusalem seven named in Acts 6 to help the Apostles administer what needed to be done in the Body. He, too, was *full of faith, wisdom and the Spirit.* The Spirit allowed him to provide *miraculous signs* confirming the Risen Christ to the outcast people in Samaria, to whom he proclaimed the gospel message of eternal life. These signs from God authenticated to them, as they did to the Jews in Jerusalem when the Apostles spoke of the Christ (see Acts 5:12ff), that these men and their message of God's Mercy and Grace came from the Risen Lord. Acts 8:12ff tells us that when Philip *preached the good news of the Kingdom of God* (the Gospel), *and the name of Jesus Christ, they were baptized, both men and women.*

Further, (8:14) this obedience by the disciples to the Lord's command to make disciples outside the city was so genuine, and so amazing in the minds of the church, that when the church in Jerusalem heard of the Samaritan converts made by Philip and the Holy Spirit, they sent the Apostles Peter and John to them. On arrival, they prayed for the new converts *that they might receive the Holy Spir-*

it, because He had not yet come upon any of them. When Peter and John placed their hands on them, they received the Holy Spirit.

Acts 8:16 states that these new Samaritan converts had not received the Holy Spirit when they believed, but (8:17) only received Him when Peter and John laid hands on them. This was contrary to Peter's promise to the crowd gathered to hear his first Gospel sermon—and heard him say, *you will receive the Gift of the Holy Ghost* (Acts 2:38). Nothing further is mentioned in Acts 2—so we can assume the Spirit was immediately given in Jerusalem.

Why—you may ask—did not the Holy Spirit come immediately after repentance and belief to the new believers in Samaria, as they did in Jerusalem? And why did the Apostles have to come down to them, pray for them, and invite the Spirit to enter inter these new believers, well after they had repented and believed in the Lord through Philip's preaching? I wrestled with these questions too, studied Scripture with the *Spirit of Truth* within me, you, and every believer—and concluded that the following is a correct scriptural understanding of the **"Samaritan new converts, temporarily without the Spirit," problem** requiring the Apostle's prayers.

Readers undoubtedly will recall, from their reading of Christ's **first mission** to the Jews, His assembling of twelve Apostles and other disciples, teaching them, and finally, sending them out to *seek and save the lost of Israel.* No mention was made by Him of the Holy Spirit. He and the Jews, as People under the Law and the Prophets, of course, were told and taught that there was a Spirit of God Who came upon ancient men (Prophets) from the twelve Tribes, in the course of God's dealing historically with His Chosen People. But as Christ, His Apostles, and His few disciples went from town to town, preaching to **the Jews only:** *Repent for God's Kingdom is at hand,* the disciples were told **not to go** to Samaritans, or to the Gentiles. Samaria at that time was occupied by outcast Jews, who were not to be even talked to by "orthodox Jews" (by tradition, and Jesus' own words).

Yes, Jesus spoke to the woman at the well, in His passing through Samaria, but His first mission required that He and His disciples go **only** to lost Jews, and avoid the outcast Samaritans (and Gentiles). In understanding Christ's new church making Samaritan converts to Jesus and their placement into His new church (along with Gentiles!), we must realize that Christ's mission to Jews only had been changed by the Jewish rejection of Jesus. The scriptural truth was that His disciples now had been given His commands to *go to all nations on* **His second mission to build His church.** These events of Acts 8 in Samaria were obviously of prime importance to His church, if it was to expand to all nations in full obedience to their Lord and Divine Head of His church on earth.

Recall too, in Acts 1, after His Resurrection, but before His Ascension, He told His Apostles that they were not to leave Jerusalem but *wait for the Gift my Father Promised...you will be baptized by the Holy Spirit* (Acts 1:4,5). I have already talked about the coming of the Spirit to those gathered in the Upper Room in Jerusalem, and this, too, is explained as the result of the promise of Christ to them in Acts 1. We see how the Spirit's first arrival drew a crowd of Jews, many of whom as believers later became part of the new Body of Christ established in Jerusalem.

The Lord's disciples and Apostles who had been faithfully obedient to Him on His first mission to the lost Jews of Israel alone, were *baptized with the Spirit* in Jerusalem (Acts 1:5). Peter, giving his gospel message to the convicted crowd of Jews in the streets, answered those Jews who *were cut to the heart* by His message and the Spirit's conviction of their sin. He told them that when they repented and believed, *they would receive the Gift of the Holy Spirit.* Then, Acts says, these Jerusalem believers, with the Spirit within them as God's Gift, were added to the church by baptism, as born-again persons. Notice also that, since nothing else was mentioned about the Holy Spirit gift, except that *those who received his* (Gospel) *message, were baptized and added to the church*, we can rightly conclude that the Holy Spirit had come to them immediately and was residing in them upon their repenting and believing, as promised by Christ, and by Peter, speaking by the Spirit of God.

Summarizing, we can say definitely, basing our conclusions upon the inspired record of Scripture, that, because the Lord willed to build His church, but did not want to leave His disciples (past, and soon to be made) alone on this earth, He ensured that His Spirit would come upon His new disciples and live within them, doing the things John 14 and 16 tells us He would do for us. At first, the Apostles and first disciples from His first mission to the Jews alone were baptized with the Spirit, and thus received His power to commence building His new church, and obey His Great Commission. Then, as the second mission of Christ commenced at Pentecost in Jerusalem, the obedient disciples (aiding the Holy Spirit in His work) with Peter and the others telling the convicted Jews in the streets *what they must do* (to be saved)—the church was formed and added to by new, born-again believers, who also (Jew or Gentile) had personally and immediately received the gift of the Spirit of God.

A Temporary "Mystery": The Holy Spirit and "Milestone Events" For the New, Spreading Church.

The foregoing was a scriptural summary of the Holy Spirit coming upon the Lord's first disciples, and then upon the new disciples at Jerusalem, as the new church came into existence at Jerusalem. But I have not forgotten the temporary mystery given us later Christians in Acts 8.

Philip and other Christians forced out of Jerusalem had preached the gospel to outcast Jews in Samaria—who repented, believed, and apparently become new Christians. But when the Apostles (Peter and John) found that the gift of the Spirit had not come upon the Samaritans when they believed, as He had been given to the new believers in Jerusalem, they were amazed. We ask—why did the later, visiting Apostles, have to pray, lay hands on them, and thus invite the Spirit into these new converts? What was the Lord saying and telling them (and us in His Inspired Scriptures) about this strange new event? Why, in Jerusalem, did the Spirit come into each new believer, but not into Samaritan new converts?

I believe that if you read, study, and are taught the Scriptures as a maturing Christian in an obedient church, with the guidance of the Holy Spirit, you will reach the same conclusion that I have about this matter. It is this: I believe the Lord was telling Philip, Peter, John, the new believers in Samaria, the other Apostles, and the new church in Jerusalem, along with all later Christians, and us today

114

(through His inspired, inerrant Word) that He wanted His authority and commands authenticated on this special occasion in Samaria.

But how? By His requiring a **special act of the Apostles to** mark the required, but humanly delayed, spreading abroad of His church *to all nations* (including the outcast Samaritans). Because the Apostles were so slow in understanding, accepting, and acting fully and quickly upon His every Word in His Commission to His church, and because they seemed quite content to settle down to build His church in Jerusalem only, He used the persecution and death of Stephen to pre-cipitate—to force, even—His disciples to go beyond their comfortable existence and spread His gospel and make His disciples in all nations in an active, positive, timely way. So, to literally force full and urgent obedience upon His then-disciples (and all later disciples), I believe He decided to impress His Apostles and all believers that going to the next province beyond Judea—even to the hated Samaritans—was not unusual, but a momentous event for them and for His Church.

What better way to jolt the Apostles' unthinking acceptance of the routine entrance of the Holy Spirit in all believers than by illus-trating that He can and does act in unusual ways, in non-routine cir-cumstances? And, if you recall what Scripture says about the Samar-itans being hated as outcasts and non-conforming Jews, and Jesus' telling His *first mission disciples* to avoid them and the Gentiles, per-haps you can even have a little sympathy for the Apostles who now realized that, in aiding the Lord to build His church, His "rules" were changed. The rules (especially His commands in His Great Commis-sion) were meant by Him to be obeyed fully, and without delay, but now they knew their Lord meant *them* to obey Him promptly in all His commands to His church. **A lesson for us today also!** The appar-ently routine coming of the Spirit to believers, as shown at Jerusalem, was definitely not routine in Samaria. The Lord ensured this would be noted by the new church, and by later Christians.

The praying, and laying on of hands by the Apostles Peter and John in truth instructed them (and us, by the written Word) that the Lord works in different, marvellous ways,—often to mark a special Scriptural milestone event in the church's life. Only a few of these spe-cial events or milestones are seen in the recorded scriptural story of the growing church, but we must be aware of them if we are to be faithful and obedient to Him in all that He asks of us, His Body on earth.

In Acts 10, another church milestone of a similar nature to the Samaritan special event class takes place. The Apostle Peter was involved again. God had to shake up his thinking, and the Jewish conditioning in his life had to be re-examined, often, in the light of Jesus' Will to build His Church outside the Jewish nation and His command to *Go, make disciples of all nations.*

A Drastic Change For the Christian Church and the Apostles: Gentiles are Part of Christ's Plan.

Acts Chapter 10 should now be read again with the Holy Spirit as guide, for it describes a necessary and drastic change for the Apostles and many Jewish converts to Christianity. Briefly, a devout and God-fearing Gentile Roman officer named Cornelius, stationed at Caesarea, had a vision. An angel of God told him that his works of righteousness and his prayers had come up to God as a memorial offering. Cornelius was told to send his men to the seaport town of Joppa, a few miles from Jerusalem, and bring back a man called Peter, who was staying at the home of a tanner named Simon, by the sea. The scene shifts now (in 10:9) to Peter, in Joppa, up on the roof, also praying. Peter fell into a trance, saw Heaven opened and something like a large sheet let down, containing all kinds of animals, reptiles and birds. A voice (from God) told him: *get up, Peter, kill and eat.* Peter said: *Surely not, Lord, for I have never eaten anything impure or unclean* (Peter, a God-fearing Jew all his life, obeyed God's prohibition of certain living things as food for His People, the Jews, alone). God had long ago given food restrictions to His Chosen People. The voice from Heaven spoke to Peter again, saying *...Do not call anything impure that God has made clean. The same thing happened three times—and then the sheet was taken back into Heaven* (Acts 10:15).

While Peter was wondering about the significance of this strange event, the men sent to bring Peter to the Gentile, Cornelius, arrived and questioned the tanner called Simon, asking if Simon Peter was staying there. The record in Acts 10 continues, and says that, while Peter was still thinking about the vision, the Spirit said to him: *Three men are looking for you—go downstairs and do not hesitate to go with them, for I have sent them!* Peter met Cornelius' men and asked them why they had come seeking him. The three Gentile men replied, describing the vision Cornelius had experienced, and asking Peter to come to Cornelius' home so that the latter could hear what Peter had to say to him.

Acts 10:23b and following verses describe how Peter made the journey of nearly two days, and found Cornelius awaiting him, with his family, and close friends. Peter entered the Gentile's home and found a large gathering of people. Peter told them that it was against Jewish law for a Jew to associate with a Gentile, or even visit him—but told the gathered Gentiles how God, through a vision (coincidental, apparently, with Cornelius' vision), had told him that: *I should not call any man impure or unclean.* Cornelius, surrounded by his family and friends, told Peter of his vision, saying: *we are all here in the presence of God to listen to everything the Lord has commanded you to tell us.*

Peter's response tells Cornelius (and we later Christian church members) that he, Peter now knows that *God accepts men FROM EVERY NATION (emphasis/capitals, author) who fear him and do what is right.* Peter gives his gospel message to these Gentiles (verse 36ff and following relevant verses) and tells them of God's plan to send Jesus, as Messiah, to urge repentance to God on His Jewish nation by His people. He further tells them that the Jews rejected and killed Jesus, the prophesied Messiah, the Spirit-anointed, God-begotten Judge of the living and the dead—but that Jesus was raised from the dead (Acts 10:34ff).

While Peter was still telling the Gentiles these things, the Jewish believers who had come with him from Joppa were astonished to observe *that the Gift of the Holy Spirit had been poured out even on the Gentiles. For they heard them speaking in tongues, and praising God.* It was a similar event to Peter's and the other disciples' experience of the Holy Spirit coming on them at the commencement of the founding of the new church of Christ in Jerusalem. Peter said (vs.47): *Can anyone keep these people from being baptized with water? They have received the Holy Spirit as we have.* They obviously were believers, and the next step for them, as Spirit-Gifted believers, must be water baptism and addition to the church of Jesus Christ, as it was for the new believers at Jerusalem.

This miraculous event was also amazing because the Lord had His purpose for the church in view at this critical time in His church's building process, and wanted to confirm to Peter (and through him to the other Apostles and disciples in Jerusalem or scattered abroad as we have seen) that He meant what He had said to them in commanding them to *Go, and make disciples of all nations.* The Samaritan event was being reproduced here, with Gentiles this time as the object of God's plan. Here, with Peter preaching to Gentiles after his lesson from God about what is impure and what is not, people formerly considered unclean by God-fearing Jews, the Lord was marking a "spiritual milestone" in the formation of His church. His disciples would recognize that His purpose (and God's Grace) must be fully obeyed and recognized with obedience by His church.

I have mentioned these two events, involving apostate Samaritans and "unclean" Gentiles, so that readers will see, from Scripture, that the Holy Spirit was underlining the misunderstandings in His disciples' minds connected with the Lord's commands to *Go, and make disciples of all nations.* By delaying the Holy Spirit's coming upon the believers in these two incidents, they appear to be milestone **events recorded** by the Lord for the early church—warnings that His church must obey Him in the whole, not only in part.

The process of making disciples as the Lord wanted His church to do was certainly carried out with the aid of the Spirit when the church was founded in Jerusalem, and the Holy Spirit entered each believer there. But the Lord saw, too, that the church was settling down to remain in Jerusalem, even though some persecution was encountered—and its leaders were not thinking of actually going out to all nations. This is why I say, with the guiding Spirit of God, that the inspired New Testament record shows how the Lord emphasized His first Commission Command to all His disciples, including the Apostles—first, the *"going to all nations,"* and then the following *"making of disciples."*

118

This is why we can see that, in the case of the Samaritan disciples, the Spirit did not come upon them until the Apostles came to see the miracle of the apostate Samaritans—to see how God chose to ask the doubting Peter and John to lay their hands on them, and pray for the Spirit—Who came. It marked and confirmed the Lord's Will that His church must **go without delay to** outcast and lost peoples (Gentiles) of all nations. Through this later Gentile milestone miracle, together with Peter's enforced vision and former misunderstanding that Gentiles were impure, the Lord forced Peter and His church to face the truth, concerning His Will and purpose to build His church of believers made of all nations.

I praise God, as a Gentile—not as a Jew, but as a part of all peoples other than that Chosen race—that *God so loved the world, that He gave His one and only Son, so that whoever believes in Him shall not perish but have eternal life* (John 3:16). How happy I am, as a Gentile Christian, to know that God loved Cornelius and all the Gentiles gathered to hear Peter's message of salvation and to receive the Spirit when they believed—for I know that they, and I, will not be eternally separated from Him, but have repented and received His Son and Spirit by His Grace and by faith alone. And I know, through His inspired Word of Truth, that His Gracious Mercy and salvation is available to **anyone** in this world who **repents of sin and believes in the Risen Jesus Christ by faith alone**.

An Unchanging Command in a Changing World.

I trust that all my readers, lovers of God's Word, belong as repentant believers to Christian churches who not only preach the gospel message of salvation from the pulpit of their local church building, but have been taught the Lord's Commission to all His disciples, and have complied faithfully to His first Command: *Go, and make disciples of all nations.*

Disciples can be, and should be, made by Christian churches (both members and leaders) in many ways, in this age of global transportation and global media, as well as locally and personally (one-to-one or in groups). Church leaders can and must teach all maturing Christians how to witness for and to Christ—in their family, to neighbors over the back fence, in social hospitality groups, in hospitals as volunteers, in internet "chat rooms," and in many other ways—to fellow employees, at work or at play, joining with local churches to send missionaries to all nations for Him.

Canada, because of its open immigration policy, is becoming truly multinational in population. Racism and biased nationalism is slowly being eliminated and changing for the better, as churches of Christ realize that *all nations are often coming to them*, to be welcomed in Christ's name, invited into the church fellowship and building—there to learn the Good News of Jesus Christ, Who died for them, regardless of race or colour. There to hear the gospel invitation to eternal life!

But churches of Christ should not, as some do, leave the Pastor to do all the witnessing to Christ by himself. Nor should they sit back and let Evangelists alone carry out "Crusades" or "Missions" to all nations; or accept new believers as baptized members, but not *Teach them to obey all I* (Christ) *have commanded you.* This latter command, in Christ's Great Commission, is of course a part of making disciples and is the specific subject of following chapters of this book.

We can see, with the aid of the Spirit of God (within each born-again believing member of His church Body on earth) that Satan was and still is at work, to destroy His eternal enemy—Jesus Christ and His Body, the church. This first "Commission command" of Christ seems at first to be but one command, but it is actually in two parts: (the **Going** and the **making** *of disciples of all nations*). Some would say His first Command was in three parts—and split it into "Going" "making" and identifying "all nations."

Either way, the Spirit has inspired the Words; faithful men have written them down, and with the help of the *Spirit of Truth*, we can discover that His Words are still simple, direct, and under-standable, not complex. But many churches, in the past and today, seem to have difficulty understanding when Satan and his *false teachers* deliberately confuse the first command of Christ with worldly thoughts and cultural distractions. First, the Apostles, then church leaders and members of today's churches have been challenged with false thoughts and false beliefs in multitudinous groupings of churches, and by unscriptural leaders—many of whom have discarded the inerrant Scriptures, and rejected the Spirit in favour of *false teachers.*

Readers who trust God's Word and His Spirit can avoid unnecessarily complex and *false teaching* so prevalent today. The Spirit reveals to Christians, through the New Testament, that the way to please the Lord is to obey Him always—in all that He asks of us in His inspired Word. Sometimes today's Christians in today's churches will find themselves questioning Christ's directions for their lives in the world, and in Christ's church. They need not be confused and troubled, nor go in the wrong direction, for we have all been given **two gifts** when we believed:

One: The sanctifying Truth of God—the inspired, inerrant, infallible written Word—and

Two: *The Holy Spirit, The Teacher of all Truth, the One who will remind us of everything I have said to you* (Christ's Words in John 14:26).

Remember, too, that our Lord prayed to His Heavenly Father, in John 17, that we need not worry needlessly in our life here, for He prayed—not that we be taken out of this world—but that God would protect us from the Evil One, Satan. God protects us in this world, if we love and obey His Son, our Saviour, Lord, and Divine Head of His church on earth.

And, faithful Christians, remember also how, in this same prayer, our Lord prayed that God would sanctify us (set us apart, make us Holy) by the Truth found only in God's Word. The Apostles and members of the first church at Jerusalem needed to be more obedient, more faithful and obedient to the Lord's commands, and less responsive to their fears, customs and traditions of the past. They, and we, often forget our Lord's Will and purpose, through His Spirit and His church, to bring spiritually lost men of all nations to repentance, to belief, to forgiveness, and to reconciliation with our Loving, Holy God. This is the actual process, led by the Convicting Spirit, that He called "making disciples." His Son, His Spirit, and His Word will guide new and old believers to serve and worship our

Lord, within His Body, the church on earth. To bring lost men, women and children to salvation and growth into Christ, requires that the church of Jesus Christ first be obedient to His First Command, *to make disciples of all nations*. May we all be found faithful and obedient when He comes!

Part 3. Three Commands of Christ for His Church "He Will Build."
Matthew 16:18.

Chapter 6

Command #2:
"Baptize Them...(Into the Church)"
—Matthew 28:19

The second command of Christ, in Matthew 28:19 is a part of a longer sentence that we call, for obvious reasons, "The Great Commission of Christ for His church." Given to His Apostles by the Lord, as recorded at the end of Matthew's book of inspired events and actual conversations with Jesus Christ, His Commission commands were given to the eleven Apostles, as my readers will recall, on a mountain in Galilee. Christ had commanded them to gather after His Resurrection from his grave, and following His Atoning death and tomb burial. Matthew 28:16ff gives us the inspired record, including Matthew's comment, in verse 17, that *When they saw Him they worshipped Him; but some doubted.* Other Gospels record His disciples' doubts about whether it was really the Resurrected Christ Who stood before them. Even today some doubt His death and His Resurrection—even the Truth of the written Word of God. But **God's Word is Truth** (our Lord Jesus said so in John 17). Those who have repented and believed down through the centuries to today must not doubt Him and His Word, for the Spirit of God Who entered our hearts when we believed confirms in our spirit that Christ Lives, His Spirit lives, and His sanctifying Word lives within the hearts of all who repent and believe in the Risen Christ, in faith!

Let us consider now His Second Command of Christ's Great Commission to His church.

"Baptize them ('and add them' to My church)": Matthew 28:19

This second command of Christ's Great Commission to His church, like the first, was given after the Lord's statement about *All earthly and Heavenly Authority being given Him* (Matt. 28:18), and His loving promise that if those disciples to be included in His Body, the church soon to be formed, and later churches all obey Him, His Presence will be with us always, to the very end of the age.

What did the Lord ask of His church in this second of His three "linked" Commands? His three-part Command speaks of, first, His over-arching command to make disciples for His Body. The second action requires the church to *baptize* the new-made disciples, in a special way that would confirm them as belonging to Christ, and thus the Lord *adding them to His body, the church on earth* (Acts 2:41,47 as paraphrased by the author). Thirdly, the church acted to modify the new believers' initial status (church members, yet spiritual infant believers, as the church taught them) to that of spiritually mature believers, members and disciples—*New Creations in Christ*—all this by teaching them *to obey all that* the Lord *commanded them* (Matt. 28:20). Through these three linked commands of our Lord, the church leaders and teachers must act in obedience by making all disciples useful to the church and to Christ; able to strengthen the whole Body, and able (when fully taught) to reject *false teachings* and teachers when they (almost inevitably) appear (Eph. 4).

Detailing the Lord's Second Command in His Great Commission to His church on earth.

The second of the Lord's three "linked commands" tells the church to take newly "made" believers and *baptize them in the Name of the Father and of the Son and of the Holy Spirit* (see Matthew 28:19 and many other references to baptism and the Trinity of God). This baptism is that which we know as "Christian baptism" to differentiate it from other baptisms in the Bible—particularly in the New Testament. Let's briefly consider these now, and confirm scripturally that, while there are other baptisms noted in God's Word, only the one referred to in the Lord's Great Commission (Matt. 28:19) is true Christian baptism as fully described and identified for Christians in the Apostle Paul's inspired corrective to error, in Romans 6. It was carried out in obedience in the first Christian church in Jerusalem (Acts 2), and in most of the later churches up to the death of the Apostles. There is only one True scriptural baptism, but many churches wrongly teach and observe unscriptural baptisms, as noted here and earlier in Ch. 4. These will continue to be denounced on the authority of the inspired, inerrant Word. Read the scriptural references, with the Holy Spirit's requested guidance, as I briefly describe Christian baptism and give scriptural reasons for rejecting other baptisms as "Jewish but not Christian" or, sadly, as deliberate human perversions of True scriptural Christian baptism found in disobedient churches today.

1. John the Baptist's Baptism of Jews.

In the New Testament portion of the Bible, Mark 1:1ff tells us that according to various inserted Old Testament quotations (Mark 1: 2,3), John the Baptist came as a messenger preparing the way ahead for the Messiah. Luke 3 confirms it, as does John 1 and Matthew 3, in various inspired words. Let's refer to Mark's description of John the Baptist's baptism, however, because it is a little more definitive as to what it represents. When John appeared as a messenger from God, he knew, from the prophecies quoted in Mark 1:2,3 (from Mal. 3:1 and then from Isa.40:3), that he, John, was the person from God whose mission it was to prepare the way for the Lord, the prophesied Messiah for the Jewish Nation of God.

The question *What was the baptism of John?* is answered best from Mark 1:4. Other Gospel references merely state *John baptized repentant Jews in the Jordan.* But here, in verse 4 of Mark 1, we discover that: *John came, baptizing in the desert region and preaching a baptism of repentance for the forgiveness of sins.* Verse 5 tells us that many Jews from Judea and the city of Jerusalem went out to see him. Verse 5b says: *Confessing their sins, they were baptized by him* (John the Baptist) *in the Jordan River.* So, our question about the Baptist's baptism is answered: it was "a baptism of repentance," given by John to the Jews who confessed their sins against God and man and were immersed and washed clean (symbolically) in the waters of the Jordan—in recognition that their sins were forgiven by God. Note that John, like Jesus on His first mission, went only to the *lost of Israel.*

Some say this symbolic baptism of (Jewish) repentance, preached by John, was a forerunner of Christian baptism, done by the church after repentance and belief by faith in the Risen Saviour—first to converted Jews, and now primarily to repenting and believing Gentiles. But there is no reason to consider historical precedents when dealing with Christian baptism, for the Nation of Jews, from Scripture, are seen and treated by God as completely separate from other nations and peoples, and unique in His dealing with them. God gave the Jews (His Chosen People) their own land; their own sacrificial worship system; their own Law; their own dietary system, their own Temple, and God's Commands and Covenants—all completely separate from those doctrines and practices and faith given by Christ to Gentile believers, called Christians. Yes, we Christians worship the same God, and have the same coming King as the prophesied "King on the throne of David"—but Jews do not have Jesus Christ as Head of the church He willed to build for Gentile believers—for the Jews have a Temple and synagogues, not a church in which to worship and serve Him as part of Christ's "Body of believers." Nor do we and Jews have the same Divine Future Plan—revealed in the Book of Revelation primarily. The baptism of John the Baptist, then, was for the Jews alone. While Christian baptism, as New Testament Scripture confirms, is seen to be—and does represent—something quite different from, and unique to, Christian believers.

Aware of these scriptural statements concerning Jews and Gentiles, we can read the gospel book's inspired record with the Holy Spirit as our teacher, and say that Word of God confirms clearly that John the Baptist's "baptism" was for Jews only. It lasted only until John's death, and until Jesus Christ was rejected as Messiah by the Jews. God Willed and planned to extend His Mercy and salvation beyond His Chosen People, the Jewish Nation, as He prepared to accept the death of His Son in expiation of the sins of the world, so that whosoever believed on the Name of His Resurrected Son would be saved.

2. The Unique (not seen before or since; once only) baptism of Jesus by John.

After describing the coming and preaching of John, the forerunner of the Messiah, the Gospels, in their early chapters speak of Jesus coming on His first mission (author's term, justified when Scripture is seen to refer to this mission to Jews alone *to seek and save the lost sheep of Israel;* and to a second, *to build My church* and go to *all* [other] *nations,* i.e., Gentiles). I will use Matthew 3:13ff to describe in these inspired Words why Jesus (prophesied Messiah to the Jews) came from Galilee to John the Baptist, to be baptized by him, for a reason completely unique and Divine.

We read in Matthew 3: *Jesus came from Galilee to the Jordan, to be baptized by John. But John tried to deter him, saying, I need to be baptized by you, and do you come to me?* The *Spirit of Truth* will tell readers, in these verses, that Jesus and John knew of each other, and knew of God's initial plans for both of them (one was a human forerunner of the prophesied Messiah for the Jews; the other was the Divine Messiah, incarnate in human flesh, and sinless). I believe this, for Luke 1—in a detailed description of the foretelling of the birth of Jesus, and also of the birth of Elizabeth's son (John the Baptist)—speaks of how John would be used of God to prepare the Messiah's Way, as well (and primarily) of how the Son of God, the Saviour of the Jews, would be born of the Spirit by a human virgin. Jesus and John grew to manhood, unknowing then of their respective "missions to the Jews." It was only revealed fully to John that Jesus was the Promised Messiah when he heard God speak at Jesus' baptism, and saw the Spirit descending upon the Messiah-Son.

Returning to Jesus' request to be baptized by John in the Jordan, the latter now fully knew Who Jesus was, and told his followers that Jesus was the coming Lord by quoting Isaiah 40:3 to them. This was the reason why John said to Jesus, *I need to be baptized by you; and do you come to me?* (Matt. 3:14). But Jesus, knowing that He must please His Heavenly Father, insisted on being baptized publicly by John. Jesus said: *Let it be so now; it is proper for us to do this to fulfill all righteousness* (of His Heavenly Father). John consented, and we read (Mark 3:16ff): *As soon as Jesus was baptized, He*

127

went up out of the water (No sprinkling here; one must be immersed to come up out of the water—*author*). At that moment, Heaven was opened, and John saw the Spirit of God descending like a dove and lighting upon Jesus. And a voice from Heaven said, *this is My Son, whom I love; with Him I am well pleased.*

From these inspired words of Scripture, with the Guiding Spirit of God in each believer, we can learn these things about Jesus' baptism by John:

A. It was not at all like John's baptism of repentant Jews—to acknowledge their human repentance and forgiveness of sins by symbolic washing—for Jesus was a Sinless and Divine human. He was tempted to sin, as a fleshly human, but Jesus was without Sin in His uniqueness as the Divine Son of God, incarnate (born of the Spirit of God in human flesh or body).

B. Jesus' baptism was not symbolic of cleansing from sin, as was John's baptism of repentant Jews, but was a public, visible, and Righteous transaction between God and Himself, one that would publicly confirm and accredit Jesus as the prophesied Messiah sent by God. And thus, would show to the world His fulfilling of God's plan of Righteousness made through Old Testament Scripture.

C. Jesus' public baptism by John the Baptist, unlike the baptism of repentant Jews by John, and unlike Christian baptism (to be described later from Scripture), was an occasion at which God sent His Spirit to come upon Jesus, after His baptism, to strengthen Him and be with Him, in His coming mission to the Jews alone. And, again, both Jew and Gentile know (and we today know) through the inspired Scriptures telling us of Jesus' unique baptism, that Jesus' position as God's only-begotten Son, Messiah, and Head of His future church was pleasing to God in Heaven.

Notice that the Holy Spirit did not come upon Jews that John the Baptist baptized, and only came upon Jesus *after* His baptism—for the future church, Jesus willed that His Spirit would

128

only come upon Christians *when they believed; rarely during, seldom after the baptism event.* This will be discussed, for some Christian churches have said, wrongly, that baptism saves one, rather than repentance and belief.

3. Christian baptism as described in Scripture, and followed by obedient Christian churches.

Christian baptism—that is, baptism conducted by Christ's Body, the church upon former sinners who have repented of sin and believed in the Risen Christ, for the purpose of adding the saved person to Christ's Body in obedience to His Commission to His church—is seen to be different from John's baptism of repentant, sinful Jews. And also different from Jesus' unique baptism seen as a public consecration to God, *to fulfill all righteousness* prior to His coming mission to the Jews. Now, I will explain Christian baptism as it is shown to us in the record of the Christian church, first in the book of Acts. As we examine scriptural Christian baptism with the guidance of the *Spirit of Truth*, we must go first to the book of Acts in the New Testament. These inspired Words describe how the "First 'Baptist' church" (as we can truthfully call it) at Jerusalem was formed, under the Spirit's Presence and Sin-Convicting Power, and as the Spirit-led Apostles and early disciples obediently followed the Three Commands of Christ to his future church, in Matthew 28:18–20.

Read again (with the Spirit's counsel), in Acts 2, how the Spirit gathered a crowd of expatriate Jews (and a few Gentiles, probably) in the streets of Jerusalem at Pentecost, so that Peter could preach to them about Jesus Christ, in obedient action to Christ's Command to make disciples of repentant sinners. The listening crowd, after hearing the first gospel message preached, were convicted in their hearts by the Spirit, and asked (Acts 2:37): *Brothers* (the Jewish Apostles), *what must we do?* Peter told them that repentance of their sin was required (and belief in the resurrected Jesus, for this was his Gospel message). Then, Peter said: all repentant sinners who *received* (accepted and believed) *his message* must be baptized with **Christian baptism**—note, *not* John the Baptist's or Jesus' own).

Acts 2 tells us that *those who accepted Peter's message were baptized, and about 3,000* believers *were added* that day alone to the first Christian church Body. I can, and readers can also, justly and scripturally call these 3,000 baptisms, **Christian baptisms by** scriptural actions and scriptural Words—though the word 'Christian' was not historically used until the church expanded to all nations (see Acts 11:26). The rest of Acts chapter 2 tells us what the new believers and the Apostles did in the new Body, for Christ. It closes by confirming that *the Lord added to their number daily* (to the Body of Christ, the church) *those who were being saved* (through repentance and belief—not by baptism). Belief in Christ saves; baptism identifies the saved, "born-again" person with Christ in a special way. And by this obedient act, He adds them to the church for maturing and service to the Lord.

In summary, the Acts 2 portion is more historical than theological. The Apostles obediently followed an exciting routine of preaching the Lord's gospel message of salvation, answering questions from convicted sinners, telling them a message of offered salvation and offered Holy Spirit, and, with the Spirit convicting them, leading repentant sinners to confess and repent of their sins. Forgiven by a Gracious God, they are now born again, and must be baptized to be added publicly to the assembly of believers called Christ's church—His Body on earth. Unfortunately, Luke, the inspired writer of these "Acts" did not choose to detail such things as how and why the new believers must be baptized after belief into the new Body of Christ—but well-taught Christian readers know all these details from the Gospel records, the "Church Letters," as well as from the teachings of the Apostles and other inspired later "evangelists."

Fortunately, the Holy Spirit—recognizing man's inherited sin and tendency to listen to *false teachers*, rather than to the inspired Apostles and church members of that growing church—has given us the baptism detail we later Christians need, to counter Satan and his *false teachers* in His church today.

For **important information** about the baptismal process, as well as its spiritual meaning for the baptizers and the baptizees as conducted by the New Testament church, so that we in today's Christian church can please Christ and combat false teachings about Christian baptism, **we turn to Romans 6**. Given to correct errant baptisms, it is a Spirit-inspired corrective to *false teachers*.

In this important, inspired theological letter to the church at Rome (and to us today), we observe first that the writer, the Apostle Paul, in chapter 5 discusses sin, the Law, and Christ's work on the Cross that produces Life through Christ, as death came to mankind through Adam's sin. Then, in chapter 6, he briefly continues on the same subject of sinning, Grace and death, and says to the church at Rome (as well to all future Christians): *What shall we say, then? Shall we go on sinning so that grace may increase? By no means! We died to sin; how can we live in it any longer?* The *Spirit of Truth* shows us that Paul's rhetorical question above (Rom 6:1) hides a serious problem occurring in the church at Rome. Paul was trying to show his readers (oftentimes deceived by *false teachers*) the real meaning of sin and God's Grace and Mercy in salvation given to us believers through Christ our Lord. For those individuals and churches having the same kind of serious problem, and wanting to know God's Truth, instead of listening to *false teachers*, Paul gently reminds them (us, too!) that, if they would concentrate on our Saviour and Lord more—instead of trying to fix their sin problems by keeping on sinning, because God's Grace seems endless—they would know the truth.

As Paul continues in Ch. 6 of his letter, the Spirit gives him another argument to use with those who have (like us) *died to sin so how can we live in it any longer*. Fortunately for all the later church Body of Christ, and for those who—like me—write about its failings (and Christ's remedy), Paul uses this second argument to launch into Christian baptism in a way all Christians can understand. He writes, ***don't you know*** (verse 3) the true meaning and symbolism enacting, with every true Christian baptism, Christ's death, burial and resurrection (paraphrased by the author)? He goes on to tell them (and us today who may not clearly understand) all about it. Paul explains: As each believer is baptized by the church, he or she will be identified with the Lord both personally and symbolically with the Lord's death, burial and triumphant Resurrection to eternal life (*paraphrased by author*). But, remember, Scripture tells us **only** repentance and belief in the

Risen Saviour, Christ, saves a sinner—not baptism alone (see Rom. 10:9,10).

Let us examine Paul's inspired message of True Christian baptism as he continues in Romans 6:3–11:

> *Or don't you know that all of us who were baptized into Christ Jesus were baptized into his death?*
>
> *We were therefore* **buried with him through baptism into death** *in order that, just as Christ was* **raised from the dead** *through the Glory of the Father,* **we too may live a new life.**
>
> *If we have been* **united with him like this in his death, we will certainly also be united** *with him* **in his resurrection.**
>
> *For we know that* **our old self was crucified with Him** *so that the body of sin might be done away with*
>
> *that we should no longer be slaves to sin—*
>
> *because anyone who has died has been freed from sin.*
>
> *Now* **if we died with Christ, we believe that we will also live with Him.**
>
> *For we know that since Christ was raised from the dead, He cannot die again; death no longer has mastery over Him. The death He died, He died to sin once for all; but the life he lives, he lives to God.*
>
> *In the same way,* **count yourselves dead to sin but alive to God in Christ Jesus.**
>
> (*Emphases by the author*)

This confirms not only the true mode but the true meaning of immersion baptism. Ask your Pastor if "your church" baptizes believers in the Romans 6 inspired way of truth. I trust you will all read this scriptural passage on Christian baptism, and know the Spirit led Paul to make clear to all Christians that "immersion baptism" is inspired Truth. Every other man-made "way of Christian baptism" is false and unscriptural, and thus opposes the Word of God. Allow me to briefly summarize Paul's points that differentiate other Bible baptisms: John the Baptist's, Jesus' own baptism by John, "False," or "non-Christian baptisms," or "later and continuing false, church-perverted baptisms"—infant baptisms, or baptisms by "sprinkling" or "pouring," etc.—that differ from the Apostle's inspired and true doctrine, in Romans 6, describing the only True Christian baptism that meets Spirit-inspired requirements for His church.

1. Christian baptism must be ***by immersion only***. Otherwise, the true meaning in Romans 6 is lost on the person being baptized, or on the church members (or unbelievers) observing or hearing about true baptism. The original Greek verb ***"to baptize"*** means to ***dip***, or to ***plunge under*** and translations from it to our Bible versions correctly demand ***only*** immersion baptism to fulfill inspired Scripture.

2. Christian baptism, described in Romans 6, must and does allow the believer being baptized to identify themselves with their new Lord—through their immersion (***"burial"***), and rising out of the water ***"resurrection"***)—***with*** Christ Himself in His death, burial, and resurrection.

3. Without Christian baptism, any "affusion" ceremony purporting to be Christian baptism is not only false, but is a perversion of scriptural truth and meaning. Sprinkling or pouring will not please the Head of His church, for the inspired Paul, in Romans 6, has told us Christ's Will for us.

4. Candidates for Christian baptism must have repented of their sins, and must believe by faith alone in the resurrected Christ, ***before undergoing*** immersion baptism (Acts 2; Rom. 10).

5. As I said—as Scripture said—I am sure that the Apostles, who taught the new church in Jerusalem all that Jesus had taught and commanded them, faithfully obeyed the Lord in the process of baptizing new believers, and only then added them to the church Body there. Paul's letters to Corinth about abuses of the Lord's Supper, and to Rome about baptismal abuses, were not inspired or written to

these churches alone. In New Testament times, the inspired letters of Paul and others were circulated to all churches where possible. And they have been circulating, with the Spirit's Help, ever since. We have them today (praise the Lord!) to help failing churches recognize and correct these same abuses today, and reform them to what our Lord, through holy men, originally wanted His church to do for His Body.

Yet the pattern of church false teachings continues today, in these and many other perversions and outright disobedience of Scripture within our Lord's teachings and commands. This is why Christ told His church *to listen to what the Spirit says* (seven times in Rev. 2,3)—for the Spirit speaks of Christ's Words and teaches us the truth, even as *false teachers* pervert it.

Let me now briefly comment on some false and perverted baptismal practices that have taken place, and are still in place in many Christian churches to this day, despite the inspired truth about Christian baptism that is ours to know from Scripture and to practice faithfully to please our Lord.

Disobedient, perverted and errant baptisms wrongly practiced in the past and today.

1. Possibly the most deviant and errant distortion of true Christian baptism, as described in Romans 6, and as commanded in Christ's Great Commission for His church, is that of baptizing unknowing infants, who cannot understand or be conscious of their need to repent of sins against God or man. An infant does not understand the Gospel message concerning God's Son, His death, burial and resurrection, nor believe in the Resurrected Christ by faith—since an infant has not the capability of heart, mind, and infant body to hear, understand, and act upon the gospel message, even if preached to. The largest and best-known perpetrator of this errant baptism upon unknowing children is, of course, the Roman Catholic church (although many other Protestant denominations, state churches, etc., publicly make known their practice of this false and unscriptural doctrinal form and practice of infant baptism). It has arisen, and continues in these churches, after some centuries of false practice—although its date of origin, and particular circumstances of practice in each instance, is not known to any degree of certainty. It is a result, I know, of a basic and deliberate adoption of an errant view of Scripture. Errant teachers have substituted men's *false teachings* in place of clear, plain Spirit-inspired truth about the true scriptural meaning of Christian baptism—and many untaught members have blindly followed them.

Those who practice Scripture-opposing error, it seems, must of necessity state that—while they believe the Bible is the inspired Word of God to men, and a Holy guide to church faith and practice—"their church leaders and teachers" have the human authority and right to add, subtract, or change their interpretation of the Bible in any area. Unbiased Christians who, guided by the Holy Spirit, can and do point out from God's Word that these errant interpretations do not agree wholly with—even oppose—the inspired Word of God, are called heretics. It apparently does not matter to those church leaders who pervert and change the Word of God if other Christians consider, rightly, that these human changes, when practiced, oppose the inspired Word of God. Or, in the case of infant baptism, that they may have jeopardized the eternal souls of unknowing infants who are the subject of their *false*, man-made (not God-inspired) *teachings* and unscriptural baptismal practices.

The Roman Catholic church and others, in deciding to baptize unknowing infants, have recognized that they expect the family of the falsely baptized infants to raise them in the church, and, at a certain more mature age, teach them of God and present them to a Priest for supplemental instruction. They know they must do something more to satisfy some of their members, who might have read the truth in the Bible. This later instruction, and "Confirmation" of earlier action (also unscriptural), is meant to counter the criticism of those who say that Paul was inspired to write about the true meaning and purpose of immersion baptism, following **conscious** repentance and belief.

But what about those infants who die before they are able to "confirm" what priests wrongly "did for them" in infant baptism? The Roman Catholic church's errant teachers have an answer to this, but it, too, is Scripturally false. They say, or infer, when an infant is baptized with "Holy Water," by a "Priest" (scripturally correct, perhaps, for the Jewish religion, but not for the Christian church)—that the infant is saved by: the Priest's act, the "Holy Water," and the prayers. But salvation promised in this errant manner is not Scriptural. Inspired Scripture requires hearing and understanding the gospel message, knowingly accepting and confessing as sinners, and, if convicted by the Spirit, knowingly repenting of sins, along with conscious belief in, trust in, knowing the Risen Jesus Christ. Only then are they Biblically saved from God's wrath and "*new creations*," given eternal life now and in Heaven. Nowhere does the inspired Word of God indicate any other "way" of salvation (for lost Gentiles or converted Jews), than that given for convicted sinners in God's inspired, inerrant and infallible Word. God's Wrath will surely be upon those who oppose Scripture, assume Christ's authority, and negate the Holy Spirit's *moving* men to write in Scripture what God commanded, in order to be **born-again** spiritually.

The disobedience of some churches—who, although having the written word of God available for their guidance—perversely accept and follow *false teachers* in the Christian church, remains as one of the basest acts of *false teachers* in this book about what Christ the Head asks of His church. God's Inspired Word, and the Holy Spirit's Purpose is to Teach us God's Sanctifying Truth. But when His church disobeys Christ, the Divine Head, *He who searches men's hearts and souls* and *knows our* (false) *deeds*, demands that *we repent of our disobedience, and do what we did at first*, that is obey Him and His word. (These and many more warnings for His church appear in Rev. 2 and 3.) God will no longer permit His word to be perverted by *false teachers*, and will not accept as His bride, when He comes, a church that is *stained with sin, wrinkled and blemished* (Rev. 2,3).

I, personally, as a Christian—and I am sure many other Christian leaders and members feel the same way—have struggled with human questions about infants who die shortly after birth, before they hear, understand, and respond to the Gospel, with Scripture, and the guidance of the Spirit. The inspired, inerrant Word of God has satisfied our hearts, minds, and consciences that such infants, not yet of an age to purposely sin against God or man, will in the Mercy of God, go to Heaven upon their early death, despite having the stain of Adam and Eve's "Original Sin" of disobedience to God in them and all of us humans. Our Spirit-aided understanding rests upon our Scriptural knowledge that we have a Merciful, Loving God Who knows each human heart, as well as sure Words of Truth from the lips of God's Son, our Saviour.

The Words of truth I refer to are found in Matthew 18:1–4 and 19:13,14. I invite you, and urge those disobedient churches who wrongfully baptize unknowing and unbelieving infants (and falsely claim they are saved in the process) to look at these Words of our Saviour and Lord, and claim always and only, the Guidance—not of *false teachers* or false theologians—but of the Holy *Spirit of Truth*, to see God's Truth about this errant church problem, and reject any and all *false teachings* that oppose His Holy Word.

In the above mentioned passages of Scripture, the Lord was teaching His disciples on His first mission to Jews only—but His Words are Divinely applicable to both Jew and Christian. His disciples asked a question concerning the Kingdom of Heaven, and the Lord taught them, in His inimitable fashion—teaching by example. He called a little child from the crowd of listeners, and had him stand among them, and said to them: *I tell you the truth, unless you change and **become like little children** you will never enter the Kingdom of Heaven. Therefore whoever humbles himself like this child is the greatest in the Kingdom* (Matt.18:1–4). Later, in Matthew 19:14, after others brought little children to Jesus for Him to place his hands on them, and pray for them, we read that the disciples rebuked those that brought the children. Then Jesus said to them (and to us!): *Let the little children come to me and do not hinder them, for the Kingdom of Heaven **belongs to such as these**.*

Placing these two inspired portions containing Christ's Words together (Matt. 18 and 19) Spirit-discerning Christians can understand from Scripture that little children, by their soul's "quality and character" evidenced in their earliest naturally-humble lives ("humbleness" is the key word here) show to adults of any culture, society or nation that their lives as *infants* are *different* from the quality and character of sinful (un-humble, sinful) *adults*. As children grow to adulthood, they often become less humble and more self-centered, less loving and less caring, more sinful in what they do and say, and less honest. And thus, they become less fit for God's Kingdom. So, when Jesus talked about the spiritual character and qualities of those adults who seek to enter the Kingdom of Heaven (let alone be humanly greatest there!), He tells us a great deal about those who are in the Kingdom now, or desire to enter. He tells us adults, who desire to know who are true candidates for Heaven, that He speaks not only to adults who can and must change (i.e., repent, turn away from sin) to humble themselves, but He also says a great deal about younger, unknowing children and infants. Our Lord tells us that the Kingdom itself belongs to, or contains, *persons* like in spiritual qualities to such as these infant *children*.

The Spirit tells me, as I read the above Words of our Lord, that those teachers and churches who, in the past centuries or in recent decades, decided to listen to false men and not to the Words of Christ for His church, and who falsely instituted so-called "infant, saving baptism," are not obedient to the Head, Jesus Christ. For the Word and the Spirit tell me—and other Bible-believing Christians—that infants (or little children), *before* they reach the age where Satan leads them to actively sin—and become like sinful, unhumble adults—*belong* in humbleness of spirit and in truth to *the Kingdom* of Heaven.

I do not know why or when the Roman Catholic church and other churches, who baptize unknowing infants to "save them" and baptize them (wrongly), or "add" them to the church membership, began this errant practice so opposed to the Scriptural Truth. I suspect (but do not know for sure) that some early Bishop or church leader was probably tearfully implored to institute a new doctrine of "infant- saving baptism" by a mother or family members of a dying child. I also suspect (but do not know) that the process of this false change involved the churches and leaders appealing their church teachers instead of the *Spirit of Truth* for some theological or scriptural support for this increasingly and plainly unscriptural practice. Eventually, I suppose, the

Church Fathers, not finding agreement with the Scripture requiring "knowing, understanding baptismal candidates," (i.e., knowing believers, **not infants**) suggested "confirmation following some years of maturation" (unscriptural!)—although that, too, is adding to Scripture and opposing God's Word. Adding infants as church members and falsely stating that these unknowing infants' souls are saved would also be appealing to power-hungry human church leaders, as well as satisfying untaught and unknowledgeable church and family members. Sadly, such Scripture-opposing practices often become "church traditions," and over the years are held up as God-pleasing acts, "because they have endured for many years." But Scripture plainly says that **disobedience to God and His Word**, whether by Jews or Christians, **does not please our Saviour and Lord.** *False teachers* and their false ways, prompted by Satan, must be rejected and their sin repented of before the Lord comes again. All disobedient Christian churches must return *to do the* (Christ-pleasing) *things they did at first*, before they opposed Scripture (Rev. 2:5, Christ's Words—not this author's!).

2. Many churches, calling themselves Christian, also oppose the inspired Word of God not only by baptizing infants, but by baptizing convicted, repentant, and believing persons (who know they are sinners) in an unscriptural, and errant, manner or mode. These persons have heard, and know what the gospel message given to them by sermon or by personal witness means. They know the necessary, Spirit-led response they must give, in order to be genuinely born-again—but are often in the hands of a disobedient church Pastor. Let me illustrate what I mean, with a personal experience in a Protestant church.

I can still remember the shock I felt when our "new Pastor"—in the small church in which my wife, our two daughters, and myself were led by an earlier Pastor and the Spirit to become born-again, baptized, spiritually maturing, and worshipping and serving members—"shook up" our weekly prayer meeting. During the prayer meeting, the Pastor asked a most unscriptural question of this prayerful group of Christian members he shepherded (A hypothetical question perhaps, but obviously on his mind for some time). His question was: "What difference does the **amount of water** in Christian baptism make?" (To Christians individually, or to this

Baptist church that immersed believers.)

This new Pastor came from another province in Canada, after graduating from a Baptist seminary noted a few years earlier for their Board of Trustees inviting a certain professor from Europe to teach there. This visiting professor upset the scriptural views formerly held by all past professors in this Canadian seminary, as he shared liberal views of Scripture with new "Pastors-to-be" under his teaching care. It became very obvious that the graduating classes from this now-infamous seminary were deeply influenced by this European "liberal modernist" teacher, and his unorthodox and often unscriptural opinions on many doctrines of the Christian church.

Fortunately, when our new Pastor posed his question about Christian baptism, and what difference did "sprinkling," "pouring," or "immersion baptism" really make, there were a few Bible-believing Bible students, and well-taught mature Christians present! The new Pastor was told, in no uncertain terms by some of his new congregation (also by my wife and myself!) that **this** particular Baptist church and its members believed the Bible was inspired by God, and as the Spirit moved men to write what He wanted Christians to know about the Lord's teachings and commands, "the amount of water used in baptism makes all the difference to Christians in this world, and the world to come!"

He was told, by myself and others, that if we were not fully obedient to God's Word about scriptural Christian baptism, or any other matter or doctrine concerning our Christian faith and practice, we would be disobedient to the Head of the Christian church, whose Spirit gave us God's Inspired, inerrant and infallible Word. And, we said: if we as a Christian church changed from the only True method of baptism found in Scripture (immersion baptism), and "sprinkled or poured" candidates for membership without immediately recognizing and repenting of our error and repenting of *the* (obedient) *things we did at first* (Christ in Rev. 2:5), we would surely be out of Christ's favour as His church, just as most of the seven churches (and many others) of the past were.

The matter and hypothetical question was dropped immediately. As the Holy Spirit continued to convict and make believers of those who heard the gospel message preached, taught, and witnessed to by the new Pastor and Spirit-gifted members, the little faithful church continued to grow.

At this point I want to discuss what a present-day Canadian Protestant Christian church, the "Christian Reformed church" believes, writes and practices concerning infant baptism. I quote from a public brochure from this church, which, they say is part of the Christian Reformed Church in North America, and "... a Protestant Christian church with its roots in the 16th-century Reformation." Some "Reformation churches," when they left their so-called parent church (the Roman Catholic church), cast off certain ties such as a Pope, "indulgences," etc., but still retained some of the parent church's false "traditions"—such as, for example, unscriptural infant baptism. The Christian Reformed church pamphlet I have, and quote from, is headed: "Welcome, guests—a three-minute tour of the church." A hypothetical visitor asks in the pamphlet: "What is the furniture in front (of the church)?" Part of the written answer is this: "...A baptismal font stands nearby. In holy baptism, those coming to faith as adults are baptized here to visibly declare their conversion. Infants born into believer's families are baptized here to seal God's promise to the children of his covenant."

Reader's who have, through this book, reviewed with me Scriptural teaching concerning Christian baptism and Paul's inspired teachings on the early church's abuse and error regarding Christian baptism will understand what True Scriptural doctrine and obedient New Testament church practice requires of Christ's church of all centuries, and today, in this matter.

Paul, the missionary founder of many Christian churches, was deeply concerned with those of his day who were taught the Truth and should have faithfully followed it. Yet by evidence seen by him or reported by others, Paul knew that they were distorting the True meaning of the Christian doctrine and practice of baptism. At that time, Paul questioned the church in Rome's errant practices by saying, :*"Don't you know?"* (when they should have known)...then explained *what they should know.* They should have known (as all church-taught Christians should know that true Scriptural baptism of repentant, believing and conscious persons by immersion baptism, reveals in a striking symbolic manner that the believer in baptism is in direct experiential and personal identification with Christ's death, burial and resurrection (in clear symbolic statements relating their immersion in water and their withdrawal from the water). Only by being taught, and faithfully following True Christian baptism of repentant believers by immersion will all Christian members and leaders in all Christ's churches have confirmed in them that there is something radically and sinfully wrong about this term "baptismal font." The use of the term by errant churches is in direct contradiction to what the inspired Apostle Paul taught the errant Roman church, and us today. While one effect of adult public baptism is certainly "to declare their conversion"— adult believers being baptized by sprinkling, or pouring, ("affusion") are not being baptized Scripturally in the manner presented in the Word of God for believing adults. This cannot please our Lord, for it disobeys His inspired Word. And it is also scripturally wrong for unknowing, unbelieving infant children to be "baptized" at or in a church font for the reasons the Reformed brochure gives. Scripture rebukes (and Christ deplores) Protestant church denominations who abandon Scripture, and yield to false teachings in a parent or present church.

Let me quote my Christian scriptural beliefs, as a Bible-believing Christian, on the second part of the Christian Reformed pamphlet statement concerning infant baptism that this church says, to the public, that they practice. The Christian Reformed church does not justify its baptizing of unknowing, unthinking, infants (or of conscious children or adults) the same way most other churches wrongly do. In the same brochure I have spoken of, the church makes an incredible (and unscriptural) statement: *"**Children of believers are members of Christ's church and receive baptism as a sign of that membership.**"* The church of Jesus Christ (whether "Reformed" or not) is *never, ever told* or *taught*, in the New Testament, that "children of believers are members of Christ's church"—for true, scriptural church membership consists only of repentant believers, who, only after belief, are then baptized in order to be ***added to the church***. Never, in New Testament Scripture, are children of believers given legitimate status as church members, nor do they automatically receive baptism as a sign of membership with these false credentials. This particular pamphlet is unsupported by any scriptural references, so I can only infer where this denominational Christian church found any New Testament-inspired scriptural basis for their incredible (and false) statement. Some Anglican and Roman Catholic church public statements (some listed in this and other chapters) do shed some dubious light on where the Reformed Church found this unsupported statement, about "children of believers are members of the church, and receive baptism as a sign of that membership."

The dubious light comes first, it seems, from a false exegesis of a passage in Acts 16, in which the Lord emphasized to Paul and the new Christian church how they must faithfully *make disciples in all nations* (Matt. 28:19). Briefly, Acts 16 says Paul and Silas, on a missionary trip to Macedonia, encountered resistance from the province's citizens who disliked the new religion, Christianity, and had Paul and Silas thrown into jail. God had a plan to evangelize the Gentiles, and He acted to cause an earthquake that burst open the doors of the jail and cast off the prisoner's chains. This led the jailer to think of suicide, for he imagined his prisoners would all escape. Paul shouted, *"Don't harm yourself. We are all here."* The jailer (who had heard the talk of these Christians, and knew that they spoke of God, and the salvation He offered), rushed into the open cell, and said to Paul and Silas, *"Sirs, what must I do to be saved?"* (Acts 16:30). They replied: *"Believe in the Lord Jesus, and you will be saved, **you and your household.**"* Invited to the jailer's home, they spoke the Word of the Lord to him **and to all the others in his house** (verse 32). Then *the jailer took them and washed their wounds; and immediately he and **all his family** were baptized* (verse 33).

Before further comment, I ask readers to go to Acts 16:34—*he* (the converted jailer) *was filled with joy **because he had come to believe in God—he and his whole family.***

In this scriptural passage, if one stops reading after the conversion experience revealed in verses 32 and 33—that is, before verse 34—one can see, from the language of verses 31 to 33, that it would be possible (without reading this or any other New Testament passage on repentance, belief, and being born-again) to come to the (faulty)

143

conclusion that "whole families or households, consisting of men, women, children and infants" *could* be saved simply by having the head of the household believe and be saved! It is not possible, however, to believe this untruth about Christian belief and salvation if one continues on and reads Acts 16:34, as I have quoted it from Scripture. Notice, Christian brothers and sisters, that in this verse (34), *the jailer, after personally repenting and believing in God* (and Christ, for Paul preached the gospel of Christ to him and the others, vs. 31) *was filled with joy.* Why was he happy? He had heard the Gospel, was convicted, repented, believed, and had been born again. His sins were forgiven—he had received the gift of the Holy Spirit, as promised by the Lord, because he was saved and now had eternal life! But what about the others, to whom Paul and Silas witnessed in the jailer's house? *Verse 34* clearly states, in unequivocal language, *he was filled with joy because he had come to believe in God—he and his whole family.*

There should be no doubt in the reader's mind (if there is, ask the Spirit to explain it) that the joy of salvation was not only the jailer's, but belonged to *all those in his family* who had listened to the Gospel, *understood it,* were convicted and *repented of* their sins, *believed* in the Risen Lord *and had joy in their salvation*! All these things were explained by the missionaries (Paul and Silas), who would have never taught that unhearing, unknowing infants and children in the family *could* be able to understand and respond to the gospel message. Nor would (*could*) they feel or express the joy of salvation as their saved parents in the assembled group would. "Household salvation" is a myth, a falsehood and not scriptural.

The Christian Reformed church, and many other mistaken, untaught and errant churches, obviously teach their members Scripture-opposing falsehoods, on the testimony of this small brochure handed out to the public. They advise visitors to "their church" that children of believer-members are "household members" of Christ's Body—and receive baptism in "their church" as a sign of that (false) doctrine. But they should realize that in this unscriptural doctrine, they oppose the Lord's clear plan of *making disciples...baptizing them...and teaching them.* According to Scripture, churches that teach falsely are disobedient, just as most of the seven churches in

Revelation 2,3 were. They should realize that their false teachings are *held against them* by the Lord they claim to obey. See Part 4!

Many other churches also baptize unknowing infants, and I have mentioned some, but not all of them. All, to my knowledge, are forced to justify their Scripture-opposing errant baptism, through deliberate **manipulations** of Scripture by *false teachers*. Here, the Christian Reformed church uses **some** relevant verses of Scripture, **but not all,** and hopes their members, or visitors will not find their error. Classes for visitors wishing to join the church probably will not examine Acts 16:34 (with the Spirit)—for full scriptural truth revealed would destroy their statement about "infants being part of the membership of the church," because they are in the "family household of believers." "Part-Truth doctrine" is favoured by non-Christian cults, also.

Some errant churches, calling themselves Christian, try to justify unknowing infants being baptized "as a sign of their church membership by virtue of their being in a believing family or household," by other Scripture portions. I have heard, as I'm sure many readers have, of Christian churches who justify infant baptism by going back to the Jewish religion, and saying things like: "God required all male members of **Jewish families** to be circumcised a few days after birth, as a sign and seal that they are acceptable to God" (True!). Since circumcision is a sign of God's favour for male Jews, they say, **wrongly**— "baptism at a very early (unknowing) age of children (male and female) of Christian families serves the same purpose, and is equally pleasing to God." But God's **Covenant Law for Jews** is **not for Christians,** Paul wrote ...*but* we (Christians) *are not under the Law under Grace* (Rom. 6:15). Christians have been given, in the New Testament for the church, their own (symbolic and spiritual) sign of God's approval: namely, Christian baptism, for convicted, repentant and understanding believers only—not for adults only, but also for any conscious, understanding, repentant and believing child.

Often these errant church acts with regard to infant baptism, after all these centuries, are now being wrongly justified as Church traditions—but they are still wrong. No Christian would deny that true, scripturally-based "traditions" are useful to keep the church "family" together—but only if they agree entirely with God's inspired, inerrant Word. All church traditions are not sinful; only those that are of men, *and not* confirmed as truthful in God's Word.

I have a book in my library, called *Your child's baptism*, written by Frank Colquhoun, Vicar of Holy Trinity, Wallington, Surrey, England (Church of England). Its subtitle says it is "A book for parents and 'godparents'" (scriptural?—writer) "who are prepared to think seriously about Baptism." On p. 44 of this book, the author quotes the same Scripture, as in the above example: Acts 16:31. *Believe on the Lord Jesus Christ, and thou shalt be saved, and thy house...he was baptized, he and all his family were baptized* (from the King James version of the Bible—other translations are similar). Colquhoun comments on verse 31, saying: "Here is the preaching of 'household *salvation*' (unscriptural, says the author!) in accordance with the covenant principle" (NB: Jewish, not New Testament, Covenant—*author*) "and it was accompanied by the practice (unscriptural, says the author!) of *household baptism*: '...he was baptized, he and *all his* straightway' (Acts 16:33)." He continues: "It is clear that the apostolic church accepted the Old Testament teaching concerning the relation of the 'family' to the covenant and the visible church." The writer, from the Church of England, has suggested faulty and unscriptural teaching in an effort to justify 'his' and many other churches' today baptizing unknowing, unbelieving infant children. Yes, Acts 16: 33 states that *he* (the jailer) *and all his family were baptized*"—but who, exactly and truthfully, were the only ones baptized? I must repeat my earlier explanation for emphasis: Acts 16:34 of Holy Scripture provides the answers, but *false teachers* often do not discuss this verse, for it defeats their (false) elaborate theory that Christian baptism is for unknowing and unbelieving infant children. Verse 34 is quite clear: *the jailer...was filled with joy* (why?—*author*) *because he had come to believe in God* (through faith, after hearing the Gospel, and being convicted by the Spirit—*author*)—*he and his whole family*. There is no other meaning hidden here, and Acts 16:34 justifies the True scriptural position for all Christians of all times, on Christian salvation: conviction and repentance on hearing the gospel of the Risen Christ, belief in Him by faith alone, then baptism by immersion—always and only for those who are **able to hear, and respond in knowing faith**. Those who cannot hear, understand their sin, have faith, or respond to the Spirit cannot—and must not—be baptized.

Throughout history, *false teachers* in the church have desperately tried to apply a completely different religious system (that of the Jews, for example) to the Christian faith found in the inspired New Testament for the Christian church. In this documented example, readers will see that the churches from whose writers I quote, are caught up in a web of Satan's deception. The Anglican (Church of England) church, arising from the earlier Roman Catholic church in England, which was long ago "cast out of England" by a sinful "King" (but called secular Head of the Church of England now), can be seen in public knowledge and history as adopting the continuing Roman church false position of early centuries on infant baptism. The Roman church does not usually quote Scripture to defend their false doctrines, but rather has often chosen to state (wrongly!) that their "Pope," advised by "Church teachers" expects the members to accept without question—and in fear of excommunication—every and any doctrine the Pope puts forward as "Vicar of Christ" (also an unscriptural title). This assumes, wrongfully, that the "Pope" or his "Successors" have assumed the mantle or authority of Christ, the Divine Son of God, Who **only** has **all authority in Heaven and on earth** (see Matt. 28:18).

The Divine Head of the Christian church, Who gave us, His church on earth, His Great Commission we are studying now (Christian baptism in this chapter), also gave us inspired instructions as to the Overseers and Deacons who would guide and shepherd each part of the church on earth (see 1 Tim. 3). There is no mention anywhere in His Teachings in the New Testament for the church, of any "Pope," "Vicar," "Royalty as Secular Head," "Cardinals," "Bishops," or even "Priests" as church leaders. Whenever a Christian believer finds unscriptural church officers, unscriptural organizations, and unscriptural "traditions"—including infant baptisms or "household baptisms" or mis-applied Jewish Law stated as governing Christ's church—there one will find the *false teachers* that the Apostle Peter wrote of in 2 Peter 2:1, *introducing false heresies…and bringing swift destruction on themselves.*

I do not write about these examples of a few publically seen and known sins of Christian churches of the past and today with a spiteful, hateful, unloving spirit. I write rather, with God's "Agape love" in me—not to destroy my brothers and sisters in Christ in His churches today, but to warn them, with the Spirit and the Word, of Christ coming again soon.

Our mutual Lord, some 2,000 years ago, warned all His church that they must "wake up," discover their sins, repent and reform, and return to do as they did before for Him, their Saviour and Lord—or suffer terrible consequences as referred to in Revelation 2,3. Hear and obey our Lord, for He is coming soon.

Part 3. Three Commands of Christ for the Church "He Will Build." Matthew 16:18.

Chapter 7

Command #3:
"Teach Them to Obey All I Have Commanded You"
—Matthew 28:20

With the explanation of the three individual, yet united, Commands of Christ to His church on earth; with the Aid of the Holy Spirit of God, Who is in every Christian believer as the gift of God, I will have brought before readers *"The Great Commission of Christ"* for His church on earth in Matthew 28:18–20.

Without the full and complete carrying out of His Commission, by the church, several calamitous things will occur, as Christ tells us in His Inspired Word. If any local church Body of Christ on earth fails to obey any one of the three unified, yet separate Commands, then:

1. Christ's Body will fail to grow, and many lost persons will never hear of or gain eternal life, if new disciples are not made everywhere in the world. And the lost world itself will not know *that God sent His Son to save them.*

2. If, when **disciples are made (with the Spirit's Help)** they are not **baptized by immersion** in the only True scriptural way of identifying the new believer with Christ in His death, burial and Resurrection, and in the Commanded way of adding these new believers to the local Body of Christ, **Christ and His Word will be failed.** New disciples, wrongly and disobediently baptized, will fail to receive the full benefits of becoming members of His Body **on earth.**

3. If disciples are made, repentant sinners are made "born again believers" by the Spirit and the gospel message received, **but they are not taught** by the church *to obey all that Christ commanded us*—again, Christ is failed. The church will neither be strengthened, nor will the new "spiritual *infants*" have the ability to fend off *false teachers. False teachers,* under Satan's influence, will inevitably come to cause the church to fail and disobey Christ, the written Word, and the Holy *Spirit of Truth*. They are behind past and present-day church problems (Recall 2 Pet. 2:1).

What Scripture is saying is this: Christ's Will and purpose is to build His church, as outlined in the three short, individual, yet unified parts of His scriptural plan to build *one completely Unified body* on earth: *His Body, of which He is Head* (Eph. 5:23), *and the One who gave Himself up for her* (Eph. 5:25), *to make her Holy* (Eph. 5:26). His Commission must never be considered suggestions only. No—*these three holy, authoritative Commands MUST be OBEYED.* For our Lord, Jesus Christ, said: *all authority in Heaven and on earth given to me* by His Heavenly Father (Matt. 28:18).

As we consider the third and final Command, let those who need to review Divine Scripture, with the help of the *Spirit of Truth*, do so with fear and trembling. For without faithful obedience of *all His* commands in *all* our churches today, we *forget Who* is the *Divine Head*, and *forget* that *if we love Him, we must obey Him* (John 14:15).

If we forget, and remain in disobedience, and in spiritual sleep, we show we do not love HIm who saved us from eternal death. And *only if we obey Him, will we remain in His love* (John 15:10, paraphrased by author). Remaining in His Love means, and requires, full obedience to His Commands. Disobedience and failure in any respect *will lead failing individuals and churches to lose their Promised Rewards, and worse, they will cause Him to reject us, when He Comes.* He seeks only a *Radiant Bride, " radiant church without stain or blemish or wrinkle of sin"* (Eph. 5:27, paraphrased by author). What will He discover when He comes to find such a Bride—"our church"—and discovers instead, a *"wrinkled church, stained and blemished by disobedience and outright sin"* (converse to Eph. 5:27, paraphrased by author)? We do not and will not really know the answers to these questions, until we come to the point in our knowledge (and in His time) of our Saviour and Lord that marks every church member's and leader's spiritual maturity. What will be the Christian's state then? Read Revelations 2 and 3.

The inspired Paul, in his letter to the faithful saints at Ephesus, and to all later Christians, including us, tells us something of the spiritual state and marks seen in all faithful saints (and churches) when they achieve spiritual maturity. Ephesians 4, inspired and written under the Spirit's "moving," tells us that (when we are well-taught by the church): ...*we will reach unity in the faith and in the knowledge of the Son of God and become mature, attaining to the whole measure of the fullness of Christ* (4:13). Then, wonderful things will happen to the individual Christian, and to the "Body of Christ" of which he or she is a unique part, if the church overcomes trials and remain faithful. Read Ephesians 14:1 ff with the aid of the *Spirit of Truth*, and you will learn (or relearn, if you have fallen "spiritually *asleep*") the full purpose of Christ for His church on earth. These things said, let me turn now to the third Command of Christ for His church, and let us all discover (or re-discover and re-teach) how every Christian may reach spiritual maturity, strengthen the "Body," and serve the Lord in faithful and obedient works of righteousness and service to the Divine Head Who loves us and gave Himself up for us.

A Crucial Command of Christ: "Teach Them to Obey All That I Have Commanded You" (Matthew 28:20).

An Introduction:

In the previous chapters, I spoke about forms of church disobedience—from outright refusal to obey what He scripturally asks of us, through members' tolerance of *false teachers*, "lukewarm" approaches to serving Him, and "sleeping" (not being alert), to not doing *the things we did at first* for Him (Rev. 2,3).

From a few past and present church examples of several disobedient acts (most directly opposing the Lord's Word), I went to the Great Commission of our Lord for His church—choosing His three vital and related Commands in Matthew 28.18–20 as important subjects for church discussion. Our Saviour and Lord's many commands and teachings to His disciples—to direct the lives of both Jews and Christians, who must not neglect them—would take a library of books for adequate comment. My burden in this book is to show from Scripture, specifically, how those who make up His Body are required to mature spiritually, and ensure we all are faithful, we all are one, and we all are able and willing to carry out His Will and purpose for His church.

Some Christians may find that, in truth, they have not fully obeyed Him, their Saviour and Lord, in all that He has taught, asked, or commanded them. They will discover they are not alone in these errant acts. They may receive a scriptural answer to their cry, *What shall I* (we) *do to be saved* from the consequences of my (our) sin? I pray that disobedient churches, members or leaders might discover their sins against their Head, take His advice, *repent, wake up, and return to their first love,* and *do what they did at first* (see Rev. 2,3— Christ, the Author).

Teach them. Our modern generation, particularly in wealthy, Western technological societies, realizes the importance of good secular education and schooling. Backing this realization with tax funds, we have created a generally good secular school system, with well-educated teachers. We provide generally better-educated professors (teachers, basically) in our universities and technical schools, for those students seeking employment in skilled trades and higher-level vocations, while seeking worldly success in materially-oriented lives. But secular, or "worldly," education, while important for young and old, men and women today is but a part of the Christian's life while he or she is living in this world.

We read in God's Word that man is created by God with a soul or spirit (often used synonymously) that is immortal (lasting beyond physical death, and destined to live a future life (or death) in God's plan. Christians believe all mankind must realize that we must not only learn to live out our human lives on this earth—we must prepare, if we are wise and obedient to our Creator, for an "everlasting life," the conditions of which is dependent upon whether or not we accept and obey Him, or disobey and reject Him in this world. The soul within all humans (whether some know of its existence, or deny it and God's Love, Mercy and Will for our eternal future after death) is what the Bible and I speak of now.

In this book, then, I want to relate this idea of teaching or educating young and old people, not only secularly in the "school system," but religiously—particularly, spiritually-directed teaching of Christ's inspired inerrant Words, by the church to all Christian church member/believers.

Christ's Teachings to His Christian Disciples in His Church on Earth.

It is clear from Scripture that when Christ gave instructions to His future church and His Apostles—after His death and Resurrection, but before He went up to be with His Father in Heaven—He knew his first disciples' hearts, minds, and spirits. His Great Commission Commands told them that they must *make disciples*, take these new believers, baptize them, and thus, add them to the church Body. Then, *teach them* in the church to *obey all that He had taught them* (in His time with them on earth, and later through His Spirit). At another time, He told them that He would, when He left them, send His Spirit to Empower, Convict, Teach and Guide each one in building His church. He knew men's hearts. He was God, they now knew, and they now knew also the future of His church. His old enemy, Satan—although defeated by Christ's Resurrection—was still wandering the earth, seeking to pervert Christ's purpose and gain men's souls. The Lord knew, too, how Satan would infiltrate the future church with *false teachers* trying to persuade church members and leaders alike to follow Satan, and their own wills and purposes, and ignore what Christ had told and taught them to do. These things—His Authority, Omnipotence, Omniscience, and all His Godly attributes (assumed fully when He returned to Heaven)—were part of Christ's Will and purpose to build **His church**, with the help of His faithful disciples, and the Teaching and Guidance of the Holy Spirit. His Spirit came into the hearts, minds, and spirits of His disciples at Pentecost in Jerusalem, and when He came into new believers—that day and later—in His church

These Three Commands of Christ are really one integral Command, expressing His Will that all people be *born again, baptized* into His earthly Body, and *taught* to be obedient and useful to Him now, and until He comes again.

In Command #1 to His future church, Christ told His Apostles and disciples to begin to build His church, after His Ascension, in Jerusalem. The Lord said He would send His Spirit, and the Apostles would then form His church with Spirit-filled "born-again believers" (disciples). The Apostles would preach and tell lost sinners of God's New Mercy in extending His salvation to all nations, rather than restricting it as in the past to only His Chosen People, the Jews. His church was not to be a social club or association of religiously-minded people who considered Jesus Christ to be a great teacher. Nor was the church just a human assembly who had God's favour, because He did many miracles among the Jews and Gentiles living among them. Now was the church to be just a human assembly who had God's favour, because He did many miracles among them. The church was to be His own, united, Body on earth, with His Spirit guiding them in carrying out His Will and purpose, according to His Commission.

This new assembly of born-again believers, contrary to some today, was first to be told of what God had done, in sending His Only-begotten Son (as the long prophesied Messiah of the Jews) to call the disobedient Jews to repentance of their sins against God and man, because the "Kingdom of God was near." Then, the Gospel (or Good News from God) was to continue to speak of how the Messiah, this Jesus of Nazareth, was rejected by His own People; how He was betrayed, falsely convicted, and went to die on a Roman cross at Calvary for the sins of the world. He died to carry their sins as the Holy and Just, yet Merciful God required. Then, the gospel message continued, Christ was buried in a tomb for three days—but was raised in the Power of God, and lives today in Heaven with His Heavenly Father. Because He lives, those who listen to the gospel and are convicted of their sins by the Spirit of God, those who repent and turn from their sins in faith, and believe in the Resurrected Son of God—these new believers are born again, and are *new Creations; the old has gone* (2 Cor. 5:17).

These new believers,"'adopted' Sons and Daughters" of God, must not return to the world's evil ways, to sin. They must be baptized by the church, and in this special way, become added to His Body. Not just added to a group of people with religious interests, but to a special, born-again, and unique group whose Head in Heaven calls them *His Body* on earth (1 Cor. 12:13)—His church.

"Teaching them..." Matthew 28:20.

All new believers—after being scripturally baptized by, and into, the Body of Christ—must be taught. And all new as well as old believers (who might not have been taught previously, or who have not learned well) must learn to *obey all that I have commanded you*, in teaching classes or groups in the church. Details of the "Who, What, and Why" of an obedient church teaching process follows.

The New Testament church was first formed under the preaching of Peter and the work and actions of the Holy Spirit, in Jerusalem, in the streets. They had neither buildings then, nor church structure built for the worship, teaching and preaching activities Willed by our Lord. They did have the Jewish "Temple Courts" available to them, at least in the early days, weeks and months, before intense persecution of Christians by Jews began (see Acts). And, after and during persecution, the church did meet in member's homes then, as they often do now in hostile countries in the present-day world.

If we examine the very early days of the church in Jerusalem, particularly before the spread of the church forced upon Christians by Jewish persecutions and the death of Stephen (see Acts 7), we find, in connection with this Third Command (*Teach them...*) that the early church in general was faithful, in this and in all three Commands of His Commission.

We discover next, in Acts 2:42, that, in obedience to the Third Command: *They devoted themselves to the apostles' teaching...* There are many other references to the fact that **the church was in truth obedient in the Lord's requirement to teach new believers in those early years.**

155

Added to the Apostles' immediate knowledge of Christ were inspired teachings of others, such as Paul, Barnabas, Timothy, Luke etc., by whom the church taught and learned individually and together to obey all that Jesus had taught the Apostles, and later disciples. Thus, we read how the church obediently and faithfully *grew to spiritual maturity from being spiritual infants* (Eph. 4, paraphrased by author)—as well as in numbers of members and of growing and spreading churches in the relatively small Roman world.

Acts 2:42 does **not** say, "**some of the new disciples attended classes** " or "children's classes were set up" or "Adult classes, with voluntary attendance, were set up" by the early church. **No**, it appeared that the church of the Apostles' time was truly **devoted to** *the apostles' teaching* (Christ's own teachings). The current, errant approach to Christ's universally-commanded "Christian Education," by many churches today, was not in force in those days. **Faithful obedience was Christ's rule** under the Apostles in the New Testament church.

New Testament Scripture for the church speaks rather briefly of the Church teaching process for all new believers. Rarely does the inspired Luke, the inspired human writer of the "Acts" tell much of the process other than in Acts 2:42; 6:4; 11:26, etc. Luke was a church historian, communicating to Christians what Christ wanted to remind them of Him and His Will to *build His church* by means of His disciples, and with the Holy Spirit.

It remained for other inspired writers, such as Paul, Peter, John, and others to move away from historical things and discuss some really practical items related to vital details of the Lord's Will and Commands. One of these "vital, vital details" underlies my burden for the church, and concerns many Christian members and leaders today. Lukewarm churches must be reminded that Christ's commands must not be taken lightly, ignored, or perverted to the extent that what the Lord asked us to do for His Church body on earth is rarely done faithfully. The results of not fully and faithfully obeying His commands is that His church will not be found Holy, Radiant and Blameless, unstained by sin (disobedience, false teachings), when He comes again to claim His Bride. Therefore, although the inspired book of Acts is important to give the history and acts of the leaders and members of the new Christian church, under the workings of the Holy Spirit, it does not provide all that the church needs to know about His third Command, and how to carry it out for the Lord, the Head of His Body on earth. This is why the Spirit inspired other holy men of the New Testament age (moved them *'carried them along'* to write—2 Pet. 1:21) to give the new and spreading church more scriptural details in Letters concerning these specific Commands of the Lord.

For example, when we turn to some of Paul's inspired writings concerning the various *Gifts of the Spirit* to men in the church (Rom. 12; 1 Cor. 12; Eph. 4; Heb. 2:4, and many other places), we find that the Lord has given us in Scripture much more information as to what we are to do in His church to carry out His Will, purpose, and Commands. I speak primarily of His "Teach them" command, but Scripture's words apply to all parts of the Lord's Will and Purpose for who make up His True, Obedient, and Faithful Body on earth.

We can all see, with the help of New Testament Scripture, and the guidance of the Holy Spirit, that we should lack neither Spirit-Gifted preachers and teachers in the Body, nor full knowledge of what we must teach all new believers in Christ's Body— for the Spirit provides His Word *and His teachers!* We know too, from Scripture, that the teaching process was a long-term one, lasting over a year in the case of the Antioch church. But note that Christ did not set a time limit on His Command. By modifying His Command with words descriptive of *what* they must *teach* the new disciples—*to obey all that I have commanded you* (Matt. 28:20)—He gave the church all the curriculum they need: namely, all the Scripture containing His Words to us (and to Spirit-inspired holy men in the New Testament days!). Moving on to this second part of verse 20, I will now expand my concerns about the church's often-seen neglect of the Lord's full "teaching process"—such a vital part of His church-and disciple-building process that He Wills for all members or leaders to do obediently for Him until He comes again.

157

(Teaching them) to "Obey All that I Have Commanded You."

Christ's Command, to teach all His (new and old) disciples—and to teach them to obey all His Words—has been strangely and sadly distorted by many perverse and disobedient churches today. A modern sociological survey undertaken by most churches today would reveal astonishing statistics, I believe, if it asked one question of each member, such as: **"Have you personally been taught, in this or any other Christian church,'to obey all that Christ commanded you in His Word?'"** From my own church experience, going from spiritual infant to mature adult, to Bible student and teacher in several churches, I would suggest such a survey, conducted in today's churches, would reveal that fewer than 10% in most churches have been taught as Christ commanded. I have been a part of some faithful "teaching churches"—as have many of my readers, I know—but I also know of many others whose teaching has been sporadic, brief, incomplete, and not mandatory or at all consistent with Christ's Commands to teach and obey. Nor have they been consistent with Paul's inspired teachings in Eph .4 as to the *purpose and Will of Christ for all members* (and leaders) to become fully *spiritually mature* in His Body.

We can observe again, for example, the Roman Catholic church, in the past and today. Instead of teaching all that the Apostles taught of Christ's teachings, this Body of Christ on earth has—observably for many years (centuries even)—taught members only a brief summary of *some* Bible truths, and asked only that new "Confirmation candidates" attend *"Catechism classes,"* in lieu of full scriptural teaching requirements by our Lord. Looking up the words "Catechism" or "Confirmation" (or infant baptism for that matter) in the Bible is useless, because neither word is there. "Catechism" and "Confirmation" are part of men's added and false teachings, not at all part of God's inspired Word—especially the New Testament Scripture for His Son's church.

As well, the Roman Catholic church, upon the advent of other Bible versions than the Latin versions used mainly by priests and other leaders, have in the past refused to allow "their" mem-

bers ("lay persons") to read the Bible, God's Word. Their justification for disobeying the Lord's Commands to *teach* new believers *to obey all that* He *has commanded* us? They have no scriptural
justification at all, but rather have adopted a (false) way to avoid
having *false teachers* enter the church and lead untaught members
astray. Their public stance and (indefensible) argument seems to
be: that the priest would, in the "Mass," and in the "Sacra-
ments," and in brief homilies, sermons and catechisms, convey to
them everything they need to know of God's inspired Words to
His church. (Don't bother looking up either "Mass" or "Sacra-
ment"—for they, too, are inventions of men, and part of the autocratic leadership control of the members of this once faithful and
obedient Body of Christ.)

Don't misunderstand me here. Words assigned to describe
unscriptural and errant actions in any part of Christ's Body on earth
or disobediences are not the real sin. It is false (according to Scripture) words, doctrines, and religious "ceremonies and dogma," not
in accord with Inspired, inerrant Scripture, that offend and disobey
Christ and His Spirit's Words of instruction, that are a concern to
believing Christians. All of these false, limited, contrary and disobedient, weak and unscriptural teaching, doctrines, and acts are
observed in this one very large "Christian" church, as well as in
many other churches who emulate part or all of these disobedient
and false practices of the Roman church. Some churches, formed in
the "Protestant Reformation," so-called, from former Roman
Catholic members (excommunicated or otherwise) did not in fact
either cause the Roman church to reform, nor "repent and reform"
error in their new resultant churches when they left the former very
large "parent" church centuries ago. Instead, many held on to the
Roman scriptural distortions, additions, and subtractions to Christ's
Words to all His Body. We have today many more Christian bodies
who do not obey their True Head, the One Who died for us all. They
teach things that oppose God's Truth—Holy Scripture.

The members of these churches, Roman Catholic, Anglican,
"Reformed," or any of the hundreds of "denominations" called Christian (but often they are not, fully or completely) are my brothers and

sisters in Christ. I do not feel any hate or worldly emotion other than pity towards them and their deprived members—only spiritual sadness concerning their leaders' unrepented sins against the Lord's Word. I have asked Christian "Catholic" friends about their knowledge of Christ and His Word—and found an unforgivable void. Their church must repent and return to the Word of God alone, and soon.

I write this book, and I quote the Inspired, Inerrant, Infallible Written Word of God in support of what I write. As they read (about disobedience, repentance, revival, and True reform), I pray they see their failure as displeasing Christ, the True Head of His church (all of it) and act to return to do the things they did for Him before. Yes, my prayer is that someday, some Roman Catholic, or other laymen (probably not the leadership hierarchy) will be truly convicted by the Spirit of God as they read Scripture—perhaps even this book about disobedience, repentance, revival and reform—see their false teachings vividly compared with the Word of God, and realize their disobedience and failures to Christ. **They,** and all who are warned by this book, which echoes the scriptural Words of the Lord, **must return to Bible reading,** and **particularly Bible teaching**—for these acts alone can, with the Spirit, break them away from *false teachers* of the past and return them to His sanctifying Words of Truth.

I do not believe, from my reading of Scripture (with the *Spirit of Truth*), and from my observation of what goes on in many churches of the past and today, that there are "degrees of disobedience" to Jesus Christ. I say, and echo Jesus Christ's Words, that quite literally, sin is sin. Christians cannot condone or excuse it by speaking of "human error," "unfortunate lapses by an early Bishop or Pope," or "categories of sins." Yes, all our sins, Scripture says, can be forgiven by God (except for *the one unforgivable sin of blasphemy against the Spirit* [Christ, in Matt. 12:31] *that will not be forgiven*).

When the Lord, *Who searches our hearts and minds* (Rev. 2:23ff) finds sin and disobedience in our individual and church lives, words, and deeds, *He Will repay each of us according to our deeds.* This sounds as though some in the seven churches of Revelation 2 and 3 will get off with a "tap on their wrists" for "minor sins" against

160

Him. Not true, according to Scripture—read Revelation 2 and 3. You will see there are no minor sins, and no minor discipline by Christ. In truth, His Word says that even those who do not participate in *false teachers'* evil work in the church (but only **tolerate** what goes on—as is the habit of some in today's churches!) will suffer in the future, because they have not *overcome evil and sin* and *have not done the Lord's Will to the end.* Some may think that they will be exempt from the Lord's taking away His Rewards from them as they lackadaisically (or deliberately) offer him their *lukewarm, tolerant, sleeping* teaching support in His church. This is not true—according to Scripture. **Christ says that His Word and His Spirit must be heard, and every Command must be obeyed.** Read John, Chapters 14-17.

Nor can church members or leaders think that following errant "Traditions," and a theology that is based upon unscriptural false teaching, or allowing a church to have little or no Bible teaching for **all** members, will be considered as **overcoming** in the Lord's eyes. He will not excuse them because "this is the way we have always done it in our church." Even the idea of "their church" reveals spiritual ignorance and sin.

We members of Christ's Body must surely see, if we read Scripture with the Teacher of Truth helping us, reminding us of the truth, and of all that Christ said to us in very many passages about teaching new and old disciples, that Christian education for all believers is vital for the church to carry out fully and completely. I remind churches disobedient to Christ to again examine what they do in carrying out Christ's command "to teach them," (all their members), while comparing what they do with what the Lord has asked them to do. When disobedience is found, only repentance and reform to the Lord's Will is the remedy, if we are *to remain in His love.* Even the best of sermons is no substitute for mandatory Bible teaching in accordance with Christ's Commission Command—but many lax churches do not insist on members knowing Christ's teachings. *Teach them...to obey...* With little or no teaching, where is spiritual maturity and obedience?

I would be remiss not to emphasize again, in talking about Christian education for all Christians in Christian churches, Christ's Words in this Third Command of His Commission for His church.

Not only does He require that the subject matter (*all that I have commanded you*) be fully taught, but *OBEYED* by ALL members and leaders of the church.

The Lord and Head of the church says, in His teachings received by the Apostles, and Commanded to be passed on, that He must be obeyed not only by the members being taught, but by *the teachers and leaders also*. The Apostles taught new church members what Christ commanded in the First Jerusalem church—however, they at times were, themselves, guilty of delaying or procrastinating on one of His Commands to them: *To go and make disciples of all nations.* After persecution of Christians by hostile Jews forced all but the Apostles to leave the city, Acts 8 tells us that the *church was persecuted, and scattered* throughout Judea and Samaria. Godly Christian members, including men like Philip, went out and preached Christ to Jew and Gentile unbelievers. Later in Acts 8, we are told that when the Apostles heard *Samaria had accepted the Word of God,* they sent Peter and John to investigate. The Word describes how the now-obedient Jerusalem church finally went out to make fully taught disciples of all nations, rather than remaining partially obedient in Jerusalem.

Acts 8:25, with the guiding of the Spirit, tells us that when (Peter and John) *had testified to the new believers and proclaimed the Word of the Lord, they preached the Gospel in many Samaritan villages.* This speaks of part preaching, and part teaching, given to those who *received the message* (the Gospel) *and repented and believed in the Risen Christ. ...Then the church throughout Judea, Galilee and Samaria enjoyed a time of peace. It was strengthened; and encouraged by the Holy Spirit, it grew in numbers living in the fear of the Lord* (Acts 9:31). This tells me, and all Christians today, that the early church had finally fully received and acted upon Christ's Three-Part Commission to them in all that He required— *Make disciples...baptize...teach...* and obey.

Similarly, the missionary effort by the scattered believers from Jerusalem continued, as we learn from Acts 8 about the Spirit-guided mission of Philip to the Gentile Ethiopian, and Philip's teaching the Gentile convert concerning Jesus (*the good news about Jesus*—the Gospel message, Acts 8:36). When Philip saw conviction, repentance and belief in the Gentile foreigner, he knew he was born again. The new believer knew it too, and, recalling Philip's teachings about Christ's church doctrines, exclaimed *Look, here is water. Why shouldn't I be baptized?* The new Gentile believer stopped his chariot, and Philip baptized him (by immersion baptism, note, for the words *they went down into the water; they came up out of the water* denotes immersion baptism, not errant sprinkling or pouring).

Philip was snatched away; the now Christian Eunuch went on his way, rejoicing—saved! Later "missionaries" undoubtedly reached Ethiopia, and taught the small weak churches they found there!

Later in the Acts record of the early church, we discover that while the church members in Jerusalem had no misunderstanding about what Christ's *Go and make disciples of all nations* meant, in relation to doing so in Jerusalem City, the Apostle Peter had—it seems—difficulty understanding that the Centurion Gentile's conversion (Acts 10) revealed how God, by means of a vision, had to stress the necessity of the church actually going out—despite Jewish historical shunning of all Gentiles.

"Teaching disciples" in the early church spreading out to all nations.

We have seen in Acts that the First church of Jerusalem was obedient to the Lord's Teaching Command locally. Then, as persecution forced Christians out of Jerusalem, we saw that Christian men (*full of the Spirit and wisdom* as Acts 6 tells us) witnessed to Christ in the provinces of Judea and Samaria. There, they made disciples, faithfully baptized them (we are sure but are not told so directly), and taught them about Christ's Will and purpose for them as part of His Body in their own towns and villages.

We learn also from Acts that, when the Christian persecution by Jews eased, several Apostles (Peter and John primarily, it seems) went out into these provinces and confirmed Christ's Will that the Jews and Gentiles be granted salvation upon repentance and belief in the Risen Lord. Later chapters in Acts tell us that the initial few new Christians in the adjacent provinces beyond Judea gathered into small "bodies of Christ"—and, with the teaching of Christ's "missionary" disciples, and occasional visits of the Apostles from Jerusalem, we can be sure that they, too, began the teaching process the Lord required to strengthen and mature both the disciples' and the church's mission.

As I noted in Acts 10, the Apostle Peter was brought to full realization of what the Lord required in His Commission to the church. Simultaneous visions, given to Cornelius and Peter from God, brought about the conversion of many (but not unknowing infants!) in this Gentile family at Caesarea. We know also, from Scripture, that after they believed, these converted Gentiles, now Christian believers, were baptized and thus formed a Christian church. Because Peter stayed with the new believers for a few days (Acts 10:48), we can be sure that those days were filled with teachings concerning Jesus Christ and His purpose for the new church, of which they were now a living part.

Acts 11 tells us of the further spread of the Christian church— to Phoenicia, Cyprus and Antioch—initiated by those disciples driven out of Jerusalem by persecution following the death of Stephen. Here, the disciples often first went only to the Jews. This indicates that, like Peter, these early missionary disciples were converted Jews, still bound by their traditions. They did not fully understand that Christ's Will for the church was for them to *go to all* (Gentile) *nations* to make disciples. But Acts 11:20,21 tells us that not all went only to the Jews—some (Gentile believers from Cyprus and Cyrene) *began to speak to the Greeks* (Gentiles) *in Antioch about the good news of Jesus Christ* (the gospel message). (The following is paraphrased by the author) *The Lord's hand was with them in Antioch, and a great number of People believed and turned to the Lord* (NB: Also ...baptized, added to the Body, and taught).

As with the earlier work outside Jerusalem, the Jerusalem church heard this good news about many believers being born again in Antioch. They sent Barnabas to observe how the Spirit had led many Gentiles to the Lord. See also Acts 4:36 and 9:27 in connection with Barnabas befriending Saul (now Paul) after the latter's conversion, and coming back to Jerusalem to meet with the Apostles.

Acts 11:25,26 describes how Barnabas—after encouraging the new Christian disciples in Antioch, and leading many more to the Lord—saw the need for help. He went to Tarsus to find his Christian friend Saul, and bring him back to Antioch. As I write about the Lord's Commission to His church, I am particularly interested in what Saul and Barnabas did for the Lord in the new church. The disciples there were called Christians first in Antioch. What they did, as Spirit-gifted teachers, is described in Acts in verse. 26: *So, for a whole year Barnabas and Saul met with the church and taught great numbers of people.* This prepared Paul to write to the churches (us too!) his Ephesians 4 teaching passage. Ephesians 4:12–16 is particularly important for churches to act upon.

From the brief snippets of facts gleaned from Luke's inspired "Acts," we understand that not only the *Good News of Jesus Christ—the Gospel message of God's Gift of salvation to those who repent and believe in the Risen Lord*—but the verbal teachings and commands of Christ were taught to the new Christians, with the Holy Spirit's gifting and guidance. The teaching process (and obedience required by the Lord) was a direct verbal line, at first, between Jesus, the Apostles, and earliest disciples; then, from the Apostles and more mature disciples in the Jerusalem church, to the great number of new believers. And, from the scattered, Spirit-gifted believers, to the new believers in Judea and Samaria. Then, passed on to new believers from the scattered believers in more remote parts of the Roman world, by disciples like Barnabas, and specially-gifted men like Saul. All fully realized and obeyed the Will and purpose of Christ's required teachings and commands. Would that today's churches would return to full obedience!

The church today must now surely realize that limited, superficial, and incomplete teaching by the church is both unsatisfactory and disobedient to Christ. "Catechism-type teaching" (its brevity, not its Truths), "voluntary learning," limited content of church teaching, and classes for some members but not for all, is the opposite of what the Lord requires (and what the early church provided to all disciples). Believe me—these are not opinions I have formed by talking about Christian education, or being a Christian teacher of spiritually immature believers (although I have been part of the Christian education process in many churches). They are Scriptural Truths, that come from the inspired, inerrant written Word of God, as conveyed and taught to Christ's Body over the centuries by the Holy Spirit, the *Teacher and Reminder* of all those things our Lord wants us to know and to be in His Body, and in this world.

If you wish to please God in His church today, teach all members as Christ requires.

Should you discover, having read this chapter, that you yourselves have not been taught—I pray you will ask your church teachers to include you in their next class on "Christian fundamentals 101" (author's idea of a joke—except he is deadly serious!).

After you have graduated, with a "Degree" in "Pleasing Christ in His Third Command," why don't you ask the Holy Spirit, in prayer, **to grant you** His Gift of teaching others in the church? You may find, as I did some 40 years ago, that He will grant you this very special gift. If He does, you may be certain that you will never regret it—for others will then be able to learn from you all that our Lord wants us to know on this earth. Others will spiritually mature, and the church will be strengthened, to carry out all Three of His special Commands we have studied in His inspired, Holy, infallible Word.

Chapter 8

The "Seven Churches" and "Ours" —Faithful, Disobedient, or Asleep?

Throughout this book, I have used New Testament Scriptures to remind church members and leaders that our Saviour and Lord wants us to serve Him faithfully, with the Holy Spirit as our guide, obediently following His Inspired, Inerrant Words of instruction and command as we build His church for Him. He said, in John 14:21, *If you obey my commands you will remain in my love.* This requires absolute obedience, as we faithfully build His church in the world. Previous chapters have also raised other important related subjects for the Christian church, both to recall and do for our Divine Head, with His Will and purpose always in mind:

- The inspiration and inerrancy of the written Word of God as the church's primary Word of Truth

- The gift of the Holy Spirit, to convict us and the world of sin, and to be our Holy Teacher, Counselor, and Guide (with our Spirit-gifted human church members and leaders)

- The Will and purpose of Christ to *build My church,* with each member an essential part of carrying out His plan

- The Lord's plan to have each repentant sinner and new believer, after being baptized and added to His church, taught by the Body to grow from spiritual infant to spiritual adult—thus, strengthening the Body, while being able to resist *false teachers,* and to serve the Lord better in the church and in the world; and,

- The Lord's Great Commission for His church on earth, with its three related commands that express His Will and purpose for all church members and leaders, under the Head, Jesus Christ, while revealing God's Love, Mercy, and Grace to a lost world.

But this review of Holy Scriptures, that many readers—I am sure—received as children, youth, and (perhaps) as adult believers in their church, or from their own Bible reading and devotions, is now over. It is time, the Spirit leads me to believe, *to hear what the Spirit says to the churches* (Christ's Words in Rev. 2 and 3).

Christ's own Words of truth, included in these next two book chapters, are taken from the Lord's Revelation to the Apostle John—the last New Testament Book, called "Revelation"—and given by John in writing to the Seven Churches of Asia, as the Lord asked him to do. Readers, make no mistake about it: these two chapters of Revelation are not just historical discussions about ancient (mostly bad, but some good) churches, long forgotten by some as dead history. They are clearly and obviously seen, with the *Spirit of Truth's* counsel, as eternal examples of early Christian churches—who, like later churches and ours today, contain typical faithful and faithless, good and bad, obedient and disobedient, active or sleeping Christian members and leaders—not much different from our churches today.

And do not, dear Christian readers, listen to those *false teachers*—perhaps in "your church"—who wrongly tell you the Revelation 2 and 3 Churches "are from a different (and ignorant) society and culture, and cannot possibly be identified with Christ's dealing with our wonderful modern society and churches today." But this is an error; Scripture tells us, rightly, that neither Holy God nor sinful human nature changes. Without His forgiveness of human sin, in the world and in the church, God's Mercy would not be blended with His Justice for all. Fortunately for His church today, the Heavenly Father, according to His Word, will judge and deal both Mercifully and Justly with those who reject Him, His Son and His Spirit, while on earth. Christ, as the Head of His church, will carry out His unchanging and authoritative Will and purpose for His unstained Church Body on earth.

The purpose of my book is not to judge my fellow Christians—but only to warn them to wake up, and hear the Spirit says in God's Word and His Son's commands. The warning is Christ's own warning against churches who disobey or fail Him.

The Spirit speaks today—but He **does not** (as some falsely say) **speak a different, or unclear, or uncertain Word** for each and every human church congregation, in the past, and down through the centuries to today. No, the Spirit speaks for the Head of the Christian church of all time, and does not change in one iota the consistent and eternal things He asks of us, despite the centuries that have elapsed since our Lord formed His Will to *build* His *church*. These Divinely-Given Words in Revelation 2 and 3 have been preserved over the centuries by the Spirit of God and of Truth, for the universal purpose of speaking to the churches of all ages—including ours. **Commendation or condemnation—which will our Lord speaks to us in His church when He comes?**

A Worldly Analogy to Scriptural Truth for the Church.

I have entitled these next two chapters (8 and 9)—somewhat facetiously—**"Christ's first Divine 'Audit and Review' of His church—Rev. 2,3."** "Audit" and "Review" may, at first sight, appear inappropriate to the language and understanding of men and women of Jesus' time and missions on earth; nor do they fit well with the churches of the Middle Ages, nor of the time of Luther's "Reformation." But they do fit well in the "church age" we live in—our modern, technological and materially-oriented (secular), Western 20-21st-century industrial societies. We in the church today must struggle to discern Christ's Will and purpose for His church, and bewildered disciples' lives within it, so that we can serve Him faithfully *in the world*—but not take part in its evil practices under the *Prince of this world, Satan* (John 14:30).

I use the phrase "Audit and Review," then, purely as an attention-getter for modern readers—both members and leaders under the Head, Jesus Christ. No matter what words were used in the past, the problem is the same as it is today—**His disciples must understand, obey and apply Christ's universal and unchanging teachings and Commands to our day**, our service, our lives for Him—and be faithful to Him in all He asks.

It is important for this writer to communicate the truth that Christ and His Word are Eternal and unchanging to "modern" church readers, often told falsely that the words of our Lord spoken to ancient churches cannot possibly be applied to our churches today. And it is vital for churches today to read, preach and teach His Word to His church Body of all ages. This book of warning must stimulate readers' interest by adopting a strategy they recognize as both familiar and fitting for **them** to apply to **their church** (really and truly "His church"!)

When a businessman or woman builds a worldly business firm today, he/she will wisely write down instructions (in the form of a charter, a business plan, written articles of constitution, etc.) as to how employees are to carry out the "president's" or "head's"—or "founder's"—will, desires, and plans. This is done so that, even in his absence, the company will become a success in the eyes of the one who founded the firm. The businessman is even wiser (especially if he is required to be away for long periods of time, and must trust his employees to be honest and faithful in their work for him) if he arranges for a periodic *"audit and review"* of how employees carry out their duties and responsibilities. This secular-based audit or review process (as seen in today's world) usually results in written statements of audit, with unbiased examiners reviewing and listing both commendations and condemnations. They often require corrective actions, such as "discharge of unfaithful employees," or demotions for unfaithful work. So, what we are about to read (or re-read) from Revelation 2, and 3, in our Lord's often symbolic language, should not be completely foreign to us today!

As with most analogies, however, I and you cannot often directly apply what we read in the Bible to modern business practices, or vice versa. But, as Christians, we hopefully can become more interested in following God's ancient scriptural writings. We should see that what Christ said and did in His very similar (but not identical) audit and review process of some very early churches (Rev. 2and 3), are, in truth, very *applicable and pertinent* to all later churches, and to ours. The material, sinful world in which we Christians must work, grow, and please our Lord may be very different from that of the early churches in the primitive Roman world of Revelation 2 and 3.

But His words whether of commendation or condemnation are universal in time, and in His Nature. However the Spirit has led you before to think of His Words to "Good, bad, or lukewarm churches" of those times, it is important that we all know now that His soon-to-come audit and review of many of His churches today is Divinely Just, Truthful, and always applicable to all churches of any age. God cannot lie and He is Unchangeable, Merciful and Just. Our sinful natures are unchanging, too, until we become **new creations through** His Grace and Mercy, as we become Christian in His scriptural Way.

Like the businessman of today, writing down for his employees all that is necessary for them to know to conduct his business honestly and effectively, our Lord has **written down for us,** in His Word, exactly how He wants his "Church business" to proceed, ina faithful and obedient way.

Unlike our hypothetical businessperson, Christ has not left us alone with only a Plan and Purpose written down in Scripture (comparable perhaps to a written business "charter or constitution"). No—He has, in His Providence and Love, provided every born-again member of His church with **His own Living Spirit,** to live in each of us—when He was required to be absent from us, and until He comes again as He has promised! This Spirit of God has many functions, but for church members and leaders, He is also a vital *Teacher of all Truth* and One Who *will teach you all things, and will remind you* (us) *of everything Christ has said to us* (*paraphrased by author*—see John 14).

For forgetful, weak, and sinful unsaved humans—living in the world, yet trying not to be a part of this world's evils because they have a God-given conscience—a well-written business plan may or may not allow them to sleep peacefully in their absentee human president's absence! But, for we often forgetful, sometimes sinful, "humans, Christians in Christ's Body, the church," it is comforting indeed to not only have in writing (in inspired, inerrant Scripture) what we must do in His church, and in the world, but equally comforting to have our Lord's Spirit always present and available to us to Guide and Remind us of all that He requires us to be and to do for Him.

An absentee "president" may, without mercy, discharge, demote, or fine us for cause (failure), when he returns from a trip to find we are unfaithful and disobedient, or have listened to false advice contrary to his "business plan." Our Lord, in His Written Word, knowing that His Spirit is with us in His presence and guiding roles, tells us that even when we disobey and fail Him—when we listen to *false teachers* rather than to Him, when we fall *asleep* at His business, or *lose our first love*, when we differ from or oppose His instructions—He will forgive us when we repent of our sin and disobedience, and return to *do what we did at first* (His commands).

Before we review our Lord's first audits of the Seven "Asian" churches of Revelation 2 and 3, let me say that He is Merciful and Just in all things. Yes, the All-Knowing (Omniscient) Head of His earthly church knows that *some* of His churches—from Jerusalem at Pentecost, down twenty centuries to today—have been faithful, unstained by sin, obedient in all things He has asked us all to be and do for Him. His Word (especially Rev. 1–3) told the early church, and tells all His Body, that He recognizes our efforts to please Him, and do His Will in carrying out His purpose of the Great Commission, and every other purpose He has for all of us. Yes, He tells of rewards, crowns, and a wonderful future for all who will obey Him in all things in the church.

Read this book, and you must receive the Truth that God is Holy, Just and Merciful. Even as you read my quotations from His Inspired Word, advising that the Lord speaks often of His Wrath and destruction in store for those in His Son's Church who sin against Him—do not forget that He Loves His church and desires that we obey Him. False teachers often deny these Truths, but all True believers are given the Spirit within us to Teach and Guide all to God's Holy Plan and Purpose.

In the material to follow, a Christian church member or leader may gain the impression that Christ speaks (and I echo his words in my writing) only of doom, wrath, and destruction of those who fail Him. If you think or feel this, you are probably not studying and reading God's Word with the help of the Holy Spirit, given to each *new creation* who believes in the Risen Christ. I urge you, as the Spirit will do if He is asked to lead you to the truth, to drop all false premises, bias, and teachings of men. Read the Scriptures—by hearing and obeying the Spirit, and the Word, you will be able to discern whether you, and His Body are faithful and obedient, or the converse—so that when our Lord observes His church today, of which **you are a part,** you will be able to accept His rewards or wrath—now, or when He comes soon as He promised (Rev. 22: 7,20)—knowing you have earned it by your own acts. It is your (and your church's) choice, as I hope all will come to realize before they read the conclusion to this book!

A Brief Scriptural Review of Seven Early, Yet Typical Churches:

"If readers will turn now to Revelation 1, 2 and 3 and observe..." (I'm a teacher at heart, and can't help writing as a teacher speaks—forgive me! Forgive me, too, for being impersonal at times. I am with you, and for you, as I and you are all part of Christ's Body on earth, as Christian members and leaders). Let's ask the *Spirit of Truth* to show us, from this inspired Scripture, the truth in it for those early Christian churches of an ancient remote land, as well as the truth that will speak to our hearts and minds in the application of it to our own bodies of Christ, and our part in it as Christians in His Body, here and now.

Revelation Ch. 1. Introduction, from Christ through the Apostle John.

The first few verses of Revelation 1 are a prologue by the Apostle John, telling us how he came to write down the Lord's Revealing to him these things *that must soon take place* (verse 1). Late in his life, the Apostle John tells us, he was on the island of Patmos. The Lord came to him in a vision, and commanded him *to write on a scroll what you see.* It must have been a few years since most of the Seven were established by the Apostle Paul, and others, in the early years of missionary church growth described in Acts and Letters of Scripture. From the words and context of the letters to the Seven, we can infer that the church of Christ had been in existence for some decades, because of the type and kinds of sin practiced in and by the church then, and the **commendations or condemnations spoken** by the Lord. John, an older man when he received Christ's Revelation, was told by His Lord to write what he saw and heard to these Seven established Churches of the Roman province of Asia, in turbulent ancient times for Christians then.

Although many Christian students have attempted to "date" the year of Christ's Revelation to John, we only know it was in yet another time of persecution of Christians. It is not important that we later Christians fix the exact date of writing, although many scholars past (and present) still argue endlessly about it. By their arguments and differing conclusions about relatively unimportant matters, the church is, thus, continually divided. What is vital, Scripture and the Spirit tells us, is that we hear and obey Jesus Christ. And equally important is for the church *to hear what the Spirit says to the* (mostly sinful) *churches* (Rev. 2 and 3).

The Apostle John, in Revelation 1:12ff, not only tells us that the Lord told him to write what he was about to see and hear relevant to these Seven Churches, but describes the continuing vision of the Lord's Revelation to His church through metaphors and symbols. John was shown a vision of the Lord Himself—the Omnipotent, Omniscient, All-Powerful "Son of Man," Jesus Christ, Head of His church on earth; dead, yet Resurrected, and in Heaven. Again, as He did prior to His Great Commission of Matthew 28:18–20, the Lord states His Divine Authority to speak the things He is going to convey to John for the church of all centuries—and us today. In Revelation 1:17, He identifies Himself as *the First and the Last* (the *Alpha and Omega* of the Greek), the *Living One* Who is God—dead, yet gloriously Resurrected, and the Divine Head of His church of all ages.

He is the Eternal God, Who holds the keys of *death and Hades; the Living One* Who, these Words remind us, **Willed to build His church**, the church He commanded to *make disciples, baptize them…and teach them to obey all that* He *has commanded.* Do you see and understand why these Words to His church are timeless? They come from our Lord, Himself!

In this same portion of Revelation 1, John—speaking of the church down through time until Christ returns to claim His *radiant* Bride—tells us in 1:19ff that, in his vision, Jesus has in His hands *seven stars.* They represent the *angels,* or perhaps leaders, of the Seven Churches to whom John is to write. He also tells John that the *seven golden lampstands in His Presence* (1:20) represent *the seven churches* (and us today—author).

The Risen, Triumphant, and Glorious Jesus also tells John, and we later bodies of Christ, what is happening now, and what will happen to them and to us in the future—for He expects us to listen to Him (...*hear what the Spirit says to the churches*). Notice that in each letter, to each exemplar church, He repeats this phrase, knowing frail Christians in every age **need** to remember and obey it. Note, too—the Spirit reminds us of what Christ has already said to us!

With this introduction to the Lord's Words for His church, I am now able to remind my readers of the Lord's purpose of communicating His special Words in Revelation 2 and 3 (together with His introduction in Chapter 1 to us all). **Hear Him and obey Him** in all He says and commands us to do.

An overview of the successes, failures and failings of the Seven Church "examples"

Since a full analysis of all that is contained in Chapters 2 and 3 of Christ's Revelation to the Apostle John (and to His church today) would not fit into this humble volume, I have, with the Spirit as my guide, condensed the "Seven Churches'" successes and failures into a short list. In the following chapter, the disobedience and failings of ancient churches are analyzed more extensively.

If you are ready (i.e., have asked the *Spirit of Truth* to help you as you read again Revelation 2,3), I will prepare these "lists" in this chapter and the next, also with the Spirit's counsel.

"Successes and failures" of the Seven churches of Asia
(Some Scriptures are paraphrased).

1. **The church in Ephesus** (Rev. 2:1–7).

A. Successes: *I know your...deeds and...hard work;* intolerance of *wicked men;* testing of *false Apostles; perseverance, enduring hardships for my name; ...Not grown weary* (Rev. 2:2,3, some paraphrasing by the author).*You hate the* (sinful) *practices of the Nicolaitans* (a heretical sect within the church, that made a compromise with pagan society, and practiced idolatry and immorality).

B. Failures, disobedience: *Yet I hold this against you: You have forsaken your first love* (Christ); *fallen* from a great (spiritual) *height.*

175

C. Action commanded to reform and return to full obedience: *Repent and do the things you did at first.*

D. Recommended process to start reform: ...**Hear what the Spirit says to the churches** (a universal warning and closing Words of Christ in these chapters for the Seven Churches, as well as for all Christian churches, past, present and future).

2. **The church in Smyrna** (Rev. 2:8–11).

A. Successes: *I know your afflictions...poverty... slander* you endure.

B. Failures, disobedience: None, apparently, at present. But future possibilities of failure under coming persecutions, even unto death. And future possibility of weak Christians in the church not knowing that their present afflictions and poverty disguise their true spiritual *richness* in Christ.

C. Recommended process of reform: *Hear (and obey) what the Spirit says to the churches.*

3. **The church in Pergamum** (Rev. 2:12–17).

A. Successes: *I know your deeds...you live where Satan* (has his throne), *yet you remain true to my name. You did not renounce your faith* when one of you was martyred, *put to death in your city.*

B. Failures, disobedience: *Nevertheless I have a few things against you.* Some Christians among you hold to false teachings of a false god (Balaam, See Num. 25:1–2; 31; 31:16; Jude 11); *you also have those among you who hold to the* (false) *teaching of the Nicolaitans* (see also Smyrna church).

C. Recommended reform: **Repent** and **hear what the Spirit says to the churches**.

4. **The church in Thyatira** (Rev. 2:18–29).

A. Successes: *I know your deeds* (good deeds), *your love and faith* (for and in Christ); *your service and perseverance, and that you are now doing more than you did at first* (for Him).

B. Failures, disobedience: *Nevertheless, I have this against you: You tolerate* (accept the false teachings of) *Jezebel* (a Biblical name—obviously, an unnamed female member of the church) *who...misleads* the disciples *into sexual immorality,* and practices forbidden by the church.

C. Recommended process of reform: The guilty persons must *repent; the rest of* the Body *must hold onto what you have* (the true faith) *until I come.* Again, the Lord's universal injunction to: ***Hear what the Spirit says to the churches*** (All that Christ's disciples have taught of Him).

5. The church in Sardis (Rev. 3:1–6).

A. Successes: *I know...* (and He sees through their inaction and deceit, for we see that they have no successes in the Lord's eyes; they have failed Him in their service to Him in Sardis) *a few* in the church *have not soiled their clothes* (allowed sin and "spiritual deadness" to overcome them).

B. Failures, disobedience: *You are* (spiritually) *dead* (and a failure as His Body). *Your deeds are not complete in the sight of God.*

C. Recommended process of reform: *Wake up. Strengthen what remains and is about to die....Remember...what you have received and heard* (through the Apostles' teachings, through the "missionaries" who founded the church, and trained the leaders); ***Obey*** what you have heard from my teachings; ***Repent*** (and act to reject sin and become obedient). ***Hear what the Spirit says to the churches*** (NB: in all cases preceded by *"He who has an ear to hear, hear what the Spirit says."*).

6. The church in Philadelphia (Rev. 3: 7–13).

A. Successes: *I know your deeds...you have kept my word* (despite your little strength), and *you have not denied my name* (when Satan and public pressure from those loyal to 'other gods' tempt you; and when hostile Jews attacked you); you have kept my command to endure patiently. (Paraphrased by the author.)

B. Failures, disobedience: Apparently none, although some might question their *little strength* and suggest they did not work hard enough to "make disciples," despite the intense hostility and pressure to deny their Lord from those sinners surrounding them.

C. Recommended process of reform: None needed; nevertheless, the Lord repeats His "universal" injunction for all these churches, **and ourselves today,** in Christ's Body—to **hear what the Spirit says to the churches** (For this is the key for all types of churches, in all kinds of evil social and sinful environments—to keep in touch always with the Spirit—one of Whose roles it is, to remind us of all that the Lord has told us to be and to do (John 14). Without hearing the Spirit speaking to us, we cannot become, or be, the fully obedient bodies He requires us to be in this world.

7. **The church in Laodicea** (Rev. 3: 14–22).

A. Successes: Few indeed, for this is an example of a *lukewarm church*—one that is **neither** *"hot"* and fervent to do the work of the Lord at all times, nor *"cold"*; one that completely rejects what the Lord has told them to do, as believers in the Body of Christ in all nations.

B. Failures, disobedience: A continual state of **lukewarmness** that the Lord **hates**, and even *wishes that you are either one or the other.* Like lukewarm food or drink, Christ says, *because you are neither hot nor cold* in My service, *I am about to spit you out of my mouth.* Additionally, the Lord notes,you say you are *rich* and *have acquired wealth and do not need a thing*—but this is not their true spiritual condition. The Lord says *you do not realize that you are wretched, pitiful, poor, blind and naked* (spiritually lost).

C. Recommended process of reform: Christ counselled the Laodicean church in this example for all of us in the past and today, by especially denying as worthy this type of self-deceived, lukewarm church and prideful condition. He counsels them (3:18) to return to the refined *gold* of His Life and Way and Light. To become *new creatures in Christ, the old* sin *has gone* (2 Cor.

5:17). They must be *earnest and repent* of their sins and spiritual 'blindness.' And, again, He urges them—as all Christians through the centuries, today, and until His return are urged—to **hear what the Spirit says** (has said, is saying, will say continually, in the Name of the Head), **to the churches**.

Now that I have, with the Spirit's directions, extracted the basic elements (His Words) constituting these seven church "examples" from the early days of the church, **I will assemble them in a simple list.** I believe I should not concentrate on making a vague, unclear list some would agree with, while others might say "that's a cultural error, not applicable to our highly-advanced society"—but a faithful scriptural listing, using our Lord's own Words.

In my study of the historical churches, when they are placed against the New Testament church, and both studied with the inspired Scriptures (and the Spirit), I find that *false teachers* in the past and present church often oppose Scripture, and want to teach the church to obey their own (false) teachings, even if **they oppose God's Word.** So, all who are truly interested in obeying God's Word, Christ's teachings, and the Spirit's counsel must overcome false opinions, teachings, or false doctrines—standing firm on His Word, principles, teachings, and commands alone.

I do not believe that our Creator-God, His Son Who Willed to build His church, and the *Spirit of Truth* (the Holy Trinity of God) would ever say, do, teach, command, or move men to write down for we Christians (or for Israel) something that purports to be only applicable to a cultural, or human situation, that does not agree always with the Holy Scriptures. To the contrary—everything that is in the inspired Bible is not only inerrant (and infallible), but is God's Eternal Truth. Truth that is applicable and recognizable in any society, then, down through the centuries, today, or in any sort of cultural or societal or national situation we can imagine.

Sin of any and all ages is still sin—whatever human form or name is attached to it by Satan and *false teachers.* God knows, understands, and speaks to the heart of ancient mankind and "modern" mankind alike, with Eternal spiritual (scriptural) principles, church doctrines and practices that can be understood and applied in Spirit-led church teaching in any century. None then, the Word and the Spirit tell us, can oppose the clear, inspired teaching of the Word, or pervert, add, or change His Word for any human reason, without sinning and offending God, His Spirit, and His Son, our Saviour, Lord, and church Head. *God's Word is Sanctifying*, Infallible, and sufficient for us always.

Jesus Christ was being Divinely Omniscient (All Knowing) when He told us that the world will hate us Christians, just as the world hates Him (John 15). For example, He inspired the Apostle Paul to write to us, in Romans 1, about the spiritual condition of sinful men who ignore or reject God and become evil and deceitful in their lost lives of wickedness, and often in their opposition to God. He also inspired the Apostle Peter to write to tell Christ's church, in 2 Peter 2:1, that *there were also false prophets* (speaking first of Israel and the time of the Prophets) *among the people, just as there will be false teachers among you* (in the church and in the world—now speaking of *false teachers* in later ages). He inspired the Apostle Paul, in Ephesians 4, to write about the vital necessity of ... *teaching them* (new disciples in the church) *to obey all that Christ commanded us.* For, until all disciples are fully taught, they are unable to mature spiritually into the *whole measure of the fullness of Christ* (Eph. 4). And they will not be able to discern, reject, and overcome the Scripture-opposing *false teachers* in the church—and in all sinful churches who will not repent and reform their evil ways, and fail Christ.

It is most important that today's church be warned about Satan's leading in this regard. Christian readers must recognize and reject false teachings, accepting only the Spirit's counsel when we read and study and apply Scripture.

Discerning readers, who read the Revelation chapters I spoke of with the guidance of the Spirit, will have noted that I have not talked about **all** that Christ talked about to the churches of that time! I have omitted certain things—not because they are unimportant, for nothing the Lord says to us is irrelevant or unimportant, but because they tend to divert and channel my reader's thoughts unnecessarily as I prepare this general list. I do so by category, of the good, bad, and indifferent (lukewarm) commendations and condemnations of Christ to the Seven church examples He has given us as instruction for His Body in every age. But first let me add something else about the Scriptural summation of Revelation 2,3 that I have compiled previously in this chapter.

I have entirely omitted the whole subject of *rewards* and special considerations given now or in the future, to faithful, obedient, and persecuted church members. Certainly, these things must be taught and explained to all members of Christ's Body in the past, and today, for they all a part of the spiritual maturing process that Paul talked about in Ephesians 4 and elsewhere. And, certainly, they all fall under the ... *knowledge, the whole measure of the fullness of Christ,* the Christian faith, and all that are a part of the disciples' strengthening of the church Body, resisting Satan, and serving Christ, etc. But they are not necessary in the purpose of this book—which the Spirit has led me to write to use Christ's Words, and Spirit-inspired Words of Apostles or disciples—to reveal to disobedient, failing, or failed churches what displeases Christ and what they must do to correct their **own** errors and return in faithfulness to their Head.

My omission of these regards in Christ's Words to His church should be viewed, not as detrimental or in opposition to His Words, but as clarifying the churches problems. This, so disobedient churches can more readily see, grasp, repent and correct (reform) **their possible** disobedience to Him.

Christian Church Disobediences—A Basic Classification by Category, Observed in Many Past and Present Churches and Society:
(based upon "types" seen in Rev. 2 and 3). These are Christ's very Words, in italics below, not the words of men.

1.A. *You have forsaken your first love* (Ref. Ephesus church).

> **Explanation, comments:** Literally, forsaking Christ means that, through sin or love of the world, one has turned away from the Lord Who died for Him, and saved him as *a new creation,*

181

to serve Him in His "Body" the church. Forsaking Christ leads to a multitude of sins and disobediences within the church, along with an inability of the church to witness to and affect the world or society around it.

Although we may be sincere and loving at first, this failure and disobedience results in members' hating rather than loving each other, a divided Body of Christ, and in Satan's representatives entering the church and finding a fertile ground for him. *False teachers* soon lead to *spiritual infants* being *tossed to and fro by every wind of* (false) *teaching.* The church, once strong and faithful, erodes. A failing love for their Saviour and one-time Lord (despite their past obedience, and works of faithfulness)—unless restored—will mean loss of future rewards, and worse.

B. *You have...Fallen* from a great (spiritual) *Height*
(Ref. Ephesus church).

Explanation, comments: This differs from the **A** type, above, perhaps only in that this allows one who has *forsaken* their *first love* (Jesus Christ) to consider what they have done or not done from a metaphorical perspective. Their rejection of Christ is illustrated as a physical fall, from a great height of well-being to a lower abyss of failing Christian and church existence.

These two types of church disobedience—really two types of the same sin, as they are metaphorical—need to be placed alongside present-day or traditional past disobedience to see if they fit Christ's categories of conduct that He *holds against them*—and other churches that would do the same.

2. *You have a Fear of persecution (unto death)*
(Ref. Smyrna church).

Explanation, comments: This indefinite type of possible disobedience may be seen only times and places in which Christian or Christian church persecutions exist. Besides Smyrna, we noted in Acts 5, cases in which the Apostles were persecuted, and in Acts 6, where the persecution was against the

Jerusalem Christians following the martyrdom of Stephen. In neither of these cases in the New Testament church's early days was there any question that the church did not (or might not) remain strong in the face of persecution. But here—probably several decades after the church was spread abroad to all nations—we get a hint, I believe, that the Lord is questioning whether this small church (probably mostly Christian Gentiles), set in the midst of a very hostile Jewish population, would be able to withstand present and future persecution in His Name. The threat of imprisonment and persecution, even unto death, might be in their future, the Lord says. The church is asked to *continue to be faithful*—to Christ's Words, and to Him, personally. I list this "possible disobedience" as a type that may occur today. It should be watched for by church leaders, as we seem to be in the *end times* when we Christians must watch for His coming, without failing Him out of fear. There is little doubt, too, that all Christians, of any age or society, are subject to subtle and not-so-subtle persecution. Perhaps not *unto death*—but who has not been rebuffed, as a Christian, for not "going along" with the practices of today's sinful, material world?

3. **Some Christians in the church** *holding to false, "cultic" teachings* (Pergamum church).

   Explanation, comments: Nothing indefinite about this type of disobedience—variations of this error have occurred down through the centuries, even as Peter warned us about *false teachers*. The "cult" will vary with the society, and culture, as new false gods and teachings about them occur, under Satan's pressures on weak Christians. We have "New Age" cults today—watch for, and avoid them!

4. *False teacher(s) in the church* (Ref. Thyatira church).

   Explanation, comments: This kind of false teaching does not attract weak Christians in the church to false cultic gods, but often the teaching leads to human sexual immorality, to a pattern of false worship, and to other evil church practices that cast shame upon the Head of the church, as the "world" considers the church's God and whether or not He sent His Son into the world to draw all men to Him. There are *false teachers* in many Christian seminaries today also, as I have observed in this book's examples. Seminary Councils, or "Governing Boards" must keep alert and observe the faith of "professor applicants" for signs of past or present defections from the inspired, inerrant, and infallible written Word of God.

5. **Christian churches and members** *who are 'dead' spiritually,*

    Explanation, comments: Here, the metaphor compares the actions (or inactions) of living men, faithful and obedient in their Master's sight, with those who are "dead" spiritually— and who, thus, can no longer produce complete (i.e. God-pleasing) works of righteousness, as faithful disciples of Christ. Spiritual and watchful Pastors can observe what sort of spiritual *fruit* or *withered fruit* is observed in the lives of their members, teachers, etc.—and ask the Lord to prune the *vine branches* where required.

6. *"Little strength,"* and subject to failure when persecution or temptations come along (Ref. the Philadelphia church).

    Explanation, comments: While seemingly similar to the church at Smyrna, the phrase *little strength* that the Lord uses with that church leads us to consider, with the Holy Spirit, what lesson we may derive from the service and works of this small, early church. Like most of the other Seven, it was complimented on many of its efforts, *works, faithfulness, and obedience* in carrying out His will in troubled times, difficult surroundings and persecution. But we realize, as we place the picture of Seven troubled Churches in ancient times against *"our"* churches today, the Lord is not only warning them of trouble present and trouble ahead, but teaching us—in our weaknesses, our strengths, our imitations of their problems, our *pride,* our *sleepiness,* our *deadness,* our *tolerance and acceptance of false teachers,* of what we must be for Him (or return to) to win His praise and rewards for *overcoming evil, sloth, pride and circumstances.* How many baptisms have occurred lately in "your" church? How many new teachers have been recruited lately? The answers may surprise you, and cause you to wonder if **your church** is "spiritually weak," too—needing the Spirit's Help for reform.

7. *"Lukewarm"* **in His Service;** Pridefully rich in their vanity; yet *wretched, pitiful, poor, blind and naked* in truth and in His sight (Ref. the Laodicea church).

   Explanation, comments: I find the example of this church to be the saddest, most useless Body of Christ imaginable. Perhaps it is to the Lord, also, for He reserves one of his most terrible metaphorical treatments and language for it. He is about to *spit them out of His mouth,* like cold food when one expects and needs a hot meal. Others may disagree, but as one compares the degree of severity of His threatened treatments of disobedient churches (which I shall soon do), few examples from these Seven Churches can compare in terms of the Lord's utter disgust with their actions and inactions.

Before I close this chapter, listing church problems of the past, and comparing them to the problems of the later churches and today, please allow me to prepare a list of some *"consequences"* that the Lord speaks about in connection with the disobedience and sin Christ reveals in Revelation 2,3. Using both lists, in the next chapter, I may be able to show you how they apply to the "process" of examining our local Bodies of Christ, and how we should scripturally act to **repent, reform and remove** what we find that the Lord *holds against us* when we disobey Him and His Word.

Consequences of Revealed Disobedience in the Seven Churches;

When repented of, and when continued, despite warnings from the Lord (Readers note: In Rev. 1,2,3, *lampstands* represent the individual Christian churches, hopefully kept in His Presence):

185

1. *Ephesus church.*

If sins repented: *return and do the things you did before.* If unrepentant: Christ will remove their *lampstand* from its place (NB: Rev. 1:12 tells us that in John's vision, Christ appeared to him *in the midst of the seven lampstands,* representing the Churches in the Revelation). So, the consequence of Ephesus continuing unrepentant would be the denial of Christ's presence with the failing church (**with others**, if we consider the many unrepentant, disobedient churches in history and today). A terrible fate for an unrepentant church!

2. *Smyrna church.*

If repentant of disobedience, or continuing to be faithful, the church would receive *the crown of life.* They would not then lose the gift of Everlasting or Eternal Life, received when each member repented and believed by faith alone in the Risen Lord. Smyrna and we are told that, for continuing to be faithful, they and we would be *overcomers* not hurt by the *Second Death* (and the *lake of fire* mentioned in Rev. 20:14; 20:6 and 21:8).

3. *Pergamum church.*

The Lord promised that repentant churches such as Pergamum, who *overcame,* would be given some of the *hidden manna* (see Ps. 78:24) as well as *a white stone with a new name written on it, known only to him who receives it.* The white stone metaphor would be better known (as would the *new name*) to converted Jews in the Pergamum church. For Gentile believers, it would be accepted as a reward given in the future for those who *overcame* evil by their Christian faith. For the unrepentant ones, Christ tells them—and us—that He personally will come to *fight against those in the church who 'hold to the false teachings'* offered by non-Christian sect members in the church. He will use *the sword of My mouth,* referred to in the Revelation 1 vision, meaning the sword of Divine Judgment, as spoken of in the Old and New Testaments (Isa. 49:2; Heb. 4:12). How can we accept thoughts of our Saviour and Lord coming to fight against us? Give up false teachings now!

4. *Thyatira church.*

For repentant churches such as Thyatira, the Lord will give these *overcomers* and *those who do His will to the end, authority over the nations,* quoting Ps. 2:9. He also observes that this reward of authority will be given (just) *as I* (He) *have received all Authority* (from His Father) (see His Great Commission, Matthew 28:18). Finally, for repentant believers as well as faithful overcomers, He will give them *the morning star* (Rev. 22:16—another name for the Lord, given to the churches). The Lord also says to unrepentant sinners, in Revelation 2:23, something very significant for all these as well as unrepentant, disobedient churches: *…I am He who searches hearts and minds, and I will repay each of you according to your deeds.* He Who is Omniscient, Loving, and Just is aware of all our sins and disobedient deeds. And He **will repay our** errant deeds by a just **repayment**, or Divine Penalty—proportionate to the disobedience, in His eyes and the eyes of His Heavenly Father. To me, this statement expresses clearly how the Holy One, our Lord, Who says, *If you love me, you will obey my teaching* (John 14) will respond to those who show clearly they do **not** love Him, and instead following and obeying *false teachers* in and out of the church.

5. *Sardis church.*

For spiritually *dead* churches, as characterized by the church in long-ago Sardis, the Lord uses the metaphor of a sleeping person whose waking life is a ruin, caused by lethargy and useless dozing. Repentance is necessary, of course, for such churches, but the Lord substitutes here the phrase *Wake up!* The "waking-up process," carried over into the truth of a spiritually dead church, means *repent and strengthen what remains and is about to die.* This is truly a terrible situation to consider! What if some churches today wake up—as perhaps some Spirit-convicted member or leader reads (**hears**) what **the Spirit says to the church** in the Word of God, and suddenly realizes (*wakes up*) that it is "their church—no longer His (except in name)" imitating the Sardis church. What should failing churches do? Surveying the dead and dusty remnants of a once faithful church Body, the

Spirit and the Revelation of Christ tells them to *strengthen what remains* of His Body. Their *good deeds are incomplete* because they have failed He Who gave Himself for His church. Is this possible? With Christ, all things are possible; but in the things that he abhors, church repentance and reform is necessary—and a return to full obedience.

Yes, repentance is necessary, as is *remembering what they have received* (from Godly teachers) *and heard* (from other Godly disciples, as well as from the Spirit Who speaks to the churches). Obedience is also necessary, if they are to avoid the implicit threat that the Lord gives them in His Revelation to John. Revelation 3:4 concludes with the Lord saying to them, through John's letter, *if you do not wake up, I will come like a thief, and you will not know what time I will come to you.* Brothers and sisters, I do not know what punishment or spiritual loss of reward is meant by this—or even if the Sardis church "woke up" before it was too late. But His threat is sufficient cause for every disobedient church to **hear what the Spirit says** *to* (their) *churches.* It should, an must, however, cause them not only to hear but obey, before He comes again to claim His Radiant Bride.

If recipients of John's letter of Revelation from Christ woke up, corrected their failing work for the Lord, repented, and returned to full obedience, Christ's words tell them and us that *all who overcome* (few or many) **will walk with me, dressed in white.** This is "good news" for faithful Christians. Our reward, of walking with the Lord, unstained by sin, in symbolic white (not sin-stained) clothes, will be more than a sufficient reward in our everlasting lives with our Saviour and Lord.

6. *Philadelphia church.*

Seemingly blameless, the church here is nevertheless known by Christ to have little strength. In spite of persecution from hostile synagogue Jews, they had kept His word, and did not deny His Name. Consequences of disobedience in their not acting to *make disciples* in their difficult situation is not discussed. However, the Lord speaks to them—and us—by saying

He *will keep them from the hour of trial...* that he will send to test them and us. The Lord also encourages them (and us today) by saying, *I am coming soon.* He says, too, as He has to others in this group of churches: *Hold on to what you have, so that no-one will take your crown.* He says "consequences" are given, not to this faithful but persecuted Body, but to those Jews who are harassing the Christian church at that time.

7.   *Laodicea church.*

This prideful, complacent, *lukewarm church* realizes that the Lord still loves them, for Revelation 3:19 says *Those whom I love, I rebuke and discipline.* Because He loves them, and does not want to discipline or reject them outright, He asks them *to be earnest and repent.* The awful consequences for non-repentance is this outright rejection of *spitting you out of My mouth.* For the repentant ones, *who overcome their pride and uncaring service* to Him, the Lord promises them—and us, if we are found guilty, yet repent of these or other sins—*the right to sit with me on my throne!*

A Brief Summary and Conclusion:

The Lord tells all Christians in all His churches, in Paul's inspired writings to His *dear son Timothy* that *All Scripture is God-breathed and is useful for teaching, rebuking, correcting and training in righteousness, so that the man of God may be thoroughly equipped for every good work* (2 Tim. 3:16-17). I hope to use what we all have learned, or relearned, in the past chapters and in Christ's Words, in order to carry out my purpose and His. That is—to use His Words of command, condemnation, commendation and warning. I urge those churches who are *lukewarm,* or *disobedient,* or *asleep,* or *faithful in part but not in all* to examine themselves against Christ's Words and Standards, and to reform what He *holds against them.*

All of His Words (as He says, in 2 Timothy 3:16,17) are important and valuable, but allow me to select just a few Words of truth from our Lord that will emphasize and expedite Christ's Will and purpose for each Christian and every church, especially the failing ones.

He who has an ear, let him hear what the Spirit says to the churches.
This is of prime Importance to failing churches (perhaps yours, perhaps mine). For, if some do not hear (or remain *deliberately deaf* to His
Spirit's Admonition, Counsel, Guidance, and recalled Remembrances
of Christ's other Words of Truth to the churches of Christ), they will
surely continue to disobey and fail Him. Some who read this Seven-
times-repeated phrase, in the Lord's Revelation to the Seven Churches
that we have just studied, may tend to skim over it and not discern its
importance, in their spiritually-dead condition. Others may encounter
and ignore it, because they do not understand it, or its value to them
in their modern, but often errant church. This failure to teach and
understand our Lord's Will and purpose for the church is the fault of
the church, in not teaching what Christ has asked us to do and be for
Him. It is certainly of Satan, and confirms the present condition of spiritual immaturity in many Christian churches today.

Yes, the *Spirit of Truth* continually speaks to the churches
through God's inspired Word—when revived church members and
teachers will seek His Willing Aid to help interpret, guide and counsel those who will read it.

The second vitally-important Word of Truth that I wish to mention
concerns the **Words of Truth about His Authority** and about Who He is
to those who *hear what the Spirit says to the churches.* He says (in
Rev. 1–3): *I am the First and the Last. I am the Living One. I was
dead and behold I am alive for ever and ever. I hold the keys of death
and Hades. I will give you many rewards* (things that only God Himself can give). *I know…your deeds, sins, and disobedience* (only God
Who *knows and searches men's hearts* can know this). *Repent…obey
me* (with the forgiveness of sins, and the Over-arching Omnipotent
and Omniscient Authority of the One True God).

The third tremendously important Word of Truth from this Revelation of Christ is this: it is not only important to the Seven Churches
of the past but to every Christian in every Church, His Body on earth
that has been formed by His Spirit, that *we must obey and serve Him
in the building of His church.* Regardless of His church's human "flaws,"
the Lord keeps on seeking our loyalty and obedience until His return
to claim His *Radiant Bride* (but not a *wrinkled, sin-stained, errant*

body). But remember, He is a Just God—rewarding obedience, and condemning disobedience.

Fourth, these scriptural understandings add significantly to all that the Lord's Revelation to John has told us about church obedience, disobedience, overcoming sin, pleasing or displeasing Him, in Revelation 2,3. Very near the end of the Revelation message to John (Rev. 22:7,20), Christ says: *I am coming soon.* I want to relate this prophetic statement by our Lord to all that He has said to His churches in Revelation 1–3, as well as in Ephesians 5:27 (that He will present His church to Himself when He comes again, as a *Radiant church—without stain, or wrinkle or any other blemish of sin*). These two Scripture passages (Rev. 22:7,20 and Eph. 5:27) fit perfectly with all of Scripture relating the Lord's hopes, Will, plans and Purposes for His church, made up of born-again Christians of all ages. And they fit perfectly with other Scriptures that I, this writer (with the Spirit) have chosen to include in this book of warning to disobedient churches of the past and today.

Fifth, finally and importantly, I must mention our Lord's great desire (expressed in prayer to His Heavenly Father near the end of His human, God-Incarnate life)—the prayer that all His disciples, in all of His churches then, in the future, and today *might be One, as the Father and I are One* (John 17:21–23). The churches of the New Testament were close to oneness, but later churches and today's are certainly **not one** (united fully as in Christ's definition)—due to our continuing disobedience. Again, we must hear the Spirit, and act to **repent and return to full obedience and oneness** in our love to Him, our Saviour, Lord, and coming Bridegroom.

Chapter 9

Disobedience in Christ's Church: In Scripture, Church History, and Now

If readers have found Chapter 8 of this book rather "heavy going," imagine how hard it was to condense Chapters 2 and 3 in our Lord's Revelation to the Apostle John, and then to summarize the material from His "Audit and Review" of Seven later New Testament Churches' actions or inactions, so that it could be applied (as it must be) to His church down through the centuries—to "our" churches today! It is not an academic summary, but intensely personal for the reader. I, too, love the Lord and His church, and agonize over disobedience in the Body.

Some readers may even have found reading suggested scriptural passages to be difficult—either because they were simply not used to studying the Bible, or because they had never done so by first asking the Holy Spirit to carry out His "role" of *Teacher and Counselor*. I sympathize with those who, because "their church" does not provide Bible Classes for all ages (and spiritual maturity for them!), nor make them mandatory for *born again* members to be taught *to obey all that I* (Christ) *have commanded you*, are literally having to "go through the throes" of learning to study alone and try to absorb these Holy Words. Some of you, possibly, have never even heard of the inspired Apostle Paul's words in 2 Timothy 3:16, concerning the importance (necessity I believe!) of studying Scripture, so that it may make each Christian church member in a local Body of Christ *spiritually mature*, as Paul also says in Ephesians 4.

193

Some churches, in past centuries, but not so much today, have even told their members NOT to read the Inspired Word of God to man—and that they will receive all they need to know about God, Christ, and the Spirit, from priests' brief "catechism", or extracts from the Bible or from church sermons or homilies given by church authorities. But this kind of Bible teaching and learning—especially as a response to our Lord's Command to " teach baptized disciples to obey *all* that He has commanded us" is insufficient, incomplete and unsatisfactory. The church **must** teach *all* disciples and so do to make disciples mature, and able to live useful lives for Him. Not teaching, or teaching too little, is disobedience!

Scriptural Teaching on Obedience, and Lessons from the Past: An Overview.

I want to make a brief analysis of the overall spiritual findings and probable results of another, modern-day "Audit and Review" of His church today, by Jesus Christ, when He comes soon as He promised (Rev. 22:7,20). He Himself says *only the Father* (God) *knows the hour and day and year of My return* (*paraphrased by author; see* Matt.24:36, etc.). He has said, too, that if we do not return to our former full faithfulness, and hear and obey what the *Spirit says to the* (His) *churches* (Rev. 2,3), many churches will not be fit, as a *wrinkled, sin-stained Bride* (Eph. 5:27) to have Him, the Sinless Bridegroom, for a Divine Husband (in this Divine analogy to a human marriage). Instead of being a spiritually Holy, a fully obedient *"radiant* Bride"when He comes again (see Rev. 22:7), unrepentant, unreformed churches will remain stained with sin. They will not be fit to be in His Divine Presence, without repentance and reform to full obedience (Rev. 22:5).

I want to try, then, to place before the Christian church today the urgent necessity of Christian church member and leader self-examination, with, as your "Aids" or "Helps," the inspired Word of God, and the *Spirit of Truth.* This can be done best by comparing your local church's **present** "life and works, words and actions" with the Divine, Holy, and Righteous **Standard** of God's inspired and inerrant Word. But self-governing local churches, under local scriptural leaders and the

Divine Head, Christ, must do this "comparison and review" action by themselves, with the Word and counsel of the Spirit in each believer. My human role is but to *alert and warn those churches who have forgotten, or not been taught the truth, and who have rejected our Lord's Words.* My purpose and actions carry no authority at all—only Christ has been given such Divine authority (see Matt. 28:18). An *advocate for the Lord* who draws your attention to *what God has provided in His inspired, inerrant Word,* I only point out *to the present-day church* of Jesus Christ, using Christ's inspired Words (plus some from Christ's inspired New Testament disciples) *that He is coming soon* (Rev. 22:7,20). His Words (such as in Rev. 2,3) give me, and all Christian churches, a terrible burden and concern. Are we ready to meet Him, our Lord?

Once again in this book, I urge all readers to *seek the Spirit's Counsel* in personal and corporate (church) prayer and Bible study, as they read Christ's commands and pleas in the Scripture I quote, and seek His Strength, Will, and His Spirit's guidance to lead them back to full obedience before He comes again to this earth. Read again John 14 and 16 for the Spirit's roles in all we say and do for Him.

How far have we come today in our understanding of His Will for us? In all instances of spiritual and practical disobedience, His first "scriptural Audit" of His church revealed that Christ, our Head, abhorred, disliked, hated, and held their sins against the disobedient ones. Moreover, He demanded that they repent and return to Him in full obedience, or He would act against them. His scriptural Word reveals, too, that He Who *Searches our hearts... knows our deeds... and those who "overcome evil,"* will *repay each... according to our* (sinful) *deeds* (Rev. 2,3). His *"Audit"*— as I call it to interest modern church members today—concludes with many other consequences of unrepented sin, including the awful (but little-known) statement that, *if you do not repent, I will come to you and remove your "lampstand" from its place* (Rev. 2:5).

This rarely-addressed removal of failed churches from the presence of our Lord and Saviour Himself, as described to the Apostle John in Revelation 1:13,20, must be preached to *wake up the whole body.* The full consequences of unrepented disobedience of failed and failing churches cannot be fully assessed by our finite minds until He comes, I believe.

My warnings to all failing and failed churches (really Christ's Warnings) *can and will* lead to the return of all disobedient churches of today to His Love, Favour, and rewards, and to His Divine Presence. That is, if they will only *hear, repent and reform* their Scripturally disobedient words and sinful deeds. I pray that many Christians in Christ's "Body, the Church" will return in repentance to do what they did at first—to please Him, before His imminent Return.

More Words of Advice From Our Living Loving Lord, on the Subject of Church Disobedience to Him.

Inspired scriptural writings by the Apostle *John* (Ch. 13–17 especially) give us all many of the teachings and prayers of the Lord, as He tells His disciples that He must leave them and return to His Heavenly Father. He tells them He will not leave them alone when He returns to Heaven from whence He has come, but will send the Holy Spirit to live within them. And, as He prays for all future disciples ("made" in accordance with His church Commission to be applied after He leaves them), He comforts them and prays that the Father will not take them (us) out of this world, but protect them from the Evil One, Satan. We Christian disciples are not to be "left as orphans," but Christ says *I will come to you* (see John 14:18—our Lord speaking to early disciples and to us).

The Lord tells us many of the other things that are on His Heart, for He must be obedient to His Father's Will and purpose in extending His Mercy through the church, to a lost world of Gentile unbelievers. He knows all our hearts, and all our deeds, and says these things so: *...all the churches will know that I am He who searches hearts and minds, and I will repay each of you according to your deeds* (Rev. 2: 23).

In John 13–17, our Lord also spoke much of obedience, praising it when He finds it in His churches—yet not hesitating to condemn those who disobey Him, and who listen to *false teachers*, rather than to His Teachings and to the *Spirit of Truth*'s counsel and guidance. He says to us, for example, in John 14:23: *If anyone loves me, he will obey my teaching; My Father will love him, and We will come to him, and make our home with him.* In John 15:9,10, He continues with this obedience requirement, and says: *Now remain in my love. If you obey my commands, you will remain in my love, just as I have obeyed my Father's commands and remain in his love.* I emphasize that this teaching, although made to His early disciples, **is for all we disciples** in His then-future, now present, church. Read Jesus' Words of prayer in John 17:20, too, in which He prays not only for His early disciples, but *for all who will believe in me through their message* (all believers and Christian churches down the centuries to today).

All of His teachings and commands will be reinforced in our hearts and minds and "born-again soul" by the Holy Spirit, of Whom Christ speaks in John 14:16,17: *I will ask the Father and He will give you another Counselor to be with you forever...the Spirit of Truth. The world cannot accept him, because it neither sees Him nor knows Him. But you know Him, for He lives with you and will be in you.* And in John 14:26, He says to us: ...*the Holy Spirit, Whom the Father will send in my Name will teach you all things, ...will remind you of everything I have said to you.* I repeat these things to you, and ask my readers to **invite the** Spirit of Truth to remind you of **everything** Christ has said to you, commanded you, and desires of you in His inspired Word to you and to all in His obedient church.

As I continue to discuss church disobedience, please understand (and refer to the Contents page of this book) and realize that Part 5 will talk of consequences of disobedience and sin by church members and leaders—while reminding us all that we have a guide and Teacher of Truth, repentance and reform in each of us believers. If read and understood with the Spirit's aid and guidance, the following chapters and Scripture passages will lead churches to return to the only way to please Christ, the Divine Head of His church.

Examples of Disobedience in Christ's "Body, the Church" in New Testament Times.

In the previous chapter, we saw that the early churches' disobedience could be classified in "types" or "categories of sinful acts." Some of these **types of sin** bore the names of various men or women cult members. Others showed the signs of Satan's work in the church. Sin, we found, could be grouped and applied so that we could examine church disobedience of the past, the middle ages, and today—and relate them to scriptural "types" or "categories" of disobedience. This is what I want to do now *as a teaching tool,* for Christ has made it plain in the inspired New Testament Scriptures (particularly Acts 2,3) what He *hates* or *holds against us* when we disobey Him. His inspired Word also clearly says that all *disobedience,* whatever its type, has its roots in Satan's influence on sinful men and women—who say, in effect, "I will not obey my Saviour and former Lord, for I want to do what pleases me." We have to only look back to Adam and Eve's temptation by Satan, their "Fall," and its consequences down through the ages, to recognize that pleasing ourselves is really pleasing Satan—who is himself disobedient to God. Satan even tempted our Lord, but failed (Matt. 4). He now tries to destroy Christ's church—His Body of believers on earth.

In my earlier study of the Seven Churches' disobedience, I produced (as in previous chapters) "lists" of the failings of individuals in those exemplar churches, as well as of general church failings to obey Jesus Christ. One list contained eight separately-named "failure categories." Sin situations where a few or many—or even the whole church listed—failed to obey Him Who is the Head, and instead obeyed false Satan-inspired teachers in the church. It is helpful (for *correction and training in righteousness* (2 Tim. 3:16) when we, in today's churches, begin to **examine "our" churches** with this book's urging and **primarily with the counsel of the Spirit of Truth.**

By itself, a list of scriptural "named sins" of the past may be confusing. When compared, however—even briefly—with failures revealed in other churches of the New Testament record, and then with later, and today's, churches, it will be revealing and very useful to those who desire to please the Lord, and reform themselves with the Spirit, to become a *radiant* Bride again when He returns.

Let me run through a few "failings and failures to obey Christ," as you and I find them, in the inspired and inerrant record of the New Testament church. Please recall that events described in the inspired book of Acts and inspired Letters to the Christian churches, after the founding of the First Christian church in Jerusalem, occurred before Christ gave His Revelation to the Apostle John. The

Lord not only chose to tell us in Revelation 2,3 about the acts of a few early churches (obedient or not) in Asia Province, but inspired the earlier scriptural record of the spread of the church *to all nations* **to teach us, in His New Testament record, that we later churches must not fail Him as some of His early churches did.**

Just a few serious disobediences will suffice, because if your church members are now obedient to Christ's Great Commission (Matt. 28:18–20),they have been taught all these things in the process of reaching full spiritual maturity in Christ. At the same time, this may be a Spiritual eye-opener to readers in failed churches. I hope and pray that acquaintance with Christ's command to "*Teach them*" will lead you to demand new (or renewed) Bible classes for *all*—not just a few—in "your" (really His) church!

A Few Early New Testament Church Failures (To Help Your Church Examine Your Failures!):

1. Acts 5—Ananias and Sapphira (Jerusalem church members):

Failure: individual church members lying to *men, God, and the Holy Spirit* concerning church and personal life.

Cause: Satan in their hearts.

Result: Ananias' and Sapphira's untimely deaths (punished by a Just and Holy God). More importantly, all members (variously weak or strong in their faith), in godly fear, **returned** to being *believers—one in heart and mind* **(in the church body)** (Acts. 4:32).

2. Acts 8—Simon the sorcerer (not then a Christian):

Failure: sought to **buy** the gift of the Holy Spirit, given to Christian believers only.

Cause: Simon's Satan-led practice of God-abhorred evil (sorcery or magic).

Result: (Peter's advice)—*repent of your wickedness, and pray to the Lord for His forgiveness.* The new believers in Samaria (as well as all who read this passage) were strengthened. They and we now know—through this example and others—that God requires all sinful men to **repent** and **believe** in the Risen Christ,

be baptized, and **taught to obey** all that Christ commanded, so the church might be strengthened, *false teachers* denied, and the Body serve Him faithfully in all things. Upon belief, they too will receive the promised gift of the Spirit (Acts 2:38).

3. 1 Corinthians 11:20ff, false teaching and practice of the Lord's Supper, Corinthian church:

Failure: Divisions within the church and abuse of church members, as a result of failure to do as the Lord Commanded as a Memorial to Him and the disciples who founded the church taught.

Cause: Basically, Satan and *false teachers* in the church.

Result: We now have (as they had then) the Lord's teachings about His Memorial "Supper" (in the Gospel books), as reinforced and reminded by Paul's inspired writing, so that all might be brought to obedience, then and now.

Another result: We now know (as they knew then) from Paul's inspired writings, that any unscriptural practice concerning the practice of *taking the cup and the bread*—not according to the Lord's command—is disobedience. Such sin did then, and will in the future, result in *weakness and sickness, even unto death* (falling "*asleep*")—1 Cor. 11:30.

4. Romans 6, False teaching and practice of Christian baptism of believers by the church at Rome (Don't you know?–Rom. 6:3):

Failure: Obviously, the church at Rome—although taught by Paul, others in person, or inspired letters—had been led astray by *false teachers*. Paul, writing to correct them, says *Don't you know?* (sarcasm—haven't you been taught of these things?— for Paul, himself, had taught them!).

Cause: Satan was still present, seeking those whom he would destroy. Disobedient and weak disciples still listen to him as he seeks to destroy their souls, Christ's work, and their service to the Lord.

Result: Falsely or inadequately taught disciples then (and many now) had this true, inspired, vital doctrine of the meaning and purpose of Christian baptism again presented to them in God's inspired and inerrant Word. This important Christian doctrine and practice, detailing the personal identification of the repentant believer (added to the church by immersion baptism as Christ requires) with Christ's death, burial, and resurrection to new life, and us, with Him, is clearly revealed to us in His never-failing Word of Truth. As seen above in connection with abuse of The Lord's Supper, false teaching, and practice, so too the true spiritual meaning and church practice of Christian baptism has been perverted and abused by later churches down to today. Paul's inspired teachings in his Romans 6 "Letter to Rome" help greatly to allow **all** of today's Christian church to throw off men's false teachings and practices, repent, and reform their present disobedience in complete accord with inspired, inerrant and infallible Scripture.

These examples of disobedience and failure did not "happen" because the churches were not well-taught by the Apostles and other godly men. The churches **chose to** listen to *false teachers* who had rejected the Apostle's teachings and later writings in God's Word, instead sowing the Devil's destructive word. Extensive and intensive scriptural teaching by all His church, as commanded by Christ in Matthew 28:20, is still needed. Remember, the church that does not teach all its members fully leaves these spiritual *infants* open to Satan and his *false teachers*. This results in immature, untaught Christians (as those in Eph. 4:14–16) being unable to discern or resist false teachings. The only recourse for such a weak and failing part of Christ's Body is a return to scriptural truths, with repentance and reform, to please the Head of His Body on earth!

Disobedience, in Some "Middle Centuries," to Christ's Words and Commands: *(By the middle centuries, I refer mainly to those centuries between the Apostles' deaths and the so-called "Protestant Reformation.")*

Our knowledge of Christian church disobedience (or hopefully, full obedience) depends upon historical records of the early churches, written by church "scholars," and upon evidence that we have of the later church in printed form. Early handwritten manuscripts, later printed documents, and—in the case of those churches who exist today—church information in print media, television, and radio, etc., are available to show us the extent of church obedience or disobedience. In some cases, public records (Creeds, faith statements, books, etc.) allow us to observe how the New Testament doctrines and practices that govern the Christian church over the centuries were actually carried out in early, later and today's churches. They help us see how much or how little past churches have pleased their Divine Head. And the records will show members and leaders of present-day "children of these parent churches" what they must do **today** to please Him personally (Who gave Himself up for us)—Ephesians 5:2.

Some churches' **"traditions"**—certain portions of their faith, doctrine and practices—are not faithfully derived and copied from the inspired, inerrant Written Word, but given to some church human "heads" by disobedient "Church Teachers" or "theologians." Wrongfully approved by the church's human leaders as equal to Scripture, some infer that such continuing, Bible-opposing "traditions" are God's Truth, blessed and approved by Him simply because they are long-lasting. Satan is smiling at these falsehoods. Such lies, worthy of himself, will cause the wrath of God to descend on sinful men. I do not say all "church 'traditions' are false, and should be rejected." But some church "traditions" are false and are seen as such when compared with the Spirit of Truth's Guidance with God's Inspired, Inerrant Word of Truth. Some "traditions" are false; and some even oppose God's Word.

Well-taught, Bible-believing Christian Seminary and church teachers and observers can see, with the aid of the inspired, inerrant Word, and the *Spirit of Truth,* that some parts of some church traditions fall into the **false teacher** category of sinful acts of these churches. Discerning, Bible-believing readers will note, too, that some of these churches negate Divine scriptural truths by **adding** to the Word of God these imperfect, often false church traditions. Some imperfect church traditions are composed of men's errant **misinterpretations of** God's Word (**not made** with the *Spirit of Truth*'s counsel). In these cases their leader-approved acceptances of many false and often scripturally-opposed teachings, as a "supplement" to God's Written Word to His Son's church, adds to these churches' sinful determination *not* to teach God's infallible Holy Word alone to members of these churches, but rather to *control their churches* by means of "additions to the Bible"—while discouraging full oral teaching of Scripture by church leaders. While the Roman Catholic church may be the prime endorser of "Traditions" (right or wrong, according to God's Word or not), many other Christian churches are guilty of adding to, or even opposing, the Word of God, by claiming equal authority for their written "Traditions" or "Statements of Faith" or "Creeds." Does the Christian church *need these* often-errant "Statements of Faith," including doctrines and practises not found in Scripture? I believe these are human replacements and substitutes for the churches' failures (generally) to teach the Bible—including *all that I* (Christ) *have commanded you*—to *all church members*, as the Lord asked His church to do. Creeds and Statements of Faith, too, are human substitutes for His Body, the church, standing upon the *entire Word* of God alone, when under attack by cults, *false teachers*, "liberals, modernists, New Agers," and the many agents of Satan who attack a True Christian New Testament church today that holds to the *faith once delivered to the saints* (Jude 3). Some church Creed or Faith Statements are errant—either because the are incomplete, or add to Scripture, I believe that all of these "external statements" (of often errant men)—purporting to define and guide the Christian church in *addition* to God's inspired, infallible and *sufficient* Word to the church—are completely *unnecessary*, and may be Satan's words in disguised biblical forms. Errant Creeds lead to church division, not church Unity, as Christ requires (John 17). No creed can state Bible Truths fully; discard them in favour of the full Bible.

So many evidences of disobedience and false teachings and practices are observed in the churches of these middle centuries, that I must limit their number to just a few. Let me now quote a few more disobedient acts of historical, traditional or present churches. Consider them (with the Spirit) as Christ does—lovingly, but justly and truthfully.

1. Church "Hierarchical" or "Organizational" Disobedience.

The Spirit reveals what God and His Son require that His church know, and be, and do in obedience to Him. First received in person from Him by the Apostles, the Lord's teachings and commands were given orally to the early New Testament church Body. The inspired Apostles, together with other Spirit-Gifted men, taught and led the then-small Body to do all that the Lord Commanded. With only the occasional visit to outlying regions, *the Apostles (with later "Elders) formed the Jerusalem church leadership organization,* together with the "seven men" chosen by the church (Acts 6). These later inspired men's duties (as *Deacons* or *"church servants aiding the Elders"*) were to carry out church ministries not required to be done by the Apostle/leaders, and thus relieve the latter to carry out *the ministry of the Word* of God...*and prayer* (Acts 6:3,4). The church grew and spread to *all nations,* as Christ commanded, with the Apostle Paul, Barnabas, Philip, and others going in obedience to many cities and countries of the then-Roman world, where they formed new churches of Christ from the disciples that they made, baptized, and taught. These missionary leaders *taught the new disciples-believers in the new churches to obey all that Christ had commanded the first disciples.* Some founder/leaders stayed (as at Antioch—Acts 11) and taught the new believers, as Christ had commanded (Matt. 28:18–20) for more than a year! Teaching the Word fully matures all members—and leaders!

It was the Apostle Paul however, inspired by the Holy Spirit, who saw the need in the new churches for wise and godly male leaders, *full of faith and the Spirit of God,* to guide teaching, church growth, worship and practices, and minister to the new disciples' needs for, knowledge of, and obedience to, Christ the supreme Head of the church. Leaders, under Christ the Divine Head, were needed to guide the church, teach disciples and oppose *false teachers* who had crept into the church (Ex. Tit.1; 2 Pet. 2:1). The Apostles, it seems, belatedly felt led to go to Samaria and Judea, but not much further than Antioch, as the book of Acts describes some of their journeys. The Spirit led

Paul and his assistants to establish more remote Christian churches on three missionary journeys; stay awhile to baptize and teach new believers; appoint wise and godly men as Elders (or Overseers) and Deacons, before moving on to new opportunities to serve the Lord—always led by the Spirit.

In Titus 1:5, the inspired Paul tells Titus to appoint Elders in the Body everywhere a new church was established, and describes their qualifications as church leaders, under the Divine Head. Then in 1 Timothy 4:14, Paul reminds his protege-helper (and church leader or "Overseer"), Timothy, not to neglect *the gift* he received when a *body of elders laid hands on you* (to ordain him as church leader at Ephesus). In chapter 2, Paul advises him on worship in the church, and goes on in chapter 3 to describe **both elders and deacons as leaders,** with their qualifications for these two **unique** "offices" of male leadership in the churches, under Christ the Head. Note too, that in 1 Corinthians 12:28, in his great spiritual letter to the church at Corinth, with all its problems and difficulties, Paul speaks under the Spirit's directions about *the Spirit's gifts,* and says to the church (all churches and us today): *Now, you are the Body of Christ, and each one of you is a part of it. And in the church, God has appointed...* and he goes on to speak of all disciples who are Spirit-gifted to meet the needs of the members, to carry out Christ's Will for His Body, the church. All disciples in the Body are not all apostles, or prophets, *nor do all have all the gifts of the Spirit.* But certainly church leaders, and teachers, and those with Spirit-given gifts of administration, and of helping others, etc. are necessary for the church. Men with special spiritual qualities are chosen by the Spirit and appointed by the church as leaders and helper/Deacons to guide the Body under the counsel of the Spirit and the Headship of Christ, also appointed by God (Eph. 1:22).

It is very important that we hear the Spirit and apply the Word, as given us in Scripture through Spirit-led men in the early church, to the subject of church leadership organization . We know from the Word of God that Christ's Body, the church, was then—and must be now—led on earth by certain gender-specific and unique leaders, with certain special qualifications, and duties—and no others. All are under the Headship of Christ, and guided by the Holy Spirit. Scripture and the Spirit reveal that— except for the unique case of the "First Baptist Christian church at Jerusalem" (as I call it, from scriptural descriptions of what it was and did, as Christ's first church formed)—*all other* local Christian churches in the whole world, through all the centuries until the Lord comes again, must have *male leaders only* (called "Elders," "Overseers," "Pastors," "Shepherds," or infrequently, "Bishops," (all synonymous) by scriptural definitions, with Deacons or Servant helpers). Additionally, according to the inspired New Testament Scripture for the Christian church, we will see no more unique Apostles assigned to lead the later church; nor will there be any human "Head or Heads" of groups or "Empires of churches" or "denominations," *or any other unscriptural "hierarchy" of human organizations over local churches.* For Scripture states: Churches of Christ must be self-governing, with human "overseers" guiding each local Body with the aid of the Spirit, under the Divine Head alone. Any human attempt—past, present or future—to pervert and set aside Christ's sole and only Divine "Headship" of His Body, or His human leadership organization in the Christian church on earth, is wrong, inspired by Satan, and must be repented of by such hierarchies. They must be dismantled, and reformed to agree with the Lord's inspired Word, before He comes to claim His *Holy, sinless and Radiant Bride.*

We know, too, from Scripture (mostly from Paul's inspired writings on the gifts of the Spirit, given to all believers in the church only as He wills, to meet Christ's Will and purpose for His Body) that all these believers, with their diverse gifts, are valuable to Him and essential to those within the local church Body—but that not all members may serve in leadership positions, defined as "Elders" and "Deacons" in Paul's inspired letters to the church. I hasten to add that the Apostles, Christ's chosen 12 (reduced to 11 with Judas' betrayal), leaders under Christ the Head in His First Church in Jerusalem, according to His purpose at that time, lived and died as leaders of only one church, and were not appointed by any other New Testament churches to be "Elders" to other bodies.

Yes, in 1 Corinthians 12, Paul speaks of God appointing, and the Spirit giving, gifts to the church—and he includes "Apostles." But I believe that he was speaking generally, while not listing all the gifts that the Spirit "Wills to give"—and I believe that other inspired Scripture, by the same inspired writer, tells us that, following the Apostles' deaths, only **two** "church leaders" (defined in 1 Tim. 3, as "Elders and Deacons") are needed and required (by Scripture and the Lord) as church leaders. *False teachers'* and false leaders' attempts to add upon Scriptures' two leader positions is false teaching, disobedient to God's written Word. Church members gifted with other Spirit gifts, as spoken of in 1 Corinthians 12, Romans 12, Ephesians 4 and elsewhere, are not to be leaders of the church as are Elders (or Overseers, or Pastors—synonymous titles), but are men **and** women equipped by the Spirit as helpers to the Elders and the congregation (as are male-only Deacons), who meet Christ's Will and purpose for His Body. **Two male scriptural church officers only (1 Tim. 3)** (NB: Officer means leader in Elder or Deacon positions.)

The only two scripturally-required and spiritually legitimate church "leadership positions" (offices) for the Christian church are the offices of "Elder, Overseer, or Pastor (all synonymous)" and *the office of "Deacon,"* with additional helpers (not in a third "office," but gifted by the Spirit *to serve and meet all the further needs* of any particular local church Body not supplied in the two noted church offices.)

But after the deaths of all the Apostles, and in the centuries following, and up to today, *what do we find in many churches of Jesus Christ, in terms of leadership offices, under Christ, the only Divine and True Head* (Eph. 5:23)? Sadly, we find—in very many churches—a great many unscriptural (therefore false) church offices. These represent a complete departure, from the Inspired Scriptures and from our Lord's desires, as given by the Spirit through inspired New Testament writers to His Body on earth. We find, from history, and knowledge of past churches, and from many churches continuing on to today, that disobedient churches have established not only scriptural "Elders" or "Deacons" alone, **but added offices not inspired, written down for the church by God, or required by the Spirit or the Lord.**

We find local churches led by *"Priests,"* in contradiction to the inspired Word of God. A priest is certainly biblical, often referred to in the Old Testament record of God's provision of a religious system and a Temple of Worship to His Chosen People, the Jews. But we are instructed in the New Testament that the Law, the Prophets, and the Jews' religious system are not given to, or binding upon the Christian church—only given to the Jews (see the inspired Paul, and others, in Romans and elsewhere). Additionally, 1 Peter 2:9 states *we* Christians are *all a royal priesthood*, and therefore we are all priests in a "ministering" sense. How can churches appoint a leader called **priest** over members who are scripturally all priests? The Truth? Such an unscriptural office is wrong and opposes Christ's Written Will for His church. I have quoted much New Testament Scripture in this book describing problems caused in the early Christian church by some "converted Jewish Christians," as well as the converted Christian-Jewish Apostles, themselves, who often were bewildered in their "church" misunderstanding of what Christ wanted of them as Christians. Their Lord led the Apostles out on His first mission to preach the gospel of salvation at first to the Jews alone. Then, after the Jewish leaders' rejection and hostility, the Lord Willed to build His church and extend God's Mercy and salvation to all races— spoken of as Gentile unbelievers. Many early Jewish converts, even the Eleven Apostles, did not understand or seemingly support the Lord fully in His Will and Purpose for the church to go to *all* (Gentile) *nations.* Today also, Christian churches sometimes confuse the Jewish **religion** (given to Jews alone by God), and the Christian **religion** (the church Willed into being by Christ, mainly for Gentiles)—and wrongly try to urge their followers to apply God's separate, uniquely- and specifically-given Laws to **both** groups. Christian readers should all be aware that they are not under Jewish Law, as the inspired Paul writes in his letters to various churches (Rom. 3; 6:15 and elsewhere in Scripture). Christians must follow inspired instructions found in the Christian New Testament only for the church.

The use of the office of "priest" in the Christian church, is contrary to the New Testament Word of God, inspired and inerrant. The naming and use of any church leader other than male Elders and Deacons (see 1 Tim. 3) opposes Scripture and should be repented of, and corrected, by the disobedient church.

Many church organizations in the past, and today, have added such "church offices" as **"Bishops"**—not over one local Body, as Scripture requires, but as some men's wrongful desire for an "Extended Elder" over many local churches—**"Arch-Bishops"**; **"Cardinals,"** etc., all topped up by a scripturally-foreign "office" called the **"Papacy"** over their great hierarchy of churches. All this is foreign to New Testament organizational commands of Christ, the sole Head, given us by inspired, holy, scriptural writers. Adding false church leaders, created by *false teachers*, also divides the whole Body of Christ that our Lord prayed would be *one as* He *and the Father are One* in all things —John 17. Some Christian churches today and in the past are observed to be led by "Supreme leaders" called "Popes" or "Patriarchs," and also have, wrongly, a multitude of lesser, unscriptural church "dignitaries," culminating in this foreign (to Scripture) local church "head" called a "Priest." Other Christian "state churches" (unscripturally state-assisted, financed, and controlled) have as their overall "head" of many local Christian church bodies, a **"King" or "Queen" as an unscriptural "head."** Whether nominal or not, these unnecessary, unscriptural church offices all have the false distinction of being placed in or over their church bodies in defiant opposition to the inspired, inerrant Word of God in the New Testament for the church— which states that Jesus Christ only is True Head of His church on earth, and allows only Elders or Deacons to guide His church.

When disobedient church bodies, who claim scriptural authority for their hierarchies, and multiplicity of offices, names, and duties are examined with the Spirit of God, the New Testament Scriptures, the Words of Christ and those of inspired holy men, they give the lie to their false organization and claims. Many of these disobedient bodies, too, claim complete allegiance to the Bible—then *add their claim* that their church has authority to interpret the Word of God to please themselves.

Error (sin) category:

When compared to the examples derived from the "Seven Church Types" seen in Revelation 2 and 3, the above error can be clearly seen to be that of allowing *false teachers in the church* to distort Scripture, substitute their own interpretations (made without regard for God's Word or the Holy Spirit), and claim authority over and above the Word of Truth. In fact, they deny the inspired Word of God, and choose to elevate themselves above the True Head of the Church (Jesus Christ) as many of Israel's Kings did (over God) in the past in their religion.

2. Unscriptural Infant Baptism, followed by Unscriptural "Confirmation" in Later Years.

This has been discussed previously in this book, but is inserted here, because it is a very large and serious sin problem in many churches of past centuries and today.

Error category:

Present in many "Catholic" as well as many "Protestant" churches today, This error is also in the same category of error as 1 above—namely, that of *false teachers* in the church (2 Pet. 2:1). Those that practise this, in defiance of Scripture, face important eternal consequences—for it affects the souls of those baptized and saved (they say) as infants, as well as making their so-called "confirmation" a mockery: a sham and a deceitful act, for human motives of (possibly) pride and power in the numbers "added" in this errant way to the church of Jesus Christ.

3. "Lord's Supper" Disobedience.

Churches that are guilty of these problems are scripturally

condemned by God's written Word of Truth. *False teachers* in the church is a convenient categorization. It is not only this, but represents also the categories of *being dead spiritually, being asleep spiritually,* and even *forsaking their first love.* These deliberately disobedient acts, taught falsely, oppose His written Word to His church members.

In disobeying the *Lord's Supper* command and the Divine teachings of Christ—reinforced again in Scripture by the inspired Paul—we find, if we examine church history extending down to the present, that the Lord's direct teachings about His Supper in Matthew 26, Mark 14 and Luke 22, have been, and are now, often distorted by many errant church leaders in continued disobedience to the Lord's Words to His church.

Though they may call it a "Mass" (from the Latin "*Missa,*" probably taken from the Roman church's "concluding dismissal of attendants" in their—not Christ's—remembrance ceremony), these errant churches I describe depart drastically from the *Lord's Supper* instituted personally by Christ as read in the Gospels noted. Christ gave **first the bread** (representing His Body), and then **the wine,** (representing His soon-to-be-shed Blood) to **all** of His disciples present. Luke records that the Lord, when handing all His disciples the bread, said *do this (all that I do—*author) *in Remembrance of Me.* Paul, in 1 Corinthians 11, tells the disobedient ones in the church at Corinth who had abused the Lord's Supper, that He had *received of the Lord* what he had *passed on to them* and described how the Lord had asked His Body members to **each take** the bread, and **each take** the wine *in Remembrance of Me.* All the records (Matthew, Mark, Luke—and Paul, by vision) **report faithfully what the Lord said and did** in this "Remembrance Ceremony to be observed in future by all in His church:" He gave **each disciple** a portion of the "broken bread" and the "wine," symbolic of His soon-to-be crucified Body and His Blood shed for the whole sinful world on Calvary's Cross. The Word is inerrant; only men distort the truth.

After this three-fold description of the Lord's Words and actions with and for His disciples then, and us in the future,

what did the Roman Catholic and many Protestant churches do (and still do today) in their false and unscriptural observances in "their" churches? Instead of offering **both His** symbolic "Body" **and His** symbolic "Blood" (i.e. both the bread and wine) to **every Christian** believer-participant in the Lord's Supper, they offer only the symbolic Body (bread) to members, and the **"priest" alone drinks** of the wine of Remembrance. The observance commanded by Christ for all in His church to observe in solemn and grateful remembrance of the One Who died for them was **divided** into two Scripture-denying parts, **in disobedience to the Lord**, and against His commands.

In addition, the Roman church (and other Protestant churches) distorted the True scriptural meaning, intent, and purpose of Christ's "Supper" of "Remembering our Lord's Sacrifice for us all," by their *false teachers*, with the support of unscriptural church heads. They twisted the Lord's clear statements about the bread and the wine as representing or picturing **symbolically** His Body and Blood. The Roman church (and others) declares, on the church's authority—men's, not Christ's—that the priest and his words **change** Christ's material Supper elements into the **actual, present, body and blood of the Lord.** This is false teaching, obviously meant to gain power and control of their untaught members. Christ Himself was physically present (His Incarnate Body, and Blood) when He instituted this first *Lord's Supper,* as we call it now. He was observed by real disciples, in His real Body, coursing with real Blood, at the very moment He declared (holding up, first, the humanly-produced pieces of bread, then cups of humanly-produced wine). He said, *This is my body ...this is my blood.* No reasonable, unbiased Christian, guided by the Holy Spirit, could read His Words and confuse His real Presence, Body, and Blood with the symbolic representations of these in the human food offered. Some churches, however, wrongly do this to this day. "Transubstantiation" is the coined errant scholar's word for the Roman Catholic church's faulty interpretation of the true, scriptural (Christ's) **symbolic presence only** in this Christ-ordered act of **Remembering Him until He comes again.**

212

Error category:

Undoubtedly caused by *false teachers in the church,* (2 Pet. 2:1) this is also, by its very nature, a deliberate negation of what Christ wanted. As they ate and drank the **symbols** of His Body and Blood, and thus were drawn closer to Him, Christ intended His disciples to experience and remember Him in His death, burial, and Resurrection. It is futile to try to trace the origin of this errant "Lord's Supper." But note, Paul said, *Whenever you eat this bread* **and** *drink this cup, you proclaim the Lord's death till He comes* (1 Cor. 11:26). **Withholding the "cup" from Roman Catholic participants withholds something spiritually necessary and precious from the believer's Remembrance in that body.** What is withheld, I believe, from Christ's own Words, is the Divine Presence from the believer-participant. What is lost to them—unless the church repents and returns to the True Supper, celebrated faithfully in the way the Lord told us to do—is the true, full Remembrance of His atonement act on Calvary. Also lost is their true part, as full members of His Body, in proclaiming His death (once for all, and **not** repeated every time in an errant "Mass"), and proclaiming His coming again in glory. No one knows the effects of these false teachings, except Christ.

4. The Church organization "Gender and Authority" Disobedience Problem.

In 1 Timothy 2:11,12 the inspired Paul, says to the church: *I do not permit a woman to teach or have authority over a man.* In verses 13 and 14 of the same chapter, he is inspired to give the reason for this admonition, going back to the Creation of man. Paul addresses Eve's first submission to Satan's temptations and her first disobeying of God's instructions to Adam and her: *You must not eat of the fruit of the tree of the knowledge of good or evil or you will surely die* (Gen. 2:17). Paul adds, in his inspired teaching on this subject to the church, *and Adam was not the one deceived* (first —writer); *it was the woman who was deceived* (first) *and became a sinner* (1 Tim. 2:14.).

In the same Letter to Timothy (1 Tim. 3), the Pastor of the church at Ephesus, Paul was *moved by the Spirit* to write on the subject of Christian church leadership organization. He wrote: it is to consist **only** of **male Christian Elders, Overseers, or Pastors and male Deacons** guiding, teaching and helping the church members, under Christ the True Head of His Body. These paraphrased words, when examined in detail, with the Spirit, are God speaking to us through an inspired man, and the facts of man's fall from grace in Gen. 3 support Paul's inspired teachings to the church.

Most Christian churches, over the early centuries since the First Christian church was established by the Spirit (guided and taught by male Apostles, then by gifted male leaders and male members), have complied with the written Word of God I have just quoted. Certain women caused difficulties in some early exceptions, noted especially in Christ's Revelation to John (Ch. 2 and 3), by trying to introduce false teaching of cults into the church.

Within the past century, many formerly faithful Christian churches have listened to the false teachings of women (and some men), who denied the Apostle Paul's inspired words on church offices, and have countered with their irrelevant, often out of context Scriptural passages concerning "the equality of men and women in God's eyes." Many church Overseers or Pastors have discarded the clear, unequivocal teachings of Christ in the inspired New Testament, and adopted, falsely, the recent "modernist movement" by women in some churches. Some women, defying Scripture, have taken errant places in the church, assuming authority over men, and teaching men in the church, in contradiction to the inspired Word of God (1 Tim. 2:12–14). Scripture, in 1 Timothy 3, confirms that the gender of "Overseers or Elders, and Deacons" is male only (*husband of one wife*). Many of today's churches, opposing God's Word, are appointing female Pastors and Deacons as having equal scriptural "rights" with men. This is wrong, and Christ some day will *repay* these "errant deeds" *in kind, according to their deeds* (see Rev. 2:23).

214

Women in the Church (ancient and modern) have many other important roles to play for Christ in His Body the Church. Scripture tells us that Christian women can be, and often are, *gifted by the Spirit* to teach women and children, and exercise gifts of helping, hospitality, and service—as well as any other gifts He may give them *as He Wills.*

Nevertheless, many women in the church today, tempted by the Devil and false male teachers, try (and sometimes wrongly succeed) to teach and *have authority over men* and have set their hearts wrongly on these very, forbidden things. Satan, false male advisers, and many of these women in today's churches, say things such as: "...since Jesus, His disciples, Apostles, and ancient male teachers lived in a patriarchal society, and wrote things reflecting this society, it is an error to say that we, in our modern, technological society—where most women have many more "equality rights" than in the past—should follow Scripture of the past."

Part of what they say may be true (about "patriarchal societies" of the past, only). However, true Christian believers cannot deny that the Head of the church, Jesus Christ, and His Spirit Who moved holy men to write His Words, is dealing with His Body only—not with worldly "societies," or "cultures" outside the church, patriarchal or some other form. Whether Satan, *false teachers,* or falsely taught and supported women in the church like it or not, God, in the Person of His incarnate Risen Son (Whose Word does not change), has told us how to organize and establish His spiritual Body, the church on earth, for Him. *If we love Him, we are to obey His every teaching in His inspired Word.* Women's, and men's, "modern errors" come from insufficient Bible teaching in the church today.
Error category:

Allowing church women to *teach* and *have authority over men* is obviously within the general category of being prompted by *false teachers* in the church. It is just as obviously related to other categories, described by the Lord Himself in His Revelation to the Seven Churches of Revelation 2 and 3, and to all churches down to today. Disobedience on the part of some churches, in allowing women to *teach* and *have authority over men,* and appointing them as "Elders" or "Deacons," or falsely, as "Priest," in some state churches—contrary to Scripture—may be seen by these churches as small and insignificant steps closer to their human, prideful, desires.

Like it or not, if churches of past centuries and today (all members and leaders) cannot and will not accept the written Word of God (particularly the New Testament for the church) as fully inspired, inerrant and infallible in all that the Spirit led holy men to write about, they are disobedient and failing churches, with only two choices. These are, paraphrased in the Words of Christ: "Repent, and *do the things* of mine *you did at first,* and receive your rewards"; or, "Continue to deny Me and God's sanctifying, Holy Word of Truth, and receive a terrible punishment for disobedience" (cf. Rev. 2 and 3 for Spirit-led confirmation). Scripture is God's Word to men; not men's word to men. To this writer, and many faithful Bible-believers and true Christians—and to God, Whose Word is sanctifying Truth—this fatal step will lead to further false and disobedient steps that oppose Scripture, and cause the errant Body to further displease and wound Christ. ***They do this by doing deliberately what He asks us not to do.***

A good test for members and leaders in the Christian church today is to ask themselves what the converse, or opposite of John 14:23, *If anyone loves me, he will obey my Commands* means to them. In all of Christ's Words of Teaching, Command, and Love, a common thread of Holiness and Justice is seen. If we deny His Holy inspired Word, and substitute the false teaching of men (and women) who pervert and disobey Scripture, His Holiness and Justice requires that we, in disobedient churches, will pay for our tolerance, apathy and false deeds, before, or when He comes again (and soon, Rev. 22:7,20).

Part 5. Eternal Consequences of Church Disobedience
to the Divine Head.

Chapter 10

Loss of Rewards;
Dismissal From the Lord's Presence
...Or Worse?

As I move on in my Spirit-led purpose, to warn disobedient churches today on behalf of Christ, again I urge my Christian readers to read the scriptural Words of truth that I quote from the New Testament, always with the counsel and guidance of the *Spirit of Truth*. Each person who hears the Gospel, is convicted of sin by the Spirit, who repents of sin and confesses belief in the Risen Christ, the Son of the Living God, experiences this **Spirit of Truth**. God's own Spirit, His gift to every believer, will lead us to God's Truth always—trust Him!

Consequences of Christian church failures and disobedience:

Loss of "rewards."

In previous parts and chapters, as we studied Christ's Revelation to the Apostle John—particularly the first two or three chapters of the inspired New Testament final Book of "God's Revelation to man"—we noted that the Lord, in speaking to the *Seven churches* (and all His later churches) spoke words of condemnation (many!) and words of commendation (a few!) to these Seven Church examples. *Jesus wept* over disobedient Messiah-rejecting Jerusalem (Luke 19:41); He weeps too, over His failing disobedient church today, spiritually *lukewarm...sleeping...forsaking Him* and His inspired Word of Truth!

In my study and brief analysis of my purpose in writing this book, and of Christ's Purpose in building an effective, *sinless, blameless, Radiant* church in this evil world, I tried to extract a few of the many ancient church "sin variations," and diverse problems for reader's study and consideration. I made a list of the seven churches' (Rev. 2,3) failings, and commented upon Christ's promises of *rewards* that He would grant to those who repented (turned away) from sin, and returned to faithful obedience. It is important for members and leaders of today's churches to recall these sins, and rewards, for our Lord is coming soon and look for obedience and faithfulness—not failure and outright and deliberate disobedience to Him and His Word. Churches, do not take His Words lightly—examine yourselves for error before He comes.

Our Lord and Saviour, Head of the church that He *Willed to build,* with mostly Gentile believers making up His "Body on earth," did not hesitate to ask John to write to the Seven (as well as to all later) Churches. Nor hesitate to not only talk about their disobedience (and our sinning against Him), but to speak of their future if they *overcome* their failings, by *repenting* and *doing the things they did at first.* He spoke too, in Holy Scripture, of His *rewards* to be given to repentant sin-*overcomers,* when He returns to claim His *Radiant Bride* and take her to Heaven. **But what if He finds many of His churches wrinkled, and stained with sin?** Remember—He, God, does not change.

I do not hesitate to suggest that many of my readers (with the exception of a few members, leaders, and professors of religion) would read my summary today, and say, **"I never knew that!"** A few decades ago, the percentage of scriptural knowledge taught and retained would be much higher in the Christian churches and in the seminaries that taught Pastors/teachers. Churches then (not all, but some) were much more faithful to Christ's Commission Command to...*teach them* (new believers) *to obey all that I have commanded you* (Christ's Words to His future church in Matthew 28:20).

Now, let's turn again to Revelation 2,3 with the *Spirit of Truth* to guide us. Our Lord talked often in these chapters about one eternal good consequence—that is, eternal *rewards* for obedience and faithfulness on the part of a few, many, or, hopefully all of His Body, the church. Let's talk now about some of these *rewards* for faithful and fully obedient Christians. First, what they are not. They are not material, not worldly, and are not given until Christ comes again, and the *radiant churches* (Eph. 5:27) meet him in the air and return with Him to their heavenly home (cf: 1 Thess. 4:16ff). They are not given to churches as such, but are given to faithful individuals who compose **His church "Body"** (many "local churches" united in one Body on earth).

The rewards are spiritual, for faithful Christians go to a spiritual Heaven with glorified bodies. Second, while they are spiritual and heavenly in nature, they also reveal a future practical conveyance of authority, and a revealing knowledge to others that the reward is given for faithfulness, by this Christ Who alone has been given *All authority in heaven and on earth...* (Matt. 28:18).

Third, what His rewards for faithfulness are is difficult to explain in earthly terms—simply because, while they will be given and used (or revealed to others) on earth perhaps as well as in Heaven, they differ so greatly from worldly human expectations, and standards of earthly rewards, that they are hard to comprehend—even by very well-taught and spiritually-mature Christians.

Nevertheless, with the counsel and guidance of the *Spirit of Truth* in every believer (and much less reliance upon the teachings of men, who may be and often are tempted to yield to Satan), we can examine these *rewards* offered by Christ to those who *overcome* evil or who repent and reform disobedience, and see rewards with the *mind of the Lord* (1 Cor. 2:16). With the Spirit, too, we can see what they really are, as explained in Revelation 2 and 3 to these Seven ancient Churches (and to us today!).

Examples of Future Rewards For Church and Individual Obedience and Faithfulness:

The church at Ephesus (Rev. 2:1–7)

After speaking of their great failure—*You have forsaken your first love...You have fallen* from a great spiritual *height*—Christ, in Revelation 2:7b., says: *To him who overcomes* (these failures) *I will give* (a reward:) *the right to eat from the tree of life, which is in the paradise of God.* Most Bible students will agree that *the tree of life* is a direct reference to the creation and placement of mankind in the *paradise of God* which is called Eden. Here He speaks of the *over-comer's reward* as the future state in which faithful believers will be restored to the perfect relationship and fellowship with God our first ancestors once had in the beginning of created life on earth.

The consequence of continuing in sin and disobedience, and of not overcoming evil, is directly implied in Verse 2:7b. That is, if the members of the Body of Christ, the church, do not overcome evil, they will not receive the reward of eternal life in righteous fellowship with God hereafter.

The church in Smyrna (Rev. 2:8–11)

To the *faithful in Smyrna* (and to later churches, and us! — *author*) Christ says, *Be faithful, even to the point of death, and I will give you* (His reward) *the crown of life.* This church represents those who Christ predicts will experience an increase of persecution, even to death. Such circumstances have existed in the past, exist today, and will exist in the future—because Christ told us, in Mark 13, of terrible things that will occur before He comes again to claim His *radiant* Bride. The reward given by the Lord, for faithfulness of Christians in their churches and in the world, is *the crown of* **(eternal)** *life.* The Greek word for *crown* does not refer to a royal crown, but rather is a type of garland worn on the head, as given to an athlete who wins an athletic contest. The symbolism is a confirmation that Christians in the Body of Christ who remain faithful will receive eternal life for *overcoming* as promised in Scripture.

The consequence of unfaithfulness, however, must be the direct opposite of receiving *the crown of life.* It must be **a withdrawal of** unfaithful Christians from eternal life, because they have not repented and reformed their disobedience to the Lord on this earth, while they were part of His Body, the church.

The church in Pergamum (Rev. 2: 12–17).

To the *overcomers of evil*—evil represented by following *false teachers,* and tolerating teachers of false cults and religions in their church midst, Christ says: *I will give some of the hidden manna.* "Manna" refers to food from Heaven, given to the Jews who travelled in the desert towards the Promised Land, led and supported by God (Ref. Ps. 78:24). *Hidden* means it was hidden from Pergamum in contrast to the unclean food of the Balaamites, the food sacrificed to their idols, that was openly tolerated by unfaithful Christians within the church. Secondly, if the disobedient ones *overcame* this, and other evils and false teachings in the church, Christ would also give them a second reward for faithfulness with repentance—namely, *a white stone with a new name written on it, known only to him who receives it.* Bible scholars—familiar with the many false, pagan gods, and "religions" of those ancient days—tell us that certain kinds of stones were used as tokens for various purposes (meaningful to the wearer and observers). They tell us that, in the context of a future Messianic banquet, such a stone would probably be used for the purpose of admission. The *new name*, they say, likely refers to such a name as mentioned in Isaiah 62:2—a name revealing the righteousness of the wearer. Again, the rewards for overcoming sin, noted by Christ in His Word to this church and future churches (such as the ones we serve Him in today), must also have a Divine and Blessed consequence. Those who do not, and will not, repent and overcome evil, must endure the direct, terrible, opposite consequences mentioned by Christ throughout these Revelations to His church.

The church in Thyatira (Rev. 2:18–29).

Christ says to the faithless, disobedient ones in His Body, the church: *I will repay each of you according to your deeds.* His rewards, I suggest, must also (but not necessarily) reflect the good deeds that the faithful, repentant overcomers do for Him, Who is the Head of His church on earth (and for others). He speaks of His direct punishment of evil *false teachers* and their adherents in the church, making them suffer for their deeds. But for His Body members, *who overcome (and do His Will to the end),* He says: *I will give* (him) *authority over the nations—just as I received authority from my Father* (Ref. Ps. 2:9; Rev. 3:26,), referring to the future times of His second coming and millennial rule. Here, too, Christ offers a second reward for overcomers: *I will also give him the morning star.* Referring to Revelation 22:16, we see the Lord Himself referred to there as the *Root and Off-Spring of*

David and also as *the bright Morning Star.* The Apostle Peter refers to the latter title as the Person of Jesus Christ, in 2 Peter 1:19, Who will "rise" for believers in their hearts, as a new day dawns and the morning star lights the earth, with a promise of a new day and a new life. These *rewards* for overcomers, given by the Lord to all overcomers in all His "overcoming bodies," are remarkably similar in that, while they use imagery from both the Old and New Testaments, they are applied here to Christian believers and Christian churches of all times, all cultures, and all societies. They speak of rewards for all faithful members of Christ's church of all ages, to confirm His promises for faithfulness (full obedience) given to us in His unchanging, inspired Word. And once again, rewards for faithfulness, and lack of rewards for unfaithfulness and unrepentance show us the consequences of both opposite actions by His Body, the church, of all ages.

The church at Sardis (Rev. 3:1–6).

In this *spiritually dead* church, just a few disciples were found to be unstained by sin. For the faithful, the Lord promises: *they will walk with me, dressed in white* (symbolizing their unstained—hence pure white—souls). This is their reward for faithfulness in a spiritually dead church. Although it is not called a "reward," it is a wonderful promise. To be able to walk in Divine Fellowship with their (and our!) Lord in the everlasting Future (Heaven). For the remainder of the "dead" church congregation, for those who *hear what the Spirit says to the churches,* who *wake up,* recognize their sin, **and repent of it**—they, too, will be dressed in white. And because they have repented, the Lord tells them, He *will never blot out* the repentant overcomers' names *from the book of life.*

This book of life is first mentioned in Ex. 32:32–33, when the Lord speaks to Moses concerning a *registry* of those who sin against Him. But in this context, with Christ speaking to Christians in His church on earth, it is much more likely that this is the *Lamb's book of life* noted in Revelation 21:27, where impure souls (unrepentant, and thus, unrestored by God) cannot enter the *New Jerusalem* but *only those whose names are written in this book.* The consequences for repentant "overcomers" is a happy one, for they will be in Heaven, forever with their forgiving Lord. Those who are *spiritually dead* and do not *wake up* and *repent* of their sins (Rev. 2,3) will suffer the final deletion of their names from the Lord's *book of* (future, eternal) *life*, the consequence of which is eternal death.

The church in Philadelphia (Rev. 3: 7–13)

In this relatively obedient church, under persecution from hostile Jews, and of *little strength*, the Lord finds Christians are still faithful, for the Lord *knows their deeds*. They have kept His Word, and have not denied His Name. They have also kept the Lord's command *to endure patiently* (as paraphrased by author)—and because of this, His reward (although not so-called) is that He will keep them from a world-wide future trial: the *tribulation* (Rev. 7:14). Although the Raptured church will be spared, through the Lord's Mercy, the tribulation will test all those who still live on the earth on that terrible day.

The Lord reiterates a wonderful phrase I have quoted often in this book: *I am coming soon!* He asks the Philadelphia church (and all those weak but faithful churches down through the centuries to today) to *hold on to what you have* of His teaching and faith—so that *no one will take your crown* (see Smyrna). To the overcomers, who hold out against the Evil One and his hostile, persecuting agents, the Lord promises to make *a pillar in the Temple of my God*. Extreme symbolism, perhaps—but how wonderful a promise, to be seen as an upright, righteous, outstanding and faithful disciple of the Lord, in the New Heaven and/or the New Earth!

The church in Laodicea (Rev. 3:14–22)

To this *lukewarm church*, one that Christ wished was either hot or cold, but not the way it was, He says *I am about to spit you out...!* **What a terrible consequence to fall upon a failing Christian church!** Besides being *lukewarm*, the Laodicean church was prideful and probably materially rich. Yet spiritually they were *wretched, pitiful, poor, blind and naked* in Christ's eyes. They needed to obtain spiritual *gold* to be truly *rich* in the Lord's favour; to have *white clothes* (representing sinless lives) to cover their spiritual nakedness—and spiritual *salve* to put on their blind *eyes*. They, like many in today's disobedient churches, have not sought, nor perhaps have they been taught of the spiritual riches of the Word of God, and especially not taught to *obey all* that Christ *has commanded* (and taught) us from His inspired New Testament **Word of Truth** *that sanctifies us* (John 17:17).

Christ wants Laodicean-type churches today, too, to overcome their spiritual failings—to be earnest (i.e., steadfast, unwavering and faithful) in what they do for Him, and to repent of their sins of pride and disobedience. To those who overcome their failures and sins, He promises *the right to sit with me on my throne*. This reference probably relates to Revelation 20:4, where the thrones offered are for those to whom the Lord gives authority to judge the world, rather than the reference in Matthew 19:28, where the twelve thrones are offered to Jewish disciples who will judge the Twelve Tribes of Israel.

Christ also encourages the Laodiceans, and His later failing churches, in this matter of overcoming evil and those who counsel falsely. He states, in Revelation 3:21, that He will give those who *overcome the right to sit with me on my throne*—and says, in encouragement, *just as I overcame* (the evil ones, His opposers on earth, and death) *and sat down with my Father on His throne*. If only all we Christians, *Sons* (and daughters) *of God* (Rom. 8:14) by **adoption and faith**, and hence now part of the spiritual family of God, would recognize the truth of these Words, and strive—with the Spirit's guidance—to "overcome" all those who oppose us. And not yield to *false teachers* or false leaders, or succumb to spiritual *sleep*, or *lukewarmness* in His service. **The cure for these things that Christ hates? It is to listen to what the Spirit says to the churches and repent, reform and do the things we did before** (in full obedience to Him). **What the Spirit says to the churches** is what Christ has said to us, His church today (see John 14:26—Christ's Words).

Today, Will You Not Hear What the Spirit Says to the Churches? (Rev. 2,3)
—Seven times repeated by Christ to those who must hear and obey.

Christ has spoken of *rewards* for *overcoming* and faithful churches, all their members and leaders, and His disciples forming His Body on earth, in these Seven representations of early exemplar

Churches. He closes His statements to these Seven Churches, to whom He asked the Apostle John to forward His Words in letter form, with the revealing warning that: *He who has an ear to hear, let him hear what the Spirit says to the churches.* His truthful, loving and just Words apply to us today!

Hear what the Spirit says is a general but very pertinent scriptural statement, applicable to the entire Christian church Body of any century, including today—**to all Christians in all churches.** I combine this statement with Christ's earlier Words, given to His disciples about His not leaving them alone but sending this same Spirit of God to each believer, to Counsel and Teach and Lead them to His Truth. **This same Spirit makes Christ's teaching complete to us, as He tells us all that He expects.**

And He tells us how to achieve success in obeying the Lord with the help and Guidance of the *Spirit of Truth.* He (and I, echoing His Words) also remind the churches of everything He said, taught, and commanded them while He was yet with them. It would be brought to their and our remembrance by this same Spirit in all believers. This same *Spirit of Truth* continues to speak the Words of Christ to the churches, until Christ comes again, present to speak to us Himself. Through His speaking to the spirits of those believers who are in the church, and form Christ's Body, it is clear to me—and will be also to those who read this book based on inspired Scripture—that the early churches (including the Seven Churches of Rev. 2,3) were largely disobedient, unfaithful, "Spiritually *asleep*," etc. etc., and were all counselled (whether they were good or bad) to *hear what the Spirit says to the churches.* We, too, must "listen to the Spirit speaking" in His Word and to our hearts, before it is too late.

"General" Consequences of Disobedience to Christ By His Churches.

Christ talked, too, in these Seven Letters to the early church we have been studying, about the **opposite** of His *rewards*—namely, "consequences of disobedience." For purists, the word "consequence" is not to be found, as such, in the Letters to the Seven Churches of Revelation 2 and 3. Instead, we find it in shorter, but more significant, alternate Words of Christ, such as: *or, if you don't..., repent therefore...,* *otherwise I will...*, and His Words, *Do this, Repent,* etc.

Christ tells us something about these terrible consequences to be given to those in the church of the New Testament (and to us, in later ages) who do not, or will not, now repent and return to complete obedience and faithfulness, to *do the things* we *did at first* in full obedience.

If readers dismiss what I say (from Scripture), and discount my words (His Words!) as simply those from "someone who doesn't belong to 'my church,'" I simply ask once more that they seek their own resident "Holy Counselor" and ask His advice! No, I'm not talking about your Seminary professor, knowledgeable member or friend of your church, or renowned church leader from today or the past who has written a book, perhaps on this subject. I'm speaking only of Christ's advice for **doubting Thomases** of today, to *...hear what the Spirit says to the churches* (the quoted phrase begins with Christ's words of emphasis: *He who has an ear...*). Both the Lord and I do not speak of physical anatomy. We speak of a spiritual symbolism that includes a willingness of a reader of Scripture to discover Truth from inspired Scripture, rather than "hear or read" ***men's often false teachings but not hear or read what the Spirit of God says and has said to us***—as preserved by Him in the form of Christ's imperishable Words of truth that never fail. ***Hear the Spirit; consult Him as you read His Word; obey Him, and give up false teachings*** that can be "tested against inspired Scripture," and often are found lacking by this same Spirit within each of us believers!

To counter these *false teachers* (or your suspicions of this writer's Christian integrity and intentions) I ask everyone, in Christ's Name, to not do what I tell you to do, but do what our mutual Lord tells all His true and faithful disciples to do...*hear what the Spirit says to the churches* (Rev. 2,3). If what I repeat from Scripture is God's Truth, the Spirit will confirm it to you, relating it to the written Word of our Lord. If it is false teaching, I also urge you to ask the Spirit, the *Spirit of Truth* (John 16:13) to speak to your spirit, and confirm not only that every Word of God's Word (not men's) is His sanctifying Truth (John 17:17), but that His Truth applies to you, me, and all believers.

By this Divine means—**this consulting of the Spirit of God**—even unfaithful and disobedient members of failing or failed Christian churches will be led to the truth, to repentance, and then to reform. Return to the faith once delivered to all the Saints. Then you will gain His promised rewards for being entirely in His Will. But not listening to *what the Spirit says to the churches*, and **not acting** and repenting and reforming and returning to what Christ desires for His church, will mean terrible *(but just!)* consequences for failing, as the Lord says in Revelation 2,3 and elsewhere in His Word.

Some Particular and Terrible Consequences for Failing Christian Churches.

All **disobedience will reap punishment by the Head of the church.** He says, in His letter to the church in Thyatira (Rev. 2:23ff): ...*I will strike her children dead* (this evil 'Jezebel,' leading the church astray) ... *Then all the churches* (and us today!) *will know that I am he who searches hearts and minds, and I will repay each of you according to your deeds.* The Lord's "repayment," as we see in these Seven Letters (as in the case of Ananias and Sapphira in the first Jerusalem church, where "repayment" meant the sinners' deaths) can be terrible indeed.

In the case of the exemplar disobedient church at Ephesus, it means that **if disobedience continues, and there is no repentance, no "overcoming"—their lampstand will be removed from its place by Christ Himself.** In Revelation 1, the introduction by the Lord to His "letters of warning" tells us that their lampstand represented the entire local church. Its expected and obedient *place* in Heaven is with the Lord—with Him in the midst of all the other faithful *lampstands* (Ref. Rev. 1:12,13). If this disobedient church, and other, similar churches in the future, did not repent and return to *their first love,* the terrible consequence of their disobedience would be removal by the Head from His Presence and Love—as well as being separated from the fellowship of other churches, other believers, in Heaven.

We are mercifully not told more, and I won't comment further other than to say: what a terrible fate this will be for any church! Will we *hear what the Spirit says to the churches* (what Christ says to "our" churches in His Word), or will we postpone needed, Christ-commanded repentance and a return to the Head's desires, only to find ourselves lost—separated eternally from His Presence and love?

Consider the case of the *lukewarm church* example (Laodicea). Here, worst cases are translated into actual facts, as we read the Lord's angry reaction to one of His "bodies" whom He wishes were either spiritually *hot or cold*—but not *lukewarm*, lethargic, and effectively useless to Him and the lost world around it. His reaction, in analogy, is the same as ours when we taste food or drink that we expect to be either hot or cold (depending upon our needs and the climate we are in at the time!), and find it disappointingly "lukewarm!" We would reject what we expect to be something else, and spit it out—and the Lord does the same. He threatens to (symbolically) spit the lukewarm church out of His mouth if they don't repent and return to His favour and love. We cannot comprehend what this means, for we do not know the full extent of Christ's love for the church He *Willed to build*, which He gave Himself up for, and *of which he is the Saviour* (Eph. 5:23)—if not their Lord! He said these things to the church in Thyatira, and to us today, in Revelation 2:23—said, as the One Whom *the churches will know...searches hearts and minds*—that *I* (He) *will repay each of you according to your deeds.*

If we do not listen to what He and the Spirit say to the churches, can we expect that He is only joking, the One Who has been *given all authority in heaven and on earth?* Do we honestly think or expect Him to "laugh off" or "dismiss as unfortunate" the things that we choose to do, as part of His "Body on earth"? Do we really believe that He will continue to accept our disobedience and unfaithfulness as the "norm" for His disciples, supposedly *new creations in Christ Jesus?*

No, sadly, I accept and believe what the Lord says to disobedient members of His disobedient churches. I do not fully understand what He says He will do to us, if He Who *searches our hearts and minds* finds us unwilling to conform to His commands and teachings, to *overcome* evil, and instead fail His Will and purpose for His church. Will my readers, in any of the almost endless "varieties" of so-called "Christian churches" observed in today's world, understand that **God's Word is,** and remains forever, **Truth**? (John 17:17). God's only begotten Son, *The First and the Last, The Living One Who holds the keys of death and Hades* (Rev. 1:17,18), means what His Spirit (and He) *says to the churches* about their sinful deeds! Christ's warnings that I write about from Scripture are sure and clear. *Our disobedience (and those of past churches) cannot be condoned or be misinterpreted even by those churches who are lukewarm, asleep or almost spiritually dead—even if we do not know what His coming to us as a thief at an unknown time (Rev. 3:3) really means.*

If my readers are feeling as I do now, after contemplating such necessarily harsh words from our Lord of Love, and are wondering in their hearts if the Lord is speaking about "**our local** church," or "denomination," or "Christian movement"—take time out to be in prayer to God, while His Word is on your heart! Will you ask the *Spirit of Truth* to touch your heart and convict you of what you and "your church" (really "His," if you are honest) must do to receive His rewards always, rather than His *discipline,* His *consequences,* and His *repayment in kind* for our disobedient actions? Yes, God and His Son and His Spirit, the One, United, Triune Creator-God, is both Merciful and Just. His Son has said (Rev. 22:7,20) that *I am coming soon.* Will you and I, as members of His Body, the church on earth, be ready? Will we be found repentant, reformed and forgiven, revitalized, and following the Spirit's counsel and teaching, as well as Christ's commands? *I pray so, for when He comes, He tells us He will claim His faithful church as a Radiant, Holy, Sinless, and Obedient Bride. And take Christians, those who have overcome, with glorified bodies, to Eternal Life with Him in Heaven.*

In closing this chapter, I must remind my readers of some of "today's religious responses" to Christ's teachings and commands that are often heard (or unheard) from "Christian pulpits" these past few decades. I refer to some church Pastoral responses heard on radio, television, and in many local churches in your or my cities—responses to dealing with God's Truth, salvation, Heaven and Hell, consequences of disobedience, and need for church or personal reform.

I had a Christian friend, who, until he recently went "Home" to be with His Lord, used to discuss with me what we had heard or viewed over the past few years, concerning many basic Christian doctrines and Christ's teachings and commands. I used to say to him—"When was the last time you heard the doctrine of Hell or Heaven preached from a Christian church pulpit?" He would say, "I can't remember!" I would say to him—"well, what have you heard preached from a pulpit about the fate of someone who is not a believer in the Risen Christ and who rejects God?" He would say, "It seems to me that the last sermon I heard, talking about an unrepentant unbeliever's fate after death, was to the effect that the man's soul would simply wander in space, and it would only be 'separated from God.'" (A half-truth, hence a lie!) We would speculate why it was that Scriptures' sanctifying Truths were never or rarely talked about in many churches these past few years, and why the pulpit spoke to the pew only about the "social gospel," or why their church needed more finances, or when the next "bingo" or "garden show" would take place in the church or parking lot.

My Christian friend and I used to agree that, over our Christian lifetimes, the inspired Bible seemed to be less and less relevant to today's more technically advanced, yet more spiritually lethargic society. We also noted that church "sociologists," and their Christian "surveys" of Pastors and people of the multitudinous churches, denominations, sects, and "reformed" churches observed today, were predicting serious declines in their church attendance, declining faith, and outright disdain for most of today's diverse and disunited "brands" of so-called Christianity.

Before he died and went to be with His Lord, with rewards, I am sure, for faithfulness, I told him of my burden from the Lord to write and warn failing churches. He encouraged me to continue, and I did! I doubt if he can leave off his praising the Lord to see my work, but I know the Lord sees and approves of this necessary warning, taken from His inspired Word. Will you pray with me that this humble book may be passed on to those churches who desperately need to know about His Will for them?

Part 5. Eternal Consequences of Church Disobedience to the Divine Head.

Chapter 11

Action Words: "Overcoming"; "Failure"; "Repent" and "Reform"

Members or leaders of today's disobedient churches, if convicted of their sin, spiritual lukewarmness, or inaction, must now recognize some "action words." These words represent what Christ asks *them to do* to take action on their inaction, by *overcoming, by repenting, and reforming their failure.* Read on...

Now, I must discuss more of the Lord's Words of both *commendation* and *condemnation* to the Seven Churches (and to all later churches, and us today), and focus upon actions, reactions, or inactions of "overcoming," "failure," "repentance," and the necessary "reform," or return to full obedience, by churches that accept His chastisement for their failures.

In writing these chapters—based upon both scriptural New Testament church failures and historical failures observed in the sad record of the churches after the death of the Apostles, as well as failures actually experienced today—I sometimes find myself discouraged. Of course, *today's* divided, divisive, lukewarm, sleeping, proud, falsely- or little-taught church membership, with evidence of *false teachers* in such churches, even *spiritually dead churches,* is what concerns me most (as well as being our Lord's ever-present concern). How about you, my readers? *Do you sometimes, or often, feel sad, knowing that "your church" (really "His," if you believe God's Word!) will fare much like one or more of the Seven (mostly disobedient) Churches of Revelation 2 and 3 if your actions do not change?*

Do you find that you and your brothers and sisters in Christ in your nation—and the world—are often **divided** by false doctrines, false teachings? The sinful world is creeping into many local churches, despite Christ's teachings, commands and warnings for us to shun these evils. Does my repetition of certain phrases of Holy Scripture, telling us, reminding us, urging us, pleading with us to return to *do what we did at first* for Christ (Rev. 2:5), strike your heart and plague your mind with remembrances of your personal church life, your personal loyalty or lack of it, to the Lord? I hope so, for I want this Spirit-urged book, if it does nothing else, to cause you spiritual discomfort if you tolerate false teaching (resulting in disobedience to Christ and His Word) in your church.

But *if you and your church say* in your pride, by your actions (like the Laodicean church example) **I am rich, I lack nothing—*I hope you will stop and listen** to *what the Spirit says to the churches* (and to you and me) **and do something about your discomfort, my concern, and the Lord's Will and purpose!**

Overcoming.

If you have read the Scripture quoted in this book, you will remember how Christ used the phrase, *He who overcomes*, or the word **overcomes**, itself, often in His Revelation through John to certain bad church examples in the past. I want to discuss this scriptural term (Christ's word) **overcomes**—what it means for us today; and something about how we can overcome our own (and our church's) particular and diverse disobedience to Christ in all its forms, ancient or modern. We later Christians, through Revelation 2 and 3, can discover what **overcoming** means, and what will happen to those who overcome trials, temptations, spiritual deadness, failure, tolerance of the false, and lukewarmness to His Word of Truth in their relationship to Him as Body members of Christian churches.

On reading the Letters to the churches in Revelation 2,3, it is fairly obvious that six out of the Seven Churches of Asia were told to **overcome** something involving their church. Only the Philadelphia Church was told by the Lord, because of their faithfulness, to

Hold on to what you have, rather than that they needed to overcome something specifically disobedient that He *held against them.*

From the context of the word **overcome,** in Revelation 2,3, we in later churches must realize that, when *He who searches our hearts and minds* (Rev. 2:23) "audits and reviews" our local church, our chances of being told we need to overcome some particular sin, in the form of unfaithfulness, tolerance of *false teachers,* divisiveness, etc., are about the same as the scriptural Seven Churches—about six out of seven! Even if our deeds and our faithfulness were the same as Philadelphia's (although chances are we are not, at the moment—at least in Western democracies—under any form of overt persecution), it is very likely we would be told by Him to *Hold on to what you have...*for *I know that you have little strength* (Rev. 3:8).

The church and its members (and leaders of course) who overcome disobedience and evil, repent of their sinful personal and corporate actions, and do the Lord's Will to the end will receive *Crowns* and many other types of rewards that Christ speaks of often (in symbolism) in Revelation 2 and 3. Most mature and spiritually faithful Christians would rightly deny they only serve Christ and overcome sin and error for His rewards—for true service to Him is based upon love and obedience (John 14: 23,24). Without spiritual maturity (Ref. Eph. 4) new Christians cannot reach true *unity in the faith and in the knowledge of the Son of God...attaining to the whole measure of the fullness of Christ* (verse 13). And, without being taught to *obey all that I* (Christ) *have commanded you...*(Matt. 28:20), they cannot strengthen the church (Eph. 4:16), nor mature so as to resist false teaching in the church (verse 14).

The Lord, *who knows* and *searches all men's hearts,* knows that the joy that comes to Him from the knowledge of His disciples serving Him faithfully and well, out of love, is reciprocated in the hearts of His serving disciples. Rewards, then, like obedience, are a recognition of our mutual love for the One Who died for us. The ones who trust Him by faith alone, and serve Him faithfully to the end, do so not for rewards but out of gratefulness for His saving them—although His rewards are bestowed, and received, too, as a recognition of the mutual love of Master and servants.

The faithful ones in His church, who, when faced with a wide variety of opportunities for sin, turn away from them—and turn towards the Lord—are the real **overcomers,** because their faith is strong, and the presence of the Spirit in their lives reminds them of what the Lord **overcame** in His human, Incarnate, life for **them.** The Spirit *reminds them,* as is part of His role (John 14:26), that Christ, the prophesied Messiah, when rejected by Jewish leaders and temple priests, **overcame** unjust betrayal, an unjust "trial," and a terrible death on the Cross for all sinful mankind. And, because of His ultimate saving act of Redemption on behalf of all men, Christ overcame and received *the right to sit down with* His *Father on his throne* (Ref. Rev. 3:21). He overcame Satan, *the prince of this world* (John 14:30), and on our behalf, gave us victory over the Evil One at the root of troubles that beset the church of the past and present—including His Christian Body today.

Facing and **overcoming sin**—in the church and in the world—for Him, will result in our not only receiving His rewards, but being confirmed in His love and in His promises of a future in Heaven beyond our present understanding. The *Spirit of Truth* in each believer will guide and lead us back to Truth at all times (John 14,16).

Failing *Our Divine Saviour and Lord, the Divine Head of His Church.*

In this chapter too, I want to discuss this human term—not in human, but in scriptural terms—as the Lord used it in Revelation 2 and 3 to describe how *lack of faith, lack of obedience, and lack of persistence in and for Him and His Word and their results, constitutes "failure" in His eyes.* This word, and its variations—"*fail,*" "*failings,*" etc., in the scriptural, religious, and often spiritual context—means failing to do something that a person (Christian in this book) has been told or taught, and knows is just and morally right. Something that the failing person knows will bring *repayment or recompense in accordance to the failing deed involved,* from Jesus Christ, the Head of the church to which the failing person "belongs," by original faith in the Risen Lord. Evidenced by sin and disobedience to Christ in many diverse areas of church and personal life, **failure** comes about, for Christians in Christian churches, through the influence of Satan directly, or through his human agents who infiltrate the church. They act as supposed "wise men," bringing "fresh, new, and 'modern' ideas" (but often scripturally false doctrines and practices) on many Christian subjects, doctrines, and theology, often directly opposite or opposed to God's inerrant Word.

Agents of Satan are not new in the church—or out of it. Satan acted directly upon Adam and Eve's minds in the Garden, after their creation, by speaking the first lie: *Did God really say...?* (Gen. 3:1). Through their *failure* to obey God's sole prohibition to them, they suffered His penalties. Not only did our original ancestors suffer the penalty of physical death, after their eviction from Eden into a sin-corrupted world—a "Fall" from Grace, and from immortality to a deserved limited span of human life—but they "carried and transmitted" their Original Sin on to all their progeny in the now-fallen and corrupt world outside God's Paradise. The earth, too, was corrupted by their sin and *failure*, leaving Adam and all men to earn their "living" by the sweat of their brow; Eve and all women to suffer pain in childbirth—all of which is the penalty of *failure* to obey God, on the part of sinful mankind.

Down through the history, first of the Jews, then of the Christians, Satan ...*your enemy, the devil, prowls around like a roaring lion looking for someone to devour* (1 Pet. 5:8). We Christians must be self- and Spirit-controlled, and alert always, or we will *fail* in doing our Lord's Will. Later, Satan acted upon Ananias and Sapphira, in the First Christian church in Jerusalem. These church members "fell," and lied to God, the Spirit, and to Peter. Through New Testament history, as recorded in Acts, the letters of the inspired Paul, and elsewhere, we have much evidence of *failures* in the lives of Christian church members—*failures* that result from disobeying the Head of the church, Jesus Christ, under pressure from Satan through His agents, *false teachers*.

Through later church history, we also find *failures* of both members and leaders of the Christian church to obey their Lord. They have, instead, spiritual... *infants, tossed, back and forth by the waves, and blown here and there by every wind of* (false) *teaching, blown here and there by cunning craftiness of men in their deceitful scheming* (Ref. Eph. 4:14ff). That's *by the overcoming waves* (of ever-changing doctrines and

235

false teachings of men) resulting in church members remaining spiritual *infants* in the church of Jesus Christ. I have previously noted the Apostle Peter's counselling that *there will be false teachers* in the church. As the first century (and later) churches tried to fight off their great loss of the (mostly faithful) Apostles in their teaching, preaching, praying, and corrective actions for the spreading Body of Christ in the world, Satan and his agents continued their destructive work in the church.

Augmented by the divided church's adoption of unscriptural leaders, who introduced Scripture-opposing doctrines, Satan's agents in the later church (*false teachers* predominantly) maintained their errant actions. They opposed Christ's scriptural Will and purpose by spreading false teaching that caused new disciples, largely untaught concerning the scriptural Words of Christ, to be *tossed and blown about by every wind of teaching from these false, scheming and deceitful men in the church* (Eph. 4), just as the inspired Paul wrote about earlier in his New Testament Letters for the church.

These conditions continued in the following centuries, and were not greatly ameliorated by Martin Luther's so-called "Protestant Reformation" in 1517 A.D. Called a "half-way reformer" by some reformers who wanted a **full and faithful return to Scripture**, Luther, at the time, seemingly wanted only to discuss certain, current, errors—Papal authority, false doctrines on such matters as "dispensations," etc.—and seemed genuinely surprised by the furor caused by the Papal hierarchy on their reception of his "95 theses" (or discussion list) of Roman church flaws in their Headquarters in Rome.

The church's condemnation of Luther, culminating in his excommunication for heresy and his being cast out of the Roman church, seemed to many to be destined to bring about a desirable "splitting off" of many reform-minded Christians from the failing parent church. Renewed, or at least new, churches then tried, and promised to, reform their earlier errant ways by returning to a pure (and obedient) New Testament faith, doctrine, and practices. But students of both history and the Bible, upon examining the schismatic process and its evident results within both the "parent church" and its Protestant "reformed (children) churches" over almost five centuries, find only a partial, **not** a complete Reformation.

Those Christians who today applaud this splitting-off process called "the Protestant Reformation" must surely realize that the process itself was absolutely contrary to Christ's prayed-for condition, of **unity of all His many bodies on earth.** The Divine Head of His future church prayed to His Heavenly Father that His church *may be One, as I and the Father are One* (John 17). **He included His reasons for complete church unity**—*May they be brought to complete unity to let the world know that you sent me and have loved them even as you have loved me* (Jesus' prayer in John 17:23). But history and unbiased students of His Word give the lie to unity claimed for His Body, then and now. While I have spoken of this earlier, I will continue to discuss herein some of the sinful effects of the "Protestant Reformation," in both the Roman Catholic church and the resulting multitude of divided churches.

I urge all participant church bodies who exist today to re-examine "their church's" full obedience to Scripture, or not, and observe that their "splitting off" processes have largely failed. **Failed**, for the world's presently divided 'Protestant' churches often oppose Christ's plea for a completely united "Body," completely obedient to Him in all things. While Luther and his Christian friends of that day undoubtedly felt they would be able to achieve unity and true reform by their actions, they were sincerely wrong, according to Scripture. Their own failure to reform all error from their faith, doctrine, and practices was a **failure.** Christ's Desires, Hopes, Will and Purpose to have a *completely United Body* full obedient to His Inspired Word in Scripture have failed to be shown to the world by many churches today because of men's lust for power, unwillingness to return to *do the things they do at first* and refusal to faithfully obey Him, the True Head in all things.

Church histories of the Roman Catholic churches, the "Protestant churches," "state churches," and, indeed, the many other later churches not part of the worldwide "Christian churches" of Luther's and following days, reveal—and it is public knowledge for the most part—that they are not truly "Reformed," in the sense that Christ wants us to be reformed, and return to Him and His Word, faithful and undivided. Many open and clearly-evident heresies, false doctrines, false teachings, and false, unscriptural "traditions," in these and other churches are still present—in many cases, because Lutheran and other "new" churches, formed by the breaking away of those who had been Roman Catholics in European countries, only disagreed with **some** of the false practices, doctrines and "traditions" of their former parent church, **but not all.**

These errors, false traditions and teachings of the church were, and are still, errant and sinful—because they did not, then, and do not, now, agree fully with the New Testament teachings of Christ, nor with the Spirit-inspired teachings of holy men such as Paul, Peter, John, etc. HIstory shows, many so-called "Protestants," in the past and even today, cling to some of the false human practices, doctrines and teachings of the corrupt Roman church, and have added many of them to their so-called **reformed** churches. Then and now, sinful churches must return, with the Spirit, to the Bible alone—or carry the title "**Failure.**"

One example here will suffice, perhaps, to illustrate what I mean about churches breaking away from an earlier church, calling their part in it a "Reformation movement," yet retaining many of the false practices of the earlier parent church. I previously commented in this book upon "scriptural Christian baptism," by which Spirit-Convicted sinners, hearing the gospel message of salvation, recognize their sins, repent of them, and, believing the Message that Christ died for them and rose again, accept Jesus Christ by faith alone. Then baptized by water immersion (Ref. Rom. 6), they are thus "added" to the Christian church (Refer part 3, chapter 6 of this book). The **true scriptural baptism**, outlined for errant churches by the inspired **Apostle Paul**, alone represents the Lord's meaning and purpose of baptism for Christian believers. I also noted that Scripture requires that all persons being baptized must be capable of: understanding the Gospel and recognizing that they are sinners; forming, recognizing and understanding true repentance, and acting on it; of believing with their heart and confessing with their mouth that they believe in the Risen Lord; of recognizing the gift of the Spirit in their heart when they believed; and, finally, asking the church to baptize them as believers and add them to the Body of Christ.

Do I need to repeat that infants cannot understand, much less do these things, and therefore should not be baptized by any Scripture-led church? I think I do! For the "Protestant Reformation," some 500 years ago, and its resultant multiplicity of "Reformed churches," with their public history, did not, in God's Truth, change all sinful church matters requiring **reform**—in fact, many churches continue to teach and practice Scriptural errors today.

All of us in professed Christian churches today must hear Him, His Word, and His Spirit—and obey Him. We first must understand what He requires, by re-reading His scriptural Words concerning failure, disobedience, sin, error, and the need for "overcoming them." **Failure** of any kind, in His church, requires repentance and reform—with the aid of the Spirit of God in each of us. Again, — **we must know what repentance, reform (and failure) mean, and how to act upon them with the counsel of the *Spirit of Truth*, to overcome them and achieve true reform.** That is, we must return to doing *what you did at first* and not *forsake[ing] your first love,* Jesus Christ (Rev. 2,3). This is what He asks us all to do when He tells us to *hear what the Spirit says to the churches* today.

Through this book, referring always to Christ's own Words and pleas, He (and I, and very many faithful Christians) **want(s) only to see genuine obedience in all things, just as He wants to see all His disciples one, as He and His Father are One.**

As Christ directs His disciples of all ages to the errors, especially, of the Seven Churches of Revelation, I want to point out, in genuine *agape* (God's) love, that little has significantly changed in the history and life of the Christian church down the centuries to today. Men's basic spiritual natures have not changed—*all have sinned and come short of the Glory of God* (Rom. 3:23). But wait—something has changed, beginning with the formation of the "First Baptist church" in Jerusalem, under the Apostles' gospel preaching, and the Spirit's Convicting Power! Repentant sinners, then and now, have believed in Jesus Christ, Risen from the dead—and Scripture tells us that they are *new creations; the old has gone...*(2 Cor. 5:17). Their sins forgiven, they are baptized by immersion and added to the Body of Christ, the church; there to be taught to obey all Christ's teachings and commands, to grow spiritually, and serve and strengthen the Body in Christ's service in the world.

Despite this Good News of the gospel in Christian lives, Satan's efforts to destroy Christ and His disciples' souls, and His church, never changes. In fact, as I am sure many Christians reading this book (and its scriptural references) will agree, today's "modern" Christian church's problems reflect the ancient churches' problems—only worldly societies and cultures have changed. God, His Son, and His Spirit remain unchanged and unchangeable. God's inspired written Word is unchanged; much of unsaved and spiritually lost mankind remains sinfully lost (unless Christ's church acts to save them). Satan seems to be now concentrating upon a failing Christian church, but Christ is still coming soon to claim what He hopes will be a *Holy, Radiant, unstained and blameless church.*

Yes, what has changed for the church of all ages—formed first in Jerusalem by the work of the Holy Spirit and the faithful Apostles, and continuing to spread *to all nations* by disciples faithfully obedient to the Lord's Great Commission to His church—is the surprising Revelation of Jesus Christ, made some decades after the Jerusalem church was formed. A small portion of this Revelation (Chapters 1, 2, and 3, centering upon His church) was given to tell His church of all ages that we must hear His Spirit and His Words, obey His Commands, and repent and reform every disobedient act, doctrine, or church practice—or suffer terrible consequences. I am certainly not saying the church should ignore the other chapters of Revelation—not at all, for they are Christ's Words of advice and counsel concerning what will be coming next in God's Plan. I am saying, however, that these early chapters (1–3) must especially neither be ignored nor forgotten (as they appear to be, in part today). Today's churches' response to—or rejection of—our Lord's Word, affects their (our) eternal future, if they *fail* to *hear what the Spirit says to the churches* and *fail* to act obediently upon His Words. The Christian church must return to the Bible truths, and reject *false teachers*—or pay God's Price.

Repentance

When disobedience to the Lord, or any church or personal Christian failure is discovered, through reading the Word of God with the aid and counsel of the Holy *Spirit of Truth*, Christ and His Word tells us that **repentance** is both required and necessary. Always, the Head of His church, Jesus Christ—not a "Pope," "Patriarch," "Bishop," or human, unscriptural "head," but the Risen Christ alone—tells us that He requires that we **repent**, turn away from our sin, and return to *do what* we *did at first*. That is, **turn away from** disobedience to His teachings and commands, and **get back to** doing what He Who has Divine authority over all has told us, in His Word, to do and be for Him in the church and in the world. Human leaders can counsel this; only Christ has the authority of God to ask it of us.

Just as being *born again* (the salvation process), conviction by the Spirit, and **repentance** by the sinner is demanded before he is accepted by our Holy God—so too, **repentance (*turning away from sin, and returning, forgiven, to God, in the Person of His Risen Son*)** is commanded from church members and leaders of His Body on earth when sin is discovered, and before their restoration is accepted by God the Father and God the Son. The Spirit, as always, is ready, willing, and able to Convict, Urge, and Counsel us to full restoration (reformation), through commanded **repentance** on the church's part, and forgiveness on Christ the Head's part (God, through Christ alone!).

Repentance is not only human sorrow or agony of heart respecting sin and wrongdoing, although it may certainly be present when the Spirit convicts people of these things in their lives. **Repentance** is, rather, a spiritual change of mind—a reversal of mind-set, a turning away from past sin to a new life found only in Jesus Christ. It is sometimes used as a synonym for "belief," but when the Bible speaks of repentance, it is used in two instances:

One: In the "salvation process," where convicted sinners hear the gospel message of Jesus Christ, and are convicted by the Holy Spirit. They realize that they are sinners, and know that they must turn away from their

sins, give them up, and take a new Way with Christ—
through belief in Him by faith alone. And,

Two: *Repentance* is found in the New Testament in several
places, including Revelation 2 and 3, where Christ
tells believers (Christian members and leaders of His
church) to repent of their disobedience and sins (also
to *overcome*, to *wake up*, etc.), and return to full obedience to Him, their Saviour and Lord. *Repentance* is
the only way back to Christ's True Way of life.

Reform—Planned Change From What is Wrong to What is Right

Reform in the "man-made," often "religious" sense, is a word
used to justify many of the changes men feel are necessary as a
way to return to Christ's commands and teachings. The true Christian sense of the word *"reform,"* however, comes from the **Living
Word**. Jesus uses several sentences in Revelation 2 and 3 to more
clearly state what He requires when He, *who searches hearts and
minds* finds that change for the better is necessary. For example,
He says (meaning this act of *"reform"*), *do the things you did at
first...*(as opposed to the errors you are committing now, Rev. 2:5);
buy from me gold refined in the fire (spiritual truth and behavioural
standards need correcting, Rev. 3:18); and *Wake up!* (Reform your
disobedient "acts and actions!"—Rev. 3:2).

As we read about the need for *"reform"* in the Bible (in one of
Christ's equivalent phrases) we must realize that repentance always
precedes *reform's* changes, itself preceded by self-examination and
recognition of sin. *Reform* is necessary when the church member,
leader or "Body" perceives (with the guidance of the *Spirit of Truth*)
that they have been too tolerant, too lukewarm, too weak, and too
accepting of *false teachers* in the church. But how do we know what
to do, and when and how to act, if we are relatively untaught believers? The answer, of course, is to return to Christ's Words and seek the
Spirit's help. Most weak and sinning Christians (members or leaders)
cannot find the answers to their spiritual questions in their own

weak, finite, sinful humanity and experience. No matter how they may say publicly, as the church at Laodicea says in Revelation Chapter 3: *I am rich...and do not need a thing*, they—and the *wretched, pitiful, poor, blind and naked* churches of long ago and today—are deceived and need to acknowledge that they are one with that church, in their pride and disobedience.

Examine **your true spiritual life and condition** with the *Spirit of Truth* (see John chapters 14,16). Self-examination is not only thing we must do. We must recognize the sin and disobedience in our individual and church lives as His Body, then act to continue to follow His Word to true reform. **Revival, repentance, reform and full obedience** are required until He comes—all with the Spirit of the Living Christ to strengthen and lead us back to what we *did at first* for Him Who is the True Head, the True Way, and the True Life.

More Examples of Church Disobedience Opposing God's Word and Divine Standards.

I recall vividly my own experience as an older new Christian. I remember how incredulous I was when I was taught what Christ wanted His church (and me) to be and do for Him, and to remember always. As I grew spiritually, I was even more incredulous to find how far apart many churches were from His ideal and Will, in actual church life. The Head of His church, *who searches* our *hearts and minds...* will *repay each of* us in His church, *according to* our *deeds* (good and bad!—Rev. 2:23). He is the One Who says: *those whom I love I rebuke and discipline*—those who disobey Him (Rev. 3:19).

Never, ever, my brother and sister Christians in the true Christian church, think that our Lord gives His commendations and condemnations lightly or without Heartache (Recall, *Jesus wept*, John 11:35). Never listen to *false teachers* in some churches today, who say that He was simply talking to a few ancient churches (in Rev. 2,3)—not to us now. God hates all sin; all disobedience to His Word (teachings and commands) is sin. But since we cannot humanly repent, reject, or reform alone, we are fortunate that the Head gave us His gift of the *Spirit of Truth,* in every true believer, who will, when asked, Counsel, Guide and Aid us to overcome all of Satan's wiles, and show us the way to return to full and faithful obedience to Him. ***Don't overlook sin, but overcome it!*** We must get back to the New Testament for the church, assess our failings and act positively.

Sexual Immorality in the World and in the Church Today.

God and His Son are Holy, Sinless, and Divinely Moral; their Righteousness requires that we Christians must be moral also—or lose fellowship with the Divine Trinity of God. Moreover, throughout the Bible, God and His Spirit has inspired Prophets, holy Men such as Apostles, and Christian disciples to write to churches, counselling them to avoid immorality—or suffer terrible consequences. For my purpose, I choose to outline what God has said (through the inspired Paul, in Romans 1) regarding sexual immorality and its consequences. In Romans 1:18ff. (ff means: and several following, pertinent verses—author), the inspired Apostle Paul speaks of the *wrath of God* exercised against men and women, who *although they knew* (of) God, *neither glorified Him as God, nor gave thanks to Him as Creator.* Paul speaks of what happened to these Godless people (of all time):

> *Their thinking became futile and their foolish hearts were darkened. Although they claimed to be wise, they became fools, and exchanged the glory of the immortal God for images made to look like mortal man and birds and animals and reptiles* (Rom. 1:21–23).

Some read this, and proudly say, "we are not like such men—for we are Christians, and attend Christ's church." But wait, and read on as Paul begins to talk about what happens to those whose lives show they have other gods, and who reject our Holy Creator-God. Paul tells us (as the Spirit spoke to him, and us) how such men and women act immorally, as *God gave them over in the sinful desires of their hearts to sexual impurity, for the degrading of their bodies with one another.*

He speaks specifically of what we call, today, "homosexuals" (men) and "lesbians" (women)—or just "homosexuals," in reference to both genders. They carry out sinful desires and lusts of their hearts by engaging in sinful acts of sexual immorality: men with men, and women with women. Romans 1:26 states: *they exchanged natural rela-*

tions for unnatural ones. It is clear, from this New Testament passage alone, that God considers homosexuals to be depraved sinners who, since they have rejected Him, practise evil, immoral acts, and do only what their sinful, lustful, nature leads them to do. God loves all His Creation—but, as Holy God, **hates their sin!** We Christians must do so, too; many churches, however, accept homosexuality as simply a **way of life, not sin;** and (Scriptural-defying) **natural, not unnatural.**

Notice that the clear meaning of this Romans 1 passage is that homosexual acts are the end result of deliberate **choices** made by men and women—and, thus, are **not in any way** the result of **genetic inheritance.** Today, however, these particular types of deliberate sinners try to defend their immoral, ungodly, lustful acts (sin) by looking for favourable support from modern Godless scientists and researchers, who say: "homosexuality is a 'physical orientation' that comes through inherited genes, and only affects those who have these genes." I call them Godless scientists, for they will not accept God's clear statements, in His Word, that these people are **not** innocent victims of a transmitted "bad gene," but rather are simply God-rejecting humans, expressing the sinful desires of their carnal hearts, carrying out sexual immorality, and degrading their bodies with other sinners (male and/or female)—as a matter of personal choice against God. To my knowledge, no scientist has ever proved, nor do I believe ever will prove, that homosexuality is brought about by genetic "sexual orientations." Romans 1 and other biblical passages state unequivocally that no other reason than deliberately opposing God explains immoral, perverse and lustful acts between men with men, and women with women. They choose to reject Him as Adam and Eve did, listening to Satan or to *false teachers,* and committing **deliberately chosen, conscious acts of sin and lust.** Bible students note: Romans 1:24 (God gave them (these sinners) over in the sinful desires of their hearts). God allowed sin to run its course in disobedient, unbelieving sinners as an act of Judgement.

I am speaking here of what is sin in God's eyes, and in His inspired Word—not of what Godless societies today think are "good or bad, moral or immoral acts" of men and women. I write herein only for Christian churches, who, by God's Mercy and Grace, have accepted

His Divine, Sinless, Morality because He sent His Only begotten Son to this sinful, Godless world, *so that whoever believe in Him* (and in the One Who sent Him) *shall not perish, but* (their souls) *have eternal life* (after physical death) with their Saviour and Lord (John 3:16). But what about Christian churches who accept unrepentant homosexual sinners as members of Christ's Body, the church, and tolerate "Godless scientists' opinions" rather than upholding God's Word—and even accept homosexuals as church leaders and teachers?

Newspapers, magazines, television screens, and many conversations today, are filled with stories of "gay (homosexual) rights" and privileges—in the Western world, at least. But this is in our society, not in the church—and our society is only nominally Christian. It often borders on the pagan, because our churches have made little impact upon the world by making few disciples for Christ in it. If the church obeyed Christ fully, made disciples (new Creations), baptized them and taught them to obey Him fully, society would improve morally, and in every other way as well as live Godly lives—with a Heavenly future.

As I close this discussion of homosexual sin, I would be remiss not to mention that dismissal of unrepentant homosexuals (men or women) found "hidden" in the Christian church Body should not be the final, or only, action of a Bible-believing church. Christian church leaders should always take admitted, active homosexuals aside, and tell them that their sin is not irrevocable, or unchangeable—but that our Lord can and will forgive their sins, if they come to Him in true repentance. He can, and will, change them into a *new creation in Christ Jesus* (2 Cor. 5:17). He will remove their lust, blindness, evil thoughts, and actions, if they will ask Him to heal them. Many former homosexuals have come to the Lord in true repentance, sought His Mercy and overcame their lustful tendencies and acts in this way. The world, and all the psychologists and psychiatrists in it, cannot do this—for it is not a matter of worldly "therapy" to overcome an annoying "habit" (really sin against God, genetic or not). Christians must love the sinner, and hate the sin, as Christ does. Forgiveness of confessed sin is truly life-changing, if conviction, repentance and reform is sought from our Merciful God!

Only Christ can make a person a *new creation,* in whose changed life, now and in eternity, *the old* (sin, immoralities, disobedience to God) *has gone, the new has come!* (2 Cor. 5:17). The sins and lusts of the world have gone, as the person repents and believes and becomes *born again* (John 3:3). Christ does not do this by a public "miraculous act," but through His church—who, in a reverent atmosphere, with the Spirit and sincere prayers, provides His gospel forgiveness and salvation to all repentant sinners. Only as they experience God's Truth and forgiveness will new believers come to see that their sins are forgiven, and they are "right(eous) with God." Homosexuals can be "cured"—not by worldly counselling, but through salvation by faith, a holy life, and reliance upon a Merciful God. But the church must not accept, as part of Christ's Body, those who do those immoral acts that are directly condemned by a Holy God in His written Word of Truth, and who do not acknowledge their sin, repent, and ask His forgiveness and Mercy.

Outside the church, in the sinful world, *false teachers* advise all men, worldly or Christian, that since "God loves us all equally," we in the church must be loving to all sinners (true!)—even to the extent of declaring them members of Christ's redeemed, born-again Body on earth (false!). These *false teachers* are partly correct in the statements above, but also partly wrong—which is a half-truth, and in Truth, is a lie! Discovered sin and disobedience to the church's Divine Head must be seen as such by church leaders. Sinners must be counselled with God's righteous, sanctifying Truth, the unrepentant must be cast out, and the repentant sinner must be received in God's Name, with shouts of praise for Him Who gave Himself up for the church, His Body on earth!

God loves all men, but by with His Divine Attributes, cannot condone their sins—for He is Righteous, and sinners are unrighteous. *All have sinned, and fall short of the Glory* (and Righteousness) *of God* (Rom. 3:23). But, thanks be to God, Romans 3 continues with the wonderful gospel message (verse 24): sinners are *justified freely by His Grace through the redemption that came by Jesus Christ.* Church members and leaders, continue to love the sinner (of whatever sort or kind) as God does—but don't leave the sinner to his certain fate, without lovingly telling him or her God's Truth about how to become "right(eous) with Him" by hearing the Gospel, repenting, believing, and being baptized into Christ's Body on earth!

Women "Priests" in the Anglican Church of Canada and Church of England.

As an example of a modern church disobedience problem, I have a newspaper clipping from the Associated Press, in a Canadian newspaper (July 20/98) about the Anglican (church of England) 1998 "Lambeth Conference," at which "Bishops" from 164 countries around the world met to discuss and debate "their" church and societal problems. In this clipping, speaking of controversial subjects and debates occurring during their church Conference, I noted that at an Anglican church in central London, an admitted "lesbian" (homosexual) woman had became the first openly lesbian "priest" to celebrate communion in Britain. I have also noted, among other news clippings in my collection, that many female Church of England "priests" already serve in both England and in Canada—despite scriptural injunctions opposing female "Elders or "Overseers" in the church (1 Tim. 2,3). Christ does not recognize national borders—but I, a sinner saved by Grace, am disappointed when I read that the "Canadian Anglican Church" took the (sinful) lead "by being one of the first nominally 'Christian nations' to appoint women 'priests' in the world—and then was followed by the Church of England." Leaders in Christ's scripturally-defined church are to be in the world (serving the Lord) but are not to be a part of the world's scripturally-opposed and sinful life—and, now, church style. Speaking of the Church of England's disobedience, the same July 20/98 news clipping draws attention to another subtle church sin against our Lord—namely, the seemingly innocent statement that "guests [at the Church Conference] included Prince Charles, who will be the **secular head of the Church of England** if he becomes King."

The "subtle sin" I note is that there is only one scripturally True Head of the Body of Christ on earth: the Divine Head, Jesus Christ, whose Spirit is in us—the One Who gave Himself for the church He Willed to build, and the One Who is coming soon to claim His *radiant* Bride, the sinless church. **Nowhere in Scripture do we find any "supreme head of Christ's church on earth,"** be that a "secular" King, a Pope, a Patriarch, or any other human being. Yes, there are scriptural Christian church leaders, Overseers, or Elders, (Pastors) and Deacons (both male only) appointed leaders and overseers of each individual, self-governing church. But Scripture reveals no "overall" Supreme leader of Christ's churches except the Divine Head, Christ—no priest (except for the Jews), nor any other human head but those shown to us in 1 Tim. 3, etc. His church on earth is **guided, shepherded and overseen** by human disciples, the Holy Spirit, and the written Word of God. And nowhere in the New Testament for the Christian church do we find the Divine requirement for any church Body of Christ on earth to have a human "Head," other than the Divine Head Who rules from Heaven.

Christ's Words and teachings state that the Spirit of God, within every true Christian believer in His church in the world, **represents** the Divine Head of every local Body of Christ. The Spirit Speaks, Teaches and Counsels each and every member, and Spirit-Gifted "Church *Overseer*," and *Deacon*/helper, to obediently carry out all of the Divine Head's teachings and commands.

I pray, and so should believers everywhere pray, that sinning, disobedient churches also *hear what the Spirit says to the churches* (Rev. 2,3...in Christ's Words)—before it is too late, and He comes to claim a **faithful, Holy, unstained Bride,** but finds instead **a wrinkled, sin-stained, blemished and disobedient church.**

A Personal Experience With Evidence of Southern Baptist Seminary Errors.

Over twenty years ago, I was a member and Deacon of a very small Canadian Baptist church. We (His church) experienced great shock and sadness to discover sexual immorality in an earlier Pastor, found it necessary to discharge him. We asked our Association to see that he not be allowed to serve as a Christian church leader again, since he showed no evidence of remorse or repentance.

Later, a new Pastor—a Canadian and recent graduate of the Southern Baptist Seminary at Louisville, Kentucky—was located, agreed to serve as Pastor of the small church I speak of, and came with his wife and young family, to serve the Lord in this small community. While offering him and his wife hospitality at our home, we naturally discussed the new Pastor's training, as well as his relative inexperience as a Pastor. We discovered at this time, that his wife had also been trained as a Pastor, at the same Seminary in Louisville—and that she had aspirations to become "a woman Pastor," in Christ's church, someday.

It was my first encounter—especially in connection with a Baptist church, after becoming a Christian believer—with a female graduate of a well-known, seemingly faithful, Baptist Seminary, aspiring to become a Pastor, and even training for it in a (former) stronghold of the Christian faith. I should mention, here, that the Baptist Pastor who earlier "led me to the Lord" in Canada, by his preaching and teaching, who baptized my wife, myself and our children, and added us to my baptismal church, was himself a much earlier, but more faithfully trained, graduate of this same Louisville Southern Baptist Seminary!

Returning to my shock and surprise, upon hearing that this Christian woman (the wife of our new Pastor) aspired to become a Pastor of a Christian church some day—and had even trained for it!—I questioned her about her aspiration. She said her professors at Seminary believed that the Apostle Paul's writings in his Letter to Timothy (1 Tim. 2 and 3) were not Spirit-inspired writings, but were, rather, only personal injunctions given by Paul—based upon his patriarchal society, and his personal beliefs and views as a former Jewish rabbi. That is, these professors neither upheld the scriptural faith of Christians (Baptist Christians in this case) of the past—*all Scripture is inspired and inerrant*—nor defended **the whole Bible as God's inspired, infallible, and sufficient Word of Truth**, to be followed faithfully by all Christians in all His churches on earth.

I spoke in Christian love to this woman, and her Pastor-husband, about their scripturally errant training in this formerly well-respected and faithful Christian Seminary—to no avail. The wife described a little more of her Louisville Baptist training, and said that she was taught, and believed, that God can (and did) ***call anyone, male or female,*** to ***any service*** to the Lord—including the two male church offices of Elder and Deacon—and that the Spirit would honour "His call" by "gifting her with the necessary gifts of preaching, and teaching to both men and women, as future Pastor of a Christian church." I spoke of the New Testament (1 Tim. 2,3) injunctions or prohibitions against women teaching or having ***authority over men*** in the church, and pointed out that confirmation of this could be found in the scriptural qualifications (and gender) of New Testament Pastors and Deacons. I also reminded her that this prohibition was based upon Paul's inspired statements concerning the events occurring in the Garden of Eden (Gen. 3), and that the early church accepted, as God-ordained, that woman's (Eve's) first and primary disobedience to God ruled against women teaching or having *authority over men* in the church. And, that this was also confirmed in the inspired Paul's teachings on male-only Overseers (Elders) and Deacons in the church (1 Tim. 3:2;3:11). It was useless—her *false teachers* had convinced her that her "personal call" to be "Pastor or teacher of men" overruled the Word of God. Indeed, she was also told that 1 Timothy 2 and 3 were only the words of men, not of the Spirit.

My brothers and sisters, do not have the Lord *hold this against you...that you have forsaken your first love,* and His Word of Truth (Rev. 2:4). Our Lord urges that you repent and correct any errors in this matter of women Pastors and Deacons in His Body on earth, or any other errors you might discover, with the help of the *Spirit of Truth.* All Christians, men or women, members or Spirit-approved and faithful leaders, need to ask for the Spirit's guidance to all truth, especially the Sanctifying Truth of the inspired Word of God alone. All Christians must be taught God's inspired Standard of Truth in their reformed New Testament church—and not listen to *false teachers* in the church or Seminary.

Part 5. Eternal Consequences of Church Disobedience
to the Divine Head.

Chapter 12

Listening to "What the Spirit (Not Men) Says to the Churches"

Part 5 of this book has been an examination of what Jesus Christ had to say to, and about, a small group of churches on the mainland of the Mediterranean Sea, north of the Island of Patmos, nearly 2,000 years ago. So that the church might avoid the consequences we have been speaking about, I—with God's Word and the Spirit's guidance—must emphasize not only disobedience in the early to middle centuries and today's church, but reiterate the plea of Christ to His Body of all ages: *hear what the Spirit says to the churches.*

In a few decades of growth, the churches learned the truth of the Lord's final statement of His Great Commission—for He surely was with them *always, to the very end of the age* (Matt. 28:20). Persecution, *false teachers*, disobedience, and spiritual *sleeping* were present, as well as errors and abuse concerning the Lord's Supper and Christian baptism, as we have seen and read in Scripture. But the Lord truly was with them. Questions were asked and answered by the Apostles and the local church leaders, with the Spirit's Aid. Yes, there were mistakes, even sin and grave errors encountered and overcome in those early years. And yes, as Christ told them, Satan was present among and around them in his agents, his *false teachers*, and often in the hearts of weak members of the church. But, God, the Holy Spirit, the Apostles (while they were still alive) and the overseeing Elders kept the churches steady on the Plan, Purpose, and Way that Christ taught them. The churches grew, in number of "widespread local churches," and in numbers of maturing new believers. Through persecution by hostile Jews, pagan cults, and *false teachers*, persuaded by Satan to lead weak believers astray and thus destroy his enemy, believers in Jesus (in his "Body," the church on earth) continued to spread, to all parts of the then-known world. The early church tried, but often failed the Lord in those early years. We know this as we read Revelation, Chapters 2 and 3.

Even a small sampling of the early Seven Churches reveals that most of them harbored disobedience, *false teachers, lukewarmness,* even spiritual somnolence or death. The problem is that His churches had been listening to false teachers not always *hearing what the Spirit says to the churches* (Jesus' Words, in Revelation 2 and 3, at the close of His first "audit and review" of His early church).

What False Teachers Have Said (and Still Say) to Christian Churches in the Past.

This subject is of vital importance to the purpose of this book for Christ. For if unsuspecting (untaught) believers in the Christian church are not aware of the fact that *Your enemy the devil prowls around like a roaring lion looking for someone to devour* (1 Pet. 5:8); then he, Satan, the devil, the old snake of Eden, infiltrates *false teachers* into the church Body. Such teachers will *introduce destructive heresies, even denying the Sovereign Lord* (2 Pet. 2:1), and these untaught, unsuspecting believers will, in their ignorance, be led to church disobedience, sin, and failures. And, *if church leaders and Spirit-gifted teachers do not teach all that Christ commanded* them to teach (Matt. 28:20), and obey Him as the inspired Paul wrote about in Eph. 4, *how can untaught disciples recognize heresy or any false teaching or disobedience creeping into the Body of Christ, then or now?*

The inspired Apostle Peter told God's elect in many of the growing churches of that time: *But there were also false prophets among the people* (of the past and the time of which he was speaking) *just as there will be false teachers among you* (2 Pet. 2:1).

After Saul's (now Paul's) conversion on the Damascus road, he became a *born again* believer. Told by the Lord of many things, including his new mission and *what you must do for Me* (Acts 9:6), he was brought, much later, to the newly-founded Christian church at Antioch by Barnabas. There, *for a whole year Barnabas and Saul met with the church and taught great numbers* of the believers (Acts 11:26). This verse is a rebuke for churches today who teach little to church members, instead of teaching them to obey **all the Lord commanded us**.

The new church at Antioch grew spiritually and thrived. When Saul and Barnabas finished their teaching mission, they took John Mark (after visiting the Jerusalem church) and, led by the Holy Spirit, were commissioned by the Antioch church to go on an evangelistic journey and mission to the lost and unsaved people in Asia province. The book of "Acts" continues with their mission until, in 14:26, we read *they sailed back to Antioch*. There, they found that something disturbing had gone on in their absence. But first, *they gathered the church together and reported all that God had done through them, and how He had opened the door of faith to the Gentiles. And they stayed there a long time with the disciples* (Acts 14:27,28—undoubtedly carrying on His Great Commission!).

Acts 15:1 tells us what concerned them: *Some men came down from Judea to Antioch and were teaching the brothers: "unless you are circumcised according to the custom taught by Moses, you cannot be saved."* These men, "brothers" of the mainly Gentile Christians at Antioch, were obviously Jews from Judea, converted by the initial work of the Jerusalem Christians and scattered by persecution from Jews in Jerusalem following the stoning of Stephen (Acts 8:1). These converted Jews, raised with Jewish religious customs, were **wrongly teaching new Christians**. Their "salvation" statements did not agree with the Christian doctrine of the Apostles. Paul and Barnabas disputed their false teaching concerning "circumcision of Gentiles required for Christian salvation." Obviously led by the Spirit, *Paul and Barnabas were appointed, along with some other believers,* from Antioch, *to go to Jerusalem to see the apostles and elders about this question* (Acts 15:2).

The church, at this time in Christianity's history, was maturing spiritually in several ways. For one thing, the Body in each new geographical location was being taught Christ's purpose for them, **as individual, self-governing bodies (under Christ the Head)**, as well as homogeneously—**each being part of His united body** although scattered about the then-known world—by the Apostles, and other, inspired, Spirit-gifted members. Although the Lord spoke of His Body as a singular entity (*my Body*—which it was, spiritually, yet represented by human disciples, or members), He knew and ensured that the church's Apostles and teachers knew, also, that they were to be **scattered** on the earth, **but not divided as to His Will and purpose.**

I personally am reassured in my Christian faith, when I read the inspired passage just quoted in Acts 15. The church at Antioch, separated by distance, individual, and autonomous—yet all Christ's disciples, being one in Christ, as the Father and the Son are One (John 17), was able to discern false teaching from error. Consultation with the Apostles and the brethren at Jerusalem would ensure that false teaching would soon be corrected at its possible source, lest it infect other churches, and destroy the unity Christ prayed for. The Apostles, with the Holy Spirit, formed the first Body of Christ at Jerusalem, and were, at first, the church leaders and teachers of the new and only church of Christ. But as the first church grew, with thousands of new converts to Christ, it became obvious to them that they, the Eleven Apostles (plus one to replace Judas Iscariot, the traitor) needed help. They appointed *seven men* (Acts 6:3), *full of the Spirit and wisdom*, to do the church's "administrative," or "social church work"—thus releasing the Apostles for *preaching, teaching and prayer.* As the church spread and grew, the Jerusalem church needed *elders*—church leaders under Christ and the Apostles, overseeing what Christ required of His Body in His Great Commission. So, we see, in Acts 15:6ff., that when the Antioch church delegation, together with the itinerant evangelists Paul and Barnabas (the latter a past "envoy") arrived at the Jerusalem church, they were met by a **group of leaders** consisting of the **Apostles** and male **Elders** (or "Overseers"), as described in 1 Timothy 3 by the inspired Paul.

I digress here deliberately, because my digression relates directly to the purpose of this book. Untaught, forgetful, *sleeping*, and disobedient church members and leaders, who read this scripturally and Spiritually-guided book, are to be made continually aware that **all they say and do in and for the local church**, to which they belong, **must** be in accordance with the Word of God—**not** with the words of *false teachers*, who reject or distort the inspired Word, and substitute their own false views. For disobedience to the Lord brings serious consequences from Christ.

A very few years after the new Christian church was formed at Antioch, then, the church was maturing in faith, knowledge, organizational structure, policy (church polity, as some say), sound doctrine, and wise, Spirit-urged actions. They had learned to be self-governing, yet always under sound teaching of what Christ Willed and commanded, under the Spirit. They had appointed men *full of faith and wisdom* as leaders, under the Divine Head, as well as men and women to *go* to the mission fields of *all nations*. And they also learned to recognize and reject doctrinal error. They learned, too, to seek the counsel, not only of the Spirit, but of the Apostles at the First church of Christ in Jerusalem! They knew these Apostles were not to be considered as human co-heads of the church, but were chosen ones of Jesus, to go before the Lord on His first mission to *seek and save the lost of Israel alone.* They had then been chosen to form, with the Spirit, His initial church of many in foreign lands and over ages of time. Since these Apostles were wise in their knowledge of church problems caused by *false teachers*, they and elders were consulted by the delegates from Antioch church—by Paul, the evangelist and teacher, and by Barnabas, himself *full of the Holy Spirit and faith* (Acts 11:24; also see Acts 4:36).

Acts 15 in my (NIV) Bible is unscripturally "sub-headed" with the words of a modern editor—*"The Council at Jerusalem."* These words of men—especially the phrase, "The Council"—lead immature and untaught believers to think that God, in His Bible, arranged this particular meeting at the First church at Jerusalem as a formal "Church Council." Some readers might say, "I have read, in church history" (not in Scripture), "about various human 'Councils of churches,' set up by certain divided groups of churches in the past. Some say that these must be seen as a 'God-arranged, and therefore, approved new pattern of Councils.'" *False teachers* could then—by deceitful schemes, and by adding unscriptural, uninspired words to various Bible versions—lead some untaught church members and leaders to think this Acts 15 meeting was a **scripturally-ordained "First Church Council meeting."** Later centuries' gatherings of divided churches (called "Council Meetings") could then also be assumed to be legitimate, and approved by God. This is untrue, unscriptural—and wrongly presented centuries later as approved by Christ or Scripture, or a future unscriptural "Pope," heading groups of churches! ***Consultations with other, autonomous churches—yes!*** But *Councils* under spurious, "outside, Supreme" *church leaders*? ***NO***!

Like false "Traditions," so-called "Councils of churches" must not oppose inspired Scripture, add to, or pervert God's Word, be divisive, or not represent ***all of His Body***. While the wrongful dubbing of a discussion and consultation between two Christ-Headed churches as a "council," in a Christian Bible "explanatory heading" nineteen centuries later may seem a small mistake, many, if not most, church sins and errors of past centuries (continuing today) have started out similarly and ended up opposing Scripture and God's Will and purpose for His church, as errant "Traditions."

The meeting of Acts 15, with those present, and their conversations well-described in the inspired text, is ***nowhere called—in Scripture***—"The Council at Jerusalem." It was clearly never intended by Paul to be anything more than a ***consultation*** with the first church leaders, the Apostles (unique to the Jerusalem congregation), and Elders of the First church at Jerusalem, by a Christian delegation from a remote, later-formed and independent (yet, in Christ, united) church.

The ***consultation*** was held on a Christian doctrinal issue important not only to both autonomous bodies of Christ, but to all other scattered bodies of their One Lord and Head. It was a theological crisis, precipitated by *false teachers* wrongly infiltrating the Antioch church. The problem was presented at this "consultative meeting of two Christian churches" (*my phrase, supported by Scripture—author*), and after much discussion, some other ***Jewish converts*** to Christianity in the First church spoke up in defense of what the Antioch church delegation felt was "false teaching." The Jewish converts at Jerusalem who spoke, it seems, were members of the Jewish *"Party of the Pharisees"*—as was Saul, now Paul, before his conversion. They had become Christian believers through the gospel preaching of the Apostles, and the Spirit's work, but they wrongly brought certain false beliefs with them. Namely, that Gentiles must be "converted" first to Judaism, and be circumcised—as male Jews, **alone,** must be—to be eligible to be saved by faith in Christ. But Christians, not under the Law, were then and are still under Christ alone.

It was another Gentile/Jew "religious" problem with which the Jewish Apostles, particularly, had struggled. They had much difficulty, at first, accepting that God intended to extend His Grace and salvation to the Gentiles. The Apostles were told by Jesus **not** to go to either the Samaritans **or** to the Gentiles, on His **first mission** to seek and save the lost of Israel **alone** (cf. Matt. 10:5). Now, building Christ's Body independently of the Jewish religion, their Lord Jesus Christ had commanded them to *Go* and *make disciples of all nations* (including Gentiles).

After Christ's rejection by certain Jewish leaders, and knowing that He must go to the Cross, and die, Jesus began to instruct the Apostles about God's new Plan to extend His Mercy to the Gentiles, and how He Jesus, hand an obedient, concurrent Plan to *build my church* so the Gentiles (in His All-Nations command)—Matthew 28, were now to be offered God's Salvation. His Commission (Matt. 28) spoke of Christ's new Mission (it was God's Plan, too!) to go out to preach the Gospel of Christ to these formerly outcast races of sinners. The Apostles, earlier were willing, but lacked understanding. Peter, himself had to be "shaken" in a vision from the Lord, before he would accept God's Truth and Message that Gentiles were no longer impure—because God declared them pure and wanted them to hear His Gospel and turn to Him.

Christ's church, established by the Holy Spirit and the Apostles, had spread, urged on by the Spirit. Believer/disciples from the Jerusalem church went into Judea, as well as on to the previously forbidden outcast Samaritans, and beyond. The Apostles were gradually led to see and to understand that God was now extending His salvation beyond the Jews, to the making of disciples in *all nations*, not just their own people. Peter had been convinced—by the extension of the church Christ Willed to build into Judea, Samaria, and to the ends of the known earth—and by the vision from God, telling him to "wake up." He now realized that he, too, must be obedient (even as a Jew by race and upbringing) to his new Christian duty to Christ, to *make disciples of all nations.*

Note here that the Apostle Paul—although he at one time had been a strict Pharisee (a sect of the Jews, ref. Acts 26), and a feared persecutor of Christians and the church—had been wonderfully converted by Christ on the Damascus road. The Lord was using him now, as His servant, to grow and spread His church, as well as teaching him to teach His church what He wanted them to do. Now Paul and Barnabas, with several members of the Antioch church, were "consulting" *the Apostles and Elders* (Acts 15:4) on this question, in Jerusalem. They wanted to talk to the first-formed church leaders about a problem similar to that encountered by Peter, with regard to Gentiles hearing and receiving the gospel message (Acts 10), and becoming Christians.

Primarily because the church (and Apostles) at Jerusalem **appeared** to have sent the Jewish converts from Judea with false instructions to Gentile believers in the Antioch church, Paul, Barnabas, members of the Antioch church and the Apostles and Elders reached an agreement not to *make it difficult for the Gentiles who are turning to God* (Acts 15:19,20). All present agreed, then, that a letter should be sent to Gentile Christian churches from Jerusalem, stating that the Apostles and Elders of Jerusalem did not, in truth, send the *false teachers* of Acts 15:1 to Antioch, but they *went out from us without our authorization* (Acts 15:24). The Apostles and Elders were human, too, and did not want anyone to blame them for someone else's sin! Peter and James were the principal advocates, with Paul and Barnabas, of the decision to write a letter *to the Gentile believers in Antioch, Syria, and Silicia...from the Apostles and Elders, your brothers* (NB: *"your brothers"*—**not** *"your superiors"!*) in Jerusalem.

It was a wise compromise decision, reached with the Spirit's help. Stating their regret that *some disturbed you, troubling your minds by what they said* (about "not being saved, unless first circumcised"), they agreed *not to burden you,* the predominantly Gentile Christian churches, in the areas noted, with anything beyond the requirements that *you are abstain from food sacrificed to idols, from blood, from the meat of strangled animals and from sexual immorality*—and, they said, *you will do well to **avoid** these things.*

These things, to be avoided by Christians of that time, society, and culture, were a combination of local evil customs occurring in pagan territories, and sinful habits repulsive to Jews living nearby the Christian churches. The "sexual immorality" problem was endemic (common) among the Greeks of those territories, and also occurred in pagan cult worship affecting the Gentile Christians in these Gentile regions by its continual presence. The "list" included in the letter was reasonable for the situation, because it satisfied the teachings of Judaism—God's teachings—on morality and His food restrictions to the Jews, while avoiding tension between Jews and Christians. At the same time, the list would be seen by the Christian churches as reflecting the moral and spiritual standards of Jesus Christ, as taught by the church and missionary evangelists. The letter was to be taken by Paul, Barnabas, Judas, and Silas from Jerusalem to Antioch, and thence to other area churches. We read it now and see it as the Spirit's work in the New Testament Word for the church.

At the very least, the Jewish converts would be told that all believers (whether Jew or Gentile) are equal in the sight of God; at the most, it ensured that the circumstances at Antioch or other pagan areas, the consultation with the Apostles and Elders, and the resultant compromise letter to Gentiles, would be credited to the Spirit (Acts 15:28). I'm sure that the Jewish—now Christian—Apostles (and Paul and others present) would finally realize that the Messiah, Jesus Christ, the coming King of the Jews, and Divine Head of His Christian church "Body" were one and the same, acting upon God's separate plans for Jews and Gentiles. And finally, that it would all be recorded in the inspired Word of God. In this way, the Christian church of later centuries would have an example of the spirit of Godly (and scriptural) compromise necessary, ***if all believers are to be one, as the Father and Son are One*** (John 17:20). The particular problem between Jew and Christian occuring at Antioch (basically the Jewish convert's misunderstanding Christ's Will and Purpose to "postpone" the Messiah's full acceptance by the Jews, until He fulfilled. God's Plan to have His Son's church extend God's salvation

Mercy to Gentiles) seemed acceptable to all present at this discussion. The conflict between Jews and Christian—over many Jews in the past and today not accepting Jesus Christ as the prophesied Messiah—was not then, nor is yet resolved; nor will it likely be before Christ comes again. Until He comes, both Jew and Christian must become fully obedient to the Triune God, as He has ordained for each separate Body. Christians must be obedient, holy, and united, while not under the Law which is for Jews alone, according to God's good pleasure, and in His time.

The evidence of human conflict between Christian church leaders of that day was not resolved entirely, however, for we see in Galatians 2 the recurring problem of *false brothers* (verse 4) who had infiltrated the church there, as well as conflicts between Peter and Paul (2:8) arising over similar Jew/Gentile-Christian problems as had occurred at Antioch earlier.

Speaking as a Bible teacher and student, since one of my burdens from the Lord is the obvious fact that the Christian church is divided today, as as in the distant past, these evidences, in the inspired New Testament, of problems with *false teachers* in the church, as well as the early and continuing hostility of Jews toward Gentile Christians down to the present, confirms in my heart and mind that this book of warning, written on the basis of the inspired Word of God, is now urgently necessary. Once all disobedience is removed, and then only, will all the Christian churches will be truly *one in Jesus Christ*.

The inspired Paul, in Galatians 2, recognizes and writes about the conflicts we have observed in the early church, extending to the later church and today. He writes: *through the law* (of God to the Jew) *I died to the law* (in becoming a Christian) *so that I might live for God. I have been crucified with Christ and I no longer live, but Christ lives in me* (Gal. 2:19,20). It is a great pity that both Jewish and Gentile Christians, in all centuries, have not and do not entirely today understand and live out their lives for God, as Jew and Christian, as His Word tells us to do. As Peter observed in 2 Pet. 2:1, and now Paul observes in Galatians 2:4, *false teachers* (sometimes brothers) in the church do enormous harm in their deliberate distortions and misunderstandings of God's inspired truths for both Jew and Christian. *False teachers*, in teaching seminaries, also influence the Christian church today.

What False Men Have Said to the Churches of Today.

I am always in a quandary when I select examples of false teachings from my experience in the church, from church history, or from public information sources such as newspapers and magazines—because there are simply too many of them for a reasonable size of book. However, I will give some practical advice to readers, so that when, if, and as the Spirit moves members and leaders of possibly disobedient Christian churches to examine their "own" church for sin and error, the self-examination will proceed quickly and thus please Christ, the Head. But obedience long-delayed, like justice, is not true obedience.

One recent example comes to my mind. I will write it down as I recall it, from a newspaper report in Canada about a Canadian church. Again, let me reassure my readers, and those from the church "denomination" I speak about from the public record, that I do not report this problem of *false teachers* in the church out of personal "religious bias," or lack of Christ's love in me. I do not speak of this public incident for any reason other than to further my warning—on behalf of Christ—to other churches. I desire only that churches tolerating sin and *false teachers* today may understand, *wake up, repent* and return *to do the* (obedient) *things you did at first* (Rev. 2,3—our mutual Lord speaking).

Here is a public example of a church listening to what men say in, and to, some churches today. On Nov. 1, 1997, a newly appointed (August of that same year) "Moderator" (unscriptural office!) of the United Church of Canada—reputedly the largest Protestant "Christian denomination" in Canada—stated, in an interview published by the Ottawa Citizen and the Edmonton Journal (among others), some of his startling religious "views." This is what the editorial board of the Ottawa Citizen newspaper reported in print: "An activist moderator is rocking the United Church of Canada. Rev. Bill Phipps wants to 'mend a broken world' by exhorting his flock to focus on social issues, not religious doctrine." Quoting Rev. Phipps: "Those who say the United Church is drifting away from the Bible haven't read it themselves." And: "I don't believe Jesus is the only way to God. I don't believe he rose from the dead as a scientific fact. I don't know whether those things happened. It's an irrelevant question." Phipps is quoted: "Is heaven a place? I have no idea. I believe that there is a continuity of the spirit in some way but I would be a fool to say what that is." And: "Rev. Phipps told the Citizen 'he doesn't accept the Bible as a valid historical record, and questioned the idea of Jesus as the son of God.'" Phipps also often "refers to God as *'she'* when he speaks," the interviewer said (*Notice the influence of false female teachers here—author*).

These startling views held by the then- United Church of Canada Moderator came under a rebuttal (of sorts) when its "governing Board" met with the Citizen editorial board, and told them, in effect, that the new Moderator or any other member of *their church*, could say what they pleased in *their church*. "The United Church," they said "has a wide range of membership views," and they didn't intend to "suppress any comments made by their leaders or members." Little—if any—mention is made, in these statements, of God's inspired written Word, of the Holy Spirit's work, or of anything scriptural. Their members' or leader's points of personal view or beliefs, instead, often opposed the inspired Word of God.

In a Dec.10, 1994 report from the same Ottawa Citizen newspaper, passed along to the Edmonton Journal newspaper, the news reporter gave the results of a report commissioned by the same United Church of Canada, researched and published by an Alberta sociologist, Reg Bibby.

His report says, in brief: "Canada's largest Protestant church has to act now to become relevant to its members or it will die." He continues, "The United Church...has a rapidly aging and shrinking membership, and its leaders and parishioners are at odds over what its priorities should be." Bibby called the United Church a "denomination in demise." Bibby's sociological report assesses survey results and assigns percentages to the United Church's membership's responses across Canada. It reports, as well, the "views" of its local church leaders, its governing "boards," and the public and private opinions of its appointed but unscriptural "Moderator"—and poses some conclusions about its probabilities of a long or a short "life" as a professed Christian "Body" in Canada. Statistically—and practically—many churches are failing Christ and their members. But the real question sought by this group of churches, themselves resulting from past church schisms—and incorporating members from several earlier Christian "denominations"—should be: "What does Jesus Christ, the Divine Head of His true and faithful churches, think about the 'United Church of Canada?'" Is this church truly "united" in all things, *as the Father and Son are One*? Is it a scripturally faithful church, or does He *hold certain things against* them? Does He think of them as *sleeping, lukewarm*, or even *spiritually dead*, as some New Testament churches of Revelation 2 and 3? What does Jesus Christ think of the diverse and unscriptural views and offices in this church?

I personally recall an "edict" (perhaps only a "suggestion" issued by the Sunday School Board, or "Board of Christian Education") of the United Church of Canada more than 30 years ago, to those churches using its (U.C.) Christian Education materials for teaching purposes. It stated that *"Sunday School teachers using our (teaching) materials can now teach the Bible to their pupils as either 'myth' or as God's truth."* Either "view" was acceptable to their denomination at that time. The material itself was subtly altered, in certain areas, to fit their Board's new "mythical" views of the Bible. At that time, I was a member of another denomination which used the U.C. material. But we also believed in an inspired, inerrant, infallible Bible, completely true in all that God, its Divine Author, caused holy men of old to write down. So, "our local church" dropped the new "mythical" teaching aids from the United Church—and our teachers resumed teaching new and old Christian members the Bible as God's Word of Truth to men of all ages and societies, and containing the gospel message of salvation that would lead sinful men and women, to true salvation and *new life in Christ.*

I am being neither judgmental, nor deliberately hateful, in listing any of these public examples of Christian church error and disobedience. Jesus Christ judges their acts and words and will judge

all men. I point out His Holy Words here,only to warn all the churches of what will happen If they continue along their willful, sinful and
disobedient path of denying, rejecting, opposing, and distorting
God's written Words of Truth, and teaching **their errors** to **their**
members. Declaring that they can have, and teach to their members, their own views of Divine Truth is also disobedient to God and
His Son's church; it shows that this church is not at all **one** nor is it
fully obedient as Christ urges in His Word.

Jesus, our confessed Saviour and Lord asked His Heavenly Father
(in praying for His future Church—its members and leaders) to *Sanctify them* (all Christian disciples by the Truth; *Your Word is Truth*,
John 17:17). Those of us who are Christians, know from His Word,
that Christ is Divine (John 1:1), and was sent to earth not only to
seek and save the lost of Israel, as the Messiah, but, when rejected
by the Jews, He followed God's Plan to extend His Mercy and Grace
in Salvation to the Gentiles. It was God's Plan, too, to have His only-
begotten Son *Will to Build My Church* (Matt. 16:18), and said—*the
gates of Hades will not overcome it.* Our Lord gave the Gift of His Holy
Spirit to each repentant believer in the Resurrected Christ, who then
became our own "resident Counsellor, and Spirit of Truth in the
Lord's temporary absence in Heaven. He gives us the Will, Strength,
and Knowledge of God's Word to carry out His "great Commission,"
to grow the church, and extend God's grace to all nations of unbelievers. Hades (or hell) will not overcome the Christian church, but
Satan and his *false teachers* may, and have overcome **some** churches
in the past, and today. If the churches do not *wake up* (Christ, Rev.
2,3) and *do the* obedient things *they did at first,* disobedience,
neglect or opposition to the Inspired Word of God—if continued,
and not reformed, will cause sinful churches to suffer Christ's Wrath
and terrible consequences (as found in Rev. 2,3).

Is the United Church of Canada, since its formation as another
schismatic Body (they called it a "reformed church" just a few
decades ago), disobedient and failing Christ in many areas, as the
Seven Churches of Revelation 2,3 were in many instances? I believe
so, for their leaders have publicly stated their unbelief in Jesus
Christ's Divinity and Resurrection from death. They have annulled

Christ's Great Commission to His Body (the making of disciples of all nations), and instead are pursuing what they call (unscripturally) a "social gospel" (i.e., looking after unbelievers' bodies, not **both** soul and Body).

The religious sociologist's reported study of the views of their church members reveals that many members and local church leaders hold different views from their leaders—but what does this secular study mean in the eyes of Christ? The Divine Head of His Christian church in this world commands obedience to His Word, and desires our unity—as He and His (and our) Heavenly Father are One. He demands that the believer/members of His entire "Body" be united, *in the faith once entrusted to the saints*, to do and be for Him all that He requires.

The so-called Christian or "church head" who does not believe—or is taught about Christ and His Word and cannot, in his disbelief, confess these eternal, inspired things—is not a true Christian, and cannot be "added to" or be allowed to remain in a true Christian church—unless he and they repent. It also means that the church that does not make true disciple/believers in the True scriptural Way, or baptize them in the only True Way, and/or does not teach the disciples (so made and baptized) all that Christ asked them to do, has failed Christ, and will fail His "audit," as shown in the New Testament (Rev. 2,3—see Part 4). Christ is the One Who *searches the hearts and minds of men* (Rev. 2:23), and He will *repay each* of us *according to* your *deeds*. "*False teachers*," "false leaders," and "false churches" must be warned of their fate, before Christ comes again, as He has promised in Revelation 22:7,20.

False teachers and false teachers who claim that every Christian in their church or divided denomination has a **right** to individual opinions and views of Scripture are **wrong**—for they and we must recognize that **it is not "our church," but the Lord's church in question now.** Only the Divine Head of the Christian church, Who Willed to build it for His Divine purpose, and Who gave Himself up for His church "Body" has the sole right to determine our beliefs. Any person in this world can, and often humanly does, "will" to build "his" or "her" so-called "church"—and persuade a group of persons to join, in worship, service, and obedience, the human leader (or a false god). But **they cannot name their "church" a Christian church, unless they faithfully obey Jesus Christ's Will and purpose, as completely defined and outlined in Holy Scripture alone.** Nor can they, when Christ returns to earth, avoid His Divine wrath, if they have disobeyed Him in any part of His Will and purpose.

In these last times before Christ comes again, as He promised, to claim His *radiant* Bride, the obedient Christian church on earth, there have been and will be many *false teachers* and false churches. Often they call themselves "Christian"; a branch of the Jewish faith; or a name unique to themselves. These false "churches" refer to "a god," to a "heaven" (but not a hell!), to a "new home" on some planet in our universe. Recent history reveals that these lost souls often follow their false leader to suicide and death by poison, flame, or self-destruction. Men and women who reject the One, True, Creator-God—known as *Heavenly Father* and *God* to true Christians—often completely separate themselves and form a new sect, whose "god" is their charismatic leader and *false teacher*. Too, a small number of these find their way into weak Christian churches, where they teach—not the inspired Word of God to other weak "Christians"—but false and perverted versions of the One, True, sanctifying Word of God. These false teachings do not set apart the listeners for Christ's service, but weaken their faith. The members remain spiritual *infants* (Eph. 4:14), useless to both Christ and His church.

Hear now, from Holy Scripture, *what the Spirit says to the churches* (Rev. 2 and 3). Regardless of what churches down through the ages to today think about the Divine Head and His revelations, He is still *The Alpha and the Omega...who is, and who was, and who is to come, the Almighty* says the Lord God (Rev. 1:8). He is the Saviour and Lord of all true believers in His "Body," the True Church on earth. And He has *all authority in Heaven and on earth*. His warnings are made to all failing and failed churches of all time. Churches who have not repented of their disobedience to Christ will suffer their Lord's repayment in kind (Rev. 2:23) when He comes for His *radiant* Bride. The unrepentant churches will have their *lampstands* removed from the Bridegroom's Presence (see Rev. 1,2 and 3). His

Word says that only those who repent, return to their *first love*, and *do the things* they *did at first* (obediently) will please Him and allow Him to withhold His judgment and discipline.

The New Testament Book called "Revelation" is the last Book in the canon (rule or standard) of the New Testament for the church of Jesus Christ. In it, He reveals to all mankind—as well as to His Christian church of the New Testament era—*what is now and what will take place later* (Rev. 1:19). His beloved Apostle John obediently wrote down Christ's Words and Vision (and the Spirit preserving it), so that we later Christians would know with certainly *what will take place later* in God's Time on this earth for both Jew and Christian. Without this inspired "Book," men would live their lives in rebellion to God—rarely in full obedience to our Saviour and Lord. With it, as part of the inspired, inerrant Christian Bible, Christians especially must face up to our duty and responsibility, as part of His world-wide "church Body"—or face the clear consequences of sin and disobedience.

The Book of Revelation is somewhat daunting reading for new Christians, as well as to many Elders (or Overseers, or Pastors) of today's Christian churches, for it is written in Divine symbolic language. For this and other reasons, this Revelation of Jesus Christ to the Apostle John, is often, it seems, treated as either incomprehensible to the "average Christian," or is falsely interpreted and taught by men who indicate that only they know the "hidden truth" buried deep within it. The Spirit of God, however, can, and will, Guide Christians who read it, to the Truth of God (John 16:13). It is no mystery to those who seek the Spirit's Guidance (John 14,16) and obey it fully in faith. But the true view of this important, final Book of the "Christian Bible" is neither **errant**, nor **hidden**. What it is, of course—to Bible believers and Christian scholars guided by the *Spirit of Truth*—is nothing less than God's infallible Word to God-fearing men, preserved over the centuries to teach and guide us to His Truth. By "us," His Word tells us, Christ means the entire Christian church Body on earth, of all eras.

Only if we accept the Bible's inspired, inerrant teachings as from God the Father, God the Son (Church Head, too!), and God the *Spirit of Truth*—only then will God's Word to men be accepted

and used rightly as our Creator-God intends. I pray, too, that all my readers in Christian churches today discover what the Bible describes itself as being for us all (I quote from 2 Tim. 3:16,17): *All Scripture is God-breathed* (i.e. inspired, or Spirit-moved) *and is useful* (absolutely essential, I would say!—author) *for teaching, rebuking, correcting and training in righteousness, so that the man of God* (i.e., righteous Jews and Christians) *may be thoroughly equipped for every good work.* While read and discussed often in symbolic language, we Christians (new or old) should need neither fear nor shun the Book of Revelation, nor **any** part of the Word of God, because Christ often explains His symbolism, and the Spirit, if asked, will Guide us to His Truth. Choose Spirit-guided teachers for your church!

We also have the Word's assurances that the same Spirit gives gifts *to each one, just as he determines* (1 Cor. 12:11), including the gift of teaching the Word to all members of the church as He has Commanded (Matt. 28:18–20). With Spirit-led teaching, all spiritual *infants* (untaught Christians) **become strong and spiritually mature**, and are able to both **strengthen the whole "church body"** and **withstand false teachers in the church** who often lead them astray (Ref. Eph. 4. For gifts, see Rom. 12, 1 Cor. 12).

Near the close of each "Letter" to the Seven Churches in Asia, we find Christ's Words of **excellent Counsel**, namely: *He who has an ear to hear, let him hear what the Spirit says to the churches.* Whether having spoken Words of *commendation* or *condemnation*—or both—to each church on the list, Christ decided, in His Omniscient Wisdom, to repeat this Divine sentence to everyone in those churches (and all future churches). **Why did Christ give each church His Words—about their good works, or their disobedient works—and then feel it necessary to add that they should listen to** *what the Spirit says to the churches?* It is, I believe, because our Lord, Head of His Body, the church, knows our human frailty and tendency towards sin. Down through the scriptural history of God's dealing with mankind, even to this day, Satan has been trying to tempt men and women to disobey what He has said to them. But through His Death on the Cross, God's Only-begotten Son has fulfilled all righteousness by dying for the sins of the world. Both obedient Jews and obedient Gentile Christians have had God's

Grace extended to them. A wonderful future, in the New Heaven and New Earth, is spoken about in His Word and is open—according to God's plan for the earthbound Jews and for Heaven-bound, faithful Christians—to all who believe and obey Him and His Son.

The "antidote" for sin, disobedience, and immature members of His church of all ages, is **not only** to *hear what the Spirit says to the churches*—but **act upon what He says** in a way that is pleasing to the Head of His undivided and obedient Christian Body. If some of my readers are fully carrying out all that our Lord has taught and commanded them, I say "Praise the Lord for your church" (really "His church")—and thank you for reading this far! But if you have any doubts—after reading this book and all the Scripture passages herein—I, with our Saviour and Lord, urge you to examine your church and all it does or does not do for the Lord, with prayer and the Spirit's guidance. Repent and reform any sin, and return to Him in love.

Chapter 13

The Scriptural Reform Process Required for the Disobedient Church

In this last Part (6) of this book, as a fellow Christian believer and member of Christ's Body, the church, I seek to warn members and leaders of disobedient churches of Christ in this world, about two urgent scriptural facts that will soon affect "our" future personal and corporate church existence:

- First, Jesus Christ, our Saviour, Lord, and Head of His church—to which you and I, and countless millions all over the world are joined by baptism after belief—is coming back (Rev. 22:7), soon, to claim what He hopes will be a *radiant*, sinless *church*. To claim us, His church of believers, as His holy Bride, *without stain or wrinkle or any other blemish* of disobedience (see Eph. 5:27).

- A second, scriptural fact is that the Head of His church, the coming Divine Bridegroom, has told us in His Holy, inspired, and inerrant Word—many times, and in many ways—what He expects us to do and be for Him to make His whole church fully loyal, obedient, and faithful in all He has asked and commanded of us. Included in the second fact, are our Lord's Words of reward and punishment.

Previous chapters have concentrated on the scriptural details concerning these two major facts, but of course they do not stand alone on the book of Revelation. The Gospel Books and the Letters to the Churches also have told us all that we need to know to carry out what He asks of every Christian church member or leader, in every true Christian church in the past and today.

We know too, and I have emphasized it often, that the Lord wants us all to be one united "Body," just *as we* (the Father and I) *are one* (see John 17:11,22). Yet, the church of Jesus Christ today is in schism. It is divided by false teachings—often by *false teachers* seeking to have their own views of God's scriptural Will and purpose for His church put in place, rather than obeying the inspired, inerrant New Testament for His church. Today's churches are also split apart by "man-made" false doctrines, traditions and practices, instead of being united in all things. The Christian church today must get "back to the Bible" **only**. For the church this means, primarily, back to the New Testament truths.

Christians also know that Christ links obedience directly to our love for Him (see John 15:9,10). If we are found disobedient to Him, it is because we *have forsaken* our *first love* (Rev. 2:4). We show that we do not love Him, our Saviour, and the One we falsely call "Lord" in our disobedience (John 14:23).

The Gospel of John contains a veritable treasure house of Jesus' truth, love, and teachings, all inspired and preserved by the Holy *Spirit of Truth*, who enters each Christian believer when he/she first repents and believes in Him. John 13–17 contains much of what we know about the Holy Spirit, and His work in our lives—or can learn, if we invite Him to Counsel, Guide and even Remind us as to what Christ has said and is saying to us in His inspired, written Word. I have made much of the Holy Spirit's role, for I strongly believe (with His often asked-for Wisdom) that Christian and Christian church failures, the evil influence of *false teachers*, and Satan's work in the world and in the church could all be **overcome** if we would but *hear what the Spirit says to the churches*—and obey Him (Rev. 2,3).

With the Spirit's loving aid, it is time to further examine ourselves and our local church for disobedience or failure to Christ, the Head. We must seek to be revived again, to repent of discovered sin, and to move to true reform, in accordance with His Word alone. Then, with heartfelt prayer, we must act to become *holy*, *radiant*, united, faithful and loving—at last, fully obedient to the True Head of His church on earth when He comes again to claim His Bride (Eph. 5:27).

A True, Scriptural Reform "Process" for Disobedient Christian Churches.

I hope my readers will forgive my introduction of an unscriptural term ("process") in this chapter, as I did similarly in Part 4 when I used a secular phrase ("audit and review") in describing Jesus' words to the Seven Churches in Asia in Rev. 2,3. I only write these things to create some urgent interest for my readers—who, after all, live in a technological world, a materialistic world little interested in the future of mankind.

The words "Audit and review," I hope, stimulated interest in a portion of the Bible usually only studied and taught by 'dry old Bible scholars,' and taught to 'dry old church members' as a purely optional Bible study class in most churches. As a Christian Bible student, teacher, and member of our Lord's church on earth, I, too, have had a secular career in our material world. I have been involved in several secular audits, reviews, seminars, and like learning experiences. So, as many of my readers did, I'm sure, when we encountered Revelation 2,3 chapters about the Christian church, I almost immediately thought—"why, what Christ is doing by His audit and review of some early churches, is just what I and my business associates have done: examined, identified, and corrected problems in our own business situations."

When we did our "performance reviews," of our employees' faithfulness and good work, we commended them for loyalty, and hard and faithful work, and promised them rewards and a better future if they complied with what we said! If they conducted themselves wrongly, however, they received a warning of what would happen to them if they didn't correct the problems found. These are the spiritual things that Christ did for the benefit of the Seven Churches in the early church, some 2000 years ago, as well as for the benefit of all later churches over the centuries.

Depending entirely upon my readers' scriptural and spiritual knowledge, and spiritual maturity, as well as upon the spiritual faithfulness and maturity of the Christian church to which they belong, they will have understood or misunderstood what Christ, through His Word and His Spirit, says about what He expects of His church. If the Spirit has led even a few members or leaders of a few disobedient churches to enter this Christ-urged "process" of self-examination, it will be worthwhile. For it will act as a "Divine seed" which, when sowed with the Spirit's aid, will certainly bring forth a faith harvest noticed by other disobedient Church members (and known by the Lord) who pass by these "fields of truth" and consider studying and applying Christ's Words to their own situation.

A Scriptural "How To" List.

In our busy lives, we often compile "lists." Rather than considering volumes of detailed contents which may be scattered over many pages of Scripture, let me list again what we must do for Him as encountered in the Word, with the Spirit's guidance.

Here is the list I compiled, from Revelation 2,3 and other portions of Scripture, of the minimal elements of a scriptural and Christ-urged *"process of reform"* leading to the **end result** of churches returning to *do what* they *did before*—that is, becoming **fully faithful, obedient, unstained, blameless**, and spiritually *radiant*, in accordance with all that our Lord has asked and commanded His churches to be and to do for Him.

Let me outline for you why this process of reform, to succeed, must contain these 8 elements (at least): PRAYER; THE HOLY SPIRIT'S COUNSEL; SELF-EXAMINATION; REVELATION; SELF-AWARENESS (DISCOVERY AND CONVICTION), REPENTANCE, REVIVAL, AND REFORM, and produce, finally, a Radiant, sinless, Christ-pleasing church.

1. PRAYER.

A crucial element of personal and corporate worship, revealed and taught by the Lord, is prayer to our Triune God, in the Name of His Son, our Saviour, proclaimed Lord and our church Head. The early disciples saw, and were Spirit-inspired to write down for future disciples, how important prayer was in Jesus' life. They even asked Him to **teach them to pray**. We have an "example of Holy prayer" in Scripture, as well as written "samples" of His prayers to His Heavenly Father. Often we neglect to pray. Often we are not taught by church leaders and gifted teachers to pray, and do not read in Scripture our Lord's prayers concerning His love and hopes for us, or even his gentle reproof: *If you obey my commands you will remain in my love* (John 15:10).

Prayer is necessary in entering into this reform process. Christian church members or leaders who try, without prayer, to achieve reform—or even find out whether their church is fully or partially obedient in all things to the Lord—invite Satan to enter into these proud or weak Christians, confuse and divert them, and lead the failing church Body away from our Lord's Will. Effective prayer is absolutely necessary to help the necessary reform process by leading every participant to the Truth of God about their concerns. Ask the Holy Spirit, the *Spirit of Truth,* to assist in this particular effort of self-examination before reform, for another of His roles is to *remind us of everything* Christ *has said* to us—see John 14:26. The Spirit within each of us Christians, new or old, spiritual *infant* or mature adult, must be consulted, in prayer, for another of His duties is to *guide us into all truth* (John 16:13). **What better Teacher can we find and consult than this SPIRIT OF TRUTH?**

Prayer directed to God, our Heavenly Father, in the Name of Jesus Christ, His Obedient Son, is important too, in every single area of our concerns. Even if we find our church disobedient or confused in some respects as to what the inspired Words of Christ ask or command us to be and do for Him, and feel uncertain what to do next, we should pray that the Holy Spirit will convict us of our failings, counsel us to ask forgiveness, and provide direction in what we must do to appease a Just and Holy God, and His Son, the only True Head of the church He Willed to build.

2. THE HOLY SPIRIT'S COUNSEL.

When we have asked the Spirit, in prayer, to draw near and guide us, and He has done so—and we begin to ask His help to go to the next step in the reform process—we can speak silently to the Holy One within us, called the *Counselor* in John

14:26). His inerrant counsel and Divine advice will be given to all who ask, as the process proceeds. This is exactly why the Lord told His disciples that He would not leave them alone (for He must go soon to His Heavenly Father), but would send His Spirit to help them (John 14:16–18). I ask each member and leader who desires to enter into this "process" I speak of, to first read the Lord's Words concerning His Spirit, in John 14 and 16, before doing anything else. Then the *prayer* element will be "on target" (focused, as we say today!).

In this process, too, unlike worldly business "audits," "seminars," and "business meetings," these necessary elements of prayerful personal and church self-examination will lead to frequent pauses, in which the church members seek the Counsel, the Truth, and the Reminders of what Christ has said to His church from His Spirit in prayer. Thus strengthened, we can go on to the next step in the process of restoring (renewing) the church Body to faithful and full obedience. In summary, if you examine the scriptural "lessons" offered by the New Testament church to the later church and to us today, you will find that every time the early church tolerated, or allowed *false teachers* into the church, they got into trouble. But they got out with the Spirit's counsel and Divine aid—and, I'm sure, always with fervent prayer to God!

3. SELF—(or CHURCH) EXAMINATION.

The church moved by the Holy Spirit to examine itself for possible failings, in the light of Christ's teachings and commands, with prayer and the *Spirit of Truth*, begins to do so with a Christ-like purpose in mind. They will enter into the process of becoming His True obedient Body in the Will of the Lord, by seeking to please Him.

I will use this chapter to "set the stage," so to speak, for this necessary step in the process of achieving full and obedient church and personal Christian reform. And, in the following chapter I will put all these necessary steps together in a practical format that churches, from the smallest to the largest, **can please Christ** by finding disobedience and casting it out. Then

278

only can they return to full obedience (with revival and renewal) to our Lord's teachings and commands for His church.

I must remind you that if Reform is found necessary, it must be carried out quickly, and on an urgent time-table, for our Lord has said He is Coming Soon (Rev. 22:7,20).

Self-examination is both a personal and a church process—done, I suggest, both personally and together as a church Body. It should be carried out with much prayer and much calling and reliance upon the Holy Spirit to search our minds and hearts, and counsel us to return to truth.

The "church Body examination" process should be prepared for by the "Elders" of the church (also called "Overseers" or "Pastors" in New Testament Scripture). In the "job description" that the Spirit inspired the Apostle Paul to write down in 1 Timothy 3 for this *noble task* of Pastor (verse 1), we see the faith and character qualities outlined that will allow each of these human leaders of the Christian church (under the Head, Jesus Christ) to lead and take care of the Body, with the help of the Spirit. So, the Elders (or Pastors, or Overseers) of each church must ask the Spirit's guidance, and be freshly committed to self-examination through an "audit and review" process based upon and compared with unchanging scriptural truths as set out in the New Testament for the church. Through prayer and the Spirit, they will shepherd His flock to the Truth.

Self-examination—whether individually before the Lord in the quiet privacy of our homes, or done in our "church home" (members only)—must have the same goal, to please our Saviour and Lord. By bringing our corporate, "bodily" actions, conduct, words and deeds into the open meeting, honestly, in the full sight of our **brothers and sisters in the Lord**—and in the full knowledge of the Lord and His Holy *Spirit of Truth*—we must **examine what we have done in the past**. When this is done, when the "Body" have laid themselves and their acts before Him *who searches our hearts and minds* (Rev. 2:23), and found sin, pride, spiritual apathy, or find themselves spiritually *asleep*—the self-examination must continue by comparing these deeds, that the Lord *holds* *against them,* with His Words of Truth. Note: Churches should also examine their Creeds, Statements of Faith, or Doctrinal "lists," if they have prepared such things, rather than "taking their stand upon the Words of Christ alone." For many Creeds, Catechisms, etc., are incomplete, and contain men's words, rather than God's. Sincere members and leaders seeking necessary reform must return to God's Word alone.

Church Elders and members who have Spirit-given gifts of teaching others (added to by their Spirit-inspired Scripture studies) should work together with the Spirit to guide the church Body (perhaps not all well-taught or spiritually mature) to the teachings and commands of Christ, and discuss how to cast out unscriptural false teachings or doctrines unwisely adopted in the past.

What will come from this step, I pray—and every obedient member and leader of every Body of Christ should pray—will be a Christ-like and **true reform movement**. It may be small or large, depending upon past and present faithfulness or lack of it in the church under self-review, but it will ensure, among other things, that Christ's Great Church Commission is now and always carried out faithfully and fully. Only then will the inspired passage of Ephesians 4 (concerning the teaching and maturing of **all** church members, required by the Lord in Matt. 28:18–20) be fully and faithfully carried out. No more "voluntary" Bible classes—a full range of mandatory Christ-ordered Bible studies must be instituted for members of all ages (not just Sunday School for the children). Only this will satisfy Christ's Will and purpose for the church to teach all believing members to *obey all that I have commanded you.* No more "catechism" classes or brief summary statements from the Bible; no more substitution of Bible extracts, homilies or weak sermons for the full teaching requirement of all members by the church. Nothing less than full church Bible instruction of **every member** of **all that** the Lord requires of His church in His scriptural Words of truth (Matt. 28:20) is to be done.

Scripture tells us that repentance, revival, and **reform back to what Christ "asks us to do"** is not easy, or without cost—spiritually, and in every other way. The New Testament teaching of the Lord's Words, by inspired Apostles and holy men—about error and *false teachers* in the church, and what was necessary to correct the many errors that crept in during even a few decades of church planting and attendant persecution—tells us it is common for Christians of any age to fail God. But it also tells us, as the Lord teaches us in His first "audit and review" of the Seven Churches (Rev. 2,3), it is necessary to **overcome and recover from our sin** and failures **and return to full obedience,** or the penalties will doom us forever in His wrath. Rewards and punishments as described by Christ will surely follow in His Time—whether today, tomorrow, or when He comes again to claim a *radiant church, without stain or wrinkle or any other blemish* (Eph. 5:27) of our sin and disobedience. This is why we must enter fearlessly, with the Spirit as our guide, into His scriptural "repentance and reform" process, with all the help we can get, from Scripture, the Spirit, faithful church leaders under Christ, and Spirit-gifted members of the church Body. Above all else, review and discard forever **all church traditions not supported fully by the inspired, inerrant Word of God.**

4. REVELATION.

Revelation, in this reform context (spiritual and scriptural), means a revealing by the *Spirit of Truth* from God to the Body of Christ. I have listed this "step" as a necessary process part that each member and leader of the church of Christ must accept and understand from His Word, and make part of their lives, actions, and words, as church members. Especially must they understand this in connection with the church's *self-examination step* of review leading to reform of personal and corporate disobedience (past and present) to the Lord. I learned it as any Christian can—and must—learn it, from Bible study and teaching, and experienced it with the *Spirit of Truth* as my *Teacher and Reminder* of all things that our Lord requires of us (John 14:26). The **"revealing"** by the Spirit in this context **is a revealing of God's Word of present Truth**. Not something completely new, as some *false teachers* announce to their followers. God's Spirit, when asked, will guide us to all truth, the Truth of God's sanctifying Word (see John 17:17), *already given by the Spirit* to us in the Bible—New Testament and Old.

I learned, as I matured from being a new spiritual *infant* to a church and Spirit-taught adult, that whenever my teacher, or I, or other students in church (or private) Bible study classes ran into difficulties correlating the inspired Word of God with what some human teachers said or wrote about religious matters, or church, or personal Christian problems—we could find revealed Truth and trust inspired scriptural solutions seen in God's written "Revelation" from Scripture. These "Revelations" neither come, nowadays, in the form of visions, nor as direct speech from the Lord (at least in my Christian church experience and knowledge). I am thinking of such past "Revelations," as recorded in both Old and New Testaments, in which God revealed in a very direct way what He wanted Prophets, Apostles, and holy men to pass on to others, or do for Him. God revealed Himself in a vision to Peter, in Acts 10, concerning the necessity for Peter to cast off His Jewish prejudice against Gentiles and do what Jesus Christ Commissioned His church to do—*Go and make disciples of all nations* (Gentiles). I am also thinking of the Lord appearing to Saul (now Paul, the great church-planter after his conversion on the Damascus Road) in Acts 9. Other such direct "Spirit-Revelations" take place a number of times in the New Testament inspired writings.

Today, there are few, if any, genuine "Direct Revelations" of Jesus Christ to Christian members or leaders of His church. There is a reason why this is so—I believe it is simply that there is **no need now** for the Lord to act in isolated personal "visions," for He has given His church, in centuries past and today, two other forms of Revelations to members of His Body, the church on earth that He Willed to build so long ago.

In New Testament days before and after the death of the Apostles, He revealed His Plenary (full, complete) inspired, inerrant Word and His Will to the church—verbally, at first, from those who had either been with Him while He was sinless man,

God-incarnate in the flesh, or those who had been *moved by the Spirit* to speak and teach His Revelations to the church. A few inspired and written-down Spirit-teachings, received by holy men, were passed as "letters" among the Christian churches of those days. And of course, the Spirit within each believer revealed the Lord's teaching to every Christian, member or leader, in those early years, as He does now through the same *Spirit of Truth* in every true believer.

The church of the "middle centuries" received, copied, and distributed these ancient, Spirit-inspired New Testament manuscript documents that we know as the "Gospel books," "Acts," and "Letters to the churches," and of course, the final "Book of the Revelation of Jesus Christ to the Apostle John." I am not excluding the rest of the New Testament canon—just emphasizing a few here, as used in this book. All of the New Testament books, passed to the churches of those days, were consulted—literally—as God's Word to the church. Finally, as church and secular history tells us, the printing press was invented, expanding God's plan of putting all these sacred documents into print, and allowing an increasingly literate church Body to have them in their own language in each country—rather than restricting them to a few literate "priests" (unscriptural "Elders") and other, scriptural, *Overseers (or Elders, or Pastors)*.

The printing press opened up the possibility of ideally allowing every member of each church to have God's Word in a form easily taught, read, and acted upon. But first, it seemed, the Christian church, with the Spirit, had to sift God's Truth from men's false teachings *about* His inspired, inerrant Word. The Christian church of the past centuries met in *conference,* at various gatherings or "Councils"—man-made, not a scriptural term— and examined the many "religious documents" on hand as a result of centuries of amassing human collections of every sort of church "religious writing." This was done, as far as history reveals, by church representatives, church leaders, church "Fathers," church teachers and theologians—with the aid and counsel of the Holy Spirit. By this time in church history, Peter's prophetic statement about *false teachers among you* (2 Pet. 2:1) had come true—both in the New Testament era, and in later centuries. There were many false sects and false teachers in the Christian church outside it then, continuing through the years. The later churches had Spirit-given Truth (God's Word) in their hands, but also had in their congregations many *false teachers* whose advice and writings, to Elders or Overseers, opposed God's Word. Writings from men who opposed Scripture were also circulated in document form. These had to be compared, with the help of the Spirit, to the true Scriptures, in these church gatherings, so that the false, spurious and secular could be removed—leaving the Truth of God's Word clearly revealed for compilation in a "canon," or rule and standard of Divine content.

Christian Bible scholars and historians tell us that the "Council" agenda was (with the Spirit's guidance and teaching) to list for church approval, in church-approved format, only those scriptural and holy writings—books, letters to churches, doctrinal theses, etc.—that bore the recognizable, authentic "imprint" of God's inspired record of His New Testament dealings with the church. As well, the compilation of the Old Testament books was reviewed, with the Spirit, from much earlier times.

The Councils on developing a New Testament canon, according to reputable Christian Bible scholars, produced 27 "New Testament Books" (and 39 Old Testament books), identified as authentic and inspired of the Holy Spirit—Holy writings that could be trusted to be God-inspired, inerrant and infallible for use by the Christian church then and now. Some false and some doubtful documents were found and, if not discarded, sometimes retained as O.T. "Apocrypha," or as being the "uninspired, unauthoritative" work of **men only**—but thought useful. These were not found in the Hebrew canon, but retained in the Septuagint and Vulgate Bible versions by some churches. As I noted earlier, in this sub-section of Part 6, " Visual Revelations" appeared to be no longer necessary in the church age after the death of the Apostles, because Christ's Revelation (His Word of Truth to the church) became available in written manuscript form, and later, in printed form, to Christians.

Together with the *Spirit of Truth* Teaching and Counselling Christians as they read, taught, and were Guided by the written Word of God, the inspired sanctifying Word of Truth we have in the Bible is fully sufficient today to reveal to **all** His churches **all that we must do** for our Saviour and Lord. I remind Christian church members to be sure to read and teach 2 Timothy 3:16 concerning the importance and use of all Holy Scripture.

Finally, when I say "Revelation" is a key step in the process leading to church reform, please note that I mean it in two senses:

1. What His inspired, inerrant, infallible Written Word says *directly to* us to do for the Lord; and

2. What the *Spirit of Truth* in every Christian will **confirm** (reveal) to us as truth, when we read His Word and clearly understand its direct meaning and application. The Spirit will counsel us as to our Head's Word, Will and purpose.

5. SELF-AWARENESS (AND CONVICTION)

The "process" of becoming a Christian believer involves a period of time, in which we hear the gospel message of salvation, hear and are convicted by the Spirit of our sin, repent (turn away from this sin), and finally believe—by faith alone—in the Risen Son of God, dying for us on Calvary's Cross. So do we believers, in a different but parallel process, become re-aware of sin in our personal and church lives and be **re-convicted** that we must turn from what our Lord abhors, to what He expects and desires. And, of course, our Lord and His Word tells all Christians, if we sin, to *confess our sins* to God, and He *will forgive us...and purify us from all unrighteousness* (1 John 1:9).

A very urgent and necessary "process," or series of steps, must be undertaken if we are not to suffer the same fate as most of the Seven Churches of Revelation 2 and 3. Their (predominantly) sad, pitiful, yet often deliberate and disobedient actions in the early years of the growing and spreading church (mostly) led to their becoming ineffective, dead, or sleeping bodies of Christ in that early world. These things can, do, and will happen to our churches today, unless we *wake up* and return to obey Him as *we did at first.*

The key words or phrases Christ used in Revelation 2 and 3 are directly applicable now—no matter how "civilized" and "modern" our society, world, and church has become. Our Lord wanted *all* disobedient churches, *each* member, and *every* leader, to return to their *first love* (Jesus Christ, the One Who loved them, and expects them to obey Him).

Whether they were good, bad, or "lukewarm" churches, when the Lord said these things in His Letters to the Seven Churches, to the later churches, and to us today, He urged us to: *hear what the Spirit says to the churches.* With all my heart, led by the Spirit, I think He speaks with loving sadness in this final scriptural appeal to each member and leader of every church today who read His Words in Revelation 2 and 3. Do you read these Divinely inspired and revealed words, and believe, in renewed awareness, that **the Lord is speaking directly to you, through His Spirit?** I pray so, for the church today has gone beyond the early church in its sin.

Some so-called Bible teachers, professors, and real and obvious heretics, in the divided, *lukewarm* or worse churches, today and in the past, have allowed Satan to lead them away from *the faith that was once for all entrusted to the saints* (Jude 3). Some of these *false teachers* oppose and deny the written Word of God, and convince gullible, untaught, spiritual *infants* to ignore its Words of Truth as "being men's words, errant, and fallible." They, with Satan, have succeeded in dividing the church Body that the Lord prayed *might be one, as I and the Father are One.* None of these errant acts will change, unless and until the churches hear and obey Christ's call to *repent and overcome, and return in all things to me* (Rev. 2,3, *as paraphrased by author*). Churches *hearing what the Spirit says* must **act and act quickly** or it will be too late. For **He is coming soon** (Rev. 22:7, 20).

Self-awareness means recognition of how we Christians,

whether members or leaders, have actively supported, allowed, or tolerated pride, or obeyed other human motives to overturn Truth and substitute men's false words for the plain, clear Words of teaching and commands of our Head, Jesus Christ. Our Lord's teachings and commands are echoed in our hearts, minds, and spirits through Bible study, and recalled again to us by the Spirit, if we ask Him to convict us of sin, to counsel and to lead us to God's Truth that sanctifies us (John 17:17). Few churches today can truthfully say what the church in Laodicea said—that they are *rich...have acquired wealth and do not need a thing* (Rev. 3:17), and have nothing of which to repent—and be believed by Christ, the One *who searches hearts and minds* of men (Rev. 2:23). If we state: we *do not need a thing* (forgiveness, repentance, or reform of disobedience to Christ), we will receive our rightful rewards (rejection by Him). But the Spirit, the Word, and I, in this book, urge all churches to *wake up* and *hear what the Spirit says to the churches... and about you, today—about your future.*

We must see that He wants us to recognize our sin, repent of it, and turn again fully and obediently to the Lord. Jesus Christ says *I will repay each of you according to your deeds* (Rev. 2:23). **Do you believe this?** If you do, why not acknowledge and repent of your discovered sins as part of the failing Body of Christ?

6. REPENTANCE

In this scripturally-based "process" of disobedient churches seeking to reform "discovered sin," and after the steps of *Prayer,* seeking *The Holy Spirit's Counsel, Self-Examination* (and conviction), *Revelation* (what the Lord shows us—as seen in His inspired Word), *Self-Awareness* (of sin and disobedience), and acknowledgment of sin (*Conviction*)—**we then need to Repent.**

When the crowd gathered in the Jerusalem street, in the sound and presence of the Spirit, and Peter preached the first Gospel message, we read that men hearing the truth of the Gospel were convicted by the Spirit of their sin (as Jews who had sought and brought about Christ's death on the Cross). *Cut to the heart* (convicted), they asked, *what shall we do?* Peter replied (Acts 2:38): *Repent.* And told them of salvation offered to those who turn away from their sin, who ask forgiveness from God, and believe in the Risen Christ. Then, as "Born-again, forgiven believers," receiving the Gift of the Holy Spirit in their new lives, they were baptized and added as members to the new Body of Christ, the church.

Repentance is man's response to the Spirit's conviction, and God's offer of forgiveness for their sins—it precedes salvation. It means a Spirit-aided response made to God, in which the person acts with mind, heart and spirit by turning away from all sin that displeases God, to full obedience and a determination to please Him.

In this "modern process," leading to reform of disobedient churches, where disobedience and sin are discovered with the aid of the Spirit, we find that our Lord also counsels repentance (turning from sin to God) in His "first audit and review" of the (mostly) disobedient churches of Revelation 2 and 3. On the authority of inspired Scripture, we weak and sometimes failed Christian churches and members must repent and reform, also, or suffer terrible and eternal consequences. *Prayer,* and more prayer, is urged—and it must develop spontaneously, as each "step towards reform" leads past *Repentance*, with the aid of the Holy Spirit, to *Revival, Reform*, and a renewed, repentant and obedient church—ready to meet the coming Bridegroom (see Rev. 19:7).

7. REVIVAL.

In the human, sinful world about us, "revival" means resuscitation from near death of a person who, left untreated, would perish. In the religious sense, "Revival" may mean an "awakening"—something similar to a "process of reforming disobedient churches"—with all attendant spiritual and 'religious' steps taken to accomplish reform, with the help of the Holy Spirit and His inspired Word. Jesus, in His Revelation to the Seven Churches, and to all later churches, speaks in a spiritual, religious sense about one church that has *the reputation of being alive* but is really *dead,* spiritually (Sardis—see Rev. 3:1). That sinful, dis-obedient church is told by the Lord to *wake up,* which in the context of symbolic "deadness" means to become re-aware of what He and the Spirit has told them to do. That is, become self-aware, acknowledge their sin and disobedience, repent and turn away from it, and return to do what He, as Divine church Head, has asked them to do.

Some Christian evangelists conduct "Revival meetings" within churches, halls, or football fields, to carry out the first command of the Lord in Matthew 28:18–20: *Go and make disciples of all nations.* But in the context of this book of warnings to Christian churches to overcome disobedience to the Lord, church revival is used the way Christ used it in His Revelation 2 and 3 church examples to later churches, and to His church today. That is, He wants His Words to *wake up* sleeping churches—to bring back to life (**revive**) those churches who have *the reputation of being alive* to the world, but are really spiritually *dead* to the Head of His Body on earth. Churches must not only wake up, but **act** to repent and reform their known or discovered disobedience. In this latter sense, this "process" I describe involves a step of "*Revival*" that must occur when the suggested earlier steps have led the Church to true knowledge of their disobedient actions or inactions, a step toward repentance and forgiveness, and finally, on the way to *Reform* and *Radiance,* a true spiritual awakening where only spiritual death was once foreseen.

Those Christians who enter into this process that Christ advocates for His church, who are *lukewarm, asleep* or *dead,* tolerating *false teachers* in the Body, or any other form of disobedience to the Head of His Body, will experience a great sense of joy and release from Satan's grip as they recognize their sin, and turn from it in repentance to renewed life. Spiritually "revived," they will receive His forgiveness, renewed promises of rewards and a glorious future life with Him. I believe, after reading Revelation 2 and 3, and its lessons and teachings from my Lord and yours, that only true repentance, followed by true reform, will revive and prepare the church to be holy, *radiant,* and cleansed from all sin, for Him, the "Bridegroom." Remember, He is coming soon! Act now!

8. REFORM.

The reform that I speak of here, is a synonym for the things Christ asks of His disobedient church in Revelation 2 and 3 and elsewhere in Scripture. He tells us: *If anyone loves me, he will obey My teaching;* and, *If you obey my commands, you will remain in my love, just as I have obeyed my Father's commands and remain in his love* (John 14:23; 15:10). Reform in this context is simply repenting of discovered sin and disobedience to all His teachings and commands, and **actively** (through Spirit-aided reformation) going back to *doing what* we did obediently *at first*. This means returning to our *first love*, obeying His Words, and *hearing* and doing *what the Spirit says* to us in His Counsel and in His Guidance—not in false teachings, but only in His inspired, inerrant written Word.

Before writing in more detail about this matter of church reform, I will now contrast **Christ's required church reform** with men's ideas of church reform, as illustrated vividly in the so-called "Protestant Reformation" of the 16th Century. Let me say again that, while our Lord never uses the word, "Reform," He does use equivalent words that mean exactly the same. He says: *obey me... do my Will... do what* you *did at first... repent* (turn away from sin and return to me)—and His Words in Revelation 2,3 speak of His displeasure with disobedience.

Church history reveals that a former University professor, a German priest of the Roman Catholic church, Martin Luther, became alarmed with many errors he observed in his church's doctrines and practices, as well as his human leader's unscriptural assumption of unscriptural authority over this large group of Christian churches. He decided to discuss the matters he considered to be errant with superior church officials. In 1519, Luther posted 95 "Theses"(articles or propositions for debate) on the door of the Castle Church at Wittenberg, in Germany. They were sent to a secular Prince of Germany, who forwarded them to the "Pope" in Rome.

As a matter of first importance, Luther wanted to discuss what he and his friends (in the church and in secular politics) considered a serious problem for the people in his native land. This problem was the "sale" of unscriptural "indulgences" granted by the "Pope" in Italy, Pope Leo X. "Indulgence" refers to "the remission of temporal punishment for sin after its guilt has been forgiven by a priest." The Pope was outraged at what he called Luther's heretical statements. Luther, in effect, and sometimes in words, simply denied that the Pope had authority to deal with "(unscriptural) purgatory and other religious matters." The raising of church funds through indulgences was simply scripturally wrong and immoral. Luther felt the Pope should consider the needs of the poor first, rather than granting un-Biblical "indulgences" to rich men, or building a mausoleum (the Basilica of St. Peter) to house the "bones of Peter and Paul." There were many other items of doctrine and practice within the 95 Theses in which Luther, an (unscriptural) Christian priest, challenged the authority of the Pope. Since these things are public knowledge and discussed in both Roman and "Protestant" church history books, I want only to comment on the end results of this protest by Luther in 1519— a "splitting-off" from the Roman Catholic church of that day, and the consequential further ***division*** of the church of Jesus Christ into new groups of divided churches, called "Protesting Christians" or "Protestants."

The church had earlier (and wrongly according to Christ's Words about Unity or complete "Oneness"—see John 17:11; 21:23) split into two large divisions: the so-called Eastern "Greek Orthodox" church and the so-called Western "Roman Catholic" church. As a result of the expulsion from the Roman church of Martin Luther, and his Papal excommunication as a "heretic," history reveals that the immediate result of Luther's acts and statements was the formation of new, somewhat different, churches of Jesus Christ, dubbed "Protestant"—a move ***directly opposing Christ's desire that we Christians may all be one!***

I'm sure Luther and his supporters didn't intend this errant result, but it seemed at the time to be the only way for them to exist. I, and many other "Protestants" (and "Catholics," Orthodox and others) read history and sincerely wish that Luther, the Pope of that day, and others had followed Christ and His Will, had acknowledged church sin and disobedience to the True Head, Jesus—and pursued true *Reform*! Centuries later, we are still divided—and our Lord is coming soon!

My life experiences in many Protestant churches, studies in the inspired Scriptures, and constant application to the Holy Spirit for guidance so that my writings are faithful to His inspired Word, tell me—and it is confirmed in the New Testament for the church—that Luther's unplanned "Reformation" was weak, ineffectual, incomplete, and scripturally unfaithful, then and to this day. I believe this, because I, and many other unbiased, Spirit-led scholars, teachers, theologians, writers, church members and leaders, looking at the Bible, and at the divided, divisive "Christian churches" of the past and today, confirm that the "Protestant Reformation" did not truly **Reform** or **conform** with Christ's Will and Purpose for His church Body on earth. The "Act *called* Reformation" *did not truly "reform"* the Christian church (both parties), but only continued the earlier "East/West" schism. When we compare the words, doctrines, acts and actions of the Christian churches involved in, and resulting from, the "Protestant Reformation," with the written Word of God, we (and you) must see that it was not the true "Act *of* Reformation" that Christ asks of sinful churches.

Not only was the "parent church," the Roman Catholic church, **not reformed** to full obedience to the inspired Word of God in the 16th Century, but it remains in clear disobedience to Scripture in many respects today, long after the "splitting off process." Many of its false teachings are incorporated (or retained) in the "Protestant" churches formed then, re-reformed often later, and often remain scripturally errant to this very day. Luther's "Reformation" was largely ineffectual and errant because it did not conform to God's inspired Word of Truth.

Let me, in the following format graphically point out **why** the "Protestant Reformation" was largely *a failure*—not in my frail opinion, but in Christ's own Words:

1. Christ said:

I pray... that all of them (all His disciples) *may be one, Father, just as you are in Me and I am in you...May they* (all His disciples) *be brought to complete unity to let the world know that You sent me, and have loved them even as you have loved Me...*(John 17:21,23).

Men say and do*:* the exact opposite, by perpetuating and proliferating churches who are not truly "one," in all that each does, says, and teaches, but who (individually, or denominationally) falsely teach and insist on **not** doing all that Christ has told us to be and do for Him. The Roman Catholic (Western) and the Greek Orthodox (Eastern church) split on men's opinions, power, authority, and false teachings and doctrines opposed to God's inspired Word, long before Luther's attempt to discuss errors and possible changes with his day's Unscriptural leaders. This indicates, clearly, that the churches were disobedient to Christ's desire that they be one, in all things—not divided by men's pride, ambitions, and lust for power.

When Luther and his supporters heard that the Roman "Pope" considered them heretics, and realized that this was their opportunity to get out of the "clutches" of an errant and wrongly authoritarian Roman "church," the move was on to "*Re*-form new churches" (not "reform" the old, parent church). One new church (called Lutheran, after its excommunicated founder and frustrated reformer) formed a new "Body of Christ," but missed its opportunity to form a Christ-required, fully-obedient and fully scriptural New Testament Body—to throw off men's past false doctrines and teachings that had accumulated over centuries, and get back to Christ's teachings and commands. They **partially** "reformed" the "new Body," as did other "protestant" churches in different countries. Ex-Roman members *re*-formed into new churches—while retaining, in one way or another, many "man-made, but scripturally-opposed" doctrines, church organizations, practices, and beliefs fostered and added to over the centuries by the "parent church" from which they had split. A few examples are given below:

2. Christ said (through Spirit-inspired men such as Peter, Paul, Luke, etc.):

…That His church must be composed of *only* repentant believers, baptized by immersion (Rom. 6), and added to the "Body"; there to be taught by the church to mature and spiritually grow to strengthen His Body, of which they are part—and thus be able to cast out *false teachers* who might infiltrate and destroy the Body. Scripture also states that the churches should appoint *only* males as "Elders" (Overseers, or Pastors) for prime duties of prayer, preaching and teaching, and "Deacons" to assist Pastors. They were to act as sole leaders in Christ's church, guiding the church in Christ's Will and purpose with the Spirit, under the sole Headship of Christ. See inspired Scripture: 1 Timothy 3, etc.

Men (Churches) say, and do:…often, the exact opposite. They have created and still appoint men to vast hierarchies of unscriptural church organizations: Popes, Patriarchs, Cardinals, Arch-Bishops, Bishops, etc.—and even false and unscriptural "Priests," patterned after the Old Testament Law for the Jews alone. If the "protesters" of Luther's time had seized the opportunity presented by Luther's attempt to "discuss" changes in his church, and his ejection from the Roman church—and completely returned the newly re-formed Lutheran and other churches to the New Testament teachings and commands of Christ alone—many Bible lovers would have cheered, and our Lord would also have "cheered" (approved of) their obedient, scriptural, actions, words and deeds.

But they did not fully "Reform" either the Roman church or the new "Protestant churches" formed later, except in some minor ways. For instance, long-standing errors in "making disciples," in "baptizing them…," and in "teaching them," as Christ required of His Body, continued in very many of the

"Protestant" churches formed then and today—as I noted in earlier chapters in this book of warning of Christ's wrath against disobedience. We still observe, in history and today in many Catholic **and** "Protestant" churches, unscriptural *"infant baptism,"* or so-called *"household"* baptisms despite their errant origins in the false teaching of men (under the control of Satan). The false teaching and false authority of unscriptural church leaders continues, opposing Christ's clear commands. These are only a few examples of little or no reform, then and now. We still also see churches led, not by Elders and Deacon assistants, but by unscriptural officers who pervert and subvert scriptural statements on authority and control (**and gender**, sometimes leading to the appointment of **female** Elders and Deacons), with tragic future consequences, despite scriptural injunctions against these errors—as Christ reviews their sin when He comes.

3. Christ says:

All believers must be taught by the church to *obey all that* He has *commanded* us (the knowledge of the Son of God—Matthew 28) to *prepare God's people for works of service, so that the Body of Christ might be built up until we all reach unity in the faith and in the knowledge of the Son of God, and become mature, attaining to the whole measure of the fullness of Christ* (Eph. 4:12–13). The New Testament church taught the Lord's teachings and commands fully—and taught all members to obey them as He asked.

Men do and say either... the exact opposite, in the past and today. Or they pervert Christ's requirements in such a way that not only is the church **not strengthened and united**, but new and old Christians, and the church Body, are made useless to Christ, becoming *lukewarm*, sleeping, even spiritually *"dead,"* and unable to stem the evil words and practices of *false teachers* within the Body, or at its head. Church history reveals that some churches have taught—not **all that** Christ *has commanded* (i.e., **all His** teachings), but only **brief extracts** from the Bible; taught not **all**

disciples, but often only children; taught adults, but only on a voluntary basis, not mandatorily as His Word demands. In past times, some churches have not even allowed disciples to read the Bible for themselves.

4. Christ asks us:

(Through the inspired Paul and others): to carry out His two specific scriptural **ordinances**, or Orders, in connection with specific acts that will allow the church to **add** repentant believers to the church, and will cause all church members to *proclaim the Lord's death until He comes.* I refer here to His "Ordinance of **Christian baptism**" and to His "Ordinance of **The Lord's Supper**—an Act of *Remembering our Lord until He Returns again* (or communion or "Mass" as some errant churches wrongly describe it).

Men do and say: often what is twisted or distorted from scriptural statements—or they add or change the two "Ordinances of our Lord" for Christian church members and leaders, in a way that is false and disobedient to what He has asked in inspired Scripture.

As I have noted previously, often the very fact that many churches refuse to teach baptized believers fully to obey all that Christ has asked us to be and do, has led (as Scripture warns us, in the inspired Word of God) to false changes: **un-Scriptural** baptism of unknowing infants, and unscriptural later "confirmation," along with **false teaching** that baptism saves. Yet I, and others like me, are not saying the things we do out of hate or bias—only out of love for our errant brothers and sisters in Christ. Even Martin Luther was quoted as saying *"I stand on the Bible alone"*—*Sola Scriptura* (not on false teachings). Others have quoted him, at his final church trial, as saying that he could not retract what he had said and written about the Pope and his false authority, for he stood upon *"the testimony of Scripture and clear reason."*

We ask, why then did he listen to false Catholic teachers and leaders, and follow unscriptural traditions? Not only regarding cases of political sales of "indulgences," why did Luther support many doctrinal errors for which the Pope, wrongly, claimed infallible authority? This is the reason I write these things in this book—so that errant Christian churches of today might be alerted to Christ's warnings in His inspired Word, repent, and (truly) reform their scripturally-disobedient actions and words. The Lord will act—His Word tells us what He will do, when He comes and finds "wrinkled, blemished, and extinguished" churches, not *radiant* bodies (see Rev. 2,3). He *will repay* (failure) *according to* (their) *deeds*" (Rev. 2:23). Men ignore *The Spirit of Truth* and often turn to *false teachers* today.

In the Lord's Supper ordinance, too, history and experience of the past and present disobedient churches reveals that *false teachers* (and false leaders) in many churches have deliberately distorted Christ's True Words, purpose, and Will to build and sustain His church, in their errant teaching and practise of this Divine ordinance. Instead of obediently giving each believer the **two prescribed** elements (bread and wine, representing and symbolizing His crucified Body **and** His shed Blood) of His "remembrance supper," some churches give **only the "bread"** to the church believer/members, and retain the "wine" for the "priest" alone. This directly contravenes the true meaning and purpose of the supper, as taught by Christ in the Scriptures. Christ directed that **all** His disciples *take and eat...drink* (Matt. 26:26,27) the bread and the wine, so that their required remembrance of His sacrifice for them and for the world would be made real in the symbolism, even though He would not be physically present with them—except as His Spirit coming to them as believers—until He comes again to this world.

Additionally, some errant churches, urged on by *false teachers*, have taught wrongly that the ordinary bread and wine materials— as chosen and given to all His disciples by Christ and used to illustrate, symbolically, His soon-to-come offering of His very real Incarnate Body and His very real shed Blood at Calvary, as a once-for-all-time sacrifice to God for the sins of all men—was **not** to be offered as Christ instructed in His Word (and the inspired Paul reconfirmed). I refer to the errant church "doctrine" that, in a recurrent "miracle" assisted by the words and "authority" of the officiating "priest," the material bread and wine is "changed" in each and every observance to the actual, not Symbolic Body and

Blood of the Lord. But this false doctrine and practice opposes what the Lord asks us to do for Him, and replaces **His Words** with men's words and disobedient practices.

The inspired Apostle Paul, in 1 Corinthians 11—forced by the disobedient practices of the sinful early church at Corinth, who had abused the Lord's Supper—told them exactly what the Lord had said to His first Apostles and disciples, as recorded in the Gospel books of the New Testament. Still today, errant churches practice Satan's deceptions. **The Lord was crucified, died, was buried and then resurrected in God's Power once only.** When some churches celebrate the Lord's Supper by falsely stating that the Lord's Body and Shed Blood returns again and again (in their incorrect celebration of the Lord's Supper), they deny God's Truth, and lead sincere but untaught Bible-believers and church members into error. Only at the Judgment Seat will *false teachers* discover the consequences.

This book, and my continual quoting of God's inspired Written Words of sanctifying truth, is written for one purpose alone. It is, to warn forgetful, sleeping, and disobedient churches (as Christ describes them)—who continually practice falsehoods and pervert the truth found only in holy, inerrant Scripture—to come awake, recognize their false teachings (when compared to Scripture), repent of their sins, and reform before it is too *late.*

Christ Jesus, our Saviour and Lord, has said that He is the One *who searches hearts and minds,* and He knows our deeds (Rev. 2, 3). He is the One Who asks that we *overcome* evil, and, with His Spirit's aid and counsel, obey Him—and He will give us our true rewards when He comes soon. **All errant** churches of Christ, *wake up* and *do the* (obedient) *things you did before* Satan falsely led you astray. Read Acts 2 and 3, John 13–17, and the many other passages of Scripture I have quoted. In fact, re-read the New Testament for the church with the Holy Spirit, the Divine *Spirit of Truth*—and return to *your first love* (Jesus Christ), Who some Christian churches have so clearly forsaken.

"If anyone loves me, he will obey my teaching...He who does not love me, will not obey my teaching"
—*Jesus* (John 14:23,24).

Some final words of truth. In writing four previous, yet unpublished books on the same general subject—the Christian church—I have discovered that readers of my manuscripts, whether good Christian friends, publishing company editors, or professional readers, all tend to discount my claims that I write only as an advocate for Christ and His Words for His church. Most, if not all, I find, are caught up in societal, material, and traditional views and opinions—they simply do not want to talk about what Christ teaches and commands His church to be and do for Him in this world.

My life and church experiences, as well as my scriptural Bible training and teaching work (with the requested guidance of the *Spirit of Truth*) over the years, has led to my belief that very many Christian churches have simply failed to carry out Christ's Commission and third Command to: *Teach them* (all church members, not some) *to obey all that I have commanded you*!

When I realized this actual fact of most church failures to teach, I was able to write this fifth book on the Christian church (*The Spirit Speaks Today—but are Christians in the church listening?*) in such a way as to point out to untaught readers the source of their spiritual ignorance—and urge them, through a reformed teaching program, to make all members and leaders aware (many for the first time) of how little they knew of His inspired, inerrant Words of Teaching and Command! I say here, of how little they know of His Wrath, Consequences, and Will when He comes again soon.

The following Chapters, 14 and 15, should awaken very many untaught members and leaders in Christ's Body on earth today to *hear what the Spirit says to the churches,* as well as to to my scripturally-based self-examination and reform process.

Substitute scriptural teachings of the Divine Head of the Church for the *lukewarm,* lethargic, spiritually sleeping attitude of false, disloyal teachers in "your church." And always remember, it is not your church, but His church "Body"—He Who gave Himself up for us, wants to take you and all obedient Christians to Heaven with Him soon. But He only wants a sinless church. You have so little time to wake up, and do again the things that please the Head and coming Bridegroom.

My work for the Lord in this humble book is almost, but not quite, done. I have honestly and faithfully tried to describe what I and many other Christians *observe* in church history, our own experience, and public knowledge in various churches, **that is true, faithful, and obedient—or otherwise—**to the Head of the church, Jesus Christ. This book is based upon my human (though Spirit-aided) understanding of what our Saviour and Lord asked of all Christians when He taught us, commanded us, and urged us—as revealed to us in His inspired written Word—to be a faithful part of His real, yet spiritual "Body," the church on earth that He Willed to build so long ago. I speak of, and quote, the Inspired, Inerrant, Infallible, always reliable, and sufficient Written Word of God, the Bible for Christian and Jew.

The Christian Bible is, as it should be, our only source of knowledge of our Triune God: God the Father, God the Son, God the Holy Spirit, and of His dealings with mankind, from the Creation to the God-Willed and Planned future prepared for Jews, Christians, and unsaved Gentiles. In this book I have tried to focus on—and cause my Christian readers to relate to, and concentrate upon—one overarching and primary scriptural theme. That is, warning, reminding, urging, and advising (in Christ's Name, and for His and my readers' sake) of what our Lord, Saviour, and Head of His Body the church, has asked, commanded, and pleaded with us to be and do for Him. This theme has a corollary (a naturally following consequence of it). Namely: to follow up, as Christ also does in His Holy Word, on what will happen to the Christian church (and its members and leaders under the Divine Head) if they do not, or will not, be faithful or obedient to all that He asked us to be and do for Him in His Word.

Writing the chapters of this book, I have continually reminded and warned the disobedient churches called "Christian," their often falsely-taught or Satan-influenced Elders or Pastors, and their members—often untaught, gullible or tolerant (wrongly, to error), spiritual *infants* (Eph. 4)—that they must listen to Christ's own scriptural words of reward and promises, if they desire to remain faithful to Him. Or, conversely, face His anger and wrath, if they don't repent and reform their stubborn and disobedient ways.

Part 6. True Scriptural Reform—With the Holy Spirit's Guidance.

Chapter 14

Christ's Commanded Reform In Action: A Scenario For Today's Small Church

A Scenario for Church Reform.

Based upon my own recent personal experience and knowledge of some of today's churches, and their past background—and conditioned by church writings and public dissemination of their church life, doctrines, and practices—I have a very real sense that many of today's churches will resist Christ's advocated scriptural process leading to repentance and reform of disobedience. I feel, too, that Satan—even if he allows my scripturally-based book and Spirit-guided recommendations to be considered, by a small part of the membership of sinful Christian churches—will raise up opposition to my "scriptural process for reform." You see, the scriptural steps to reform of disobedience require that sin-hardened and disobedient hearts be convicted and led by the Spirit—led in faltering steps to a *spiritual revival.* The resulting re-discovery of Christ's loving commands leads then to conviction, repentance and reform of *"discovered disobedience,"* all with the Holy Spirit that many such members or leaders have not been taught to seek for His counsel and aid!

Let's face up to spiritual and worldly reality. We Christians, in the Western world at least, live in a sinful, materialistic environment in which Satan, unseen, uses his evil and sinful practices to tempt us all to ignore God, Christ, and His Spirit, the Church and living a Godly,

Holy life, serving Him in the world. Yes, Scripture says, and Christ prayed: *My prayer is not that you take them out of the world but that you protect them from the evil one*—John 17:15, paraphrased by author. We Christians have to live our life serving Him in the world while on our pilgrimage to Heaven. While on earth, we must be an obedient part of His Body, the church: learning of Christ, growing and spiritually maturing, worshipping our Creator, Saviour and Lord, and witnessing to and obeying Him, in the church and in the world. But Satan is ever-present, and attacks us while we are in the world. With help from his *false teachers*, (in the church or seminary, perhaps) he tempts us with delusions of power, pride, and, often denial of sin and disobedience to our God. We are to be "in the world but not take part in its evil practices"—and we need the Word of God to guide us.

This reality of personal knowledge of the world's temptations, lusts, and evil practices, when placed against the things Christ asks His believing members and leaders in His church to be and do for Him, simply means that even Bible-based books and recommendations, such as this book, must reach disobedient churches in worldly (but not sinful) types of presentation, to attain Christ-approved ends. For this reason, I have consulted the Spirit, in prayer and am led to present my recommendations to failing churches as a scripturally-based "process of reform"—in a worldly but not sinful, dramatic, yet real-life, scripturally-based Scenario. I pray that this will reach those who may otherwise turn away from "Bible-thumping" approaches by Christian writers.

Scenario 1, Scene 1.

The scene is set in the Pastor's study of a small "Protestant" church in a small Canadian city, at 9 a.m. on a Saturday. In the room with the Pastor are men, mostly, along with one or two women. The Deacons are male; the women, as Spirit-gifted female members of the church, help the Pastor and serve the Body of Christ by teaching women, carrying out responsibilities as church service clerks, serving others, providing hospitality, etc.

The young Pastor speaks:

Pastor:

"Welcome! Good morning to you all. Thanks for coming to this church meeting on such short notice, and for giving up your Saturday to discuss an important matter that has come to my notice…"

Deacon Fred interrupts, with a smile on his face:

"—Pastor, I'm your friend and brother in Christ. I think you and I know each other very well…but don't you know I love to sleep in on Saturday morning? I hope your 'important matter' is **really** 'very important!'"

Pastor, laughing in spite of himself:

"…Brother Fred, trust me when I say I wouldn't have asked any of you to come here today, if it wasn't something I felt was so urgent that it just wouldn't wait till tomorrow—to talk about, at least.

"The truth is, I need your presence, your support, and your advice by next week, so I can change next week's prepared Sunday sermon and include our feelings on this matter. This affects you and me, and the whole church Body… Perhaps it even involves a change in the direction, even the **life**, of our little church. It may not do this… But I need your help and ideas **right now**—not after Fred has had his Saturday morning 'sleep-in'!

"Now hear this…" (*his joking tone not matching his serious cast of expression*)… "Dear Christian brothers and sisters, I know you love this little Christian church as much as I do, even though I am a later addition—not a 'charter' member. Many of you were born here and raised in local families. Most of you, I know, have parents baptized and raised in this church, who in turn brought you to be baptized as infants here, and raised by your godly parents over your early years. You are now the second, even third, generation of Christian members. But, unfortunately, while some "our church traditions" are good—some are not. Let me explain.

"Just recently, I had an upsetting experience that has shaken me up. It has caused me to re-think some things about this church, and many others in this city and country. I won't 'beat around the bush,' for I know your time is as valuable to you as mine is to me.

This 'upsetting experience' I have had was not a physical experience, but mostly mental, with a large part of it spiritual. But no more mystery or guesses on your part... I have just read a thought-provoking, 'religious' book about the Christian church!"

The Pastor's "audience" of church workers look at each other with half-puzzled, half-humorous expressions at this comment. But they become serious as they see the Pastor is as determined in his demeanour as they had ever seen him in the pulpit, delivering a thoughtful sermon on Sunday.

The Pastor continues:

"I know something, my friends, my Christian brothers and sisters, of what you may be thinking—but let me tell you why I am both upset and serious about this book and its possible future effects upon our church and all our members—including us leaders, teachers, and helpers.

"The book I read is by a Canadian Christian author, previously unpublished and unknown to me and other Pastors in town, named Bob Williamson. His book is called, quite rightly, I think, "*The Spirit Speaks Today*." He writes about the Holy Spirit of God, and says the Spirit has spoken in the past—and still speaks for Christ, to the 'Body of Christ,' the entire Christian church Body, today. The author goes to great lengths to let his readers know what He writes about is not based upon his words or ideas, as such, but are based upon the very Words of our Saviour and Lord. Mr. Williamson quotes from, primarily, the New Testament. He says that he has a 'heart-burden' from the Lord—not a vision, as we might think—to write to the whole Christian church in today's world. He wants to tell everybody about what Christ and His Spirit said to His early church, and said to the churches after the Apostles' deaths—and *has* said in His inspired written Word, 'down through the centuries to today.'

The Pastor, pausing briefly to judge the group's reactions, sees they are hanging on his words—and continues...

"Bob Williamson became a Christian rather late in life, but God 'pursued him,' he says, and thoroughly converted him—a young 'upwardly mobile career and family man' as they say—to become a 'born-again' Christian. He tells us in his book, also written quite late in life, that God led him before his conversion—'dragged him,' he says—to a little Baptist church, where the gospel message was preached and honoured, and God's Word was taught and obeyed. The Spirit convicted him while listening to a series of sermons from the book of Romans. (Remind me to try that series here, too.) He repented of his sins, believed by faith in the Living, Resurrected Jesus, and was baptized by scriptural 'immersion' in the little church."

Hearing gasps from his small audience, at his use of the 'foreign' word 'immersion,' the Pastor frowns. They settle down and he returns to his story...

"Williamson continues, in his book, writing that the little church was obedient to the commands and teachings of the Lord. He was not just left to attend Sunday worship services on the days he was in town from his business travels. He says that he and other new and older Christians were strongly advised by their Pastor to attend special Bible classes for new believers. Because the church was 'Baptist' in denomination, they believed in a literal, where not symbolically phrased, interpretation of Christ's Words in the New Testament in many scriptural areas. Thus, he said, they believed that Christ commanded His church to thoroughly teach **all** members of the church—

not a brief catechism. All ages were to be taught to obey **'all** that the Lord had commanded them', so that they might all 'grow up into the fullness of Christ—in the faith and in the knowledge of the Lord'—he quotes Ephesians 4. Williamson continually quotes Scripture—he even had **me** hopping to follow him in the Bible!"

The Pastor looks up—his audience, quiet now, seems to sense his resolve to make some changes here. But they do not yet know his purpose, or exact train of his thought.

"But, friends, Mr. Williamson goes on to relate his experiences with other Christian churches he later attended. He speaks of his gifts from the Holy Spirit for teaching and Deacon service; about the necessity for full church Bible teaching, and worship; and about the Holy Spirit helping all Christians in their growing knowledge and study of the Word of God.

"He began to get through to me with his message—no, that's wrong. It wasn't **Williamson's** message, but **Christ's message** to the churches, that he was trying to get me to understand and obey. Mr. Williamson, as a Christian member and Spirit-gifted teacher and church worker, is no different from us, in our often weak and incomplete understanding of all that the Lord requires of us in His timeless, written Word. But this is only an introduction to his burden, *'from and for our mutual Lord and His Body, the church on earth.'*

"He continued to speak of the necessity for full Church teaching and worship, and preaching with Bible references about obedience in all church life. He had to gain readers' confidence, that was apparent—and he did, with his confident belief in the importance of Bible study with the Holy Spirit.

"Christ-commanded and obeyed teaching received in his first church had given Mr. Williamson a thirst for the inspired Word of God that he could not fully satisfy in his vocational and family life before retirement. When he retired, God led him to a godly retired preacher and missionary, who advised him to seek out a Christian seminary where he could satisfy this 'thirst for God's Word and do it without delay—for God isn't impressed with dreams, but only obedient actions'!

"Mr. Williamson thoroughly studied the Bible by correspondence, and assistance from local Pastors—and, with the help of the Holy Spirit Who, he says, 'the Bible says is within us to counsel us'—he gained a great deal more knowledge of God the Father, God the Son, and God the Holy Spirit,as well as about the Son's church. Williamson became burdened to serve the Lord in a special way—confirmed, he says, when he and his wife went to another part of Canada. In his book, *The Spirit Speaks Today—But are Christians in the Church Listening?*, he describes his personal and his church life and experiences.

"He describes how he was led by the Spirit to some radical conclusions, by his new increased knowledge of the Lord and His Word to His churches—and by experiences within several different churches. Also by—especially—his renewed awareness of the speaking of the Spirit of God and Truth in his heart, mind and spirit. In his book, Williamson then shifts from his own new awareness of God's Inspired, Inerrant, and Infallible Word and of Christ's seemingly forgotten teachings and commands to His churches of the Spirit's role in Guiding, Counselling, and bringing Christ's words to Christian's memories, and gets his reader's mind to shift—from **our views** and **our doctrines** and teachings we use in our local church—to **Christ's biblical teachings and commands.**

"Williamson is thus able to compare, effectively, in his experience and church life, what Christians often did, traditionally—but errantly— in 'their' churches. By this means, his purpose ('Christ's Purpose,' he says) to warn disobedient, perhaps, sleeping churches, using God's Sanctifying Word of Truth, can be effective.

"As I read on in this sincere, scriptural book, I found myself constantly turning to the written Word of God.

Williamson continually quoted what Christ said to us, especially in the New Testament Scriptures for the Christian church,. I, too, began to pause to seek the counsel and guidance of the Holy Spirit in prayer, as Williamson urged. Even as he kept lacing his observations and experiences with the Bible's inspired descriptions of the early and later church's trials and problems, I found, as he had, that he was absolutely correct when he said 'the church today' has seemingly forgotten much of what Christ said to them in His Word. Forgotten—if we ever knew or were ever taught—about the *Spirit of Truth* in believer's hearts, and forgotten what it means to truly obey our True church Head in all that He said. And forgotten that Christ has warned sinful churches!

"Friends—I admit to you, I began to weep as I read and examined afresh, in the New Testament inspired record, all that Christ has asked us to be and do—for the lost world and for Him. For I realized I had not included the Holy Spirit's Counsel, always, as I read the Bible, preached, taught, and lived out my life for Him in this church."

Now, the little group of listening Christians becomes absolutely still. The Pastor begins to see damp eyes, and hear almost imperceptible sobs, as his church 'helpers' follow his narrative story from this very obviously, very different Christian book.

Pastor:

"Mr. Williamson, who I really believe was under the influence of the Spirit of Truth when he wrote this book about Christ and His church, began to follow the advise of his retired Pastor friend—to learn more of God's Inspired Word—and act upon what he read. He began to write about the historical church of the past, as well as of today's disobedient churches. He wrote describing how churches could please Christ—and avoid His wrath—if churches were warned, and acted to reform error before it was too late.

"Mr. Williamson suggests that churches of today could actually *do something* about past recorded church failures *and* about their failures *today*—rather than close their Bibles and *dream* about how they are better churches than those of the New Testament or Middle Ages, and that *they need* no repentance and reform!

This book is about the vital importance, the necessity, really, of examining our own churches for disobedience. And, if sin and disobedience to our Lord is found—to actually *do something* about it, now. Williamson, insisting he is only "echoing" what Christ has said, confirms it with many scriptural references. His churches must leave behind *false teachers* and unscriptural traditions and go back to the written Word of God—especially the New Testament for His church.

In several chapters, Mr. Williamson describes 'A Scriptural Process for Reform of Church Disobedience,' using several important, but often-overlooked and untaught, Scripture passages. He uses Christ's actual Words and phrases, on subjects such as prayer, Holy Spirit counsel, self-examination, revelation, conviction, revival, repentance and reform, in the process of becoming the '*radiant church*' described in Ephesians 5:27. This scriptural 'process' is described as vital to lead disobedient churches forward on Christ's required pathway, to reform and become what He requires and expects *before He comes again to claim His Radiant Bride.*

"I will not go beyond this description of what Williamson has pointed us to in the inspired Word of God. With your agreement and help, and with the Spirit's aid and counsel, I would like to do the following, as your Pastor—and soon—for I now believe that *Christ is coming soon,* as He says in the Book of Revelation.

First, I have bought enough copies of Williamson's book, "*The Spirit Speaks Today*" that you can each have a copy. I want you to take it home and read it, if you respect my judgment—with a Bible at hand. You will need it, as I have found! And I would like you to do as Williamson wisely advises: ask the Spirit within you, as believers, to guide you as you read the Scripture passages. This so that He will Speak in His scriptural 'role,' and confirm that His Word is from God, and is completely True and inerrant for all Christian churches. However, please don't discuss the book among yourselves or other church members before you return to our next meeting.

"And, now, before you leave this morning, I want to tell you what has alarmed me, and what I plan to introduce in my sermons, next week and for several Sundays following. I won't ask for your comments or views on the book until later. But, afterward, I do want to discuss with you all that it says about church disobedience, and Christ's Words of condemnation if sinful churches fail to repent and reform their sinful actions. I want to alert you to my plans that I hope to involve you in, first. Then, if you agree to what we should do as church leaders and helpers—we should determine if there is unknown disobedience or false teaching among us in this church, and what we should do about it, according to Christ's Will and purpose.

"Here is what bothered me when Williamson reminded me about the inspired Word of God: first, I read all the Scripture references, and confirmed with the Spirit's guidance that they were indeed His Words, applied to **all His** 'Bodies'—the church of the past and today. I began to apply, in my mind, the scriptural 'process' of **self-discovery** of any failure or disobedience to the Lord here, in this little church of His. Second, I did this, as Williamson's book suggests, by reviewing, with the Spirit, what **we say and do and believe** in this church—and comparing it directly with Christ's Words, as well as the writings in the New Testament of other holy men, inspired by the Spirit to write down for us what God wanted us all to know and do personally, and in His church.

"I was shaken, physically, as well as in my mind, heart, and spirit—for I found, when I examined what we, you and I, and those early members who founded this church have been doing, saying, and acting upon as leaders of this little local Body of Christ...I found... (*the Pastor chokes on his words here*)...I...I found that we, our church, have been in grievous error, according to Christ's own Words..."

The little group looks at each other, and finding concern on every face, rushes to embrace and support their Pastor. After a minute or two, the Pastor speaks again, saying to his friends and fellow members of the church Body he leads for Christ...

"I'm all right now...please be seated ...and allow me to finish. Then you can go back to your families."

"Brothers and sisters in Christ, I found that we have been in error, according to God's Word, in at least two areas of our church's faith and practice...at least!

"The first has to do with our **'traditional' practice of 'baptizing' infants,** claiming we are saving their souls and making them thereby members of our Christian church. The second area I have discovered, with the Holy Spirit, and upon examining our practices against Scripture, has to do with our **'not teaching the whole Word of God to all members,'** but rather just having baptismal classes for adults, 'confirmation classes' for adults and children some years later, and little else. I have followed our church's 'traditional way' of 'teaching' you all, by means of my sermons. But I now know, from the New Testament church practice of often **'teaching new believers for over a year,'** that my sermons come far short of what our Lord means when He asked us to *'teach them* (**all members**), *to obey all that I have commanded you.'* Read Matt. 28:18–20. I have found, from long-forgotten Scripture, that the 'founders' of this church HAVE followed *false teachers*...not the inspired Word of God."

A deathly silence follows these words.

Pastor:

"Friends, that's all I have to say today to you. I would like you to read Williamson's book; look up the referenced Scriptures, and come back here, if possible, next Saturday morning at nine a.m., with your comments, opinions, advice and help—especially if you find, with the Spirit, what I have sadly found.

"On my part, I will commence to preach, beginning this Sunday and for several Sundays to follow, on the scriptural subjects of: Christ's Teaching and Commands for His Church; The Seven Churches of Asia ; Finding Christ's Opinion of Our Church; the Holy Spirit's Role in Christians' Lives in the Church; Consequences of Sin; Rewards for Faithfulness—and, What to do if the Spirit Speaks and condemns us personally for any of our discovered disobedience.

"I feel strongly that, when you discuss the book with me next week, you and I will be able to plan a strategy, if you agree with my conclusions on this serious matter of disobedience to our Lord. A strategy that will lead me to speak to the whole Body of Christ here, about a way to repent, reform, and cast out any sin which we find is contrary to our Lord's teachings and commands. I mean to lead the whole church first to examine what we do now, if you are in agreement with me—then hear what we 'servants of Christ in the church' say about what the Lord says. Then, if He leads us, I'll seek, through the book's 'process,' to pray and preach our whole church to repentance...and reform.

"My sermon series will prepare our members, so that we will have some time to organize the necessary prayer meetings. These, I hope and pray, will reach a mutual goal of repentance and reform, and a quick return to full obedience to our Lord. If my hopes and yours (and Christ's desires) are realized, and if you all feel and believe what I do now, I think this will mean a fresh, Holy-Spirit-inspired, new purpose for this church. Before you go, let's have a few words of prayer.

"We ask the Holy Spirit to confirm that we are in the Lord's Will and purpose for us, in His scriptural plan for this and all His local churches. His Will and purpose is not new, but has been overlooked in Scripture by many, over many centuries. Forgive us, Lord, and Guide us to your Truth, and to reform and full obedience, should we discover sin and false teaching in this church..."

Scene 1 ends here. *Standing in a circle of fellowship, the small group of men and women pray that God will bless them and keep them always close to Him, through His Spirit. And they pray that their Pastor and people will be united in love and obedience to Christ. With no further discussion, they all accept the book "The Spirit Speaks Today" from their Pastor, and quietly leave.*

Scenario 1, Scene 2.

It is the following Saturday. In the Pastor's study, the same group of men and women 'servants of the church,' with the Pastor, are present. Each person clutches a small paperback book, well-worn after only a week! We note, too, that each one carries a Bible to this meeting. The Pastor welcomes them lovingly:

Pastor:

"Good morning again my friends, and brothers and sisters in Christ! I see you have brought "The Spirit Speaks Today" with you. Our time is limited, so please let me hear from you in turn, as brief as you can be, what you found when you read the book. Let me know these things, please:

1. Did you read the book completely?
2. Did you look up all the Scriptures?
3. Did you ask the Holy Spirit to help you and counsel you?
4. Briefly, what conclusions did **you** reach?
5. Do you agree with my preliminary assessment of our church that I made last Saturday?

6. What do you think of my plan to involve the church in study, prayer, revival, repentance, and reform of disobedience found, as Christ requires?

Ladies first, please, then the men."

The two women church 'servants,' followed by the five male Deacons, each speak in turn for a few minutes. Each conscientiously tries to reply as briefly as possible to the six questions asked of them. All accounts are remarkably similar, because they have "heard what the Spirit said."

Deacon Fred:

(recall that this was the Deacon who liked to sleep on Saturday mornings and conveyed the impression that he resented being interrupted by church problems!)

"Pastor and friends, let me give my brief answers to your questions as all the others have done before me. Yes, I read the book completely—I even skimmed over it again, before I came here! And, yes, I looked up and read all the Scriptures quoted in the book, although I want to read more of the Bible passages when I have more time, for I realize how woefully ignorant and untaught about the Bible I am. Yes, I asked the Holy Spirit to help me. I've never done that before, because I never realized, until I read Williamson's book and his related Scripture references, that it is the best and only way to read Scripture—and truly receive His understanding!

"What conclusions did I reach? I reached the same ones you mentioned, Pastor, and the same ones my brothers and sisters here seem to have reached—although I am not so confident or able to explain them, as some of them were. I'm a slow learner, and haven't been much of a Bible student until now,"—*here, he grins and ducks his head.* "But I do agree, Pastor, with your assessment of last Saturday, and find I'm able to understand better now, rather than then. I now have a stronger faith and better Scripture knowledge and background, because of this past week of studying under the '*Spirit of Truth*,' as Jesus calls Him."

The Pastor smiles to himself, for this remark by Deacon Fred tells him much more of his faithful Deacon's heart than all of their associations over some years.

"Finally, Pastor, and my friends, even as I confess my weakness and poor Bible knowledge to you all, let me say that even my little knowledge, received over a few recent days, and my uncertain request for the Holy Spirit's help over the same period, has given me much more faith-confidence—even a certainty I never had before. I know now that, by following Christ's process of discovering and dealing with sin and disobedience—in my life, and the church's life—and following all the steps leading to repentance and reform of disobedience, the Pastor, with you and I servant helpers, with the Holy Spirit's help, finally can please our Lord in all things here. And that's what I want to do... please my Saviour and Lord."

Flushing, but with face aglow with a new-found inner faith and peace, Deacon Fred sits down, amid the pleased and loving expressions of Pastor and disciples present.

Pastor:

"Fred, I express to you and to all here, in the Lord's Name, my sincere appreciation for your confidence and respect for the Lord and for myself—your Pastor under Christ. You have proved to be what I already knew you to be: faithful and good Christians, a delight to the Lord's heart and to mine, and a great help to this church Body.

"I don't say this because you have agreed with me on this matter of our church's discovered sin, but because it is true, and gives me confidence in the Spirit and the Word. I am equally, if not more, guilty of perpetuating the disobedience you and I found comparing **what we do**, with **what the Lord told us to do**. Together, with His Spirit in each of us, we can—I am sure now—do His Righteous Will

315

and return to Him in reform and obedience.

"Now, as I partially explained last Saturday, I believe we should, with the Spirit, begin to plan and organize several key meetings of all the church members, as soon as I have completed my sermon series I spoke about earlier. You recall that '*The Spirit Speaks Today*' spoke often of the fact that Christ is coming soon to claim His *Radiant church*, unstained and unblemished by sin and disobedience. The Spirit truly speaks, and says the same things today, since these timeless, Divine Words come from our Lord God, Himself.

We must organize and carry out reform in the area of our lack of full Bible classes, to mature all our members, because you and I have been reminded by His Word that Christ is coming soon. He may come tomorrow, for Scripture says about His coming: '*No one knows about that day or hour...but only the Father* (see Mark 13:32). I propose we bring all the membership together, after my Sermon series, and with prayer, begin to explain what we should **do** to please Christ, rather than **continue to do what we now know is false and disobedient** in His Eyes. With the Spirit's help, and your new knowledge of Christ's Words to His church, I hope that we might persuade the entire membership to agree to Christ's desire to have us obey Him fully with regard to all errant matters we, who are leaders and servants, have discovered with the Spirit's leading. Together, we can and must implement new Bible classes for all. But infant baptism 'correction' may take some time, since it is so heavily rooted in our 'traditions,' rather than in scriptural truth; so we should act quickly if the church understands the scriptural truths involved, and approves of this necessary change.

Let's plan for church prayer meetings now, and schedule a plan, with the Spirit's blessing, that will achieve repentance, reform, and a fresh scriptural start for renewal of His Body, as soon as humanly possible!

Behind-the-scenes discussions take place between the Pastor, the Deacons, and Bible Teachers (with their Bibles and the Spirit of God).

Readers know, from previous chapters of this scripturally-based book, just what the Pastor and the Spirit will draw the church leaders to examine in the New Testament—for the *Scenario* reveals that the Pastor has been strongly convicted of his and the church's disobedience in the matter of infant baptism. His Deacons and helpers, after reading this book, refer to the Scriptures concerning Christian baptism—exactly **who** must be baptized after repentance and belief, **by what means**, and **with what results**, in the Lord's eyes. These church leaders under Christ now realize that only by following the scriptural Words of inspired Bible writers, will they be obeying Him Who loves them, and Willed to build His church. Now they know that they had formerly blindly followed a series of Pastors and false 'church traditions,' in this matter of infant baptism. And now, they know (reminded by this book, Holy Scripture, and the *Spirit of Truth*) that they must return to the foundational Christian faith of their fathers—not retain the false teachings of men in the past. They must carefully lead the whole church Body to repentance, reformation, and restoration. True Christian baptism—of knowing, conscience-stricken, sinful adults, or mature children only—must be adhered to, as the New Testament church rightly did so long ago. And, as the church before the death of the Apostles predominantly did, before the influence of Satan came into the churches—they must teach **all** members of the church to know and obey **all** that the Lord taught and commanded His Body to be and do. Now they must seek also to eliminate *false teachers* from their seminaries and Bible Schools, so that new Pastors are taught God's Truth, and will no longer listen to *false teachers* in the church.

The process of **self-examination** (their present doctrines and practices placed against the Divine Standard of the New Testament for the Church) will not be an easy one, they find. The Pastor will bear the brunt of the criticism of older church members, who accept the false 'philosophy' (not truth) of their forefathers—who "have always done it this way," and who will fiercely resist scriptural truth and change. Even as the Pastor preaches and teaches repentance and reform to those things he spoke of as part of the New Testament teachings of Christ and other inspired holy men, these 'old-timers' are certain to rebel against the inspired Word of God, and dream that the past their fathers taught them is part of their human religious "heritage" (though not always part of the Bible, God's Word of Truth).

These things are discussed between the Deacons and other Bible teachers, helpers, and assistants, and the Pastor. It is fortunate, indeed, that they have each been introduced to the power of prayer, through *"The Spirit Speaks Today,"* and to the Spirit's leading toward needed reform. The little group, meeting regularly in the Pastor's study, are helped by the Holy Spirit, Who reminds them of His Truth. The Pastor, as promised, teaches the church members primarily in Sunday sermons, while preparations are made for *"all-age Bible studies."* They all feel confident that the church members of their little "'Body of Christ" will—through prayer, Godly sermons, and Bible-teaching—soon recognize their church's past disobedience, and accept their Pastor's recommendations to change their scripturally-false practice of infant baptism.

Let's skip over further details, and move forward in time, several weeks later, to a special business meeting called by the church leaders, just after the conclusion of the Pastor's sermon series with "Obeying Scripture in Christian, but not infant, Baptism."

Scenario 1, Scene 3.

The setting has changed to the church auditorium on a Saturday afternoon. The Pastor and his faithful group of church helpers has already met and prayed for the Spirit's presence at this crucial meeting of all the members of this small Body of Christ. It seems that the whole membership (except for those who were ill and could not attend) are present. The church auditorium is filled with little knots of men and women, all clustered in groups, in which the talk is always the same—"What should we do?; What do you think we should do?; What would our parents have us do?; How I wish

318

I had studied God's Word more completely!"... Suddenly, the group is hushed, as the Pastor and Deacons enter at the front of the hall, and take their places at a table facing the church members. The Pastor, as church leader under the Head, Jesus Christ, asks that all present be seated, and opens the business meeting with this short prayer:

Pastor:

"Our Heavenly Father, we come to you today, in the Name of the Risen Jesus, our Saviour and Loving Lord of our lives. We ask that the presence of your Holy Spirit among us would calm our hearts, minds, and souls as we pause today to consider, in your Holy Scriptures, what Your only-begotten Son has asked us to be and do for Him and for You, in this world and in this church. Father, we ask, too, that your Spirit in us would Counsel and Guide us to your Truth, answer our doubts and fears, and give us the Divine Assurance and Wisdom of your inspired Written Words, as we consider other matters of concern to You and to Your little church here—Amen."

The church members echo his "Amen," some strongly, some weakly, others silently, with bowed heads.

Pastor:

"Brothers and sisters in Christ, members of this little flock of Christ in this community, I welcome you in the Name of Christ. You have all, I believe, listened to my recent series of sermons, just concluded, entitled '*Faithfulness to the Living Word, Jesus, and to the Written Word of God.*' You know from my sermon introductions, their scriptural content, and our written invitation to all adult members to attend this meeting, that you, as members of this Christian church, will be asked to vote on a two-part question this day. These questions, arising from my sermons, and later intensive Bible studies with myself teaching, and your Deacons and Sunday School teachers learning with me, are these:

'Do you agree with your leaders (myself, and your appointed Deacons) that this church has been disobedient to Jesus Christ in the past, in the matter of baptizing infant children, wrongly saying they are 'saved' and 'adding them' to the membership of this church—in direct opposition to the clear meaning of Christian, New Testament immersion baptism of conscious, aware persons only?'

"And,

'Do you agree that this disobedient practice should be discontinued immediately in this church?'

"If a large majority agrees with this two-part question, in the vote which follows general discussions amongst us all, we, your leaders under Christ and His Word, will suggest to you a process involving all of you that will do two things for you and our Lord, Who loves us and gave Himself for us.

"This proposed two-part scriptural reform process will, if followed, assure us all that we are in Jesus Christ's Will for ourselves personally, and for all His church Body here:

"*One*: We propose to enter into a program of New Testament Bible studies for all of you, whatever your spiritual progress to date, aimed at re-examining thoroughly what our Lord requires us to be and do for Him, in this church, and in the world—but not as part of its sinful nature.

"*Two*: If, as a result of these Bible studies, we find— God forbid, but it may be so!—further evidence of previously undiscovered disobedience to our Lord's Will, Purpose, Teachings and Commands for us, in His church, we propose to continue with these "**Lord's business meetings,**" as His church, so that we can repent of and reform these things, with His Spirit and Word, to please Him. We may be moving faster than some of you would like, but brothers and sisters, our Lord is coming soon. He said so in the last Book of the Bible. We don't want Him to find us living in disobedience to Him, in a sin-stained church, do we? Do you say 'Amen' to that?"

This time, the "amens" are louder and stronger. The church members' doubts and fears are diminished by the calming and counselling presence of the Holy Spirit in their midst, as well as by the Pastor's sincerity and love shining through the formal business process.

Pastor:

"Now, before the formal vote, I'd like you to pull your chairs around in small circles on the floor, of about twelve to fifteen members each. I will ask a Deacon to sit with each group, and lead the discussions on the two-part question on infant baptism, and your leader's proposal to discontinue it in accordance with God's Word. I will 'circulate' from group to group. I plead with you that you all take part, for we want a complete understanding of what you will be asked to vote upon, without any feeling that some one or two among you may verbally force you away from your understanding as to our Lord's purpose and meaning for adult immersion baptism only—and our Spirit-led conviction that rejection of infant baptism must be made **now**. If we are to please Him, the true Head of this Christian Body, we must take this next step to please our Lord.

"One more thing, if I may. I urge you all, whatever your background in this church, whatever the beliefs of your mothers and fathers or grandparents, to not let **unscriptural 'traditions,'** or other **emotional loyalties,** take the place of the inspired, inerrant Word of God concerning His Son's church, salvation, baptism, Bible teaching, and growing spiritually to serve Him in this place. I'm sure you realize, especially after my recent sermon series on our required faithfulness to Christ and His Word, that what we do here in the church must always and only be done in full accordance to His Will and purpose for His church—as described clearly in God's Word. I confess to you, I have often felt guilty before God and you members, in these last few weeks. I, too, need to work now to do what faithful Christian Pastors must do—teach you of Jesus, and how to please Him by obeying Him."

An audible sob is heard all over the auditorium, but the Pastor, after a few moments, bowing his head, continues...

"Take about an hour to thoroughly talk it over in small groups. Then, we will put the vote before God and all of you present, if you are agreed."

Group discussions take place, with a Deacon at the centre of each group, quieting those who become loudly argumentative, but urging them to continue, with appropriate words of explanation when discussion falters. The Deacons recognize the expressions of doubt and fear in their small groups. With the Spirit's help, they use the hour to urge weak and strong Christian members alike to express their concerns, and have their questions answered from Scripture.

As expected (and already well covered in the sermon series) young mothers and fathers of the "church family" are the most worried and vocal over the proposed changes: the suggested elimination of infant baptism, and the so-called later "confirmation classes." The Deacons are ready, with Bibles handy, to tell them what their Pastor has already confirmed: No New Testament church baptized infants. Baptism, they explain again, does not save anyone—only those of an age to respond to the Gospel message, be convicted of sin, repent of the same, and believe in the Name of the Resurrected Jesus, will be saved by faith alone. And they confirm from Scripture that if an infant died without undergoing "errant and man-made infant baptism," he or she would certainly go to Heaven—*for the Kingdom of Heaven belongs to such as these* (Christ, referring to the qualities of trust, innocence, and purity displayed in infants—see Matthew 19:14; 18:3). *The Deacons describe their studies of the Scriptures, under the Spirit's guidance. Many churches other than their own, as they reveal to the groups, have responded to false teachings on infant baptism, out of ignorance and fear for their children. They, like their own church, have tried to defend their practice by false teachings and interpretations of men in the past, substitution of false expressions, such as "New Testament household baptisms," or falsely relating Israel's male infant circumcisions to errant Christian infant baptisms. They explain that New Testament Scripture directly opposes these errant church practices and false doctrines. Finally, they bring to their groups' attention once more that the Pastor's sermons, quoting directly from Scripture (Rev. 2,3, Matt. 28:18–20, Acts, and others), all with the Spirit's Counsel, have brought them to face up to the incontrovertible evidence that infant baptism is unscriptural and in error. They must return to Believer's baptism, as stated in the inspired, inerrant, written Word of God. The one hour of discussions comes to a close as the Pastor approaches the table, and asks his Deacons to join him.*

Pastor:

"Christian church members, brothers and sisters, I must call you to attention now. I ask you to return to your places in preparation for the vote… Are you agreed on this church taking a vote now? All in favour, say, 'Aye.'"

There is a chorus of 'Ayes'—and the Pastor can hear no dissent.

"Now I will read, again, the two-part question that you have been discussing among yourselves at home and in . this past hour"

—he reads it slowly and clearly:

323

"Allow me to say a short Prayer to God, in our Lord's Name, for your guidance by the Holy Spirit, the '*Counselor*,' the '*Spirit of Truth*,' the One living in you and I Who will 'lead us into all Truth—God's Truth that sanctifies us who believe. We are set into this Christian church for a purpose—Christ's purpose and plan for the church.'"

The Pastor prays, in a reverent, holy hush... Then he raises his head, and says—

"All in favour of these proposals before you—say 'Aye.'"

*As if 'one,' in an unplanned movement, the believers rise and respond with a resounding 'Aye.' Now they are **truly one** in all things, as the Lord prayed for them long ago, in John 17:21,23.*

And so we conclude this hypothetical *scenario* of a little church, revived and acting to reform themselves with the guidance of the Spirit and the Word. I assure you, as the Spirit and the Word assures me in my life and writing, that if any other disobedient church today is similarly revived, through prayer and the Spirit, to carry out Christ's Will and purpose, and discover and reform their evident sins—these truly reformed churches will become, at last, what He wants us all to be—a **United**, Radiant, unstained, blameless *"Bride"* for Him when He Comes. May needy (disobedient) churches, and sinful, perhaps untaught members and leaders of His failing or failed church respond and act to take these urgent, Christ-commanded and desired steps to please the One who first loved us, and died for us and the lost world.

This Scenario was based upon a small, "Protestant" church with a Pastor and helpers, and Christ alone as its Head. Not upon a very large, authoritarian, hierarchically-organized and autocratic church, with unscriptural human "Heads" who have failed Christ, which will find it hard to admit to sin and error, let alone consider such a scriptural process of reform. I hope to show these latter churches (with 'the *Spirit of Truth*') how they, too, can please the Lord and find the Spirit's Way to Christ-demanded reform of sin and disobedience in all His church, *of which He—alone—is the True Head.*

If anyone loves me he will obey my teaching
(Jesus, John 14:23).

I pray *that they may all be One, as we, the* **Father and I,** *are One... so the world may believe that you sent me*
(Jesus, John 17:21; 17:11; 17:23).

Yes, I am coming soon...
(Jesus, Rev. 22:20).

Remember the height
from which you have fallen!
Repent and do the things you did at first.
(Jesus, Rev. 2:5).

Chapter 15

Christ's Commanded Reform in Action: Large Groups of Churches in Real Life

A writer's human path—and the Spirit's Counsel sought. During the planning process for this book of warning, in Christ's Name, to disobedient Christian churches today, and even during the writing of it, I have been acutely aware of the *Spirit of Truth* speaking to me, urging me in certain directions—and warning me away from certain other directions. Invisible "walls" seemed to be erected, as to my written approaches to certain churches, while the Spirit "showed" me clear approaches to one group or another. Lest there be any misunderstanding, I hasten to add that, as Scripture reveals, the Holy Spirit in each and every *born-again* believer "speaks" primarily of and through the inspired, inerrant, Written Word of God. But if asked, He will counsel and guide personally in the Way Christ desires Christians to take.

Before our Lord's betrayal, death, and Resurrection, He spoke to His Disciples about the Holy Spirit. Christ also said...*the Holy Spirit, whom the Father will send in my Name, will teach you all things and will remind you of everything I have said to you* (John 14:26). But, like the great majority of inspired scriptural truths, and our Spirit-led understanding of them, we must not act upon them in isolation from His Will. Our Lord, after speaking further of other important truths for His disciples, (in John 14 and 15), gave us more vital truths concerning the Spirit's work and the Lord's Will and purpose for our church lives. These, if read and understood with the help of the *Spirit of Truth*, will energize and support our Lord's concern for **all of His Church, His Body on earth.** Let's look further into what the Lord says to all His disciples in these "treasure-filled" scriptural sources of Divine Truth in John's Gospel, Ch. 14–17. The Spirit, if asked in prayer by sincere church members and leaders, will certainly *teach... and remind* us, as we learn in John 14:26.

In His **"farewell discourse"** (as I call it), in John Chapter 16, the Lord gave, to His disciples and all members of His future church, the following urgent information about the Holy Spirit: *Unless I go away, the Counselor* (the Holy Spirit) *will not come to you... When he comes, he will convict the world of guilt in regard to sin and righteousness and judgment* (John 16:7,8). Vital information for the Christian church, for this work of the Spirit, is directly related to our obediently carrying out our Lord's Great Commission Command, *...go...make disciples of all nations,* that I have written about in this book of scriptural warning to the Christian church, sleeping or wide awake, and deliberately disobedient to the Lord.

Jesus continues, in John Chapter 16, to tell us more of what the Holy Spirit will do for all of us in the Christian church today. He says (John 16:13): *...when he, the Spirit of truth comes, he will guide you into all truth. He will not speak on his own; he will speak only what he hears, and he will tell you what is yet to come.*

Do we all agree that it is critical to know of what is yet to come? And, is it important for us in His church to be led by the Spirit and the Word to God's Truths? The answer, to those who love and obey His Word and His Spirit, is self-evident! If we are to please our Saviour and Lord, and become *a radiant church, without stain or wrinkle or any other blemish, but holy and blameless* (Eph. 5:27) when He comes to transport His Bride to Heaven, we must be led of the Spirit.

I have quoted the very Words of our Lord from His conversations with, prayers about, and teachings to his little group of disciples. Concerned and worried, they have here, in John's inspired Gospel, heard for the first time that their Lord must leave them and return to His Heavenly Father. Just minutes later, Jesus further alarms and discourages them when He tells them that in His departure, they will *weep...mourn...* and *grieve* for Him (John 16:20). But minutes later too, we have the Apostle John's written recollection (in his Lord's overheard prayer to His Father in Heaven—John 17) of what Jesus, the Christ, desires of His Father for not only present disciples, but for all His disciples to be "made" after His death, and until He returns.

New disciples are to be made, baptized, and taught to obey all that Christ taught and commanded us, AND the Spirit in the new believers MUST ask the Spirit to counsel, guide and lead them to His Truth, as the obedient church preaches the Gospel, and observes the same Spirit convicting sinful men and women.

Yes, "The Spirit Speaks Today"—Not Only to Small, But to Large "Empires" or Groups of Christian Churches.

I introduced this chapter by speaking of the spiritual "wall" I encountered, as I concluded the previous chapter, *Christ's Commanded Reform In Action: A Scenario For Today's Small Church.* Christians who have read this humble book of Christian concern and warning for today's Christian churches, of all sizes, degrees of faith and spiritual condition, will discern that I have "run into" a very large and rigid symbolic "wall," with my present approach to reform of disobedient churches. The wall is similar to the wall "run into" by a studious, and hitherto obedient, servant-priest of the Roman Catholic hierarchy in Germany, some 500 years ago! I speak of Martin Luther, and his so-called "Protestant Reformation." Luther and his friends, I am sure, **thought** they could solve their church problems by dealing with their church, and the few others in Germany, at that time. They **hoped** that the Bishop, assigned by the "Pope" to oversee the German Roman Catholics, would do just that, and not bother the Pope, Cardinals, and Teachers at Rome. They were wrong, for the Bishop and other "heads" in Germany passed this significant church problem—caused by the "heretic Luther" (their term)—on to the Pope. The secular (i.e., unscriptural) church heads of this very large group of churches recognized immediately that they could not sustain their power, authority, and positions if they admitted to *any* wrongdoing at all—political, religious, and doctrinal. From the commencement of writing this book of warning to the church today, I have recognized that the problem of *"getting the Lord's warning to all*

329

churches" is very similar to that faced by Luther five centuries ago. The larger the church group, the more organizational "walls" will be encountered—and no leader (especially unscriptural in title and authority) wants to *ever* admit to making a mistake! The answer for these groups is to call reformers "heretics," and to state that leaders can do no wrong. The answer for the "reformers," conversely, is to separate from their brothers and sisters, even though this "answer" directly opposes Christ's Will that *all His church be One, as He and the Father are One, in all things.* Today, guided by the *Spirit of Truth,* I see another, more urgent crisis approaching, as churches are observably more divided and less obedient to the Lord. More urgently, we seem closer to the *end times,* and closer to our Lord's return. The Spirit speaks today, about repentance, and reform, and the divisive, divided, and sinful churches are not listening. They don't seem to hear the Spirit and the Word, and *seem further from His ideal Bride: a holy, sinless, united Body.*

It is neither a problem of timing or diplomacy, nor of God's Will. It *is* a problem of recognizing the "wall" erected by Satan and *false teachers,* and asking the Spirit for guidance as to how to break it down. For it is a wall of fear, of ignorance, and of men's pride, willfulness, and unwillingness to obey and serve God and His Son in this area of whether or not the Christian church is "Christ's Body on earth"—or "men's churches." This "wall," erected by man, unless pierced by the Spirit's aid, and the sanctifying Word of God, will resist all needed reform, as Luther and other later reformers have found.

The Bible, church history and our church experiences confirms that churches of the past and today *can sin and disobey the Lord, yet can and do return to full obedience—with prayer, the guidance and teaching of the Spirit; with repentant, reformed, and reforming leaders and members, returning to please their first love, the True Head of His church.* But under the burden of the Spirit's urging, the relevant question is *will they hear the Spirit, examine "their church" and its wall of untruths, and begin needed reform to return the inspired Word of God alone?*

Up to this closing chapter of this book about pleasing Christ when He comes, including the "scenario for today's small churches" I refused to face "the spiritual wall" I knew was there. The wall? It is, as I say, reminiscent of the same wall faced by Luther—one man and some Christian friends who tried to change (reform) "their church," despite the almost invincible wall erected by those who themselves denied they had assumed false authority, and were heading a large number of churches opposed, in many instances, to how Christ had told all men to "run it," according to His written Word and Will.

I was guided by the Spirit, that great Counselor and guide, the gift of God in **every true believer**, to write chapter 14 for **small, self-governing Christian churches**, who were obedient in most respects to Christ and His Word—yet who had failed their Lord, in not doing **all He had asked them to do for Him, in certain scriptural areas of faith and doctrine.** I know that small Christian churches today, if they sincerely believe in Christ and His Word, can, with the aid of the Spirit, return to *"do the things you did at first* for Christ*" and reform their present sinful acts, with this scenario, and the Spirit, and repentant, godly men and women willing to serve their Saviour and Lord.* Small churches, with one or a very few local, self-governing leaders, are not subject to "outside" authority—other than that legitimately claimed by Christ in Matthew 28:18, and repeated to small, mostly disobedient churches in Revelation 1–3.

But I also know, from the Spirit and the Word, as I have been led to face this spiritual "wall" in history (shored up by Satan and *false teachers* in many churches today), that seeking *"large church reform"* will not be successful in Christ's eyes, unless the Spirit counsels another approach. One that will reach the heart and minds of those men who presently guide these very large groups, denominations, and "Empires" of churches, etc., and who are aided by Satan's helpers to retain their false power, authority, pride, and continue in disobedience. I have presented a few publicly-known examples of the disobedience of these false leaders and their successors in this book—examples, I am sure, that are **not known** to most of their "church members," because they are largely scripturally untaught by their large groups of churches. And I have written that many of the false leaders' teachings, and commands to the churches, are directly opposed to the inspired teachings and Words of our Lord and those godly men inspired to write down what Christ's Body, the church, **must do** to serve and please Him—from the time the first Christian church was formed in Jerusalem, down nearly 2,000 years to today.

I am, until this year, an unpublished author because there us another "spiritual wall," erected by some "Church denominational publishers" and those for whom they publish, that is like the one presented to Luther in his attempted reformation of "his church." The "publishing wall" is a wall of denial: "Your book does not fit **our program**"..."Your material is confusing and inapplicable to **our** churches," etc. What they mean, but do not say, is that they are afraid to trouble their denominational supporters, lest they lose their livelihood. They will not say, as the Pope said to Luther, "You are a heretic, you do not believe as we do"... for the publishers and the Pope deny that they have chosen to disobey Christ, and so obey Mammon, and Satan, the "prince of this world." But Christ's Resurrection and presence has already defeated Satan, and He and His Word must be obeyed. For our Lord, the Risen Christ, has said He is coming soon to claim a perfect, sinless, and obedient Bride, the church—and take her, His obedient Body, to Heaven. Believe this; examine yourselves, reform error, and return to wait for His coming, while serving Him faithfully. Or face up to His terrible consequences, as also written and preserved by our Omniscient and Omnipotent God in His Word.

Christ's Way of Reform For ALL Disobedient Churches.

A way of church reform used by the Lord is recorded in both secular and religious history. God and His Spirit work through Evangelists and itinerant preachers, whose faithful preaching of the Word in country areas, church halls, even in the streets, has, in the past, produced "*revivals*"—in which hundreds or thousands of the lost, or "backsliders," have been invaded by the Spirit of God, have cried out to God while repenting of their sins, and have been reformed and returned to the (obedient) church to live holy lives for Him. These revivals are rare, as are true miracles nowadays, for God knows—if many church members do not—that He has Willed to build His church on earth; has given the church His Son's teachings and commands as to *mak-*

ing...baptizing... and teaching new disciples in all nations, and appears to be testing us for full obedience until He comes again.

I wrote the previous chapter (14) for small, self-governing churches, with prayer and fervent hopes that, somehow, all churches would re-examine themselves against God's Inspired Word. Then, if sin and error is found, all might, with the Spirit's Guidance come to repentance and reform before He comes—and it is too late.

Led by the Spirit, I avoided the "Wall" of large groups of obviously sinful churches, and was led to recommend the following:

The only other way of informing or warning these large groups, or "Empires" of churches (since we of today only have unsuccessful attempts at reform in the past to guide us, historically), is I believe, to **leave it up to the Spirit with a little help from Christian books, such as this one, or others—and to godly members of these errant churches, to whom the Spirit speaks today, about the need to reform.**

A Spirit-assisted Communications Project for Reform of Large Christian Groups.

The small church—with Godly, Spirit-filled, scriptural church leaders as overseers of the little Body, under the Divine Head, and with the counsel of the Spirit within each believer—will usually have **no problem** coming to grips **with their need of reform** to please Christ, if the need is brought to their attention by Spirit-awakened members. As I indicated in my hypothetical scenario for reform, in Ch. 14, these small churches need only to have the Spirit "nudge" them towards needed change to full obedience to Christ—either by a means such as this book, or through a Christian Pastor, friend, or Spirit-led sermon.

But this was my quandary in writing this book about needed reform to large groups of churches—under authoritarian, often false, leaders with terrible weapons, such as excommunication of members who did not agree with them and their errant false Traditions. How could the wall between Supreme Leaders be pierced, so that dialogue leading to real, needed, reform can be commenced? They need to be touched by the Spirit in their hearts so they could read, understand, repent, and obey **completely and faithfully** the Lord's Words (not the false teachings of past *false teachers*, blindly followed today)?

After all my agonizing consultations with the *Spirit of Truth*, allow me to tell you what advice I received from His urgings, and from God"s inspired Word. This advice is presented below in a short list that should be helpful to those Christian members of these large bodies who now see the need of true reform in their large groups of churches, and who want to communicate the need for pleasing Christ before He comes, without fear of excommunication or worse.

1. First step. See your local church "priest" or"head."

Pray first for the Spirit's wisdom and counsel, and for strength to please Christ in this way. Tell the priest privately— not in a letter nailed to the church door, or in a parish newsletter! Take a friend who is acquainted with the scriptural problems discussed here, if you are not.

Tell him that you have read a book about Christ coming soon, and that you have also read, in the New Testament (mark the passages as I have quoted from His Word), that He expects to take to Heaven only *a radiant church, without stain or wrinkle or any other blemish...holy and blameless* (Eph. 5:27), without sin.

Tell him also that the book you have read, confirmed by the Bible itself, demonstrates several practices of "your church" to be in error. Then, ask the priest whether he agrees with the evidence presented against the church errors noted, and if he plans to discontinue these errant practices.

If the priest disagrees, will not consult with a "superior," and refuses to change his Bible-opposing practices, the church member should leave, and attend a Christian church obedient to the Lord and His Word.

If the priest, however, states that ***he does agree with the Bible's position on these errors*** as pointed out by you, a church member, but that he must talk to his "superior," allow him to do so, with his promise not to let the urgent reform matter drop. Ask to be informed of the "superior's" opinion and intended action for early solution, before the Lord comes to claim His perfect, not imperfect, Bride.

334

2. Visit the "superior," should the priest wash his hands of the Scripture-opposing problem in the local church.

Pray first as in step 1. Explain to the "superior" that you have compared some doctrine and practices of "his" church with the Bible (read the problems from this book, with the pertinent biblical statements, to him—or ask your Bible-knowledgeable friend to do so). Ask the church "official" whether he agrees and will make the local church changes to agree with the Bible, or has decided to do something else.

Again, if he does not agree with the Bible, and proposes to continue past leaders' errant practices against the Bible on the grounds that they are "traditions of the church," agreed to by church teachers and officials—leave the church, and attend a Bible-believing, and following, church.

3. If these two church officials do not respond and make reforming changes to church practices presently opposing Scripture, write a personal letter to the Patriarch, Pope, Cardinal, Arch-Bishop or other person who claims to be the earthly "Head" of the church which you attend.

Pray before you write as in step 1. Explain in your letter why and how you have come to leave the church. Quote the scriptural problems and the urgent need for reformation to this official, using the scriptural references in this book, from the Bible. Explain that you have left the church, because no church official you have spoken to is willing to repent, reform, and make the church obedient and fit again to meet Christ as His perfect, obedient Bride when He comes soon.

What Other Alternatives Are There?
What Are the Chances of Success
With Large Church Reform?

There are, of course, many other alternatives—peaceful or , God forbid, destructive. But remember, *we all have sinned, and fall short of the Glory of God* (Rom. 3:23). Members and leaders of

335

Christian churches in the distant past, down through the centuries to today, have placed their own greed for power and authority before humble obedient service to God and His Son. I have not detailed, in this book, terrible events in which false and sinful church leaders have not only "excommunicated" peaceful and innocent men (and women), but have killed, without mercy, thousands of men and women who did not agree with their often errant, sinful doctrines and practices. This, although they called themselves Christians! They did not allow the Spirit of God to Counsel and Guide them to the Truths of God, preferring instead the guidance of those who often were the *false teachers* in the church referred to in 2 Peter 2:1.

My consistent burden and purpose from the Lord is to warn spiritually dead or dying; failed or failing, disobedient churches who have *"lost their First Love"*—to repent, reform, and return *"to do the things they did at first"* (for Christ)—so that they may be His Perfect Bride, when the Divine Bridegroom, Comes again... I have no other motive than to urge disobedient churches, with Spirit's help, to repent and reform all unscriptural sin, not please me *but to please Christ*, and be taken up into Heaven to be with the Trinity of God, forever. Amen.

When concerned Christians reach out to their church members and leaders, to correct things that displease the Lord (see His Words in Revelation 2 and 3, and elsewhere, as noted in this book), what are their chances of success? I believe that depends entirely upon Christ, who says in Revelation 2:23 that ...*the churches will know that I am he who searches men's hearts...* and *those whom I love I rebuke and discipline* (Rev. 3:19). We who love our brothers and sisters in Christ, can only pray, and ask the Holy Spirit to convict these disobedient ones, part of His Body, the church on the earth.

He has said, *If you love me you will obey my commands... If you obey My commands, you will remain in my love* (John 14:15,15:10). We must obey Him and warn others, but the rest is up to the Spirit, to convict and lead errant churches and their overseers back to serve Him, their Saviour and Lord. Remember, *the prayer of a righteous man is powerful and effective* (Jas. 5;16). Do not cease praying, but pray always in the Lord's Will that we may be one with His other bodies.

Announcing a Vital Part of Christ's Goal for His Entire Church Body: Complete Unity.

What is Christ's goal for church unity? We read it in His wonderful prayer to His Heavenly Father in Gethsemane (read John 17), just before He was betrayed, unjustly tried, condemned and handed to the Romans by Jewish leaders, for execution at Calvary. In this prayer, our Lord first prayed for Himself—that He might complete His first mission from God as Messiah to the Jews. In doing so, He brought Glory to God. Second, He asked God to glorify Him, the Christ, in God's presence—the glory He had with the Father-God *before the world began* (John 17:4,5). Then, in following verses, our Lord prayed for the early disciples God gave Him out of the world.

In following verses, He prayed, not for the world, but for these early disciples of His. He did not ask God to take them out of the world, but to protect them from the evil one, Satan, in the world, by the power of God's Name. For Jesus Christ had to return to the Father, and leave His present and future disciples (us too!) in the world. Earlier, Christ promised the gift of the Holy Spirit, for He would not leave us alone during His temporary absence in Heaven.

Then in John chapter 17, our Lord prayed this critical prayer for **church unity** that I spoke about earlier: *I pray...that all of them may be one, Father, just as you are in me and I am in you.* He continues: *I have given them the glory that you gave me, that **they may be one as we are one:** I in them and you in me...May they be brought to **complete unity** to let the world know that you sent me, and have loved them even as you have loved me.* This oneness our Lord desires is a spiritual and practical unity, ordered by the Divine Head of His church Body on earth. When achieved (obeyed) by every Body of Christians on earth today, it will not only please Him, but be seen in eminently practical terms—by both Christians and the lost world. For Christians, it will reveal that all churches have spiritually matured according to the Head's Will and purpose. For the lost world, true and complete unity of the church will witness to them that the One True God has sent His Only-begotten Son to save lost souls.

The sanctifying Words of God's Truth are not at all unclear—nor do they contain hidden mysteries, impossible to understand and follow. They must be believed, for they are eternal, unchanging, Divine Words. They describe a Divine Oneness in all things that God the Father, the Son, and the Holy Spirit say and do. In our Lord's prayer, His inspired, inerrant and infallible Words tell us that, until He returns again, all members and leaders of all Christian churches down through the ages *must* live for, worship, teach, and obey Him, our Divine Head, and thus by obedience in all things, come to His desired oneness (full Church Body Unity), just as He and the Father are One in all things.

False teachers I have met in Christian churches, and observed in so-called Christian literature, try to claim that the unity of all disciples was meant by our Lord to be limited to unity **within an individual church body, but not necessarily extended to unity of ALL Christian churches who claim Jesus Christ as Saviour and Lord**. But this false interpretation cannot be so, for the *Spirit of Truth* (in every true believer) tells us Christ's prayer for the Unity of all His present and future disciples *can only mean what it says*—Christ desires unity of **ALL disciples added by Christian baptism to EACH part, EACH LOCAL CHURCH, making up the TOTAL Body of Christ, in the world—in the past, today, and until He comes**. This is Christ's purpose and goal for church unity. Heed His teachings and commands for a truly obedient and **united church Body on earth.**

Present, Limited Church Unity Needs His Commanded Reform, To Please Him

Christ-ordered church reform of large, autocratic, authoritarian church groups may be found difficult to achieve, even if obvious and necessary. We already have an example from the 16th Century, involving Luther and his attempts to "reform" and "protest errors" within one church Body of his very large church group (the Roman Catholic church). The "Protesters," branded as "heretics and unbelievers," were excommunicated. Neither the church they

338

left, nor the churches they formed as part of the so-called "Protestant Reformation," effectively and fully reformed themselves, as history reveals. Scriptural errors and disobedience to Christ's teachings and commands continued to be a part of many "reformed" churches. *False teachers* continue, often, within such disobedient churches.

The only hope for true reform of very large groups, with unscriptural hierarchies of church officers, is to commence with prayer, and the Counsel and Guidance of the Holy Spirit. I have suggested a different approach to that recommended for small churches, simply because the opposition in small, self-governing churches with scriptural Overseers, Elders or Pastors is far less than that observed in Luther's attempt at reform. I do not advocate violence, nor "forceful overthrow" of disobedient church leadership—for this is not our Lord's Way. Pray, instead, for the Spirit's conviction of sin and error on the part of the authoritarian leaders. Then, in an orderly, peaceable way, approach the individual church leaders—working your way up the unscriptural, present "chain of command." Recommend to them self-examination of each church's obedience or disobedience against the New Testament Word concerning Christ's teachings and commands for His church on earth. If this is done, both members and leaders will be convicted by the Spirit of Truth and sense that He is at work in their local body—and, eventually, the entire body—for good.

I have spoken of the Roman Catholic church, as it contains many flagrant examples of sin and disobedience to the True Divine Head. But they are not the only large group guilty of rejecting God's Word in many instances, and of following *false teachers* in their Bodies. Many independent, many Orthodox, many Protestant, Reformed, Baptist, state and other churches need to examine their words, faith, doctrines, worship, etc., to see if they—like the Seven Churches of Revelation 2 and 3, need to **return to their *first love*, Jesus; to do what they** (faithfully) *did at first;* **leave their disobedient and lukewarm service for the Lord, and repent and obey He Who gave Himself for them (and us, today)..**

I pray that the Spirit will guide those Christians, in every disobedient church, to His way to self-examination, repentance, reform, and to full obedience to our Saviour and True Lord, before it is too late. He *comes like a thief in the night.* If we, who read and know the truth, do not speak the Word of Truth to sinners, we will fail our Lord also. May the Spirit guide you, and the Lord bless you, as you do your best to renew and revive "your church"—which is really His church, whom He loves and wants to find as a *radiant* Bride, the Church of Christ—*without stain or wrinkle* of sin, or **any other blemish** (disobedience), **but Holy and blameless, when He comes again, as He has promised.** Can we all say today, with the Apostle John, in Revelation 22:20—*Amen, Come Lord Jesus?* Pray with me that all our brothers and sisters in Christ may be found faithful and obedient, in Perfect Unity, Love, and Obedience, when our Lord Comes. It may be tomorrow!

Conclusion

Choose Your Future

You, readers, and I have reached the conclusion of this humble warning to the Christian churches of today. A book of warning that is supernatural and spiritual in origin, from the inspired, inerrant and infallible written Word of God to man.

I have written about the New Testament church (early and late), starting when the Body of Christ was first formed in Jerusalem in the Will and purpose of the Risen Christ, down through the ages until this very day. Then, I have compared what *He said to do and be* for Him with what the churches in the past and today *have actually done*, and are doing today.

I have listened to the Spirit since I became a Christian and began to serve Him in His Body on earth (and began to write, with His guidance). I am not better than those who read this book, but only, perhaps, more aware of *what the Spirit says to the churches—* in His Word and in our spirits—for I have learned to listen closely *to God; His Son, and to the Spirit of Truth.*

Before I close this book, allow me to summarize briefly for all the Christian churches today, how and why we all must "choose our future"—by *hear*(ing) *what the Spirit says to the churches.* Only by obeying the Divine Head of the church and by continuing to be faithful to our Lord, will we receive rewards for overcoming evil. If we follow Satan and his *false teachers*, we choose the worst of all futures, as declared by Christ in His immutable Word to man and His church.

A Summary.
What Christ Desires of His Church;
What He Receives from His Church.

A. Christ's Will and purpose for His church.

This book focuses upon our Lord's Will to build His church, after His "first mission to the Jews alone" concluded with the Temple Priests and Sanhedrin's rejection of Him as Messiah, and his unjust betrayal, Roman trial, and execution. It was God's plan, and necessary in His Sight. His Grace and Mercy could then be extended beyond Jews alone, to the lost Gentile world, through Jesus Christ taking upon Himself the sins of the world, dying on the cross, and Rising again. This, so that sinful men, believing in Him, might be reconciled to a Holy and Righteous God. Christ's Sacrificial Propitiation for men's sin procured God's Mercy, gave us salvation through Faith alone, and Eternal Life.

When Jesus, the Son of Man, understood His rejection by the Jews, and knew that He must leave His early disciples until God's future plans would be realized, He began to speak of building His church. We know His Will and His purpose for His Body, as revealed through the inspired writers of the New Testament for His church.

Besides the clear Will and purpose of our Lord for His church, I write of two sources of His Truth for and about the church that are both necessary and vital for all Christians to know—and obey:

> *One is the gift of the Holy Spirit* and His work in our lives, as Christ lives in each True believer and guides us to all His Truth.

> *The second is the written source of Truth—the Christian Bible*, written down and preserved for Jews and Christians of every age.

We should all thank our God for not only providing for our salvation, but giving us His *Spirit of Truth* in us, to guide us to know His inspired written, Sanctifying Truth, in the inerrant and infallible Bible. This so that we might serve His Son, the Divine Head of the church, and carry out His Will and purpose for the church. Every church must *teach* every member about the Spirit's work and guidance as found in God's Word—and this is part of Christ's three-part Commission for His church.

Finally, in this brief summary, I must contrast our knowledge of Christ's Will and purpose for His church, the guidance of His Spirit, and the provision of His written Word for His church, with the false teachings of Satan's "helpers:" *false teachers* in the churches. This is part of Christ's inspired warnings to the church. And it explains this book's purpose to urge all churches to **overcome Satan** and to listen and obey our Lord, rather than to the *false teachers* infiltrating many churches today.

B. The Early New Testament Church efforts to please and obey Christ.

This book examines the early New Testament inspired record, from the "First Baptist church" of Jerusalem—as I call it, in recognition of one critical facet of its obedience to Christ's Commission—to the early spread of the church in response to Christ's Commands: *Go to all nations... make disciples...baptize them... and teach them to obey all that I have commanded you.*

The early church, under the (relatively) faithful Apostles, and the urging of the Holy Spirit, tried to be faithful and obedient. And the Jerusalem church grew, even under early persecution. The Spirit guided them and convicted sinners, who then repented, and believed in the Apostle's Gospel message, and were added to the church and **taught to obey all that Christ commanded.** They had a few sin problems, but overcame them with the Spirit. Satan worked in their midst, but Jews and Gentiles were reached for the Lord. Eventually, with the Spirit's urging, the members and leaders of the Jerusalem church went *to all nations,* beginning with all Judea, Samaria, and finally to the Roman world beyond.

The little Christian church of New Testament days, under the teachings of the Spirit, the Apostles, and other godly men, grew—in numbers and in faith. They began to "turn the world upside down" for Christ. Those were difficult days, but faithful church members and leaders were truly one in the Lord in all things—and provide us today with an example of the True church of Jesus Christ.

C. The late New Testament church successes (few) and failures (many).

In order to underline and emphasize the Christian church's work in today's modern world, and their failures and successes (in our Lord's Will and purpose for His church of all ages), it is both important and necessary to point out and compare past church errors with today's churches' sins.

In several chapters, therefore, I used little-known, little-taught, but vitally important Scripture portions to remind churches today of all that our Lord had to tell us (in a vision to the Apostle John in Revelation, Chapters 1 to 3). In just a few decades from the formation of His Jerusalem church, the Lord observed His spreading church and mostly found them *disobedient, spiritually sleeping, dead, failing and failed!* This portion of Scripture, that the Lord asked John to forward to the Seven Churches of Asia, was and is absolutely crucial to the churches of **every** century—for they show, remind, and warn us all, in His Body on earth, how important it is to Him and to us **to be and remain faithful in all things to our Divine Head.**

Many churches today do not fully, teach, preach, or remind (or warn) their failing congregation of the Lord's rewards for success and obedience—or of the terrible penalties and awful future for disobeying Him. Do I misread the importance of these passages? I don't believe so, for any wise and discerning Christian of today, or the past, could observe and compare what went on in many Churches, with what Christ has them and us to do—in His Inspired Word. Activists, like Luther (a few) or writers (many) have found their complaints unanswered (or answered by cries of "heretic")—and their books rejected by Christian publishers (or "buried," indexed in church libraries) and unread.

Yes, Satan was working in the church's midst in the new church—and in the spreading church just a few years later, as Christ revealed to John (and to all later churches). Christ, and later, Peter, warned of Satan's work through *false teachers* in the churches.

This writer uses these few early chapters of Revelation, as a basic sourcebook of warning to every church today—for they contain clear warnings from Christ, as well as reminders that there are and will be rewards and a wonderful future for those who overcome evil. Who remain faithful to the end. One of the evidences of Satan's work is that *leaders often do not and will not teach all church members to obey all Christ's teachings and commands.* Nor will they preach or teach this crucial Scripture warning portion of Revelation 2 and 3. Why not? I believe it is because no church wants to be criticized (even by their nominal Lord), and they seemingly value men's false opinions over the very Words of God's sanctifying Truth.

D. Christ's Revelation to His churches of every age. His "Audit and Review."

Revelation 2 and 3 looks at Christ's review of a small part of the Christian church just a few years after it was formed, and spread to just a part of the Roman world of the Apostle's day. These Chapters of Revelation are described, in this book, as Christ's 'audit and review'—not only of the seven early New Testament churches, but applicable to all of His churches—for He and His Spirit preserved these truths down the centuries until today. My illustrations and application are intended to interest readers, and cause them and their leaders to review and audit their (really His!) churches (with the Spirit and the written Word)—to look and see if their Lord would find spiritual failure and disobedience among them, and say what He *holds against* them personally!

The Lord, He who searches hearts and minds of men... *will repay each* of us *according to* our *deeds.* **He searched the hearts and minds of those in just seven of his early churches—and found many of them unfaithful.** Yes, a few were faithful and obedient, and they would be rewarded. But the majority, as reviewed by the Head of His church were **weak, lukewarm, sinful, asleep, failing and failed,** according to His "audit and review." Without His warnings being preserved for all future churches, it would be possible for later, unfaithful churches—guided by *false teachers,* rather than wise and faithful Christian leaders—to say something like: ...we are *rich, have acquired wealth, and do not need* *a thing,* as the church at Laodicea said. But Christ, who knows His obedient own, will reply (and does say this to us today, if we *hear what the Spirit says to the churches*): *you are* (spiritually) *wretched, pitiful, poor, blind and naked.* Then He counsels them and other churches, then and now, to stop sinning and covering up their failures. He asks us, still, to return (like the Seven Churches) to their *first love...* return to *do the things* they *did at first* in faithfulness and full obedience.

This writer urges churches to consider (with the *Spirit of Truth*) what the Lord says to these seven exemplar churches, ***and to us***. He asks us all to examine ourselves for ***possible sin***, and return in repentance, reform and obedience in all things, to do what He requires of His Body on earth.

E. The church after the death of the Apostles, until modern times.

This book pursues the theme of obedience to Christ, with an examination of the churches of the Middle Ages and the "Protestant Reformation" of some 500 years ago, as well as later churches (and our own), who had lost the stability and control of the Apostles' guidance, even though they had all received the Holy Spirit to *lead them to all Truth, ...and remind them of everything the Lord had said to His early disciples.* A pattern of later church faithfulness to Christ becoming mixed with an increasing trend of Christian churches relying less upon Scripture alone (*Sola Scriptura*) and more upon ***Scripture plus men's traditions*** becomes apparent. Church history, when read with the *Spirit of Truth*, reveals that many of men's teachings and traditions taught to the later church were false (according to the inspired, inerrant, and infallible written Word of God). They needed to be re-examined. Not just briefly re-considered—but, with the same *Spirit of Truth*—the false, perverted and unfaithful words of men must be discovered, tested, and cast out of the churches.

The so-called "Protestant Reformation" was a well-intentioned reformation of ***some*** church errors—but, when it ended with the excommunication of Luther, and other church members, as "heretics," the parent Roman church was neither truly nor faithfully reformed to Christ's Will and purpose for His church. Nor did the "children of reform" carry out true reform according to Christ's plan.

Similar to some of the Seven Churches of Revelation 2 and 3, many contemporary churches remain **disobedient** to the Lord. This book on behalf of the Lord, warns the descendant churches of this failed "Reformation" of the past must *hear* (*and obey—author*) **what the Spirit says to the churches**—and return to what they *did at first*—repent, and reform their unfaithfulness to the Divine Head of His church.

F. The Christian church today:
A new audit, review, and reform is needed.

This book—by the same comparison of today's churches' responses to the teachings and commands of Christ with all that Christ has asked us to be and do for Him in all things—shows that many churches today, while professing Christ, are not fully faithful to Him and His commands. *False teachers* still lead unscriptural church members and leaders to follow false doctrines, practices and teachings.

The **warning** this book gives, urged by the Spirit, on behalf of the Lord of His Church, and in full accord with the inspired Word of God, is often never referred to in the teaching or preaching of modern churches. But they must begin to assess their church's faithfulness, or lack of it, before it is **too late**. The **consequences for failing to reform** the churches are clearly seen in many passages, such as Revelation 2 and 3. Our Lord says: *If you obey my commands, you will remain in my love* (John 15:10). The converse is too sad and dangerous to our souls to consider; therefore failing, disobedient churches must **act soon**.

G. Back to the Bible, and back to the *Spirit of Truth*.

Observe the history of the church, from New Testament origins down through to today's modern churches. **Compare it** with the inspired, infallible Word of God (containing Christ's own Words from the *Great I Am, the One who searches hearts and minds*). The church must not go forward with *false teachers*—but go "back to the Inspired Bible" and "back to the Spirit of Christ in every true Christian." If we do not carry out the Third Command of Christ in His Great Commission—**to teach all baptized believers added to the church,** to *obey all that I* (Christ, the Lord) *have commanded you* (leaders, and inspired teachers)—then the church will be unable to examine themselves for sin, for their hearts and minds will be darkened. Unless they return to the Word and the Spirit, they will be unable to repent, reform and return to become a fully faithful, obedient "Bride of Christ."

H. Christian churches choosing their futures.

If today's churches will *hear what the Spirit says to the churches*—if church leaders and members return to the written Word of God (especially the New Testament for the church)—if all see the urgency to return *to do what* they *did at first...*return to their *first love*, Christ—and if they choose to repent and reform discovered sin—then they will be ready to *"choose their futures."*

We believers all have been endowed by God, from our creation, with the power and right to choose how we all wish to live on this earth. Adam and Eve, under Satan's temptation, made a bad choice for all mankind's future after the creation of mankind. Choices made by godless mankind down through the centuries after the Fall, and through the Flood, were often bad as a result. The choices made by the Israelites to obey or often disobey God were bad, too, but God is still patient, as well as Holy and Just.

We all must make choices affecting our future in Heaven or Hell. God created us, not puppets without will, but mankind formed "in His image," with hearts, minds, and souls. We are given the freedom and power to choose Him, or gods of wood or stone, or human *false teachers*, who themselves want to be a god, as Satan does. There are bad and good choices—and they all have differing futures and consequences for mankind. The Christian church is no exception in this matter of **choosing** to obey God and His infallible Word of sanctifying truth, or *false teachers* led by Satan.

God's Word is not at all unclear as to the good or bad choices and their consequences available to, or awarded to those making up the unique institution Christ calls His "Body," the church in the world. This world is full of churches men falsely call Christian, who have made bad choices of whether to obey Christ and His Word or to accept false

gods, *false teachers*, false teachings, false doctrines, false practices, false baptism, and a perverted and distorted Scripture. Some formerly faithful churches have chosen, wrongly, to become cults or non-Christian sects, who will have *their candlestick* (the church Body) removed from Christ's presence. We will all face the Righteous Judgment of our Creator-God, to pay for our errant choices.

Self-examination for disobedience to the Lord and His Word is necessary on the part of all churches. If sin and disobedience, lukewarm service, or unfaithfulness in all or part of what He has asked us to be and do for Him is revealed, they must *seek and call upon the Aid of the Spirit of Truth, Who will lead us to His inspired inerrant Truth.*

The Urgency and Necessity of Church Reform Today.

Faithful, True and Obedient who examine themselves with the Spirit and the Word, and discover no failings or disobedience, will have confirmed in them the love and Favour of the Divine Head, Jesus Christ. They will know they will have the Peace, Mercy and Protection of their Lord, until He Comes. Knowing, too, they can claim their rewards from Him as their Bridegroom, with His Words of: *Well done, thou good and faithful servants, enter into My Presence in Heaven; enter into my Joy and eternal Favour—into Eternal Life.*

Discovered sin not repented of, or not acted upon immediately, produces spiritual sleep, even spiritual "deadness." These results of bad choices neither earn His promised rewards for faithfulness, nor prevent them from experiencing His disfavour—or worse. This book quotes Scripture in several places as to what the Lord will do if failing churches do not return in repentance and reform themselves from their failure—ranging from being *spit out of His mouth* (for *lukewarm* churches, with no zeal for His work), to His removing their *lampstand* (the disobedient, unrepentant church) *from its place* in His presence (Rev. 2,3).

Our Lord closes His Revelation to mankind about man's future (and His church's future) in these twice-uttered Words of Divine Truth: *Behold, I am coming soon...Yes, I am coming soon* (Rev. 22:7,20). He will not withhold His Wrath against disobedient

churches forever, any more than He withheld it from evil, unrepentant mankind in the days of Noah, from disobedient Jews (even
Moses), before and after their entry into His Promised Land—or
from unrepentant, disobedient Christians in the centuries following
the formation of the Lord's first church in Jerusalem. His Wrath,
from all evidence in His inspired Word, and from all events seen during these past two millennia, is, like His Creation: filled with evidences and words *urging us who love Him*, to *wake up*, and *do the
(obedient) things we did at first*, *to please Him—our Saviour and Lord.
We do not know when He will return (only the Creator-God knows this).
But He has said He is coming soon, and we must be ready.*

Reject Him, your Saviour and Lord, no longer. Disobey Him no
longer. Pray for His Spirit to come to you in His role as the *Spirit of
Truth*, Counselor and guide to all truth. Ask Him to reveal to you and
"your church" where you have not pleased Him, the True Head, and
obeyed His inspired, inerrant and infallible Word. Then, on personal and corporate bended knee—repent, reform, and return to serve
Him, as He asks, before it is too late!

Every Christian member and leader can, in deed, and in Truth,
"choose their own Future" in their personal and church life for or
against God, His Son, and the Spirit of Truth. Many have already
chosen to reject full and faithful obedience to Him who died for our
sins, and gave Himself up for His body, the church on earth. The
faithful and obedient ones, after reading this book and God's Word
(with the Spirit) know their happy Future in Heaven with their Lord
and Saviour. But I suspect many others do not know their terrible
Future awaiting who sin, disobey Him, and reject Him. This is why
I write this Scriptural book of warning. I pray that the latter, larger
group will accept God's Word quoted herein—and seek to return to
their Just, yet Wrathful Lord, in the way that I have suggested, that
will lead to revival, repentance, reform and a joyful reunion with
obedient brothers and sisters in Heaven. Don't wait long to
choose—He is coming soon!

Books Also Written by W.R. Williamson, Th.D.
—as yet unpublished

Wrinkled or Radiant (1994)
A plea for Christian church reform.
(Ephesians 5:25-27).

Christ's Great Commission for His Church (1996)
A plea for Christian church obedience.
(Matthew 28:18-20).

I pray…that all of them may be One (1996)
A plea for Christian church Unity.
(John 17:20-23).

What is Truth? (1998)
A plea for Christian church return to obedience
to God's Word of Truth.
(John 17:17).